RELIGION, CULTURE AND POLITICS IN IRAN

RELIGION, CULTURE AND POLITICS IN IRAN
From the Qajars to Khomeini

Joanna de Groot

I.B. TAURIS

LONDON · NEW YORK

Published in 2007 by I.B.Tauris & Co. Ltd
6 Salem Road, London W2 4BU
175 Fifth Avenue, New York NY 10010
www.ibtauris.com

In the United States of America and Canada distributed
by Palgrave Macmillan, a division of St. Martin's Press,
175 Fifth Avenue, New York NY 10010

Library of Modern Middle East Studies 25

ISBN 978 1 86064 571 6

A full CIP record for this book is available from the British Library
A full CIP record is available from the Library of Congress

Library of Congress Catalog Card Number: available

Set in Monotype Sabon and Futura Bold by Ewan Smith, London
Printed and bound in the Czech Republic by FINIDR, s.r.o.

Contents

Acknowledgements

Making a book is never done in isolation, although major parts of the endeavour are undertaken alone. It is a pleasure as well as a proper academic convention for me to acknowledge the many kinds of support and advice from which I have benefited during the process of bringing this text into existence.

I begin by acknowledging influences which came to me from my past, from my parents, Rosemary (1913–96), and Emile (1914–54). As I found out that I was not either of them, and so made this book my own, I have come to recognise and appreciate their part in it, and in me.

In the present I am lucky enough to have a very special sister. Lucy de Groot has been unfailingly loving, perceptive and honest, and I have really appreciated her *un*-academic viewpoint and consistent solidarity. Thanks a million and my love.

I thank colleagues and friends in York for many kinds of practical, thoughtful and continuing support. My present and past heads of department, Mark Ormrod and Allen Warren, have provided extensive practical help and shown a personal interest that was crucial to my work. Peter and Miggy Biller, Bill and Jo Trythall and many departmental colleagues have dealt with my doubts, delays and deficiencies with a degree of sense and sensibility well beyond the calls of academic collegiality. Mary Maynard and Haleh Afshar read versions of the manuscript at various stages, giving up precious time to offer advice and suggestions. Jane Rendall's editorial support in meeting a challenging deadline showed generous friendship and exemplary professional and intellectual judgement. I am grateful for the typing assistance provided by Chloe Toone, Andrea Key and Julie Bullen, for help from Paul Luft in finding the cover illustration and the efficient and vital bibliographical work of Martyn Lawrence in the final stages.

Outside York I would like to thank friends like Catherine Hall, Gavin Kitching and Dick Holt who kept contributing comments on my work and encouraging me to stick with the project and complete it, sometimes showing more confidence in me than I had in myself. Hadi Enayat provided useful comments on an early version of the text. More generally, colleagues in the Middle East Study Group, notably Floreeda Safiri, Anna Enayat and Sami Zubaida, have provided valuable expertise and insights.

Professional, collegial and intellectual support played a vital role in the creation of this book. That creative work also faced me with a number of personal challenges, and in meeting them I was fortunate to have had a great deal of non-academic stimulus and support. To Diane, Sylvie, Peter P., Peter K., Jackie, Anne, Pat, Marji, Lynn, Christy, Walter and John, who were companions on my personal journey at various times over a number of years, I want to express my appreciation in words. You were important to me, shared a lot, and gave a lot, and so have your part in my achievement. Thanks to you all.

For similar reasons I want to say particular thanks to Betsy who saw, heard, understood and worked with me as I worked to achieve what I wanted. I won't forget your insights, challenges and support.

Introduction: making stories about Iran

[there are occasionally] great radical ruptures, massive binary divisions, but more often one is dealing with mobile and transitory points of resistance producing cleavages in a society which shift about, fracturing unities and effecting regroupings, furrowing access across individuals themselves, cutting them up and remoulding them ... the swarm of points of resistance traverses social stratifications and individual unities. (Michel Foucault)

In the late 1970s, the political scene in Iran was transformed by an opposition movement which led to the overthrow of Muhammad Reza Pahlavi. This movement was more threatening than any which had challenged the regime in fifteen years, more broad-based and persistent than any mass movement in Iran for a quarter of a century, and was ultimately able to replace the regime through a cross-class nationwide insurrection unseen in Iran since the constitutionalist/nationalist upheavals of 1905–11. The success and consequences of such a movement had truly 'historic' significance, profoundly changing politics and culture in Iran, the political map of the Middle East, and the character of international interests and involvements in the region. As is well known, it was a development with highly visible religious elements (personalities, slogans, programmes), a fact which has absorbed the attention of analysts, scholars and journalists ever since. Images of bearded and turbanned religious leaders in distinctive dress, of public protest by women in concealing garments, and of demonstrations of forceful ('fanatical') religious zeal have dominated western public views of Iran; observers obsessively follow the pronouncements and manoeuvrings of religious leaders; scholars debate how and why religion came to the forefront of cultural life, political activity and ideological language in Iran in the late twentieth century.

The origins of this book lie in my own reactions to these aspects of the recent past in Iran. When the Pahlavi regime was overthrown in 1979, I responded as a European visitor to, and on occasion resident in, Iran during the 1960s and 1970s, as a historian studying past culture, politics and society in Iran, and as someone who talked and listened to Iranians commenting on their past and present. I found myself resisting both public stereotypes of 'fanatical' Muslims/bearded *mullas*/a 'return to medieval ways' and the schemes of analysis offered by experts. I was dissatisfied with presentations of the role of religious aspects of

Iranians' lives which cast them as alien and inexplicable, and with interpretations of the 'success' of religious politics which avoided the paradox of its messy contingent character and its deep historical roots. As I considered arguments against such approaches to the history of Iran in the 1970s, I wanted to offer more extended accounts of the contested place of 'religion' in the cultural, material and political experience of Iranians over a longer period. I wanted to draw on historians' skills at evoking specific situations and change over time, and look at the interactions of knowledge and power, at culture, politics and material life, and at the tensions between contingency, human agency and the structures of inequality, power and subordination. I also wanted to make ideas and information about Iranians' rich and complex past accessible without doing injustice to that richness and complexity. Such aims may be ambitious; they are certainly not privileged or unique; they are relevant to understanding the particular content and concerns of this book.

Certain images of the events of 1978–79 have become both powerful and typical – evoked decades later when US and European governments or media want to remind their audiences or electorates of the 'dangers' symbolised by the bearded *mulla*, or the angry crowd shouting religious and anti-western slogans. They have also come to overshadow, even over-determine, any account of the history of twentieth-century Iran. Two respected and widely read versions of that history (Abrahamian's of 1982 and Ansari's of 2003) have images of the 1978–79 events – huge crowds, the face of Ayatollah Khomeini – on their front covers.[1] It is as though the myriad experiences, activities and changes in the lives of millions of Iranians over four or five generations should all be seen as subsumed by that one 'historic moment'. The present text reverses that polarity and situates the 'moment' in an extended and complex range of stories and discussions. It repositions the apparent 'dominance' of religion in Iranian politics as an issue to be investigated and contextualised rather than taken as self-evident, unchanging or mysteriously incapable of rational analysis. By doing so it creates an opportunity for a fuller, more nuanced appreciation of the varied, complex and contested, roles of religious elements in the history of Iran since the later nineteenth century.

In taking this approach, the text seeks to avoid some difficulties and dead-ends. First, the high visibility and obvious power of religious leaders and of religious ideas and images in mobilising large numbers of Iranians for political action has encouraged observers and analysts to take religion as a 'given' (inherent?) feature of Iranian culture or 'character'. Scholarly writing may not follow journalistic practices of making beards, veils and turbans stand for all Iranians, but it can too easily take the persistence and dominance of religious elements in Iranian society as an assumed starting point for discussion, rather than exploring its contingent and uneven history. The fact that many, although never all, Iranians expressed their grievances and aspirations in Shi'a Muslim terms in the late 1970s should be taken as a particular conjuncture of culture, politics and circumstances needing critical explanation and comparison with other conjunctures. Defining any group of Iranians, let alone all of them, solely through religious beliefs and practices does not do justice to the complex character and history of those beliefs and practices, or to the other aspects of Iranians' past and present lives. This study maps the changing intersections of religious influences, traditions, ideas and issues with other aspects of Iranians' lives since the later nineteenth century, showing how the role of religious elements has varied over time and between different groups of Iranians. *Un-* and even *anti-*clerical forms of religious commitment, periods when religious influences were ignored and attacked, and negotiations of communal, gender, class, nationalistic or occupational interests with religious practice and belief have been important features of Iranian history in that period.

Since much of the emphasis in this text is on placing religious activities, ideas and institutions in their social and historical contexts, it consciously avoids using the abstract term 'religion', preferring to speak of 'religious' elements in those contexts. As Michael Gilsenan has observed, the term 'religion' is 'at once too general and too restrictive' a category to capture the forms, character and impact of such elements.[2] It does not express the complex, contradictory, bodies of beliefs, practices, institutions and meanings involved in religious experience, activity or relationships. It suggests a monolithic phenomenon easily separated from other aspects of human experience and endeavour rather than embedded and interactive with them. While it can be important for some people to distinguish, or even separate off, the 'sacred' and 'spiritual' elements in society and culture, this does not mean that they simply float free, nor that such distinctions will not need analysis in their wider context. It is more helpful to treat the autonomy and influence of religious elements in any situation as *relative* and *contingent*, and explore how far such elements have been autonomous, and the reasons for that autonomy, or lack of it.

Traditions of social science writing and analysis seek to incorporate 'religious' phenomena within general depictions and explanations of social structures and social change. This approach sets those phenomena in their wider context, but can tend towards schematic representations which marginalise them or present them as 'effects' or 'symptoms' of supposedly more influential elements in a social structure. Their core interest in explaining social transformations over the last 150 years, whether in sociologies of the 'first world' or development studies of the 'third world', often associates religion with 'tradition' and/or the 'pre-modern' past.

This tendency is strongly rooted in the histories of social, political and intellectual change in Europe since the eighteenth century, projected from those

3

origins to universalising models. The transformations of agriculture, transport, manufacturing, technology, medicine, commerce and government that took place in western Europe and then elsewhere seemed to be linked to the growth of forms of thought, investigation and explanation which did not rely on other-worldly or spiritual causation. Explicit contests between 'religious' and 'secular' understandings or prescriptions about evolution, democracy and moral authority, and political conflicts between clerical and anti-clerical interests, increased belief in the separation and potentially oppositional relationship between 'religion' and 'progress'. This was strengthened as professional, academic, technical and scientific knowledge was institutionalised in learned societies, university courses and departments, and technical and professional training and corporate organ-isation for doctors, scholars, engineers and so on. While rooted in real changes and conflicts, acceptance of such links and oppositions obscured more com-plex and nuanced interactions between social and political changes, religious beliefs and the growth of new ideas, knowledges and scholarly practices. It provided a powerful legacy which still influences social science, and its approach to the study of religious elements in modern societies, cultures and politics.

This book presents the religious beliefs and activities of Iranians and their specialised religious institutions and experts as active contributors to and con-stituents of its 'modern' history. It attends to interactions, negotiations and adaptations among 'religious' and other influences and interests as well as to confrontations between them. It examines 'religious' phenomena not just as fixed legacies from the past but as changing elements in whatever *current* situation is under discussion. As Michael Fischer argues: 'To rely ... on a tradition versus modernity dichotomy, as so many accounts of the Middle East do, relegating Islam to the former, is to ignore a wealth of socially critical in-formation.'[3] The activities and aspirations of devout believers, religious teachers and preachers, or innovative religious thinkers are considered as part of their 'present', whether or not they supported 'past' traditions and practices. Religious aspects of society and politics are best treated as both socially embedded and interconnected, and contingent and fluid.

Two stories from Iran in the late 1970s illustrate the point. In 1978 a lecturer at Tehran University described to me how some women students who came from the 'westernised' middle classes were adopting new forms of head-covering advocated by Muslims for women, and attending religious meetings. A few years earlier, such students had been more interested in imported fashions, music and sometimes politics, and indeed their very presence in the university suggested that they and their families wished to use 'modern' education for advancement and status. These young women's interest in religious activity and commitment was not a simplistic 'rejection' of modern life, and the anti-western, nationalistic meanings that they gave to their choices were contemporary rather than backward-looking. Religious commitment was part of their *present* rather than their past (although influenced by their backgrounds) and in acting as they did they were making personally and politically significant choices rather than expressing nostalgia or 'traditionalism'. Recent research on the so-called 're-veiling' adopted by some women in Turkey and Egypt as well as in Iran confirms that such choices are very much the outcome of women's contemporary circumstances, difficulties and wishes.[4] Whether idealistic or opportunistic, these choices and their relevance to the lives of those involved merit serious investigation.

In the same year, I talked with a group of young men in a remote town in south-eastern Iran. We discussed the rise of political protest already filling the headlines, and I asked whether they wanted a more 'religious' form of government. As they spoke, it became clear that their references to religion were a kind of umbrella or suitcase, beneath or inside which were various hopes for better lives and for a government and society in which resources and opportunities were more accessible. They told religious stories that depicted the contrast between 'corrupt'/'tyrannical' government and 'good' government, which would serve and benefit rather than oppress the people, providing values with which to judge the Shah's regime. They aspired to more control and better chances in their own lives, political 'freedom' and independence from what they saw as undesirable American influence. For them, religious language expressed these wider contemporary concerns and the influence of families or education rather than commitment to past tradition. They were young men completing local secondary school or college courses, and although geographically isolated and perhaps less culturally sophisticated than their counterparts in Tehran, they could by no means be simply pigeonholed as naive traditionalists in a provincial backwater. They wanted to improve their English and aspired to be engineers or administrators while comfortably using religious terms to express their social and political views in conversation with a visiting foreigner. Stereotypes of backward-looking fanaticism do not do justice to their ideas and experiences or explain their behaviour and opinions.

This book addresses the complex question of how Iranians' religious attitudes and activities have been 'contemporary' at the same time as sometimes invoking 'tradition' and past experience or practice, or opposing change as 'irreligious'. It argues that there have been no inevitable or necessary connections between 'religion', 'tradition', 'backwardness' or attachment to the past, and discusses connections or conflicts between 'religious' and other interests as strategies *chosen* from among real alternatives in particular circumstances. In some situations, some Iranians have identified the causes of progress or freedom with and through religion, just as other Iranians in that situation, or in others, did otherwise. The text explores and explains the contingent and chosen character

5

of support for, or resistance to, change in the name of religion. This requires attention to the role of human agency interacting with social structures and historical circumstances, and to what has been called the polyvalent[5] potential of religious world-views and commitments. This approach avoids schematic and reductive treatments of the varied and varying role of religious elements in modern Iranian history, and ensures that the success of religiously dominated politics in Iran by the 1980s will be treated as an issue for analysis rather than as an 'inevitable' outcome.

While drawing insights from the social scientific paradigms which integrate religious phenomena into accounts and analyses of whole societies, the narratives here also use other approaches. Recent work on the roles of culture in all its diversity in the making, maintenance and alteration of material and political practices offers other ways to interpret relationships between religious and other aspects of Iranians' history. It helps reflection on how the creation and use of culture and knowledge have involved relations of power and difference, as with the gender-specific organisation of learning and authority among Shi'a Muslims, the role of religious ritual in making the solidarity of particular social groups, or elite patronage of the less privileged. It also helps to reflect on the extent to which language and image have played a role in constructing Iranians' experience of their world as they made sense of that experience and communicated their understanding. The growth of the idea *and* experience of belonging to an 'Iranian nation', first among educated reformers, then political activists, and then broader-based movements, combined the making of nationalist languages, political activity and organisation in assemblies, government offices or on the streets. The meanings of being 'manly', or 'Muslim', or a member of a particular rural community, artisan group or elite family likewise developed through interactions of activity with ideas and images, interactions with histories which can be described and analysed. This study explores those histories and the role of religious elements within them.

In addition to providing a rounded account of the shifting influence of religious interests, activities and institutions, the text notes the tensions underlying any attempt of this kind. One of the most obvious is the tension between doing justice to the distinctive character of Iranian experience and creating a misleading impression of incomprehensible difference and 'uniqueness'. Attention to specificity is a core strength of historical writing, but the emphasis on 'otherness', which has characterised much work on non-western societies, unhelpfully places those societies in a category of exotic difference with unwanted consequences. It fosters views such as that the 'corruption' of African governments is inherently 'African', or that the role of Islam in Middle Eastern societies is generic rather than historical. There are dangerous differences between examining the specific historical processes which produced caste

6

systems in India, postcolonial governments in Africa, or Muslim institutions and cultures in Egypt or Iran, and the implicit essentialism which mystifies and reifies difference rather than analysing it.

One useful counter to essentialism is the comparative approach, which considers varied situations and phenomena in relation to one another, not to identify spurious similarities but to sharpen understanding of their specific features. We do this whenever we use terms such as 'family', 'government', 'worker' or 'religion' to describe relationships, institutions or activities which took particular forms and roles in twentieth-century Iran or eighteenth-century France, but which can meaningfully be said to have some common aspects. This allows for discussions of specificity and uniqueness which don't mystify, overstate or essentialise them. Comparing political religion/religious politics in Ireland, Iran, the United States and India is a way to grasp the distinctive features of each, while recognising that comparable religious and political influences may be seen in a range of societies. They can be studied as recognisable human responses to those situations rather than inexplicable behaviour by a group of people mysteriously programmed to act in particular ways because they are 'French' or 'Chinese' or 'Iranian'. This study uses comparative approaches where they clarify distinctive developments in Iranian history rather than falling back on ideas of some inherent and inexplicable 'Iranianness' to explain them.

The assumptions underlying the narrative are that stories about religious aspects of Iranian history since the later nineteenth century should not prejudge their importance, should appreciate their interdependency with other features of society, and should not treat any outcomes as inevitable. It will also be argued that those outcomes are best appreciated and understood if the stories are long ones. While the events of 1977–82 were products of immediate circumstances, and to some extent created themselves as they went along, the resources and assumptions which participants brought to their actions have a longer history. Images of martyrdom familiar for over a century, memories of nationalistic self-assertion, and long-established patterns of collective and individual self-protection, played their part alongside newer experiences and grievances. The tension between contingent and historically extended approaches to political upheaval, whether in the 1890s, 1950s or 1970s, is dealt with by combining chronologies of long-term, recent and immediate contributions to the upheavals and giving due weight to each.

In creating a rounded view of the 1979 revolution, this study places discussion of religious aspects of Iranians' lives in the past within the cultural, material and political relationships, social structures and changes with which they interacted. It will be emphasised that religious commitments, religious institutions, and specifically religious world-views, activities or practitioners shaped, but were also *shaped by*, that context. The text takes a holistic and interactive view of

7

religious elements in Iranian history, in order to understand and evaluate their shifting and contested place and influence. This approach clarifies *specific* interactions between religious and other influences in particular places, times and circumstances.

A holistic approach runs the risk of making it harder to follow clear lines of thought about any given component of a complex whole. It is therefore important to find ways of tracking particular aspects of Iranians' experience and activity over time and space in order to understand their contribution in different contexts. The strategy chosen here is to offer separate narratives, each of which addresses the central question of the role of religion in the history of Iran between the later nineteenth and the later twentieth centuries, but is a 'story' in its own right. Each 'story' deals with particular developments and relationships, and together they contribute to the general arguments and interpretation. They provide multiple perspectives on the central question, each of which is given due weight and attention, rather than being submerged in a single potentially confusing narrative.

The first set of stories, set in the framework of narrating 'religion' in its 'social' setting, address the history of the 'social' context and influence of religious thought and practice in Iran. The 'story of cultures and communities' in Chapter 1 deals with the changing ways in which religious world-views and activities have been embedded in the various living and working environments of Iranians since the later nineteenth century. It shows how those world-views and practices were constitutive *of* and constituted *by* relationships, inequities, hierarchies and linkages within and between communities in Iran, and between Iran and the wider world. It gives an account of developments in these areas in which patterns established in the nineteenth century were continued, abandoned or adapted in a period of transition from the 1890s to the 1940s and a period of intervention and innovation from the 1940s to the 1970s.

The 'story of material relationships' in Chapter 2 provides a history of the material underpinnings of religious life, institutions and practices over the period under discussion. It examines the material resources and relationships which sustained (or failed to sustain) those institutions and practices in urban and rural communities, among traders, artisans or cultivators, and among popular, elite and educated groups. The account examines three distinctive periods (1870s–1920s; 1920s–1960s; 1960s and 1970s), tracking persistent patterns and historic shifts in material support for religious specialists and institutions, and their basis in structures of ownership, production and taxation.

The 'story of distinctive institutions and vested interests' in Chapter 3 recounts the development and vicissitudes of specifically religious institutions and experts as autonomous, self-conscious and self-interested participants in social and political life in Iran since the mid-nineteenth century. It focuses particularly

8

on the evolution of distinctive institutional structures and privileges, of organised professional formation, and of explicit corporate self-definition among the *'ulama* during the nineteenth century. These developments were followed by a period of challenge between the 1920s and the 1950s and one of redirection and reconfiguration from the 1950s to the 1970s. This narrative also identifies the legacies and resources that sustained or constrained relationships between religious specialists and other groups of Iranians during the whole period.

These three 'stories' provide mutually supporting but distinct perspectives which are central to understanding the role of religious influences and interests in the history of Iran since the later nineteenth century. They establish that specifically 'religious' ideas, institutions and activities are most usefully seen as *entwined* with other productive, cultural, political and social relationships, activities and structures. They demonstrate that the social presence of religious cultures and practices in Iran had substantial if shifting material bases and cannot be understood as a purely cultural or ideological phenomenon. They move away from over-privileging or trivialising religious influences and interests, and from ideas that they are in some way peculiar or mysterious. They argue that the power and impact of religious elements within communities and cultures in Iran did not change in predictable or linear ways, and that recent developments were shaped by long-established patterns and by sharp shifts in material, social or cultural circumstances.

The move from historical narratives of the broad cultural and material settings for religious experience and activity in Iran to an account of the specific organisation and self-assertion of religious specialists points the text towards more 'political' concerns. While the development of specialists played its role in Iranians' social and cultural life generally, and had important material aspects, their active pursuit of their own particular interests was a dynamic factor in the history of political activity and ideas in Iran. The second section of the book deals with the 'political' dimension of Iranians' 'religious' activity and world-views and the 'religious' dimension of their 'political' thinking and actions. An introduction to the section outlines how the category 'political' can most helpfully be understood and used, and proposes to examine it from the three perspectives of political issues, political ideas and representations, and political movements.

In Chapter 4, the narrative deals with the 'life, death and afterlife of political issues' to which Iranians gave their energies between the later nineteenth century and the 1970s. It identifies three central areas for specific discussion and examines them in turn. First it recounts the history of Iranian involvement with the politics of 'reform' and 'modernisation', looking at the shifting alliances of interests supporting or opposing attempts at material and political change. It then looks at the history of Iranian concern with the shape of relations between

9

government (*doulat*) and people (*mellat*), giving an account of the various ways in which constitutional, populist, authoritarian, modernising and religious elements combined and conflicted. Third, it takes a similar approach to the history of nationalist politics in the period. The aim is to position religious interests and contributions in relation to other elements in the story of these three issues.

In Chapter 5, a 'story of language, symbol and discourse', the focus is on political representation as a key feature in the politics of culture and the culture of politics. In particular it provides a history and analysis of the various verbal, visual and ritual means whereby Iranians expressed political ideas and commitments. It shows that Iranians' adoption of modern styles of political expression also involved the use of inherited resources, including those drawn from Shi'a Islam, of imported ideas and images, and of creative innovations. It looks at the ways in which these elements converged or diverged, and the combinations and tensions between 'religious' and other representations, and returns to the question of relationships between lived experiences and the words, images and thoughts used to make sense of and express them.

Chapter 6 is the 'story of movements and struggles', bringing together themes and narratives from preceding chapters to provide a comparative account of three 'moments' of major political activity and upheaval: the 'Constitutional Movement' of 1905–11, the nationalist and populist movements of 1941–53 and the anti-Pahlavi movement of 1977–82. It examines similarities and differences between the role of religious and other influences on the course and character of these movements.

It is in the nature of a text with a holistic approach and a long time-span that it is more a work of synthesis than of individual research. While I have drawn on my own work on material from the Iranian past, I have also relied on the work of others in ways which I hope are fully acknowledged in the text. I also refer readers who may not have specialist interests or skills in Iranian studies to material which they can use, and so have significantly under-represented the rich range of scholarly writing produced in Persian. In addition to benefiting directly from the knowledge, expertise and insights of fellow scholars, I have sought to bring their texts into conversation with one another. In constructing the stories told here it has been enormously helpful to bring together ethnographic with textual analyses, or historical narratives with explanations of structures and symbols. In the scholarship on twentieth-century Iranians, there are often dichotomies between those that focus on the specific and experiential and those with broad structural sweeps. One aim of this book is to encourage dialogues between them, by presenting the personal and local experiences of Iranians alongside general explanations of social or political processes, and views and experiences which don't fit general patterns. Together with the use of multiple stories, this offers an open-ended approach to complex issues.

PART ONE
The 'religious' and the 'social'

ONE
A story of cultures and communities

> Identity is formed at the unstable point where the 'unspeakable' stories of subjectivity meet the narratives of history, of a culture. (Stuart Hall)

The opening narrative of this book concerns the role and limitations of religion within the various cultures created by Iranians between the later nineteenth century and the 1970s. Although the story of religious activities and beliefs in Iran can, and should, be told in terms of the material or institutional resources, structures and relationships which supported them (as it will be in Chapters 2 and 3), it makes sense to start with a cultural perspective. Religious practices (beliefs, rituals, theologies, the making of sacred images, objects or places) are components of culture in that they are creative human endeavours to make sense and express an understanding of and reactions to the world in which the practitioners live. These endeavours have histories, take informal or institutional shapes, and involve people as individuals and as groups. While a later section of the book explores the overtly political use of cultural resources provided by religion, this section deals with the cultural context of religion as an expression of solidarities and differences, of interests and inequalities, and of power and resistance in Iranian society.

The narrative follows three strands defined, but not limited by, chronology, since it will be shown that they intertwine rather than simply succeed one another. First it tells the story of the nineteenth-century legacies that embedded religious practices in the lives of Iranians in various ways; it then traces patterns of transformation in Iranian culture between the last part of the nineteenth century and the middle of the twentieth century; lastly it recounts the developments which took place between the 1950s and the 1970s. While there is a chronological line to these narratives there is also a *genealogy* whereby the features of one period are the inherited, if changed, characteristics of another. These accounts of culture are set in the context of the material life of different communities, of divisions and conflicts of interest associated with social inequalities and hierarchies, and of the creation and transmission of identities through differentiation between self ('us') and other ('them').

The narrative emphasises some important themes. Most central is a view of culture as *a set of processes created by human agency* rather than as a 'given' structure external to that agency. It will be depicted as 'made' by Iranians as they dealt with the circumstances in which they found themselves, and managed the constraints of those circumstances and their unequal position within them. Cultural practices and ideas, including those associated with religion, will be discussed as products of choice, negotiation and creative adaptation as Iranians simultaneously resisted and accommodated themselves to dominant influences, dealt with contradictions and managed many-sided identities. Cultures in Iran were expressions of Iranians' ability to combine cultural resources, to meet the demands of the powerful while protecting the subordinate, and to adapt established practices or values to new needs, interests and circumstances.

Narratives of nineteenth-century communities and hierarchies

The narrative in this section follows three interwoven strands, shaping social life relations as a context for discussing religious elements within them. Beginning with a discussion of how Iranians organised their lives within collective and communal structures, it then considers the role of relations of hierarchy and unequal power, and the local, inter-regional and global links between communities and hierarchies. The 80–85 per cent of nineteenth-century Iranians living in rural areas and practising agriculture, animal husbandry and the domestic labour which sustained households and communities founded the communal aspects of their lives on material self-sufficiency and adaptability. Settled village communities raised diverse food or forage crops, combining field cultivation, raising animals and orchard or garden production to meet their needs. Nomad communities supplemented pastoralism with cultivation, and the exchange of products with urban or village purchasers within local and regional economies. Clothing and basic tools were also produced within households and the community. Family labour intersected with collective work such as ploughing, herding, harvesting or organising irrigation, all involving co-operation within villages or nomad encampments. Foreign observers like local authors depict rural areas reliant on producing their own grain, forage and pulses as well as fruit, nuts and vegetables.[1]

Shared responsibilities for the payment of dues or crop shares to landlords, government officials or community specialists (blacksmiths or carpenters), for self-defence, and for key productive tasks, further strengthened material and social links within rural settlements. The demands of seasonal migration, of dealings with settled communities, government officials and other nomadic groups, and of raiding and hunting, similarly reinforced relationships within and between nomad encampments. The extensive arid, mountainous and unsettled terrain in Iran and consequent difficulties with communication, compounded by the lack of initiatives to improve transport facilities, further encouraged local and regional self-reliance and self-sufficiency, and the collective activities, which, while cross-cut by other interests, maintained daily existence and shaped people's understanding of their lives and identities.

Town dwellers also used local resources for many necessities, while participating in extended manufacturing and commercial networks. They relied to a substantial extent on food supplies from nearby areas, as shown by the tensions provoked by food shortages and the manipulation of prices and supplies at times of crop failure and famine.[2] Everyday life for urban Iranians was organised around the needs and activities of neighbourhoods and occupational groups. Nineteenth-century Iranian gazetteers distinguished both residential quarters and the organisation of traders and craft producers.[3] The links of apprentice, craft worker and workshop master in particular types of manufacture, of traders in specific products, or those working, living and shopping in particular neighbourhoods provided the framework for urban work and livelihoods. Collective responsibilities for craft regulation, grievances and payment of dues and taxes to guilds, religious leaders and government officials, shaped communal identities in occupational groups and urban neighbourhoods. Guilds, and other networks, gave social forms to shared material interests.

Communal and collective identities were also created in kin groups and households in village settlements, nomad encampments or urban areas. Cultivation, pastoral production and craft manufacture, like food preparation, or household, child- and healthcare work, used family and household labour divided along gender and age lines. For men trading the dairy or textile products of female household members, or parents passing on craft skills, rights to land and flocks, or access to religious and administrative office to their children, household and kin connections were vital resources. Advancement through patronage used kinship loyalties, just as marriage decisions were influenced by interests in advantageous alliances, or household production and reproduction. Women's childbearing capacity, skills and dowries, like children's aptitudes, were assets to be used and exchanged by partners and parents. The relative self-sufficiency and autonomy of Iranian communities were partly sustained by household and familial self-reliance and co-operation.

These material realities involved personal relationships and cultural resources shaping familial and communal identities. Peasants planning agricultural work, and managing or evading the agents of landlords or government, affirmed ideals of co-operation, competition and conflict that supported communal actions. Village representatives petitioned officials and bargained with landlords on behalf of the community, just as villagers made collective decisions to resettle, to defend themselves from attack, or to resolve conflicts among individual cultivators or households. Comparable elements shaped the migrations and raids of nomad pastoralists. The physical and spatial forms of walled village

15

and tent-dwelling encampment, and the organisation of collective defence and seasonal migration manifested the identity of rural communities.

Other cultural influences operated in towns, with their range of specialised occupations and social hierarchies based in manufacturing, commercial, cultural and administrative activities, and propertied, religious, merchant and government elites. Relationships and identities were based on specific locations ('quarters' or neighbourhoods), on occupations (craft and merchant organisations, religious specialists), and on social hierarchies among elite and unprivileged groups, or ethnic and cultural minorities. The spatial arrangement of craft production and trade in designated areas of the *bazar* (the manufacturing and commercial centre of Iranian towns), of bureaucrats around the *arg* (centre of civil and military administration), or of residential areas dominated by particular groups gave physical expression to collective identities.[4] The need to manage common interests or conflicts, to pursue those interests (protests by the poor over food prices, demands by craft groups for protection), and to meet collective financial obligations, created occasions for joint activity which affirmed identity.

The lives of nineteenth-century Iranians were also shaped by inequity and hierarchy. For cultivators, the key factor was access to land and the products of their labour, determined by the unequal power, rights and resources of landlords, sharecropping peasants, land-owning peasants and peasants without land rights. Absentee landlords extracted payments from cultivators on the basis of rent or sharecropping agreements, often combining this with tax collecting on behalf of government. At times of harvest or hardship, the conflicting interests of cultivators and property owners were played out in negotiation between peasants and landlords/tax collectors, supplemented by the use of armed force by landlords or flight by peasants. The princely governor of Kerman province and others described patterns of domination, subordination and manipulation embedding unequal power relations at the heart of rural life.[5]

The lives and work of the families and encampments of nomad pastoralists involved comparable power relations. Household and camp-level production and resources were exploited by leading individuals and lineages whose main source of power lay in their military and organising roles. Their material power might be achieved by renting out pasture rights, as among the Shahsevan of north-west Iran, the exaction of dues from flock owners, recorded for the Qashqai in the south-west, or management of migration as with Qashqai and Bakhtiari.[6] By the later nineteenth century, affluent and powerful 'tribal' leaders acquired land, revenues and power through links to settled elites and government, marking themselves as a dominant stratum separated from the everyday life of nomad pastoralists. Legitimised by discourses of lineage, and supported by landed wealth and the capacity to collect taxes, settle disputes and mobilise the armed

16

strength of pastoral communities, leading clans and individuals created and contested privileged positions. Use of patronage, claims to kinship solidarity, and capacity to coerce the less powerful, provided vital cultural underpinning for their dominance.

Hierarchy and unequal power relations were similarly recorded in accounts of the social structures of towns. Urban centres brought together landlords, office holders, representatives of royal government, and commercial, entrepreneurial and financial leaders, with influential professionals including religious leaders. They were centres for the exchange of manufactured and agricultural products, the production of craft manufactures, the organisation of trade and investment, and the accumulation of rents, profits and taxes. They were focal points in the networks of trade, cultural activity and government discussed below. They were bases for administrative and religious authority, and locations for public social rituals and gatherings, and displays of wealth and power. While the extent and range of these roles varied between major centres of government and production and lesser towns, some at least featured in most urban settlements.

Collective aspects of life in major centres or lesser towns were cross-cut by distinctions and inequalities of wealth, status and power. Shared activity in craft manufacture entwined with the authority and power of workshop masters over labourers and apprentices, or of merchant investors over artisan clients, and were as important as common bonds. Commercial activity relied on power relations between 'great' merchants and lesser traders, or those with wealth from land and office holding, as well as on common interests within particular areas of trade.[7] The rise of Haji Muhammad Hassan Amin-al-Zarb (c. 1835–98) from modest origins to prominent merchant, financier and entrepreneur illustrates this.[8] Accounts of shawl and carpet workshops of Kerman, or textile and metal workshops in Isfahan or Kashan or Yazd depict the shared identity of craftsmen and their use and control of paid employees. Accounts of the urban scene also describe a stratum of urban poor supporting themselves by manual and service activities, and distinct from artisans with skills, resources and authority over their workforce.[9] Dependency, patronage, hierarchy, distinction and power relations were woven into daily urban existence.

This was acknowledged in the language and perceptions of nineteenth-century Iranians. Just as they had a vocabulary for collective and communal associations (*mahalleh* = quarter; *tayefeh* = clan/nomadic group/occupational group; *khanvadeh* = family/household/tribal unit; *buneh* = plough team), so they had categories indicating rank and power. The terms *ashraf*, *a'zem* or *a'yan* used by nineteenth-century Iranian writers to distinguish urban 'notables' from lesser folk, or *malek* and *arbab* to designate landowners, or *ustad* for workshop masters, like the labelling of the tax-paying rural population as *ru'aiya* (peasants or subjects), expressed enduring perceptions of the social order in terms

17

of hierarchy. Speech conventions, which distinguished the appropriate ways of addressing social equals, superiors and inferiors, embedded hierarchy and power relations in everyday communication.[10] Records of moments of conflict and confrontation when subordinate groups challenged the power of the dominant provide further evidence of unequal and exploitative relations.[11]

Differences and inequities also operated in the intimate spheres of household and family activity. Most central were the divisions of labour, power and resources in cultivation, animal husbandry, manufacture and commerce along gender and age lines. Gender specialisation distinguished women's provision of childcare and household labour, or their processing of animal products for use and sale, from male activities such as ploughing and construction work on buildings or irrigation systems. Spatial segregation situated female cloth and carpet production within their homes, contrasted with the male production of urban and luxury versions in urban workshops. This expressed cultural conventions which separated men and women in household or public space and defined the sphere of public/external affairs as belonging to men. Such conventions in turn created specific divisions of labour to meet them, as with the role of female health specialists, female service workers or female attendants in bath-houses.[12]

Gender divisions of labour varied significantly according to social rank, age and market forces, but were a core influence in material life. Legal and customary frameworks for inheritance, marriage and the use or management of material resources (land, flocks, money) distinguished the roles and rights of men and women, with variations beween rich and poor, rural and urban, or settled and nomadic groupings. While legal or material provisions were made for both women and men, women's range of choice, autonomy and authority was often limited.[13] This was significant for the affluent, where commercial activity or the rewards of land- or office-holding were shaped by male merchants, landowners or officials, and at the modest level of local trade in cloth or milk-based goods produced by women's skill and labour where men often took charge of marketing.[14]

Just as senior males controlled women's work and resources, so they managed the lives and labour of children and junior family members. The role of family in marital and kin alliances, and in access to land, business opportunities and office was also materially significant and a concern for senior family members. We find the rising entrepreneur Amin al-Zarb manoeuvring brothers in the family business, just as Kermani landholders and Shahsevan *khans* sought to deploy and control kin.[15] While kinship and household interests relied on co-operation in the common interest, patriarchal and age-based hierarchies and authority, with their associated conflicts of interest, were part and parcel of household and community life.

The ability of the Shah's government to exact taxes from its subjects, devolving and selling that task to those with local power, or with the money and connections to obtain office, was another strand of power. The collection of taxes was often entwined with demands for rents and dues claimed by tax collectors on their own behalf to reimburse their outlay and to profit from office or tax-collecting rights. The use of physical force to assist these exactions visibly asserted dominance over the subject population, just as negotiation and resistance were the responses of subordinated groups. Other forms of hierarchy and authority emerged when leaders of pastoral, merchant or artisan communities took decisions and led action on their behalf. Acknowledgement of seniority, knowledge and experience within households, religious institutions and kin groups likewise embedded hierarchies within them.

Nineteenth-century Iranian communities and power structures operated within larger networks and relationships. Production of specialised goods fed exchange between rural and urban areas and across regions. That a district round Kashan produced at most half of its annual needs for grain, or butter was sent from Hamadan to Tehran, and the thinly populated Bam area exported surplus grain to neighbouring districts, shows interdependence as another element of material life.[16] Foodstuffs moved from villages to towns, raw materials from cultivators to craft producers, and luxury goods from artisans to elite customers. Sales of tobacco from Fars in Kerman, of pastoral products in urban markets, of Isfahani printed cloth or Kashan velvets in Astarabad on the shores of the Caspian, like those of Kermani shawls and dyes in Tabriz, Yazd or Tehran exemplify such interdependence.[17]

These exchanges involved local, long-distance, wholesale and retail traders in moving goods, money and credit within and between localities. A modest centre like Hamadan supported merchants whose 'operations extend to all the principal towns in Persia', just as merchants in Kerman had agents in India.[18] Specialisation in particular agricultural goods drew cultivators, pastoralists and landholders into long-distance links, as demand for specialist manufactures for distant markets provided livelihoods for artisans. Producing and trading fruits and nuts, pottery, leather goods and carpets, processed milk products, metalwares, tobacco, dyestuffs and specialised textiles created relationships between and within many Iranian communities.

These relationships extended beyond the boundaries of Iran to neighbouring areas of south, central and west Asia. By the later nineteenth century, the shape of long-distance trade had changed in three important ways. First, older patterns of trade with regions of the Ottoman Empire, central Asia and the Indian subcontinent were overlaid by new links to European economies with their competitive global networks of trade, production, transport and finance, and their ability to mobilise markets, labour, raw materials and investment.

Second, European demands for Iranian cotton, opium, silk and wool, success in gaining markets for their manufactures, and ability to enter Iranian tobacco, silk or carpet industries established European economic influence. Third, these competitive advantages and the global mobility of European goods and capital, reinforced by European state support for commercial and colonial expansion, shaped *international* movements of prices, markets and currency values which Iranians had to manage but over which they had no control.

Between the 1850s and the First World War Iranians lost much material autonomy. Decline in textile exports from over 60 per cent of Iranian exports in the mid-nineteenth century to around 13 per cent in the early twentieth century, when manufactured goods formed over 73 per cent of all imports, was matched by the dominance of raw material exports in a classic quasi-colonial pattern shaped by European demand. This can also be seen in human terms. The lives and choices of artisans, landowners, traders and peasants were shaped by the demand for carpets in Europe, cotton and wool in Russia or opium in Hong Kong and Iranian consumption of imported goods.[19] By the early twentieth century, dependency and interdependence penetrated and co-existed with localised self-sufficient life and production. Tabrizi merchants and British firms sponsored new carpet production for export to Europe, negotiating with artisans and carpet-making households, or creating their own workshops. Iranian merchants established agents in India, Europe, Istanbul and Hong Kong. Urban craft producers went out of business or adapted to new conditions, as Isfahani printed cloth-makers now printed local designs on imported cotton fabric. Iranian peasants and landlords juggled the risks and opportunities of using land for opium, dye plants or tobacco production for export, rather than grain cultivation for local consumption. Lower-class Iranians often wore clothes made from Manchester cotton rather than locally woven *karbas*, and had tools and cooking pans made with imported metal. Those who consumed tea and sugar relied on British, French and Russian sources at prices set in global markets. Carpet weavers faced European regulation designs or dyes and combined imported cotton thread with local wool in their work. Needy and aspiring wage earners and traders in north-western Iran became migrant workers in the Baku oilfields or traded illicitly across the Russian border.[20]

Commercial dependency was reinforced by pressures from the major powers. As the Tsarist empire expanded its territories into the Caucasus and central Asia, and the British pushed the frontiers of their Indian domains into the Punjab, Sind, Baluchistan and the borders of Afghanistan, the stability and policy of the rulers of Iran assumed growing importance in their calculations and rivalries. Intensified diplomatic and military intervention established the Tsarist and British governments as players in Iranian politics. Their influence was used for material advantage, gaining Russian and British traders favourable tariffs and commercial concessions, and later drawing Iranian governments into loans and banking concessions.

By the 1880s the Shah faced financial difficulties, partly caused by international movements of prices and currency values, to which Iranian prices and values were now linked, and partly as the result of Russian and British demands. The establishment of a British bank in Iran in 1889 was part of the settlement of the cancelled Reuter Concession of 1872, and the setting up of the Russian equivalent in 1891 followed the cancellation of a railway concession to a Russian subject. The dynamic of foreign influence and Iranian government need, leading to grants of concessions, and Iranian resentment at such concessions leading to their cancellation, shaped new forms of dependency. Cancellation of the Tobacco Concession in 1890 led to the government contracting the first foreign loans, and pledging revenues for their repayment.

By the early twentieth century, the Iranian government had foreign debts carrying service charges absorbing a quarter of its expenditure. Loans were one element of foreign financial involvement (some £30 million), which included investment in banks, transport, fisheries, telegraphs, a few factories and the Anglo-Persian Oil Company, whose value more than doubled from 1909 to 1914 and whose output quintupled in the first two years of production (1912–14). A trade deficit of some £3 million by 1913 reflected a 30–50 per cent excess of imports over exports, met by cash payments, illicit trade, remittances from migrant workers and foreign loans. This larger context of dependency constrained Iranian material activities, and connected households and communities to global frameworks of diplomacy and politics.

This shift in Iranian connections to a wider world had cultural dimensions. From elite Iranians who might adopt European luxury goods or fashions, to craftsmen depicting pianos and western armaments in tile designs, or merchants adapting to foreign competition, new concepts and images entered Iranian cultures. Telegraph offices became a focus for political protest as well as useful to commerce and government, just as long-distance traders could bring illicit political publications from Bombay or Istanbul in their caravans. European material influence and challenges stimulated cultural innovation and debate as well as political arguments about Iranian rulers' duty to protect Iranian interests. Officials, traders, intellectuals and migrant workers in cities of the Ottoman and Tsarist empires, and Iranians who maintained historic links to the Caucasus area, encountered new approaches to politics, education, law and religion. The political impact of these contacts will be discussed later, but cross-regional and global linkages were also features of cultural experience.

This compressed account provides a basis for examining the role of religion, which took three main forms. There were relationships between religious specialists and institutions and various Iranian communities and hierarchies. There were powerful contributions made to community life and power relations by the religious activity and organisation of ordinary believers. There were also verbal, visual and ritual expressions of religious influence and traditions, transmitting them among individuals, communities and generations. These cultural resources gave a religious flavour to many expressions of identity, community and hierarchy.

Central to the embedding of religious elements in Iranian cultures and communities were exchanges of goods and services between religious specialists and others in those communities. At the core of relationships between the 'ulama (the learned men of religion) and other Shi'a Muslims were payments made by village, merchant or artisan groups to such men. By the nineteenth century, Shi'a 'ulama had established rights to receive the zakat and the khums. The former was a 'poor-rate' levied on believers for charitable purposes, and the latter the 'fifth' levied for the support of the prophet Muhammad's descendants and needy persons, half of which the Shi'a saw as the 'Imam's share' – the 'inheritance' of 'Ali, the first Shi'a leader, and his successors from 'Ali's uncle and father-in-law Muhammad. These dues were paid to the mujtaheds, those 'ulama whose learning, reputation, expertise and piety gained them the right to issue judgments and interpretations that were authoritative for their followers. They supported religious institutions and specialists (schools, madrasehs [seminaries], tullab [religious students], prayer leaders and lesser 'ulama and the entourages of leading 'ulama), and gifts to the sick and poor. Since they were voluntary and based on the ability of the 'ulama to convince believers to continue payment, it linked 'ulama closely to the communities from which they drew funds and to whom they provided services.[21]

Their services ranged from leading prayer and marriage or funeral rituals, to settling legal and commercial cases over property, inheritance and business dealings, placing 'ulama close to the daily concerns of many households and communities. Provision of welfare and patronage by affluent and powerful 'ulama to the poor and dependent, or the reliance of religious specialists and tullab on material support from urban entrepreneurs, underpinned business, legal and educational activities. Tullab drew on the resources of those with money and property, on payments for their services, and on the expertise and patronage of established 'ulama; traders and craft producers involved religious specialists in their working lives; urban and rural families and communities turned to them for ritual and educational needs, marriage and inheritance transactions, or welfare, providing payments in return.

These exchanges combined the practicalities of education, money, marriage or business with cultural meanings and relationships. The role of urban groups and 'ulama in these activities met important material needs, and also expressed the cultural meanings of family, piety and community, establishing personal links of power, intimacy, conflict or co-operation between religious specialists and the wider community. These links played a part in family and neighbourhood life and popular culture. They were formative cultural influences on behaviour, expressing concerns with prosperity, respectability, power and survival. The entwining of religious elements in everyday activities and relationships linked religious specialists to households, workshops and merchant groups, shaping collective identities. Contacts among 'ulama, artisans, traders, itinerant preachers, peasants, tullab, darvishes or teachers provided religious dimensions for many basic features of daily life. Religious meanings were woven into the rituals of the life-cycle (childbirth, marriage, mourning), the annual cycle of Shi'a celebration, the rhythms of working life, and the uncertainties of health and fortune. The use of mosques, shrines and public spaces for religious activities, or of religious specialists' skills in teaching, divination or writing of prayers for amulets and talismans, regularly enacted such meanings.

The densest presence of diverse religious resources was found in urban settings. Mosques, maktabs (Qur'anic schools), and centres for religious celebration, like the use of streets and bazars for religious activity, provided physical links between religion and communal life. Madrasehs and mosques, located at the core of urban settlements, were bases for religious education and ritual, and a focus for meetings between religious specialists and members of the community for legal, ritual or charitable purposes. The physical proximity of commercial, religious, residential, manufacturing and educational premises in urban centres sustained personal and cultural connections.[22]

At the apex of these connections were the relationships of mujtaheds with those who accepted and acted on their authority. Such relationships had a growing institutional aspect and political importance, but also depended on personal links between mujtaheds and followers and the selection by particular believers of a chosen mujtahed as their 'source' of authority and 'model'/exemplar for imitation (taqlid). Definitions of the position of mujtaheds and their followers, discussed in Chapter 3, put choice and personal relationships at their core. The presence of a plurality of mujtaheds, among whom believers chose and followed a particular individual, placed emphasis on community–'ulama relations, reinforcing the impact of voluntary khums and zakat payments. Mujtaheds depended on the mobilisation of respect and loyalty, through personal networks and contacts which confirmed their doctrinal authority, and political and material patronage. Piety and reputation, judged by those among whom senior 'ulama moved and on whose support they relied, were as much criteria for recognition as the formal learning which established professional authority. They maintained their position through legal, ritual and educational functions, and, by being available to deal with requests, disputes and concerns brought by clients, allies or students, used their ability to command the attachment of supporters in pursuit of their interests.

Craft groups or residents of urban neighbourhoods might coalesce round the authority, patronage and charisma of prominent religious leaders, defining themselves as followers (*muqallid*) of their guidance, and supporting them with fees, dues or gifts. They could define themselves through shared commitment to a chosen *mujtahed*, teacher or preacher, and antagonistically through opposition or conflict with other groups. Such conflicts were often linked to *'ulama* rivalries, but also consolidated the identification of participants with 'their' grouping and loyalty to a chosen patron/leader. Confrontations between neighbourhood factions expressed a shared culture, including religious affiliation, through opposition to 'others'.[23] Since there were diverse religious traditions and practices within and outside Shi'a Islam, such affiliations could become oppositions, with followers of particular traditions defining themselves against the 'corrupt' or 'heretical' practice of others. The defiling of mosques and pulpits, exclusion of opponents from bath-houses as 'unclean', or the clash of rival religious processions and violence at debates among rival *'ulama* took conflicts into public urban arenas, linking the expression of collective identity to religious themes.

Other religious specialists contributing to urban society included lesser *'ulama* and others with claims to religious education and knowledge, who might teach or provide pious recitations in an urban quarter, self-appointed purveyors of prayer, divination, mystical knowledge or expertise with talismans and amulets. They might be established residents or itinerant *darvishes*, members of local craft and trader families, or unattached mendicants. They provided familiar valued services sustaining convention and tradition, and offered opportunities for diversity, innovation, dissidence and heterodoxy, contributing to a cultural fabric in which popular beliefs and traditions entwined with learned and 'official' contributions.

Much writing on the cultural life of communities and its religious dimensions deals with urban settings, reflecting the urban origin and concerns of many source materials. Certainly, towns were centres for higher levels of education and specialist religious training and for the religious leadership dispensing legal and doctrinal judgments and patronage to followers. Major mosques, *tekkiehs*, *madrasehs* and *huseineyehs* were common features of the urban scene. Rural settlements tended not to have such institutions, and might not even have their own mosques, although there were many rural shrines and holy places.[24] Contacts with religious specialists took the form of contacts with lesser *'ulama*, *darvishes* and others rather than everyday encounters typical of urban settlements. This strengthened informal, self-created elements of rural religious culture and their links to the distinctive concerns of rural people. This in turn contributed to their sense of the distinctive identity of their communities, and of contrasts between their own practices and beliefs and urban, or 'official', versions.

Religious elements in Iranian culture were also produced and sustained by *non*-specialist believers. Since even 'orthodox' Shi'a practices did not depend predominantly on a central institutional authority such as a papacy, local-ised authority and religious choice were important. Many religious traditions encourage the independent activity of believers, whether in the lives of individual ascetics or mystics (Hindu, Christian, Buddhist, Muslim) or by 'lay' provision of religious ritual, education and welfare (charity, pilgrimages, Methodist classes, Jewish Passover). Muslim traditions have their own historic features, notably a lack of sacraments like Christian baptism or communion in which priests act as irreplaceable intermediaries between God and the community of believers. Core religious duties such as prayer, fasting and pilgrimage are managed by Muslim believers themselves, and the authority of *'ulama* (important as it was and is) rested primarily on their role as interpreters and transmitters of texts, laws and traditions.

In Shi'a communities there were a number of key arenas in which believers played direct roles in religious culture and practices. Although the establishment of Twelver Shi'ism as the dominant form of Islam in Iran during the sixteenth and seventeenth centuries was led by rulers and *'ulama*, it also involved the development of popular, community-based religious traditions. Intense attach-ment to the persons of the Twelve Imams (especially 'Ali and Husein) was expressed in rituals of pilgrimage to shrines associated with them and their kin, and in commemoration of the martyrdom of Husein. Although encouraged by Shi'a *'ulama*, they were shaped by ordinary believers, drawing on localised mystical, ecstatic, customary or millenarian traditions.

This placed religious *self*-expression and *self*-regulation at the core of Shi'a Muslim culture in Iran. The bases of Shi'a Muslim belief and practice were narratives of the events and leaders associated with the emergence of Shi'ism as a distinct tradition, and used by Iranian Shi'a in the nineteenth and twentieth centuries to define their religious identity. These foundation narratives centre on 'Ali, identified by Shi'a as the first Imam (divinely ordained leader) of the Muslim community, displaced by conspiracy and assassination, and Husein, his son and third Shi'a Imam, who upheld his claim to leadership and was killed in battle with opponents near Karbala. Mourning for these leader/martyrs became widespread popular practice, and was encouraged by religious and ruling estab-lishments anxious to embed Shi'a Islam as the official faith. By the nineteenth century, an annual cycle of rituals associated with the lives and deaths of 'Ali and Husein, culminating in the activities of Muharram, the month associated with Husein's martyrdom, involved communities in rituals sponsored by guilds and notables, or organised at village and neighbourhood level. Processions, enactments of passion plays depicting Husein's death, gatherings of women for mourning recitations, or of young men marching and beating themselves, made ordinary believers autonomous practitioners of the most spiritually and emotionally significant expressions of Shi'ism.

These undertakings were surrounded by other collective devotional activities. The custom of visiting shrines associated with Imams, their relatives, or other holy persons, included weekly visits by groups of women to local *imamzadehs* (shrines) and long-distance journeys to major shrines like those at Mashad and Karbala. Local shrines were the focus for ceremonials celebrated by particular communities or occupational groups. Linking attachments to locality or occupation with affirmations of Shi'a commitment, and creating shared rituals, they were established and regular popular religious activities. The annual festival of the carpet craftsmen in the Kashan area, the flow of more or less affluent pilgrims to Mashad and Qum, the growth of village shrines like that at Sehkunj, near Kerman, with their opportunities for devotion, celebration and sociability or consolation, expressed that shared commitment and identity.

Central to collective devotion were the rituals associated with the martyrdom of Husein. The powerful legacy of this founding episode of resistance, suffering and conflict took various forms of collective commemoration. Rituals associated with these martyrs were conjointly undertaken by communities and preachers, reciters or *'ulama*. The major forms were mourning recitations recounting the Karbala events, and processions and dramas in the first ten days of Muharram. The growth of these practices drew on popular organisation and 'official' sponsorship by *'ulama* and rulers. Over time *rawzeh-khwani* (mourning recitations) evolved into rituals performed in public, in specially designated venues (*huseiniyehs, tekkiehs*), and in private homes where individuals sponsored recitations and invited guests. Although specialists (*rawzeh-khwans*) provided recitations, *rawzeh* gatherings were organised and funded by pious individuals or groups, and involved active participation by those attending, who expressed their own involvement in the 'Karbala narrative' in response to the recitation. The gazetteer of nineteenth-century Kerman spoke of *rawzeh* gatherings in caravanserais and private houses as well as in *tekkiehs* and *madrasehs*.[25] Notables displaying piety among peers or clients, merchants and artisans celebrating the values central to their lives, and communities coming together in shared loyalty and grief for the Imams were agents rather than passive recipients of religious culture.

Similar developments shaped the mourning processions and *ta'ziyeh* (dramatic representations of the Karbala story) undertaken during Muharram. The processions involved groups of male believers moving through streets and public spaces, chanting and striking themselves with sticks, hands, blades or chains to commemorate Husein's suffering. *Ta'ziyeh* performances combined traditions of public mourning and tales of the Karbala narrative in dramatised presentations of his martyrdom. In the nineteenth century, both sponsors and performers of *ta'ziyehs* came from the communities where they took place, drawing large and responsive audiences ranging from elite visitors to *tekkiehs* established by rulers and notables to the participants at *ta'ziyehs* in humbler urban and rural settings. Merchants and others displayed piety and status by support for *ta'ziyehs*, or providing drinking water for participants in mourning processions (a practical contribution and a commemorative/symbolic reference to the denial of water to the Karbala martyrs). As with the *rawzehs*, processions and *ta'ziyehs* moved spectators to express their own responses. Such responses (cries, tears, gestures) were personal and collective in the sense that it was gathering as groups for *ta'ziyehs* and processions that stimulated individuals and gave their responses full significance. Active involvement of believers linked religious devotion, social solidarities and the meanings of the foundation narratives of Shi'ism. Early twentieth-century photographs and nineteenth-century drawings of *rawzehs*, Muharram processions, preaching and *ta'ziyeh* illustrate this. They show specific groups (women, notables, *mullas*, servants) at an event, distinguished by dress and positioning. Written evidence similarly describes the collective presence of villagers and urban residents, the participation of specific subgroups, and shared involvement in these activities, noting how communal expressions of emotion contributed to the intensity of individuals' reactions.[26]

Material support for these events, ranging from Nasir al-din Shah's scheme for the great Tekkieh Doulat in Tehran to small donations for *ta'ziyeh* and *rawzehs*, were pious acts (*kheirat*) fulfilling personal vows and bringing spiritual reward (*savab*). They were opportunities for social display and the recognition or emulation of piety. Informal presentations of *ta'ziyeh* on carts and in available public spaces, as well as grand architectural and cultural settings and professional performances funded by the elite, indicated continuing 'ownership' and commitment by ordinary believers. Such collective commitment extended to the Iranian community in Istanbul, who organised their own large-scale Muharram commemorations in the later nineteenth century.[27]

Beyond Muharram rituals, believers were actively involved in the local cults and autonomous religious associations of Sufis, or other heterodox and minority groups. Participation by different groups in the rituals of such sects was the active expression of commitment to particular traditions, paralleling material support for Sufi *pirs*, leaders like the Isma'ili Aqa Khan, or Kurdish *shaykhs*. Ceremonies associated with local saints, shrines or sects, like the use of amulets and divination, involved the commitment and creativity of ordinary believers as well as *mullas* or religious leaders, and were often undertaken independently of the latter. A twentieth-century anthropologist considered that of eleven areas of religious activity central for Iranian Shi'a Muslims, only four or five involved the *'ulama* as key participants.[28] It followed that active sanctity and piety were recognised and associated with Iranians who were not formally trained *'ulama*, but gained respect and authority among those who knew them. The leader (*pir*) of a Sufi group, merchants like Sayyid 'Ali Muhammad of Shiraz (later leader of a new religious movement as the Bab) noted for pious prayer and study, the descendant of a sanctified lineage, and the wandering *darvish* or visionary preacher, were accepted as real, if controversial, examples of holiness.

The privileged status and expertise of the *'ulama* were concentrated in the textual and legal areas of Shi'ism. The term *'ulama* (and its singular *'alim*) derived from an Arabic root designating learned intellectual activity and knowledge rather than sanctified status. The wider spiritual, ritual and cultural areas of the faith might involve their participation or patronage, but were often organised and enacted by broader communities of believers. On the one hand there were many areas of religious activity not requiring specialist religious intermediaries, and on the other religious specialists did not have a monopoly of spiritual authority and status. The traditions of thought derived from the Qur'an (*hadith*) and the law (*shari'a*), and the expert custodians who knew and interpreted them, were augmented by other sources and traditions. There were religious ideas and beliefs controlled neither by experts nor textual authority and learning, based on popular beliefs and ideals, and expressed in the customs and activities of believers. The ideas and forms developed in such contexts included imaginative elements, drawing on myths, traditions and non- or pre-Islamic inspiration. From the appeasement of *jinn* (dangerous spirits) to the invocation of local legendary holy and heroic figures, they shaped autonomous religious outlooks outside 'official', text-based piety.[29]

Religious ideas and activities contributed to the drawing of boundaries between one community and another and the expression of divisions and in-equalities within particular communities. Accounts of Haidari/Ni'amati group-ings and conflicts in nineteenth-century settlements emphasise the clear *spatial* boundaries between neighbourhoods with different *religious* affiliations mutually reinforcing one another, and expressing both facets of identity through opposi-tion to other communities. The ritual character of these conflicts suggests that the purpose and meaning of fighting went beyond the exchange of blows and insults. Observers also contrasted the roles of leaders and other group members in such confrontations, suggesting that rank and status flavoured communal strife, as also seen in the religious practices of artisans and aristocrats, or male and female members of heterodox Shaikhi groups of Kerman or Tabriz.[30]

Any account of the religious cultures of nineteenth-century Iranians should note their association with differences in power or status, and the conflicting interests arising from them. Residents of Iranian cities who petitioned the governor for the release of prisoners during Muharram ceremonies, the role of *mujtaheds'* houses as sanctuaries for those seeking protection and refuge, or the presence of *'ulama* among the notables of Iranian communities all marked the role of power and patronage in religious matters.[31] Prominence in merchant, rural or artisan groups was often marked by a show of religious commitment through sponsorship of Muharram activities, *madrasehs* and shrines, just as the patronage of land- and office-holding elites linked their power and status with piety.

The very patterns of religious practice embodied hierarchy and authority as well as shared belief and activity. The charisma and spiritual insight of preachers and mystics marked them as sources of inspiration claiming obedience from disciples and followers. The *'ulama's* material resources and professional standing placed them among the respected and 'notable' members of their communities. At the upper levels of the religious hierarchy, *mujtaheds* had the recognised authority to issue judgments on legal and doctrinal matters which were binding on their followers (*muqallid*). This authority relied on the support of those who funded them, but also enabled them to acquire wealth and distribute patronage which placed them high in the social hierarchy. Senior *'ulama* held influential and profitable offices in the *shari'a* courts (as *sheikh-al -islam*), major urban mosques (as *imam-jom'eh*) and as administrators of shrines and religious endowments (*vaqfs*), offices which linked them to royal and elite networks and politics. The position of leading *'ulama*, like that of a Sufi *pir* within their sect, or of leaders of dissenting forms of Shi'ism, was one in which deference, authority and patron–client relations expressed unequal power and status. The *lutis* (street toughs) defending the interests of leading *'ulama*, devout followers seeking advice and support from Shaikhi *mujtaheds* or Sufi leaders, the recipients of charity from *'ulama* and pious donors, and the clients and employees of religious leaders, were all placed in a hierarchy.[32]

The authority of religious learning, spiritual charisma or legal expertise fitted a wider cultural pattern of obedience and of distinctions between leaders and disciples. They meshed with hierarchies of power and ownership in which *'ulama* gained and used wealth and status as patrons and competitors in elite or communal politics, where payments by devoted followers of an Isma'ili leader sustained his political ambitions, and *mujtaheds* were landlords and entrepreneurs.[33] Elite notions that social and political order rested on the bond between the twin bases of stable government and religious authority supported strong ideological associations between religious and political power.

The emphasis given here to religious influences and features within the communities and hierarchies of nineteenth-century Iran should not suggest that these elements were all-pervasive. The capacity of ordinary Iranians to make much of their spiritual lives for themselves created a cultural spectrum running from localised autonomy from learned religion to explicitly anti-clerical positions. Anecdotes about licentious, religiously lax, incompetent and avaricious religious specialists, like those of the nineteenth-century writer Rustam al-Hukama, gave literary form to oral and popular discourses of denigration, mockery and criticism of the religious establishment. The very diversity of practice available to Shi'a Muslims gave believers freedom to pick and choose sources of religious support. The inspiration of preachers and mystics, the spiritual force associated with shrines, the skills of diviners and amulet-makers, quite apart from believers' own endeavours, offset any claims by the learned men of religion to monopolise status and authority. Such claims stimulated critical or disrespectful scrutiny which noted mismatches between *'ulama* misconduct and their assertions of privilege based on virtue and piety.

Beyond that, Iranians had other cultural resources. Legends associated with particular places or local figures and non- or pre-Islamic stories of spirits and heroes, romances and battles were related and depicted in everyday settings. Observers reported tales of supernatural beings and fantastic animals threatening travellers, or endangering women and babies around the time of childbirth, and of magic events explaining some striking feature in a landscape.[34] Legends of pre-Islamic warriors and rulers such as Rustam, Bahram or Jamshid had spread from literary culture to the non-literate, so that servants listened to recitations of Firdausi's epic on these heroes, and urban toughs exercised to its rhythms.[35] Identity and solidarity among nomadic groups or settled elites drew on accounts of ancestry and of the past achievements of forebears providing other images of heroism, virtue or achievement. Urban notables like the Shirazi author Fasa'i, or his Kermani counterpart Vaziri celebrated forebears and fellow notables as holders of land, power and office, and skilled, loyal performers of these roles.[36] Daring, cunning, honour and the role of clan or kin provided distinctive, powerful and autonomous images and ideals. The codes of sexual and gender conduct which regulated gender-specific roles and relationships among men and women might quote religious precepts and precedents, but were powerfully grounded in familial and communal notions of honour, shame and reputation. The dramatic and violent punishments handed out to adulterous women or male pederasts expressed collective moral rejection rather than *shari'a* judgment, and were undertaken by secular authorities and outraged neighbours.[37]

In the later nineteenth century, Iranians drew on a rich cultural repertoire of non- or even anti-religious ideas, values and traditions underpinning their activities and relationships. By that period, too, new influences began to transform the familiar legacies of religious culture and to proffer alternatives. Religious debate and innovation in the middle decades of the century took dissident and critical thought and movements in anti-traditional, anti-*'ulama*, freethinking directions. The Babi movement was influenced by existing dissident forms of Shi'a Islam as it became an innovative and ultimately alternative religious tradition in the 1840s. Although its expansion was checked by persecution, division and the dispersal of its supporters outside Iran, it left a legacy of alternative belief among followers of the Babi and Baha'i movements and among wider groups of those sympathetic to their views or to freethinking more generally.[38]

This development converged with new external influences, arising from the contacts with Europeans described earlier, which encouraged some Iranians to think about themselves in different terms and added new elements to their existing cultural resources. The movement of Iranian traders, intellectuals, officials and workers to urban centres in the Ottoman Empire or the Russian-ruled Caucasus, or visits to European cities, put them in contact with a different range of ideas and experiences. In the multi-ethnic cities where Middle Eastern, Russian and western European administrators, entrepreneurs, intellectuals and military men pursued their interests, Iranians could find cultures and practices outside familiar religious frameworks. These ranged from 'modern' dress styles (suits, ties, uniforms) to different forms of urban planning, journalism, business, administration and labour relations. In particular, Iranians encountered debates and views on social and intellectual change, and on state and nation building, on offer in Istanbul, Tiflis, Cairo or Baku. They engaged with ideas about the application of 'science' to medicine or economic life, or of secular principles and knowledge to education and government, as well as the model or threat of European power and success.

The political and ideological implications of these contacts are explored in Chapters 4 and 5, but Iranians who came back to Iran with such experiences also brought new cultural elements into the communities and hierarchies to which they returned. These were sustained by links with Iranians settled in Istanbul or the Caucasus, and the regular coming and going between Iran and those areas and by contacts with Europeans inside and outside Iran. Although the groups who most explicitly took up new thinking were the educated officials and intellectuals who were to provide varied versions of scientific, reforming and nationalist ideas, migrant workers and traders also became conduits of cultural change. Interest in new ways of thinking about and dealing with social issues took a number of forms, some practical (experiments with schools, modern machinery, administrative reform), others intellectual (advocacy of new forms of education and government, scientific knowledge in books and journals, and correspondence with potential reformers).[39] Beyond that, a series of elite and popular concerns about the measures needed for the safety and prosperity of the lands or 'nation' of Iran emerged as those confronting new external interventions rethought and reviewed their world-views.

Most of the practical cultural initiatives launched during the later nineteenth century had limited impact, and were vulnerable to the fluctuating interest of government or other powerful patrons in changes that might endanger social order or vested interests. However, the debates and cultural creativity they produced began to change the terms in which Iranians understood and expressed community and hierarchy. From reinventions of heterosexual love and marriage to ideas about popular and patriotic politics or 'modern' education, new aims and discourses became available. Confined to groups of traders, migrants, office holders and intellectuals in major urban centres, they none the less become a focus of debates in the cultures around them. In doing so, they began to alter those cultures, as Iranians explored or resisted alternative ways of seeing the world and aspirations for improving it. They influenced the cultural formation of the first generation of Iranians who used ideas of reason, science and progress to think about society, government or knowledge. The hostility of some *'ulama* and *tullab* to such initiatives revealed potential conflict between religious and non-religious world-views and interests, while interaction between them was evident in others who combined critical thinking rooted in Shi'ism with these newer influences. The question of whether cultural innovation might threaten, alter or support established ideas and practices, including their religious features, was itself now *part* of their culture, as it remained throughout the twentieth century. The power and attraction of nineteenth-century confidence in reason, secular science and their potential for promoting material progress, government reform and cultural enlightenment in Iran joined other non-religious influences in the cultural repertoire. Contentious and limited as they were, they signalled shifts in beliefs and thinking, and in the composition of groups claiming cultural authority among fellow Iranians. This transition is the subject of the next stage of the narrative.

Narratives of transition, 1890s to 1940s

Discussions of the period dealt with here usually emphasise the highly visible political changes of that time. The story tells how the ruling Qajar dynasty, weakened by both its inability and unwillingness to reform, and by growing British and Russian imperial, financial and diplomatic pressures, was challenged by a coalition of urban elite, popular, modernising, defensive and nationalistic interests. By 1911 the success of this coalition in creating constitutional change and new forms of politics had run into internal dissension among its various participants, resistance from vested interests, and external opposition from British and Tsarist governments. By 1920, central authority and administrative order were crumbling, with the paralysis of government, lawlessness and self-assertion among regional elites and centres of power, and foreign invasions and interventions during and after the First World War. The ensuing chaos and insecurity were rolled back when a new authoritarian modernising regime, led by an ambitious and able soldier who made himself Shah, gained internal and external support for its combination of effective centralising authority with reform of government, law and education.

The mix of reform and repression which characterised the rule of Reza Shah Pahlavi may have tilted towards the latter by the end of the 1930s,[40] but was in any case cut short when British and Soviet troops entered Iran in 1941 in pursuit of their governments' war aims against Nazi Germany. The Shah abdicated in favour of his son and the government of Iran was shaped by the Russian and British presence (supplemented by the Americans from 1942) and by the revival of public politics following the removal of Reza Shah's autocracy. The period from 1941 to 1953 saw the flourishing of open political activity and of conflicts over Iranian independence from foreign interests, over social reform, and over representative government and the role of the monarchy. It culminated in a contest over constitutional government and national control of oil resources between the elected government, the Pahlavi monarchy and Anglo-American interests, a contest that was won by the Shah supported by those interests and by internal allies.

The dominance of these political narratives in the secondary literature, and contested views of the character of Reza Shah's regime contrasted with the 'democratic' and nationalistic politics of the 1941–53 period, have rather overshadowed questions about change, or lack of it, in Iranian communities and hierarchies. The narrative here focuses on those questions, and on transitions in the social relations, cultural practices and external linkages created and experienced by Iranians between the 1890s and 1940s. It will consider how far their religious aspects altered as a result of other changes and how this might be interpreted. While political influences on culture and society cannot be ignored, they need to be set in the context of social and cultural developments with their own dynamic and chronology.

Turning to look at communities and hierarchies, it is worth considering how far their character changed in this period. For many cultivators and craft producers, the established kin and community networks that sustained their activities continued to be central to their work and lives. Sharecropping agriculture and village pastoralism continued to dominate rural communities, while nomadic pastoralism was partially checked by state attempts to enforce the settlement of nomad groups. Urban communities were still organised around artisan production, local, regional and long-distance trading and the provision of services. Established patterns of local self-sufficiency and familial organisation, like absentee landlordism and merchant entrepreneurship, continued to be important in the collective experience of many Iranians, and their positions in existing hierarchies of dependency and exploitation. For the 70 per cent of Iranians who were rural cultivators and the 13–15 per cent who were artisans or traders, continuity in these areas was a key feature of their experience.

This said, some significant changes can be recognised. Foreign and local entrepreneurs, supported from the 1920s by state policy and monopolies in areas of trade and manufacture, stimulated industrial and commercial activity employing modern wage labour and sometimes new technology. Textile factories, printing, cement production and the expanding British-owned oil industry were noticeable areas of new development alongside construction, electricity and transport.[41] From the later nineteenth century, private and government sponsorship of new forms of education, and the work of two generations of reformers, laid the foundations for a new intelligentsia and 'white collar' class whose growth was accelerated by the demands of a modernising state from the 1920s. The establishment of a large government bureaucracy and legal system and modern educational institutions involved creating the teachers, administrators and lawyers to staff them, and some general expansion of literacy.[42]

These developments are often portrayed as a triumph of state-led modernisation, as products of an authoritarian regime, and as in some way transformative for all Iranians, a view worth examining further. Acknowledging the centrality of the state in the shifts that took place from the 1920s, it can also be seen that the regime built on earlier initiatives, and on the ideals, skills and ambitions of the groups who supported reform. The actual changes that occurred were much more significant in larger towns than in smaller urban centres or rural settlements. The quarter-million wage-workers in modern industries were concentrated in Tehran, Tabriz, Isfahan and the southern oilfields, just as modern schools, government offices and law courts were mainly urban phenomena. While the army and gendarmerie brought state power into rural areas through conscription, policing and military action against 'tribal' opponents of the state, the impact of new influences outside towns was limited. The transition which took place is best seen as a set of specific changes whose uneven impact differentiated various communities rather than a process affecting all Iranians.

There were clear areas of difference between urban and rural settlements, but also between important provincial and economic centres and smaller towns, and between Tehran and all other cities. In a number of towns, new kinds of planning and construction physically reshaped urban communities as modern streets cut through or framed existing *bazars* and neighbourhoods and new office or residential buildings, cinemas, factories or bank branches appeared alongside older structures. New work and career opportunities, albeit for a minority, modified family and occupational networks as merchants' sons entered modern professions, or members of the old office-holding elites learned new skills and made new alliances, or urban boys took jobs in factories, as their rural counterparts did in the oilfields.[43] A degree of growth increased the overall urban population of Iran from around 20 per cent at the start of the century to around 30 per cent by the late 1940s, including six cities with over 100,000 inhabitants. These cities had the greatest concentration of new forms of daily life and work.

Hierarchies within and between communities also began to change at this time. While the structures of land use and absentee ownership did not alter, the backgrounds of those who acquired and held land became more varied. In the later nineteenth century, successful merchants, senior *'ulama* and office holders invested land both as a material asset, and as a source of power and status in regional or national affairs.[44] With the changes of law (ending old forms of royal land grant) and of sources of power under the new regime, the number of successful professionals, army officers and government officials able to acquire landed property increased further. The extreme case was Reza Shah himself who, by the time of his abdication, held an estimated 3 million acres of estates forcibly purchased or confiscated from others. There is debate, fuelled by uncertain statistics and definitions, over the number of smaller landlords gaining income and influence from their holdings by the 1940s, but those figures range from a half to two million, indicating a significant element in the landed hierarchy.[45] The urban elite was likewise transformed by entrepreneurs developing new commercial and manufacturing activities through government and foreign links, or independently.

Most visible of the changed elements in urban society, and most discussed in the secondary literature, were the new professional, administrative and intellectual groups with roles in law, education, government, writing and politics. Perhaps a mere 7 per cent of the population, they had key positions in urban society and influenced general developments. Heirs to the small groups of earlier reformers committed to 'national' strengthening, by the 1920s they had the support of a regime intent on modern state building and material modernisation, which became their principal employer, regulator and backer.

The opening up of politics, intellectual life and government during and after the constitutional period, and the commitment of Reza Shah's regime to modernising law and education as well as army and government, translated into employment and new social status for these professionals. The demand for administrators, lawyers and educators and for more modest literate and office skills in the institutions created by government from the later 1920s opened up jobs for urban male Iranians emerging from the schools and adult education classes established by the government. This demand was supplemented by the emergence of modern business and engineering and new cultures of journalism, scholarship and literature as well as new intellectual and professional networks. Alongside some 90,000 government officials and white-collar employees, were privately employed clerks, supervisors, engineers and writers. The increased importance of Tehran with the growth of national politics from the constitutional era, the centralising policies of the Pahlavi regime, and the concentration of new enterprises and intellectual opportunities, gave these new groups a metropolitan and national aspect. While intellectual and press freedoms were increasingly restricted in the 1930s, the legacy of the 'constitutionalist' era and greater freedoms in the 1940s sustained reforming and dissident approaches to modernisation, politics and culture alongside the professional establishment approved by government. Many professionals and intellectuals typically had a foot in both these camps.

It is easy to be persuaded by the visible role of these classes in making significant change, and their ability to emphasise it at the time and later, that they were a uniquely innovative and dominant influence in communities and hierarchies in Iran. It is also easy to picture some sort of binary opposition between 'old' and 'new' elites or intelligentsias, marked by education, dress and cultural habits as well as by occupation, as the key feature of the period. That picture should arguably be made more complex. Many members of new professional and intellectual groups kept family and social connections to the classes from which they came, whether urban *bazari* and *'ulama* milieux or landed and office-holding elites. Many of those who had been influential in the older systems of court and administrative politics, or of commerce and education, adapted and encouraged their children to adapt to new requirements in order to maintain their roles and interests.[46] As shown in Chapters 2 and 3, the rolling back of *'ulama* dominance in law and education was met by responses that contained while not reversing their loss of strategic position. Similarly, the limited support for industrial and commercial change from a government primarily concerned with its own security allowed established entrepreneurs to negotiate relationships with both old and new economic practices. It is as important to note *connections* between the newly influential modern administrators and educators and other groups as it is to appreciate the very real differences between them and their predecessors. The prominence of suited male professionals enacting modernising roles in the narratives and pictures of the first part of the twentieth century was embedded in a context of uneven change, as indicated in contemporary texts and pictures.[47]

Communities, hierarchies and authority in Iran are best seen as being in transition in the first half of the twentieth century, with the transformations that dominate narratives of that period being as uneven as they are striking. Generalised accounts of modernisation, and the new or old agents who promoted it, should be balanced with more detailed scrutiny. Increases in the number of modern schools and pupils between the 1920s and 1950s are neither more nor less 'real' and important than the fact that education was available to males more often than to females, and to urban residents more than to their rural counterparts. The development of modern professional classes in Tehran and other urban centres was the product of new enthusiasms for change and social aspiration among younger Iranians, *and* of familiar patriarchal decisions by families and patrons about their education, careers and marriages. Assertions of central reforming authority may be less significant than the ways in which existing elites consolidated and adapted their positions within new circumstances.[48] The government's forced settlement of pastoral nomads was less transformative and lasting than its attack on the political and military power of 'tribal' leaders, just as its ending of *'ulama*-dominated legal and educational activities was offset by more pragmatic approaches to other areas of religious practice.[49] As men from established commercial and elite backgrounds added roles as shareholders and directors of modern manufacturing enterprises to existing interests, so artisan and trader 'guilds' co-existed with newer labour organisations. Accounts of activism during the 1920s and 1930s reveal both the legacy of earlier militancy and the tensions and overlaps between the different forms of urban work and labour relations.[50]

Another transitional experience for Iranians in this period affected interdependence and dependency between communities. By the 1940s, the state's drive to extend government control through military and police access to remote areas on new roads (some 14,000 miles reaching into most Iranian regions by 1941) and its modernised systems of taxation and conscription brought many communities into more direct contact with the state and each other. The pull of new economic opportunities brought rural workers to the oilfields and the industries of the larger cities, or to build the prestigious, if largely economically unhelpful, Trans-Iranian railway. Prices of key consumer goods (tea, sugar, fuel, matches) were affected by state monopolies, and local oppressors replaced, for better or worse, by state administrators. As foreign interests and government economic patronage impacted on trade and finance, and new forms of bureaucracy and representative government increased the importance of Tehran contacts for landlords and entrepreneurs, they needed to supplement local power bases with metropolitan links. The capital city became more of an economic hub as well as the centre of an increasingly interventionist government and modern intelligentsia, beginning its transition to a position of dominance that was so remarkable in the later twentieth century.

The first stages in the growth of nationwide economic structures, starting with the commodity trade of the later nineteenth century, and continuing with the infrastructural changes of subsequent decades, described above, were established by the 1950s, although only closer study can show how uneven or dominant they were. Community-level narratives illustrate complex interactions between local circumstances and the larger political and economic contexts. The emergence of more intrusive government, with a near-monopoly of the means to coerce the unprivileged by force or law, might be a stimulus to take advantage of greater security, or a greater incentive to evade and avoid state power. Foreign occupation and political conflict in the 1940s allowed the re-emergence of local exploitation, and the return of more manageable hierarchies of power. This might involve the separation of nomadic groupings from leaderships who were crushed as threats to central government. It could enable energetic individuals to seize the opportunity to bring trade and education to their communities for collective benefit as well as their own. It could mean the replacement of local authority figures constrained by custom and communal practice with more exploitative and unaccountable officials or absentee authorities. It could connect rural people to new initiatives for economic development, or push them into flight from conscription or economic insecurity and from the claims of the property owners to whom they were tied.[51]

In terms of trans-national links, while Iran continued to meet most of the food needs of its growing population, imports of manufactured goods continued to be important, and industrial and technological initiatives were heavily dependent on foreign skills and materials. In a significant beginning to new forms of trans-national dependency, oil became Iran's largest single export in the early twentieth century as western demand, and the activity of the British-owned Anglo-Persian Oil Company, known from 1936 as the Anglo-Iranian Oil Company (AIOC), expanded.[52] This growing industry was controlled by a foreign company whose decisions on investment, employment and trade were influenced by the world market and company interests, rather than local concerns. Income from oil royalties grew some tenfold in the 1920s and 1930s, and provided between 10 and 25 per cent of government revenue, while being a small fraction of AIOC's income. The expansion of production and demand for oil became central to British interests in Iran, and hence to the Iranian government. The 1933 conflict between the Iranian and British governments over the 1901 agreement on AIOC exploration and production rights drew attention to the material power of the company and to issues of national autonomy in the world power system.[53] In the 1940s, the question of foreign control of 'Iranian' oil became the iconic issue in nationalist politics as discussed in Chapters 4 and 6. Just as it was a factor in the Anglo-Russian occupation of Iran in 1941, it became the flagship cause for the political classes in their pursuit of independence from foreign manipulation of 'Iranian' interests and resources.

The notion of transition captures the uneven but significant effects of change in Iran during the first half of the twentieth century compared with the more widespread and dramatic changes of the following three decades. It is easy to show how the chances of geography, privilege and opportunity gave Iranians varying access or motivation to adopt innovative ways of work and life, but unhelpful to divide Iranians into monolithic 'modern' and 'traditional' groups. Images of such a division exercised considerable cultural and ideological power among reformers and officials during the period of constitutional struggle and the Reza Shah regime, and among the politically active sections of Iranian society during the 1941–53 period. This should not be confused with the more nuanced and complex choices and negotiations made in daily life. The teacher looking to blend Sufism with modern educational methods, pastoral nomads pursuing communal rivalries by using links to the new bureaucracy, the 'tribal' leader using established rights and authority to shift his followers from nomadism to settled agriculture and to introduce modern schooling, all practised such negotiations. So did army officers buying into land and business, artisans acquiring new skills, or intellectuals combining modern science with Shi'a piety, just as many Iranians modified 'traditional' dress rather than abandoning it wholesale.

Notions of transition and unevenness also help when considering the role of religion in Iranian cultures during this period. They illuminate the contrast between the reduced institutional power and presence of the *'ulama* and the resilience of wider contacts between religious specialists and other believers, and of the self-generated activities of those believers. They express the uneven impact of newer non-religious ideas and practices across locations, classes and genders, and the varied responses of different Iranians to that impact. While material and organisational aspects of change for the *'ulama* are examined in Chapters 2 and 3, and the impact of new ideologies in Chapter 5, it is worth reflecting on the entwining of elements of cultural change and persistence in Iranian communities and hierarchies.

Within the diverse communities of Iran, the effect of governmental or other drives for secular policies varied considerably. The imposition of new secular legal procedures or administrative controls was more widespread than the effects of modern schooling or cultural regulation. In consequence, any reduction in the role and influence of the many religious activities falling outside the state's capacities to enforce its will was limited. Communal Muharram practices and popular use of amulets, divination and shrine visits to supply spiritual and cultural needs continued to play a part in everyday life for many Iranians, as observed both by foreigners and Iranians.[54] For the latter, this might fuel images of a durable 'authentic' popular culture, arguments that restrictive ideas and practices from the past burdened many Iranians, or a sense of the uneasy relations between the two positions. By the 1940s, attempts at ethnography, social realist fictional depictions of 'ordinary' life, and critical and satirical writing on tradition and change, had opened up cultural debates discussed further in Chapter 4.[55] Within these debates new evaluations of the role of religion had a part alongside more self-consciously defensive stances by committed Shi'a Muslims. With both 'official' and 'unofficial' secularisms being put into practice, however unevenly, issues of adaptation, protection and negotiation over the religious aspects of life were now part of Iranian communities and cultures in changed and substantial forms.

Identities and communities, 1950s to 1970s

The period surveyed so far was one in which the making, reception and transmission of identities and differences were strongly based in the varied and localised settings of different Iranian communities. It was in the period from the 1950s that these settings experienced significant transformation with significant implications for the cultural experience of groups and individuals. New material circumstances reconfigured the resources and autonomy of communities and their involvement in productive labour, consumption and exchange. New cultural resources became available for the development of individual and shared versions of self, group and other. Both cultural resources and material circumstances were shaped by the influences of state power and of links to a wider world, which grew during the twentieth century and emerged most powerfully after the 1939–45 war. To make this point is not so much to argue for a linear chronology of accelerating change as to suggest that material and cultural changes were experienced differently at different times, a shift in quality as much as quantity.

Nevertheless, there were important quantitative shifts that indicated and shaped qualitative changes in the lives of individuals and communities. The more than doubling of the Iranian population (14.6 to 33.6 million) between 1940 and 1976 created a society in which half the people were under sixteen years old and two-thirds under thirty. This shift had significant implications for the creation and transmission of personal and collective identities in family, workplace or communal settings, processes in which older generations had previously played important roles. Culture and community also came to have different meanings as the proportion of Iranians living in towns increased from less than a quarter in 1940 to some 47 per cent in the 1970s. This was a product of the pull factors of expanding work opportunities in both private sector and state-led manufacturing or services and of the push factors arising from the state-led land reforms of the 1960s. Those reforms replaced the landlord/sharecropper system of land rights with a structure of landlord and peasant ownership in which over 1.9 million peasants with traditional cultivation rights (*nasaq*) received land. However, they left some 70–75 per cent of those owners with holdings too small for household subsistence needs, alongside perhaps another million landless cultivators. Rural people supplemented their inadequate resources by diversifying their productive activities, by the migrant labour of male members of the household, or by migration as the chosen solution to material difficulties. The impact of these developments was intensified by the fact that they were concentrated within the 1960s and 1970s.[56]

Iranians' activities as producers, consumers and traders also underwent similarly intense change. Lives were transformed by the expansion and diversification of wage labour, and by new patterns of consumption and of local, national and international trade. Before the 1950s, household, local and regional production had been supplemented and sometimes challenged by the importation of manufactures, and by dependency on foreign demand for raw materials produced in Iran and for specialised products such as carpets. From the 1950s, oil exports played the most dominant role in this increasingly dependent relationship, alongside imported capital and technology for modern industry. Connections with the world system formed by the earlier development of oil production in Iran under foreign control were now shaped by the renegotiated relationship between a 'nationalised' Iranian company and the foreign companies responsible for oil extraction and marketing. This also marked the replacement of British with American dominance, and intensified the combined dependency and power of the state through the use of oil revenues earned in the world market to finance economic development, to enrich the ruling dynasty, and to fund the repression and patronage sustaining the regime.

The remaking of communities and cultures all over Iran was led by external influences and state 'development policies', themselves stimulated by the state's access to oil revenues and its response to pressures from the US government. In rural areas, land reform, state regulation and and greater integration into national and global economic networks reshaped family and working lives. A pattern of land distribution that marginalised landless cultivators and left many rural families with insufficient land to support them forced many rural people, mainly males, to undertake periodic migration to seek work, and in many cases to emigrate from the countryside altogether. Of nearly 4 million internal migrants in Iran in the early 1970s, over 2 million named a rural area as their last place of residence prior to moving to a city.[57] Their labour sustained the unskilled manufacturing, construction and service sectors of the expanding urban centres. Here, too, the state-led push to finance construction, import substitution and final assembly industries, and growing demand for low-skilled as well as professional service workers in both state and private sectors, acted as pulling factors which drew labourers into towns and cities.

Such changes affected daily lives in rural communities and households as the departure of younger men, who were the majority of periodic or permanent migrants, reduced or removed their material contributions to those households and communities. Where in the past all households relied on the daily input of labour and the products in kind which men provided, increasingly their contributions came in the form of cash earnings and more limited amounts of labour as household resources could no longer be sustained solely by farming or pastoralism. Partial or periodic migration allowed households to manage

41

the insecurities of urban employment, and were particularly attractive for villagers within practicable travelling distance of towns.[58] This altered experiences and relationships within households and created new connections between rural communities and the wider society, as did permanent out-migration from those communities. The precarious viability of small-scale subsistence agriculture accelerated mobility and participation in wage labour, rural and urban, with consequences for family life and labour. The need to borrow money or purchase food as a result of government agricultural pricing and investment policies locked agricultural production and rural households into national and international markets and the money economy. This tendency was reinforced as home or locally produced manufactures (tools, shoes, textiles) were replaced by imported equivalents or Iranian factory goods (plastics, machine-made fabrics, soap), which competed in price and conferred enhanced 'modern' status. In the 1960s and 1970s, 'modern' consumption and market forces played significant roles in rural communities for the first time.

The cultural shape of rural communities, their organisation of difference and hierarchy responded to material change. As household subsistence became less closely linked to household-based production and more reliant on wage labour and purchased commodities, formerly dominant divisions of labour, and the status, identity and power relations associated with them, also shifted. It became necessary for cultivators to review and adapt existing patterns of co-operation and employment, in particular family and labour-team arrangements. The emergence of stratified rural communities with small groups of prospering farmers, larger groups of families struggling at subsistence level, and significant injections of money/market influences in the form of wage labour, cash borrowing and purchased goods, intersected with networks of family organisation and support. Rural people might create new relationships of entrepreneurial co-operation (to co-purchase and co-run tractors or trucks), joint work and fund-raising for community needs (to repair irrigation systems and paths, or to protect crops), or dealing with urban traders and former landlords. They might, in the teeth of state policy, retain old-established land-sharing practices, and certainly continued to use both close kin and extended family networks for labour and other material support. They might invent new strategies to maintain codes of family respectability and gender distinction within new patterns of work and education. While noting the impact of external forces (state power, market influences, new cultural resources) on rural Iranians, it is important to give due weight to the creative agency with which they dealt with such forces, developing new and adapted cultural practices in the process.

This kind of cultural agency is most clearly revealed in micro-studies of particular communities such as those undertaken by anthropologists Loeffler and Friedl in the Boir Ahmad in south-western Iran, Goodell looking at rural

Khuzestan, or Tapper's work on the Shahsevan in the north-west.[59] They convey the range of individual, group or family choices and strategies for protecting established interests (family honour and respect, material assets and status, manageable communal/neighbourhood relations) and for responding to threats or opportunities from state or economic forces. They show the exercise of shrewd, creative and flexible judgements within constrained circumstances and structures of dominance and subordination. A family with a school-educated daughter weighs the challenges to gender convention and family reputation posed by her taking salaried work outside the home, or living at a distance from immediate kin, against the status and money which might accrue from such work.[60] If the preservation of old patterns of land distribution and use after land reform seemed desirable for some rural people, that did not inhibit them from dispensing with traditional plough-team labour, or entering into new economic partnerships for herding, cultivation or the use of trucks and tractors. They likewise drew on both old and new practices and ideas to avoid, manage or at least minimise new forms of intrusion by the powerful, following their own judgements of the advantages or disadvantages brought by agents of the state.[61]

The cultural lives of rural Iranians can be explored from three perspectives: the cultural resources available for their use, the lifestyles they created, and the shared or opposed identities associated with them. Focusing on resources, we can see how the existing roles of kin, work associates and neighbours in transmitting knowledge, values, skill and opinions were supplemented by new ideas and information. Increased movement between different settlements, facilitated by the arrival of cycles, motor transport and improved roads, and by migration and the presence of outsiders like teachers, or other agents of the state, accelerated the flow and diversity of ideas and information available to rural people. In the 1970s, radios, cassette tapes and televisions brought other images and ideas into their culture.[62] Thus while changes in formal literacy and education were more limited in rural communities than in urban areas, their range of cultural stimuli and resources was augmented and entwined with those already established there.

The lifestyles that rural Iranians developed in contexts of material and political change, and an expanded cultural repertoire, expressed responses, resistances and adaptations to what they encountered. In part, this involved renegotiating patterns of productive activity and social relations. Male participation in migrant labour, or small enterprises linked to commercial networks outside the community, altered the roles of work, money and family co-operation embedded in their lives as pastoralists, cultivators and/or holders of land rights. The role of cash, of goods produced outside the community, and of market forces in agriculture involved new sets of decisions, and changed gender divisions of labour and consumption. This might mean greater activity by women in carpet or textile manufacture financed by urban entrepreneurs, or the reduction of productive opportunities as animal husbandry, in which they had formerly played important roles, declined.[63] New styles of house building with water supply or enclosing walls might change the arrangement of community and family, 'public' and 'private' elements in everyday life. The insecurities and difficulties of a more marketised existence and attempts at greater direct intervention by outside authorities, strengthened reliance on family and neighbourhood networks and tried and tested communal practices. While often presented as an oppositional relationship between 'traditional' and 'modern' influences, it can equally be seen as a matter of rational choice and conscious calculation, balancing the costs and benefits of existing as against new practices and priorities.

The cultures created in this context can be understood in terms both of the internal dynamics of rural communities and of broader trends. In the unequal struggle of rural Iranians to maintain their own interests and needs within the dominating forces of state and market, they developed cultures of resistance (reinforcing reliance on resources and values within their communities) and of adaptation (opening themselves to new influences and possibilities). Such cultures both produced and were produced by overlapping identities, to which elements of individuality, of hierarchy and dominance, of shared needs and views, and of gender, each contributed. While much social scientific writing on rural Iranians presents them in terms of collectivities (village communities, household/family units, peasant classes/elites), anthropological work suggests that they also had a clear sense of their own personhood and recognised and respected it in others. From assessment of the capacity of individual family members to contribute to household production and status, to the expression of personal variations in religious belief and practice, assumptions about people's *individuality* had both normative and practical importance.[64]

If personal skills, roles and characteristics sustained selfhood as one aspect of identity, so too did membership within groups and networks and differences of status, affluence or power. The role of village leaders or representatives might be grounded in personal talent and commitment, in careful management of inherited and family status or material assets, and in balancing community needs with the ties of external patronage or elite self-interest. Although office-holding tended to be dominated by the wealthier segments of a rural community, effective leadership also depended on the ability to mesh with communal norms and interests. Status and influence in the community came from recognition of hard work, civic commitment and respectability as well as material wealth or political connections. The ability to summon family support, the proper conduct of women as a signifier of family 'honour', appropriate use of both generosity or caution and force or cunning in public relationships, all sustained hierarchies of respect and influence. Divisions between those with outside connections, and hence larger cultural as well as material resources, and those without them, such as distinguished the hierarchy in Hooglund's 'Women of Aliabad', could well be the most obvious markers of 'class'. These cultural and political influences intersected with the material effects of unequal access to land, commercial opportunity, political connections and fluctuating labour markets to shape rural social divisions and power relations.[65]

Alongside hierarchy and inequality ran material and moral pressures to sustain mutuality and communal networks. The predominance of low-income and/or subsistence-oriented household production in a hostile environment put a high premium on co-operation to ensure the best use of its human resources, and on degrees of co-operation between households, whether lending tools and supplies, or partnerships for larger initiatives. The intrusions of the various agents of the state encouraged solidarity against their controlling and predatory presences, if only through shared passive resistance to unwelcome interference. The self-interest of households encouraged village networks of sociability, information exchange, economic co-operation, or communal support for transport and schooling. In cultures of relative scarcity, established practices of collective action remained valuable in the new circumstances of the 1960s and 1970s. Some of these involved particular kin groups or patronage networks, and others the whole community.

Three perspectives help an understanding of the intimate presence of religion in rural settings, the limits to its influence, and degrees of persistence and change. Most visible of these was the relationship between exponents of organised, 'official' religion to the communities where they lived or worked. The role of *'ulama* as providers of *rawzehs* and Muharram sermons in rural settlements, which increased in the 1960s and 1970s,[66] involved both affirmation of common interests and antagonism between *mulla* and community. Traditional suspicions of their mercenary approach to the provision of services, of their failure to live up to the moral prescriptions they issued, and of their preference for a façade of ritual observation over what villagers perceived as the core meanings and requirements of their faith, remained central to this relationship. Loeffler's discussions with male villagers in the community where he worked in the 1970s revealed varied comments along these lines: some contrasted the *mulla*'s preference for observation of formal prayers with the 'real' moral obligations laid on humans by Islam; some commented on demands for payment for religious services; some associated the local *mulla* with the oppressive role of landlords and not practising what he preached. It is particularly interesting that the religious outlook of the men quoted varied from liberal humanism to mystical, sceptical and conventional conceptions of Shi'a Islam, suggesting that critiques of *'ulama* did not spring from simplistic opposition between two versions of the faith.[67] Rather as villagers each crafted their own religious perceptions, the *mulla*'s practice was depicted as the undesirable 'other'. They demonstrated confidence in their own religious capability, and a preference for contrasting their personal 'genuine' views and beliefs to the 'official' suspect ones of the *mulla*.

The roles and presence of *'ulama* in villages also served other significant purposes. Villagers whose autonomous and anti-*mulla* religious views are reported by observers none the less took collective responsibility for hiring *'ulama* for Muharram rituals, where their role in focusing participation was significant, if contentious.[68] Even critics acknowledged a role for expert learning and promotion of Shi'a Muslim faith and practice, and members of rural elites and leaderships maintained contacts with the senior *'ulama* in Qum. The anti-clericalism of many villagers sat alongside use of local *mullas* as representatives in dealings with government, and *mullas* could be respected and self-supporting rather than parasitical members of the community.[69] In the 1960s and 1970s, the proportion of trained religious specialists from rural backgrounds increased, and senior *'ulama* sent their students into rural areas as resident or visiting preachers and prayer leaders. This brought 'official', *'ulama*-based Islam to rural settlements, where tapes, radios and contact with urban religious practices also brought such versions to villagers' attention. The number of villages with resident *mullas* remained limited, and religious education relied on family and communal sources rather than formal instruction by *mullas*. Observers noted increases in the practice of prescribed prayer and fasting, and in villages close to urban centres some younger people began to attend urban religious instruction. Nevertheless, discussions of the growth of support for Khomeini in 1978–79 emphasise not the influence of his religious authority and status, but his *political* message and the fact that he was seen as '*different*' from other *'ulama*.[70]

The growing material and political linkages of rural communities to a wider world of production, migration, consumption and administrative control was not matched by incorporation into external religious belief or practice. Many of the features of rural life that sustained autonomous communal practice remained central features of villagers' social world and cultural frameworks. The traditions of collective activity in the Muharram rituals, and of provision for religious needs by village prayer writers, *sayyids*, amulets or pilgrimages, continued to be prime means of religious expression. Whether the distinctive oven-blessing rituals of women villagers in Khuzestan, the resort to vows and visits to the local shrines, or the growth of religious study groups, the grounding of religious culture in self-generated activity remained strong and adapted to new circumstances. Keshavjee's account of rural pilgrimage festivals in Khurasan describes 'orthodox' Shi'a pilgrims alongside Isma'ilis, the atmosphere of collective participation, and the observance of hierarchies and distinctions of status, gender and age in the patterns of eating, ritual practice and visiting among the pilgrims.[71]

His comments on the awkwardness felt by younger participants about the 'backward' or 'superstitious' religion of older pilgrims remind us not to strait-jacket perceptions of culture and religion. The changes in rural communities already noted opened up generational differences of experience and outlook, with resulting tensions as well as new possibilities. Fathers complained that their high-school-educated sons did not fast or pray; younger villagers commuting to towns contrasted religious views or practices in each setting; villagers who acquired education or contact with modern health or agricultural practices incorporated them with older religious and communal practice; interest in *ta'ziyeh* might decline.

In the village studied by Loeffler, a religious study group set up by a promi-nent, pious and innovatory village activist drew illiterate village men into a circle of religious discussion informed by current awareness and concerns rather than custom. Villagers combined visits to modern doctors and clinics with the use of amulets, shrine visits and vows. Debates over the use of chains rather than breast-beating in the men's Muharram processions signify new urban or moral influences entwined with established commitment to these collec-tive commemorations. They may be seen as pragmatic and creative processes among villagers (Loeffler's view), or as evidence of oppositions between valued autonomous rural community and negative urban and governmental influence (Goodell's view). Whatever the case, members of rural communities actively adapted, negotiated or resisted new patterns of religious practice, rather than re-enacting 'tradition'.[72]

Religious self-activity, which formed part of the cultural inheritance of rural Iranians in the 1960s and 1970s, was neither static nor monolithic. Increased possibilities for travel might facilitate long-distance pilgrimage to Mashad for villagers hitherto limited to visits to local shrines, just as schooling and labour mobility altered their world-views and experience. Conversely, the irrelevant, oppressive and ineffective contributions of 'modernising' doctors, government officials, 'ulama or teachers encouraged rural people to reaffirm their own agency in religious practice. From participation in mourning gatherings for deceased villagers, to reliance on a knowledgeable village figure rather than the local *mulla* for ritual leadership, and creative syntheses of mystical, rational, ritual or customary versions of Shi'a Islam, this agency continued. It continued to express divisions, commonalties and hierarchies, and to mark the boundaries of community (against external interference, or for solidarity), of gender (in the name of decency and honour) and of status (in recognition of influence, rank and power).

The religious experience and activity of rural Iranians between the 1950s and 1970s do not fit neat patterns. Existing practices remained resilient but did not prevent changes and adaptations. 'Modern' influences sat beside inherited precepts and practices, as when a village teacher included reason and progress in his vision of Islam, or women resorted to both clinics and midwives and amulets and vows to deal with infertility or pregnancy, or young people adapted 'ulama prescriptions for 'proper' shrine visiting making it their own collective practice. Cars, modern soft drinks and loudspeakers or microphones played their role in Muharram gatherings. The greater presence of official regulation by the state and of urban/'ulama-generated religious authority did not remove, while it surely changed and constrained, the self-created elements of religious activity in rural settlements.[73]

While the cultural experiences of rural Iranians were disrupted and restructured by qualitatively changed forms of state and economic interventions in the 1960s and 1970s, changes in urban life looked more like an intensification of processes at work since the 1930s. By 1960, urban Iranians were already over one-third of the total population (over a quarter in Tehran), having been about one-fifth in the 1930s. Patterns of rural migration to towns began in the 1940s and 1950s, accounting for some 130,000 people a year. This quantitative change was accompanied by qualitative shifts in the urban scene as developments from the 1930s encouraged the spatial and social 'modernisation' described above.

These trends spread and accelerated after 1960 as the urban population rose from 33 per cent to over 47 per cent of the total by 1976, and in-migration rose from 130,000 yearly in the 1940s and 1950s to between a quarter and a third of a million people yearly from the 1960s to late 1970s. By 1972 migrants formed nearly 14 per cent of urban-dwelling Iranians. Over half the urban population lived in the ten largest Iranian cities, whose numbers doubled or trebled between 1956 and 1976. Above all, Tehran grew from 1.5 million to 4.5 million in that time, and by the late 1970s contained 28.6 per cent of the urban population and over one in eight of all Iranians. The impact of land reform and state-backed expansion of the industrial and service sectors, with associated demands for construction and unskilled labour, drew migrants and rural commuters into urban life and labour, just as new aspirations brought some rural young people into urban secondary schools. The ambitions of the renewed Pahlavi regime after 1953, and its rising oil revenues, funded the growth of governmental, commercial and manufacturing employment, whether directly or through the patronage of favoured entrepreneurs, while its ill-planned underdeveloped agricultural policies pushed rural Iranians into urban labour markets. These changes underpinned the rapid growth of new commercial, residential and industrial zones, and of slums and squatter settlements, in towns such as Isfahan, Yazd, Tabriz and, above all, Tehran.

Changed urban physical environments provided new cultural spaces as well as changed living and working settings. These ranged from the streets where young men strolled and loitered round cinemas and juice/sandwich bars, or families sampled or at least looked at new consumer products displayed in modern shops, to schools, parks, bookstores and new religious or welfare centres. Building sites, garages and factories shaped new workplace cultures alongside established craft workshops, offices and *bazar* trading outlets. In poor residential neighbourhoods, the intersections of alleyways and streets were locations where young men gathered and bonded socially, while young women used walks to school or the local community centre to make social connections outside kin and household. The explosion of squatter communities of shacks, tents and improvised dwellings was especially remarkable in Tehran but featured in other Iranian cities (Tabriz, Hamadan, Shiraz, Mashad, Kermanshah, Ahwaz, Bushehr), establishing distinctive poor and marginal communities characterised by shared culture as well as material deprivation. From the new styles of consumption, education and sociability offered to the affluent, to the new patterns of survival and self-definition among the deprived, the cultures of urban Iranians were significantly reconfigured.

New developments were entwined with existing urban arrangements rather than obliterating them. Although new street plans and buildings encroached on existing *bazar* and residential areas, and formerly prosperous areas became overcrowded slums for poor people, significant 'traditional' areas of towns remained intact, reflecting the continued importance of *bazar* activities. Street plans of Kerman, Shiraz, Yazd and Kermanshah as well as Tehran, Tabriz or Isfahan show mixtures of new commercial and residential areas framing old *bazar* and neighbourhood retail areas.[74] Successful entrepreneurial families might have members in both *bazari* and other commercial and financial ventures. They might lead the adaptation of a traditional production system like carpet weaving to the new consumer demands and a more centralised economy and international markets. They might use *bazar* outlets for non-traditional factory-produced and imported goods. Cultures and practices of modern schooling or banking or law, as well as manufacture and trade, co-existed with the commercial and productive work and culture of *bazaris*, whose children entered universities and professions, but maintained existing networks of common interest and association, piety and solidarity. Unskilled construction workers and street vendors might rely on the growing if unstable opportunities provided by urban growth, but embed their labouring lives in the family and communal support characteristic both of familiar past practice and of the values and strategies of the modern urban poor.

The rich unstable blend of rapid change and persistent legacies in work and daily life, and the choices and views that maintained them, shaped individual and collective 'selves' and their differentiation from 'others'. It is useful to explore these cultural questions from overlapping perspectives which incorporate rather than separate 'traditional' elements from 'modern' ones. One starting point is that of locality or neighbourhood, which was both an inherited category used to shape identities and behaviour, and the daily context of people's lives. For the urban poor, identifying with the neighbourhood or squatter settlement where they lived was an alternative to defining themselves through poverty or occupation. To be one of the 'people of Javadieh' (a slum in east Tehran) affirmed a connection to place expressed positively in mutual assistance or sociability, and restrictively as the arena where honour and reputation were judged. Communal celebration of religious events, the presence of youth groups on the streets, or neighbourhood comment and gossip enacted shared perceptions and interests, as did collective resistance to state attempts to evict squatters, or action to protect access to water, electricity and shelter. The fact that new migrants and squatters were spatially segregated from both the affluent sections of urban society and the older established working population linked their identity to other social divisions. When shanty-town dwellers referred to themselves as such, they acknowledged membership both of a particular urban community and of a stratum differentiated from other *tabaqeh* (classes/levels) in the social hierarchy.

The collective and communal cultures of the urban poor can be seen as the remaking of familiar practices of co-operation and collective self-expression to meet the new challenges of work and life for recent migrants and to establish survival strategies appropriate to a modern city. Just as struggling households in urban slums used old courtyard structures as well as refrigerators and radios, so such strategies embodied both 'old' and 'new' elements. Decline in the older forms of communal conflict opened spaces for other patterns of differentiation and opposition alongside use of established resources. In the *bazar* sections of urban society, the status of trader/entrepreneurs, the solidarity of particular craft groups and the patterns of craft workplace life were sustained by the continuing viability of *bazar* trade and some *bazar* manufacturing. Some half a million *bazar* merchants and traders, and a similar number of artisans, accounted for some 16 per cent of the officially counted workforce in the 1970s maintaining guild and craft networks and profitable niches in retailing and craft production. This capacity for material survival when faced with new competition was underpinned by established *bazar* practices, whether patriarchal workshop relations or clientage and networking among *bazaris*. The effectiveness of these practices and the culture of personalised *bazari* relations, could, as Bonine's work on Yazd shows, influence trade or craft production in newer commercial areas outside the *bazar*.[75]

These achievements underpinned the wider culture of *bazaris*, whether active involvement in religious affairs or the pursuit of collective and family interests. Merchants and entrepreneurs inside or outside the *bazar* defined themselves through public association with Shi'a Muslim piety. The continued worth of the status of *haji*, and support for Muharram rituals, formed part of the culture and identity of craft entrepreneurs, *bazar* retailers, wholesalers and owners of modern factories and commercial outlets. Such public manifestations of the role of religion in collective and personal identity and social position co-existed with other cultural expressions. For some observers the distinctive styles of dress, food or social custom associated with *bazaris* from the 1940s to the 1970s identified them as a 'traditional' element in urban society at odds with 'modern' professionals, businessmen and bureaucrats. While there are important insights in such views, they underestimate the complexity of cultural changes between the departure of the first Pahlavi shah and the overthrow of the second. Just as *bazaris* adapted to become retailers of machine-made as well as craft manufactures, or expanded and altered their role as carpet entrepreneurs, so they negotiated educational and cultural changes during the 1960s and 1970s with a blend of resistance and innovative appropriation.[76]

A second perspective is that of household and gender identities and relations. For the poor and the propertied, those who embraced 'modern' developments and those who were defensive or critical, and for members of different generations, the regulation of family, gender roles and sexuality was crucial for self-definition, and the respect of others. Questions of female segregation and dress codes, which were matters of explicit political contention in the 1930s and 1940s, played out as issues of cultural expression and contest in the 1960s and 1970s, becoming highly charged political concerns at the end of that time. The use of the *chador* became associated with poorer or explicitly pious sections of urban society, with important elements of choice and fluidity. A young woman whose father traded cloth on a small scale in the Kerman *bazar* in the 1970s argued with her mother about wearing the *chador*, abandoning it on trips to the cinema with a non-*chador*-wearing (and foreign) female companion, while retaining it when visiting family friends with her mother. Women from 'modern' professional and propertied families who generally went about without *chadors* might adopt them if attending a religious event. This suggests that concern with 'veiling' (to use a problematic term) had variable purposes and importance. It might signify commitment to particular religious values but had equally important associations with communal reputation, in poor urban quarters where it was a public demonstration of respectability, or with generational conflicts and changes between mothers and daughters as well as broader social pressures. It also continued to play an ideological role in the arguments of the state and its male critics, for whom images of 'veiled'/'unveiled' women related less to concern with substantive female needs or interests than to depictions of 'progress', 'corruption', authority and cultural authenticity.

Long-established associations of family honour and reputation with the 'modest' and appropriate conduct of its female members, and its enforcement by family elders or neighbourhood scrutiny and judgement, remained important in pious, *bazari* and poorer communities. The reluctance of poor urban women to work outside the household unless absolutely necessary, or to go about in public unaccompanied by family, shows the power of this paradigm. It marked the assimilation of migrants to existing urban cultures and affirmed material security as well as respectability. However, such interpretations seem overly functionalist if we consider the importance of honour/reputation in rural communities, and the way in which notions of respectability *produce* social identities rather than just flowing from them. Looking at women's paid employment across the whole urban hierarchy, both its restricted character and its concentration in feminised occupations (nursing, education, domestic service, textile production) are evidence of how gender convention shaped material divisions of labour. Propriety and established codes of gender difference were *constitutive* of those divisions rather than consequential upon them, a phenomenon found in European or Latin American cultures as well as in Iran or Egypt. The inherited practice of constructing public and productive spaces in gendered ways continued to shape newer patterns of urban life and culture in the 1960s and 1970s.

Nor was this solely a matter of female exclusion and the policing of femininity. Masculinity, too, was produced as a distinctive set of practices and attributes in the street cultures of young and poor urban men, and the networks of political patronage, intellectual exchange and business activity linking male groups in Iranian towns, thereby producing those cultures as gendered. Constructions of masculinity were inherited from the past practices of *bazaris*, religious education, and family or political organisation, but were also shaped by recent developments in urban life. Young men's street activities did not replicate the *luti* presence of the earlier times, but refigured gender and generation in the new settings of modern streets and migrant neighbourhoods. *Bazari* and professional networks adapted cultural activities inherited from the past to new intellectual and religious concerns with reform, writing and cultural politics. The single-sex character of their activities, and the homosociality of the cultures they embodied, were active expressions of different masculinities, from the anxious management of youthful sexual desire and aggression to the assertion of male authority and agency. The pious trader, the ambitious professional, the turbulent poor youth or the critical intellectual were gendered identities grounded in both inherited assumptions and cultural innovation.

In the 1960s and 1970s, the access of some young women to education, literacy and job opportunities contested the mutually reinforcing connection of masculine identities to politics, urban space, work and intellectual activity. Observers noted the articulate challenges of pious high-school girls to definitions of the 'good Muslim woman' as unthinking, passive and obedient, and those of female university graduates and women's rights activists to restrictions on women's status as wives and mothers, on their choices of occupation, and on access to contraception. These challenges, like those of politically active women to gender blindness or sexism in oppositional political movements, did not end the dominance of male privilege and authority, but revealed tensions and changes. In the meantime, younger men used the streets as the location for testing the limits and attributes of masculinity through their scrutiny of women as targets for sexual and emotional interest, or as potential violators of codes of decency. In *bazari* settings, codes of masculine hierarchy, solidarity and piety could be taught, learned and asserted. In professional and intellectual circles, masculine command of ideas and influence could be deployed through opinion formation, debate and the skills of cultural allusion and criticism.

As with gendered or communal aspects of urban culture, class differences expressed past as well as present. By 1950 the merchants, artisans, traders, entrepreneurs and low-status employees in Iranian *bazars* were joined by workers in new white-collar and labouring occupations. Demand for office workers and professionals, factory and construction workers, unskilled labourers (porters, cleaners, messengers), as well as drivers and mechanics, grew in the following decades, absorbing new migrants and growing numbers of high-school or college graduates. In the interstices of urban life and the formal economy, those who were unsuccessful finding other work undertook informal activities – street vending, casual work in ports or building sites, domestic service, car or shoe cleaning, or sweatshop production. While the cultural experience and outlook of these groups was shaped by residential and familial experience, and access (or lack of it) to education and literacy, it also expressed a 'class' consciousness of exploitation in production, or of inequity between rich/powerful/privileged and others.

First, we may note the language of ranks/classes (*tabaqeh*) used by casual and regular wage workers, and by slum dwellers, as they situated and differentiated themselves in relation to others.[77] Second, it is clear that such people understood this hierarchical structure in relation to family and kinship, and set it alongside attachments to areas of origin and linguistic/cultural identities. Third, there was the legacy of labour organisation and activism, suppressed by the state after 1953 and swamped by the dominance of a younger generation of workers, but occasionally surfacing in the 1970s. In interviews with worker activists near Isfahan in 1979, an older worker testified to continued radicalism from the oil struggles of the 1950s, just as a former stone-mason remembered humiliations imposed on him as a child by a Pahlavi prince.[78] It has been argued that the levels of militancy and organisation among oil workers in 1979–80 were the legacy of leftist and trade union activity during the 1940s and early 1950s, just as strikes and attempts to reshape the state-imposed unions in the 1970s evidence a culture of class consciousness.[79] Experiences of control, danger and hierarchy in the workplace as well as of the insecurities of employment and wages – for all of which there is evidence in Iranian towns in the 1960s and 1970s – could be said to form the context for class cultures and consciousness.

Nevertheless, there were strong countervailing elements. Workers' access to jobs and support came less through fellow workers than through kin and friends. Independent unions were largely suppressed. Although the offspring of factory workers were likely to go into factory work, factory workers who were first-generation migrants, or children of non-factory workers, were more likely to seek and find solidarity with neighbours or family.[80] For the huge number of workers in casual employment and/or working in small enterprises, solidarity with fellow workers was less relevant than the support of community and relatives. Since many workers were younger and new to their workplaces, contact with traditions of militancy was limited. Access to literacy, the media and education had limited effects on class culture, due perhaps to the effects of censorship on broadcasting and newspapers rather than to low literacy rates among urban workers (which, as shown by Thompson and Sewell's work on England and France, is not necessarily inhibiting). A survey of TV viewing preferences indicated the high popularity of a 'soap' series dealing with the adjustments of migrants to the city. Surveys of workers' 'leisure' activities and preferences in the 1970s suggested that they preferred to spend leisure time in their homes or in religious activities associated with mosques and *hay'ats* (religious assemblies).[81]

There was also a legacy of viewing society in terms of the people/*mellat* in contradistinction to the *doulat*/government. Cultural assumptions found in a variety of social settings emphasised the 'us' of the governed/unrepresented as against the 'them' who are the powerful elite/rulers and their agents. They expressed the historic grievances of cultivators towards landlords carried into urban life, or the general frustration and powerlessness of urban Iranians faced by the hostile bureaucracy and corrupt inaccessible patronage systems of an authoritarian state. They also took the form, used by Tehran's urban poor, of asserting the security provided by 'crown and throne' (*taj o takht*), the Shah's role as the source of favour or the righting of wrongs, and the evil role of officials in frustrating his will or keeping him in ignorance.[82] The pervasive linguistic forms through which Iranians registered equality, superiority or inferiority to those with whom they spoke, and the varied formal or informal settings in which they did so, embedded codes of social hierarchy and difference in everyday speech.[83]

While household or family were a base for the cultural formation and support of members, in the context of spatial migration and social mobility, family cultures were far from homogeneous. Gender divisions of labour and of assigned/ideal roles set up a dynamic of co-operation and contest between men and women in which concepts of *difference* played a key role. The constitution of women through their roles as mothers, carers and household managers, and of men through paternal authority and public activity, whether seen as beneficially complementary, or restrictive and unjust, was the bedrock of dominant assumptions. The mismatch between these norms and the aspirations of young women and girls who glimpsed other possibilities through access to schooling, and a wider range of media and other images, became a source of tension in middle- and lower-class settings. Cultural pressure mediated through parents and husbands discouraged women from establishing autonomous careers, or from taking paid work at all, and pressured lower-class girls to marry rather than seek other futures. Neighbourhood opinion might support a husband in forbidding his wife to undertake productive work even in her own compound, even if they co-operated in other ways. Obvious areas of conflict for lower-class girls were over freedom of movement, with parents forbidding outings with male relatives and girls using the excuse of a school or women's welfare centre commitment to go out unsupervised.[84]

This conflict was one facet of generation division within family households. The culture of parental authority was undermined by education and the access of urban Iranians, including young people, to easily available images and expectations produced outside family or community. Magazines, broadcasting and cinema became available to wider groups of town dwellers, as did contact with teachers, welfare workers and educated or affluent relatives. At a more privileged level, college and university education, and the resources available to 'middle-class' families, including travel or study abroad, similarly broadened young people's frame of reference and ability to criticise norms and conventions. For growing groups of recent migrants, or educationally and socially mobile young people from modest backgrounds, the sense that the young might be more informed and authoritative in some areas than their parents challenged traditions of parental authority and dominance. Mothers in recently migrated families acknowledged how their children had areas of expertise in urban living that they lacked. However, key life decisions on work and marriage were still made by parents on behalf of offspring.[85] Households and families were both a shared resource and protection for all classes and sites of conflicting experiences and interests.

If spatial mobility in the decades after 1950 was one powerful modifier of urban lives and cultures, mobility through education was another. As with Reza Pahlavi's earlier policies, but with greater authority and material investment, state expansion of school, college and university education, flawed and limited as it was, opened them up to non-privileged Iranians on an unprecedented scale. In 1961–62, 1.7 million school students were about 7.75 per cent of the population; by 1977–78, 7.7 million school students were over 21 per cent of the population. The number of secondary school students grew five-fold in this period, while the number in higher education multiplied nearly seven times.[86] These last two figures are particularly significant in that all higher and most secondary education was urban based and so more accessible to less affluent urban would-be students than rural counterparts. While family privilege and education continued to advantage those moving through secondary to higher education, by the 1970s there was significant change. A survey of 1972–73 showed that 64 per cent of the fathers and 82 per cent of the mothers of students in the survey had no more than six years' schooling and 42 per cent and 56 per cent respectively had little or no education at all.[87] Children of *bazaris*, low-ranking white-collar workers, even some aspiring migrants, now gained access not just to opportunities offered, if not always fulfilled, through education, but to new experiences and ideas that shifted their cultural outlook, whatever their subsequent careers. The presence of university and college students from varied social backgrounds in Tehran and a number of major towns modified wider urban cultures through their links and influence with households, communities and kin. Such links emerged in the role of student activists in both urban and rural communities during the revolutionary period 1978–81.

How did existing and changing patterns of religious influence and religious practice contribute to this varied cultural scene? As shown in the next two chapters, *ulama* were involved in protective responses to attacks on their institutional power bases in law, education and public affairs since the 1920s. While *ulama* influence and credibility were embedded in a range of urban settings in the early twentieth century, that position was at best more restricted and at worst under threat by the 1960s and 1970s. Nevertheless, just as *bazari* material and cultural practices proved durable within the changing urban settlements of Iran, so alliances of merchants, *mullas* and artisans continued to be flourishing if embattled cultural forces. The care that the regime took to manage rather than rupture relations with the *ulama*, while corralling them and checking them politically, testifies to recognition of that force. The popularity of both traditional and innovative religious publications – the largest single category of publications in Iran in the mid-1970s – indicates cultural demand for specialised religious texts and the capacity to supply it.[88]

In addition to continuing roles in *bazari* life and culture, *ulama* retained old relationships to the urban poor and developed new ones. Lack of other welfare provision created opportunities for *ulama* to sustain material links to the needy, and their credibility as patrons and sources of help, offsetting criticisms of their venality or exploitation of believers. The provision of *rawzehs*, religious classes and ritual services by *'ulama* maintained links, however tenuous, with sections of the urban working and middle classes outside the *bazar*. The perfunctory performance of such services (*rawzeh-khwans* flicking through a women's magazine while reciting) and their practice by 'westernised' Iranians as matters of convention rather than conviction (like some English church/chapel weddings today) could be evidence of declining religious influence but might also go along with interest in a refigured religious culture to which we shall return.[89]

The persistent involvement of Shi'a Muslims in self-organised practices inherited from the past was also a source of continuity. The celebration of Muharram rituals and household-based *sofrehs* (women's religious feasts) and *rawzehs*, like the continuation of shrine and cemetery visiting, divination and the use of amulets, show the extent of support for these 'traditions'. Affirmations of male and female identity through gender-specific religious activity, and of community and family identity through participation in pilgrimage or Muharram rituals, remained culturally powerful. Religious customs which were common in character, if not specific form, to both rural and urban communities may have been one of the cultural bridges aiding those Iranians moving from one to the other. It is worth noting the sponsorship of Muharram events taken on by newer members of the merchant entrepreneurial class, which suggests that such patronage was still seen as a means to express status through piety. Among industrial workers surveyed in 1970s, those who were able to take holidays used them predominantly for pilgrimage trips to Mashad and Qum.[90] *Bazaris* and the newly migrated slum and shanty dwellers of Tehran participated in the rituals of Muharram and Ramadan. Families attended mosques, *hay'ats* and *huseiniyehs* to undertake religious duties while making sociable and communal contacts.

This evidence of persistent cultural energy in the established practices of Shi'a Iranians indicates continued support for such expressions of personal and communal commitment and identity. However, it is hard to disregard the extent to which they were under pressure. The secular intelligentsia's influence in urban cultures, government hostility to *'ulama* authority and autonomy, and the opposition of many Shi'a Muslims to changes in practice, doctrine or custom, threatened to straitjacket religion as 'reactionary' and 'backward'. Responding to this embattled position and the pressures of urban change, pious urban Iranians produced innovations that reshaped some of the roles and forms of religious culture. One of these was the expansion of new kinds of *hay'ats* (religious associations) aimed at recently settled residents and offering cultural and moral support in their attempts to negotiate urban life, access to the skills and patronage of religious specialists, and affirmation of communal identities. They often focused not just on particular occupations or localities but on groups of migrants from the same area.[91] By the later 1970s there were over 300 such *hay'ats* in Tehran alone. The Hojjatiyeh organisation (originating in anti-Baha'i campaigns in the 1950s) provided speakers and teachers for religious meetings and classes aimed at urban youth, proselytising its own revivalist version of Shi'a Islam. Popular preachers more generally sought audiences through tapes and broadcasts as well as in urban religious halls. Such initiatives and their leaders operated relatively independently of the cautious 'official' religious hierarchy.[92]

The significance of these initiatives is that they addressed the modern urban constituencies of the 1960s and 1970s using a familiar repertoire of religious culture (preaching, teaching, religious gatherings). They aimed to bolster pious Iranians against the pressures and attractions of secular criticism, strengthening religious confidence and commitment in a hostile environment. They reached out to urban youth, linked by family and community to a religious outlook, but also exposed to secular education and mass media, offering alternatives to secular school and university curricula. While the declared aims of teachers and preachers were to roll back the leftist secularist influences which they saw as dominant and damaging, their real effect was to reinforce or encourage the convictions of those who already identified themselves as religious.

The views put forward in these settings varied. Some were characterised by what has been called 'neo-orthodoxy' centred on reaffirmation of belief and doctrine, and support for Shi'a *'ulama*. However, some of these initiatives reassessed or re-presented Shi'a Islam in ways which emphasised its capacity to address the concerns of a changing society rather than reasserting familiar views. Burgeoning female religious study and discussion circles re-evaluated 'traditional' prescriptions and arguments about women's role and characteristics, emphasising understanding and active devotion rather than obedience or ritual. There was active criticism and commitment to resisting the corruption of the Shah's Iran, e.g. by the adoption of *new* versions of 'modest' dress (*hejab*).[93] Such innovation had its best known expression in the work of Huseiniyeh Ershad, and its most celebrated lecturer 'Ali Shari'ati, between 1967 and 1973. Here the association of religious activism with cultural renewal and opposition to corrupting foreign influences posed the critical Islam of believers against the negative and conservative role of the *'ulama*. It combined affirmations of Shi'a Islam as an expression of popular and 'national' identity and as an inspiration to social and political change using passionate style and reformist rhetoric aimed at young educated audiences. It was a cultural intervention with considerable political potential.

Through the maintenance of established practice and innovation during the 1960s and 1970s, the cultural place of religion in Iranian towns was changed and protected if not extended. Hemmed in by official hostility and secular tendencies, Shi'a Muslims shaped some distinctive cultural spaces, taking advantage of the resilience of historic locations in *bazari* and urban poor milieux, and adapting to new constituencies, particularly those who combined piety with modern education. They benefited from the discontents of a number of key groups. For many able and ambitious younger Iranians who were unsuccessful in their search for jobs and secure lives, the apparent promises of a changing society and expanding education system were unfulfilled. Some secular intellectuals and activists, whose resistance to the regime and the culture it sponsored had hitherto taken reformist and leftist forms, were now disillusioned with failure and the regime's appropriation of key parts of their agendas and stressed issues of cultural authenticity and cultural imperialism. This led them to explore the role of religion as part of a 'popular' and 'authentic' indigenous culture of resistance to state power and the 'Americanisation' of culture and consumption, which paralleled American commercial, political and technological influence.

At the end of the 1970s, urban cultures and identities presented neither a monolithic nor a divided picture but, rather, sets of overlapping relationships and tensions. Rapid shifts in population, spatial organisation and technologies of communication, from motor traffic to television and cassette tapes, as well as in work, education and consumption, had loosened and reshuffled older features of urban life. Responses to these processes combined the seizing of new opportunities, frustration at the relations of power and inequity which denied so many people what they sought, and reliance on established patterns of thought and behaviour. Adaptation, resistance and innovation could be found in the multi-occupied old houses inhabited by the poor with televisions but without sanitation, or the attempts of Shi'a activists to incorporate religious elements into modern education. In Mottahedeh's phrase about Tehran, we are seeing an unfinished *montage*, which was also the experience of those who were part of it.[94]

This narrative of cultures and communities in Iran has aimed to convey the range, persistence and diversity of religious elements and relationships within a wider social sphere and their contingent and unstable character. It has suggested that they are best understood as *made* rather than given, in that they were products of people's agency and creativity, whether collective or individual. The story of the role of religion in the cultures of nineteenth-century Iran and its subsequent development is a story of choices, contests and uncertainties shaped by the many-sided experiences and interests of the Iranians who rejected, altered or defended particular beliefs, institutions or practices. It is a story of interwoven strands rather than opposed alternatives, emphasising the multiple meanings and changing character of ritual, the varied combinations of religious, secular and 'anti-clerical' approaches to experience, and the many facets of identity. Identities drew on various distinctions made by Iranians as they constructed perceptions of experience and of the world as they knew it (individual/collective, male/female, orthodox/dissident, innovator/ conservative, dominant/subordinate, religious/secular, senior/junior, legitimate/ illegitimate). Since the discourse of any group or individual deployed several of these distinctions, they expressed their lives and relationships in terms of many-sided meanings rather than polar opposites.

The depiction of this rich mixture has preferred to suggest density rather than to simplify. The argument that elements of Shi'a Islam remained embedded in the cultural outlook and practices of many Iranians, while changing over the five or so generations under discussion, needs that level of complexity. Arguments for persistence must be set alongside a clear view of how Shi'a Islam was challenged or disregarded as well as reinvented. Iranians found in Shi'a Islam various means to express identities as men, women, communities, classes and, as will be seen, the 'imagined' nation, and, conversely, to use gendered, communal, class and national forms to express Shi'a Muslim identities. They did not all do this in the same way, and for some Iranians it was moves away from religion, and hostility to it, that expressed the cultures and identities they made and maintained. Further around that spiral dynamic, moves away from or against religion in turn stimulated innovation and resistance by Iranians who identified with and through religious aspects of their culture. The consequences will be seen in the other narratives in this book.

TWO
A story of material relationships

In order for the analysis of religious aspects of social experience to make sense, it needs material and historical depth. While much discussion of 'religion' as a phenomenon focuses on institutional issues such as the organisation and functions of religious hierarchies, rituals or instruction, or on cultural matters of belief, texts, values and arguments, it is equally important to consider the material resources and relationships involved. In the case of Iran since the nineteenth century, this involves an account of ongoing and changing relations of property, production and economic interest which form part of the social fabric of religious activity, and of the religious side of social existence. Although some accounts emphasise a history of 'secularisation' or 'modernisation' in which the material assets or resources used for religion have decreased, further examination reveals a more complex picture. The treatment here depicts the 1979 revolution as influenced not only by political and cultural reactions to 'modernity', but by the changing but deep *material* basis of religion 'in' society.

This history is best begun by describing the shape of societies, evolving in Iran during the nineteenth century, influenced by past developments and by current needs and challenges. Material life, in the sense of production, exchange and consumption within the political boundaries of Iran, was organised within a series of distinct *regions* with a large degree of autonomy.[1] Relative local self-sufficiency was further reinforced by limited agricultural technology, variable conditions causing unreliable harvests, and the unpredictable exactions of landowners, government agents or predatory raiding groups. All these factors encouraged flexible, localised self-reliance.

Within such constraints, the material structures developed by the nineteenth century consisted of a series of regions comprising towns with their rural hinterlands, villages with associated small hamlets, and an integrated structure of pastoral and arable agriculture with local manufacturing. Material links between these regions took the form of a network rather than dependence upon a supposed 'centre'. This network was sustained by exchanges of surplus produce and specialised agricultural and manufactured goods between regions within Iran, and between those regions and areas of the Ottoman Empire, the Indian subcontinent and Central Asia.[2] It had a political dimension through repeated attempts (some more successful than others) to create and maintain systems of government using the material resources of some or all of the regions. Lastly, material links between regions had a cultural aspect in so far as localised languages and customs were offset by the use of Persian as a common language and of Shi'a Islam as the religious tradition of the majority of Iranians since the seventeenth (Christian) century. The movement of migrants, government officials, religious professionals ('ulama, sufis, darvishes) and tax resources, provided material support for the dissemination of shared cultures of popular legends and poetry, and of religious cults and customs.

The towns of Iran played a crucial role in the maintenance of this network. They were focal points for the collection and exchange of goods and money, for processing of agricultural produce, and for skilled manufacturing for the luxury and long-distance commerce organised from urban centres. They were centres of both local and central state power from which law, administration and taxation were organised, and where landowners and officials lived. They were the locations for important cultural activities ranging from the life of religious institutions to popular gatherings or elite patronage of arts and crafts. Urban markets, religious schools, public ceremonies and tea-houses were the meeting places for merchants, 'ulama or travellers, as well as for rural visitors from the immediate hinterland exchanging information and participating in education, religious ritual or recreation.[3]

While servicing the network linking the various regions of Iran, towns also provided a focus for the life of the particular regions of which they were part. Wealth, which came mainly from rural sources (rents or dues on land and crops, taxation from villages, profits from trade in rural produce) was amassed in the towns by landlords, officials and other owners of property and moveable assets. Rural produce (food, raw fibres, dyes, tobacco or opium) was brought into towns to be consumed, sold, processed or turned into manufactures, providing a living for artisans, traders and their dependants. It was also in the towns that the owners of wealth and property organised and wielded power both formally as landowners, 'ulama, judicial or administrative officials, entrepreneurs and employers, and more informally through the social and political networks of which they were a part. Lastly, towns were linked to the rural areas which provided their material support through the presence of landlords, officials, traders and religious specialists who moved between rural and urban communities sustaining these ties.

This was the basis for the influence of towns in Iranian society (local, regional or national), based on townspeople's roles in production, exchange and wealth accumulation, and in social and political hierarchies, networks and power. Landlords' authority over peasants, merchants' links to producers of raw materials and manufactures, craft and professional associations, and patron–client networks all developed wholly or partly in urban settings. These forms of urban influence in Iran altered substantially with the centralisation of economic and political structures from the 1920s, the growth of communications and international economic links, and the introduction of new forms of technology, manufacturing, government and education. This occurred in a context of urbanisation whereby Iran, which in the nineteenth century was dominated by rural settlement and production, and landed wealth and elites, and whose urban population was not more than 20 per cent of the whole in 1900, had an urban population of some 47 per cent by the late 1970s. Such changes also shifted the relationship of urban centres with the capital city, Tehran, and introduced new elements into urban life. Rather than reducing the importance of towns they reinforced it, with more recent developments complementing, supplementing and interacting with older patterns rather than replacing them.

The concentration of power, resources and elite culture in urban areas is reflected in the noticeable emphasis on towns and urban life in much primary evidence and secondary writing on Iranian society and history, as compared to rural societies and culture.[4] Recognising the difficulty, this narrative of the material aspects of religion in Iranian society nevertheless begins by looking at their roots in the urban setting. This reflects the concentration of religious resources, activities and institutions in urban settlements, based on the focal role of towns described above, and the urban basis of much political activity. The historic roles of religious specialists in cultural life, law and education, and their links to local elites and ruling groups embedded them in urban communities from an early period.[5]

In nineteenth-century Iranian towns, religion was physically present at the very centre of urban life. That centre was the *bazar*, where most manufacturing and commerce took place. It was the location not only for workshops, business premises, warehouses and shops, but also for places of worship (mosques and shrines) and other places for religious gatherings (*tekkiehs*, *huseiniyehs*), or centres for education (colleges, schools), which were under mainly religious control. Nineteenth-century plans and maps, descriptions by local or foreign observers, and the surviving historic centres of the towns themselves, reveal the physical closeness between buildings used for economic activities and those with a religious purpose. This was true for a great centre of pilgrimage and provincial government like Mashad in eastern Iran, the newly growing capital, Tehran, and the whole range smaller towns and provincial capitals (Qazvin, Kashan, Bam, Semnan).[6] Businessmen, craftsmen and traders went about their work in close proximity to the places where religious experts preached, taught and organised rituals.

This proximity of workshop and mosque, of commercial premises and religious buildings was not just picturesque or coincidental, but expressed significant personal and institutional connections between those involved in manufacturing or trade and religious specialists. Material relationships linked the two groups in diverse ways and were crucial to their daily lives, particularly through exchanges of resources and services which met the respective needs of religious specialists and commercial or artisan groups, and sustained relationships of mutual support and overlapping interests. Such relationships involved regular competition and negotiation, but were an important material force, established during the eighteenth and early nineteenth centuries. Following the collapse of the Safavid dynasty, which had directly supported a religious hierarchy in the 1720s, and faced with the hostility, weakness or indifference of its war-lord successors, the 'ulama could no longer rely on rulers. They turned to local elites and patrons, acquired revenues and properties in their own right, and established links with urban commercial and manufacturing groups which were also gaining a degree of autonomy.[7] From the nineteenth century onwards one defining material characteristic of 'ulama in Iran was their reliance on neither state nor elite resources, but on funds from Shi'a Muslim supporters, and their own properties and profits. This was a key factor in their relative material resilience through subsequent economic and political change.

By the nineteenth century, craftsmen and merchants were giving significant financial support to religious specialists and religious activities. Money from their incomes or profits supported the 'ulama's preaching, teaching and legal or ceremonial activities. Members of the religious establishment gained incomes from urban rents and entrepreneurial activities, and lesser mullas might combine artisan or commercial work with religious responsibilities. When the Englishman Fraser described the madrasehs of Mashad, he mentions new foundations established with money made in Indian trade.[8] Such resources contributed to the upkeep of students in the madrasehs and the financing of recitations, ceremonies and Muharram drama and provided resources for the charity and welfare distributed by the religious classes to those in need. It is worth noting that it was at this period that those senior 'ulama recognised as having authority to issue binding interpretations of law and religious tradition (the mujtaheds) started to claim and collect a share of the religious taxes for themselves.[9]

For their part, the religious specialists gave material support and services to the merchant and manufacturing community. As legal experts they gave judgment on a range of issues affecting craft or merchant activities, drew up and ratified business documents, and acted as guarantors and adjudicators in business transactions and disputes. As the main providers of education they offered basic schooling in the urban community and higher levels of learning. They participated in and supervised rituals and ceremonies organised or sponsored by merchants and artisans. Money from religious bodies and bequests went into building urban facilities like shops and public baths, whose rents provided income for those bodies.[10] These activities involved a range of religious men, from self-employed preachers and reciters to high-ranking government appointees in the religious law courts or major urban mosques, in close and frequent contact with key groups in urban society. At higher levels, members of the *'ulama* with wealth, political influence and social connections offered patronage and protection to allies and clients in the same manner as landowners, merchants or officials.[11]

Over time, such material bonds and mutual benefits created social and family connections, further strengthening relationships between traders, *'ulama* and artisans. Members of merchant and artisan families became religious specialists, while members of the *'ulama* likewise engaged in business activities. Inter-marriage between merchant and *'ulama* families was quite common. Evidence for this pattern of overlapping activities and interests within or between families is found in surveys of the social structure of Iranian towns by both Iranians and foreigners.[12] They record the use of shrines for trading, the association of religious buildings with particular craft workers, and the role of religious sects in financing urban building complexes containing both religious and business premises describing the patronage and the exchange of imaterial and political support.[13] Such exchanges had their political aspect, but the *material* dimension of relationships between *mullas* and *bazaris* within urban communities was a distinctive feature of those communities.

Though limited in themselves, the alliance of interests between religious, artisan and merchant groups, as well as the wealth and influence of sections of the *'ulama* as property owners and administrators of funds, sustained wider material relationships within urban communities. Iranian towns included a range of wage earners, unskilled labourers, street pedlars, animal drivers, service workers and their families, forming the poorer and more dependent sections of the community. Links between these groups and religious specialists, also based on exchanges of services, resources and support, added their own material contribution to the religious life of towns and the social position of religious specialists.

The most direct of these links was the use of *'ulama* funds and influence to assist or protect client townspeople. The distribution of food and money to the poor by *mullas* was a feature of urban life, becoming especially important at times of shortage or famine. Poorer members of the religious classes themselves depended on material support from better off, *'ulama* or other sections of the community. This support drew on the funds paid to the *'ulama* by those with resources in the form of the *khums* (the 'fifth' owed as religious tax to the *'ulama*) and *zakat* (the charitable dues incumbent on Muslims). As collectors, direct controllers and disbursers of these funds, the *'ulama* had key material roles which lay at the core of their social power, financial autonomy and collective identity.

The *'ulama* offered other services arising from their specialist skills and functions. In the performance of ceremonies and rituals or as legal experts and teachers, high religious officials, sect leaders and lesser *mullas* provided, and profited by, the use of their expertise among the urban populace. Training in religious law, which dealt with inheritance and family matters, enabled them to advise and regulate in these areas, just as they dominated the provision of what education was available in urban centres. Both *'ulama* and religious students (*tullab*) played a part in organising temporary marriages (*sigheh*), whose use by the urban poor involved the trading of women's sexual services to men in an institutionalised, socially acceptable form.[14] Such activities gave *mullas* functions, influence and resources.

This was supplemented by other material factors. Senior and respected figures among the *'ulama* acted as patrons offering protection to clients confronting the demands and pressures of other powerful men. This ability stemmed from the wealth and personal connections linking *'ulama* to other sections of the elite, from the authority of their legal pronouncements, and the tradition of regarding their houses (like mosques and shrines) as sanctuary (*bast*) for those involved in disputes with the powerful. Exercise of patronage and protection was useful to senior *'ulama*, enabling them to create bonds of obligation and loyalty among urban supporters and followers. Such patron/client or leader/follower links had practical and material aspects involving exchanges of gifts, payments and services, as well as political and cultural importance. Senior *'ulama* supported not just extensive households, but also groups of clients, hired *lutis* (strongmen) and dependants, and a wider set of connections to preachers, prayer leaders and reciters who officiated at marriage or funeral rituals, and the yearly cycle of religious ceremonies. Resourcing the everyday life of urban groups and providing incomes for those who performed such functions linked 'religious' and 'material' aspects of town life.

The dense and diverse linkages of 'material' and 'religious' in nineteenth-century Iranian towns were not necessarily harmonious, acceptable or equally beneficial to all parties, since they involved relationships based on power and inequality. The *'ulama*'s activities as collectors of *khums* and *zakat* cast them in a contentious role. The dependence of those lacking resources and influence upon religious charity and protection involved the exploitation of their needs and vulnerabilities by *mullas* in the very provision of patronage, services and protection. This informs the extensive commentary on how *'ulama* took advantage of their material position for financial gain, sexual exploitation and the pursuit of personal interests at the expense of others. Anecdotal and descriptive evidence suggests that relations of religious specialists in the urban community involved resentment, cynicism and hostility.[15] Nevertheless, these relations met the material needs of all concerned, whether through exploitation or benevolent dependency and patronage, and extended beyond the propertied classes of the *bazar* into other sections of the urban community.

Comparison of this situation with material aspects of the religious presence in rural settlements reveals differences, similarities and debatable issues. In both settings, exactions of dues by *'ulama* was unpopular, just as their distribution of welfare was welcome. Ownership or control of land and rural resources by religious figures or religious trusts (*vaqf*) represented a major source of revenue for the religious establishment, and brought the religious classes into rural areas as landowners or managers of *vaqfs*.[16] Some villages had shrines, resident *mullas* and religious festivals as the focus for the material links between religious specialists and other members of the community comparable to urban equivalents. There is evidence for the activities of *mullas* in the countryside, passion play performances in hill villages, and active peasant and tribal support for particular sect leaders, as well as for the material growth of some rural settlements around shrines and pilgrimages.[17]

However, there is also evidence that the base for religious activity in rural areas was limited. Most landholding and rural resources were not controlled by religious specialists or religious institutions. Many rural settlements were isolated by poor communications, relative self-sufficiency and low levels of prosperity, from the regular contacts with towns. It follows that the concentrations and exchanges of resources and services, and networks of power and patronage sustaining them, which were characteristic of urban communities, were less typical in rural settlements. While religious activities and associations in such settlements might have material features comparable to those in towns, it is unwise to assume that this was the case, or generalise from one setting to the other.

We can now reassess conventional views of religious life in nineteenth-century Iran as an essentially *urban* phenomenon, and modify the schematic distinction frequently made between 'town' and 'village' as ideal types. Like many conventions and typologies, they have some basis, but become mystifying and restrictive if applied uncritically and automatically. Material exploitation of rural resources was crucial to the sustainability of urban religious activities, rather than directly supporting an extensive religious establishment in villages, just as traders, officials, *mullas* and peasants might on occasion move between towns and villages. One might think of a spectrum of influences, at one end of which were the largely autonomous religious activities of rural settlements described by nineteenth-century observers and twentieth-century anthropologists. Distinctive urban and rural religious practices shaped religious aspects of the political activities discussed in Chapters 4 and 6.

67

A story of material relationships

This sketch of the material bases of religion is relevant both to any full account of social experiences in Iran, and to the history of religious aspects of society. The links between religious establishments in Iranian towns and urban economic activities and social hierarchies persisted over time, whether they were challenged, sustained, redirected or reversed. While there have been deep and widespread changes in economy and society in Iran since the 1920s, their effects on religious activities and institutions do not fit simple patterns of 'change' or 'continuity'. There is no clear-cut story of the 'decline of religion', but rather complex, sometimes contradictory, interactions between new, old, secular and religious elements, affecting material lives as well as political or cultural activities.

Four themes make useful guides to material change and its effects on religion during the twentieth century. First, there is the question of the increasingly centralised and 'national' dimensions of economic life. Second, the introduction of new forms of economic organisation and productive technologies needs consideration. Third, an interventionist state played a key role in those processes. Last, these developments should be set within the context of increasingly intense involvement between material life in Iran and global structures of exchange and investment.

Centralisation of a network of relatively self-sufficient regions began in the 1920s and 1930s with the creation of national transport structures and the beginnings of state intervention in trade and agricultural produce. While Reza Shah Pahlavi's modernising policies had limited impact, they signalled the start of a shift, which became a pattern of economic centralisation after the Second World War, paralleling the earlier administrative centralisation. The shift was partly an expression of Reza Shah's dynastic ambition, based on the application of new technologies of communication, production and organisation. Material life in Iran began to be transformed by new forms of travel and communication, new techniques in manufacturing production, and new demands for services in commerce, administration and education. These first appeared in the 1930s and 1940s and expanded between the 1950s and 1970s, a period of agrarian transformation with the ending of traditional landholding, the growth of market forces and the displacement of rural populations.

Although the role of entrepreneurial and propertied groups with these developments may have been underestimated, two more visible influences need consideration. International connections, which had been primarily commercial and relatively limited before the First World War, became an increasingly important economic factor. The influence of the oil industry since the 1920s, the role of foreign loans, investments and technology since the 1950s, and growing reliance on imported foodstuffs since the 1970s, established dependent interactions between economic developments in Iran and powerful external forces. This was encouraged by foreign investors, governments with global interests in energy resources, strategic issues and markets, and by the search of the Pahlavi shahs for material and political support for their dynastic security and authoritarian rule. The material impact of Pahlavi rule in Iran was further increased by direct government intervention in economic life in order to enhance their public status as 'modernising' rulers, and to develop up-to-date means of state control and repression. The Pahlavi state built roads, bureaucracies and an army in the 1920s and 1930s, and supported new financial institutions, land reform, and the expansion of manufacturing and service sectors from the 1950s. This directly affected investment in construction and manufacturing, patterns of service work and unskilled urban labour, and rural property relations and production.[18]

These material changes provided the context for the changing material conditions of religious activity, which were affected by significant transformations of the regional economies, of town and village communities and of urban–rural relations. The growth of wage labour (from perhaps 16 per cent of the recorded labour force in the 1940s to 34 per cent in the 1970s), of urban population, and of non-agricultural employment, involved significant population migrations (seasonal and long-term, localised, regional and long-distance). They were also associated with the expansion of production outside established forms of self-reliant household, workshop and communal labour, with increased use of money and credit in everyday life, and with greater state and market power. While these changes were uneven, they stimulated adaptations to existing forms of patronage, employment, learning and labour.

The impact of these developments on the material conditions of religious activity and religious specialists took different forms at different moments. In the first half of the twentieth century, the most visible source of *direct* material change was the state. The creation of an non-*shari'a* legal system in the 1920s and 1930s reduced the legal role of the *'ulama*, just as the slower growth of a secular and state-supported education system reduced their role in teaching and learning. An increase in students in *maktabs* (religious primary schools) between the mid-1920s and the mid-1930s (from c. 23,000 to c. 55,000) was outstripped by the expansion of state school pupils (c. 60,000 to c. 230,000) in that period, followed by decline to mid-1920s levels by the mid-1940s, by which time the state sector had over 327,000 pupils. By the 1970s, the 5 million students in elementary schools and 2.5 million in secondary or vocational schools were educated in the secularised state system.[19]

This indicator of decline in employment and income for those *'ulama* who staffed traditional *maktabs* was paralleled by a comparable decline in their legal work. From the first grant of partial rights of appeal from the *shari'a* courts to state courts in 1922 to the establishment of secular state control over the

69

registration of ownership and property documents in 1932, the secularisation of the Civil Code and courts, and the regulation of the judiciary during the 1930s, the role of *shari'a* and its expert practitioners was sidelined. While *'ulama* continued to register marriages and divorces (a key source of income), the decline of that role for commercial documents had material effects worth further study. The third important material issue for the religious specialists was growing state supervision and regulation of the *vaqfs* (bequests of land and other resources for charitable, religious and related purposes), which supported religious specialists and activities, and were often administered by *'ulama*. Although the *vaqf* regulations of the 1930s were limited, they served the long-standing aim of ruling regimes to bring this resource into their repertoire of patronage, taxation and control, and the new interventionist and modernising government agenda.

These direct changes to the material conditions of the *'ulama* were part of a wider set of material influences on religious life and activity up to the 1950s. There is no simple picture of these particular circumstances, as can be seen in the urban *bazar* setting which was the historic source of *'ulama* support and focus of religious activity. New and divergent experiences supplemented the established role of towns and cities as described earlier. The growth of a centrally controlled state bureaucracy, of state economic intervention, and of improved communications, established greater distinctions between the capital and 'provincial' centres which were now under its direct and effective influence. Entrepreneurship and production diversified, with new large-scale manufacturing in some centres (textile works in Isfahan and Yazd, sugar refining in Shiraz, Tehran and Mashad, the oil industry in the south-west) developing alongside established enterprises and techniques. Wage labour grew both in new manufacturing, service and commercial activities and in enlarged 'traditional' enterprises (carpentry, garment and shoe production) within and outside the *bazar* areas of Iranian towns, co-existing with older working relations in craft workshops. The wage-earning, poorer and more dependent sections of urban communities were enlarged by the beginnings of migration from rural areas to towns, or from lesser to more flourishing centres.

Differentiation featured in the social composition of towns more generally. Most frequently noted were new classes of administrative, clerical and professional workers in government, business, law and education, who were increasingly products of 'modern' education either in Iran or, if privileged, abroad. These occupations offered new job opportunities, both modest and powerful, and were sources of status and influence. They added distinctive elements to the urban economy and community, as did new kinds of roads and buildings, which provided for the needs of central authority, administration and commerce. Turning from description to analysis, it is fruitful to emphasise relationships between 'old' and 'new' features of urban life and their impact on one another, rather than just opposing them. Urban societies between the 1920s and the 1950s showed contrasts, but also convergence and interactions, like the ability of some *bazar* entrepreneurs to invest in new as well as 'traditional' sectors, and to use the modern state as a patron, even if facing competition from 'new' social groups. Similarly, the growth of 'new' types of employment allowed urban families, rich or poor, to have members working in 'new' as well as 'old' occupations, according to opportunity, necessity or choice. Just as new residential areas, new roads and new industrial, administrative and commercial buildings appeared alongside, or within, existing urban areas without eliminating them, so *bazar* merchants, office workers and school teachers, wage labourers and craft apprentices were distinct, antagonistic, but also interdependent actors in the urban economy.[20]

Three areas of change are worth noting. First, there were emerging constraints on urban autonomy. Central government administrative intervention, government-backed expansion of communications, and government investment or patronage in trade, began to limit the independence of regional economic networks in which major towns were centres. External influences on production, trade and consumption through state regulation, reductions in time and cost of transport, and state regulation of food and commodity prices began to establish what would become a single 'national' economy, replacing the older loosely linked network of relatively self-reliant regions. Second, qualitatively different material features appeared on the urban scene, albeit with uneven impact. The expansion of bureaucratic and educational jobs transformed employment, skills and knowledge, while varying according to the size and functions of different towns. Since it is hard to quantify the growth of this sector in this period, it is also hard to estimate its qualitative effect, or the changing power and position of established wholesale merchants in relation to state control and new competitors. The broad calculations and structural arguments of sociological approaches to this story do not wholly capture experience, although offering suggestive interpretations.[21] In particular they neglect the third important factor, the interactive relationships between 'old' and 'new' features of urban societies, which was as significant as the separation or conflict between them.

This is particularly relevant when considering the material position of religious specialists during these decades. The loss of sources of income in law and education for *'ulama* of all ranks also entailed the loss of material links to government and *bazar* activities and interests. However, this formed only part of the material support on which *mullas* relied. The continued productivity and resilience of *bazar* economies as they adapted to new circumstances, and met continuing demand for their goods and services, maintained resources and relationships which linked *mullas* to craftsmen and traders. However, these were modified by the loosening of guild controls and influence as a result of Reza Shah's abolition of guild taxes, and by the diversification of waged work which reduced the dominance of traditional craft workshop structures. Other sources of income, although not extensively researched, also continued to provide some income for religious specialists. Reza Shah's attempts to ban and/or regulate the various activities associated with Muharram did not mean that the recitations, ceremonies and prayer gatherings, with their *mullas* and *rawzeh* readers, in fact ceased, and there is descriptive evidence to the contrary.[22] The more general demand for prayers, divinations, amulets and other religious services, for which believers were willing to pay, while disparaged by the articulate modernisers and intelligentsia of the period, still generated income for religious specialists. Seen by some as undesirable survivals, they clearly had a continuing, if more limited, presence in changing urban communities, as did the welfare relations linking *'ulama* to needy members of those communities, and to their sources of *khums* and *zakat* dues. In the absence of other sources of support for the sick or poor, such relations continued to sustain important material contacts for members of the *'ulama*.

The deep and irreversible socioeconomic changes experienced by Iranians in the 1960s and 1970s are much discussed and analysed in the literature on the revolution of 1977–81. The account here gives due weight to those changes, and also places them in a more extended narrative of modernity in Iran and of their co-existence with older-established features of society, looking at the significant and disruptive developments of the 1960s and 1970s from a range of perspectives. The massive increase in economic intervention by the state via reform programmes, the expansion of bureaucratic and education systems, and investment initiatives was a qualitative shift from past practice. Using the rapidly increasing oil revenues at its disposal, and stimulated by the demands of maintaining the Shah's power and the urgings of his American sponsors, the regime deployed direct economic intervention (land reform, expanding education) and indirect stimuli via its role with banks and compensation payments to landlords as part of land reform.

This intervention had a powerful impact. In rural areas, the end of historic patterns of sharecropping and landlord power and the commercialisation of agriculture introduced Iranians in those areas to greater dependency on money, access to land for some, and new forms of material inequity. The search for work and income produced large-scale migration (both temporary and long term) by rural and urban dwellers as seasonal workers or new urban residents in major centres, Tehran in particular. Increased demand for white-collar workers – administrators, teachers, technocrats, office workers – in the hugely expanded state bureaucracy, education system and modern commercial sector involved whole strata of literate, educated and/or aspirant Iranians in work or attempts to work in such areas, again in urban settings. Explicit state support for foreign enterprise and investment encouraged an unprecedented influx of imported goods, technologies, capital and 'expert' labour, whether radios in villages, foreign backing for banks and petrochemical production, or growing quantities of food ($2.2 billion/12 per cent of imports by 1977–81).[23]

Two key features with both political and economic significance in this process were the role of oil and of the Iranian state. In the 1950s, economic development in Iran was already 50 per cent financed by oil and gas income, rising to 63 per cent in the decade 1962–72 and to over 80 per cent in 1974 following the OPEC hike in oil prices in 1973. The increase in oil revenues from $22.5 million in 1954 to $20 *billion* in 1977 placed huge resources in government hands, which funded the Pahlavi family and its supporters, and military and intelligence services to sustain the regime. It also funded the expansion of industrial, commercial and service activity in the state and private sectors, the land reform programme, and urban and communication construction. By 1977–78, oil and gas accounted for 77 per cent of state income, 87 per cent of foreign exchange and 98 per cent of Iranian exports. This single product, central to post-1945 global economies and technologies, and hence the global strategic interests of states and oil companies, was produced, priced and marketed by an international consortium, while formally owned/exploited by the Iranian state, marrying dependency and Pahlavi power. The strengthening of the autocracy, the tying of material circumstances in Iran to global economic interests (from Arab–Israeli politics, to energy capitalism and the Cold War) and the rapid introduction of 'modern' economic forces into Iranian communities formed the triangular dynamic of material development in Iran from 1953 to 1978.

This can be seen as a 'new' state of affairs which significantly altered the lives of many Iranians over that period. However, it can also be located within a longer history of Iranian involvement with modernity which established preconditions for the disruptive transformations of the 1960s and 1970s. The role of oil in the material power of the Pahlavi state and in its ties of dependency to the USA were distinctive to the post-1953 period, but rooted in earlier developments linking the Iranian state and foreign interests to the use and control of oil resources and revenues. The regime's determined initiation of 'modernising' programmes, while backed by state will and resources to an unprecedented degree from the 1960s, were in the tradition of state-sponsored modernisation which had influenced reforming, dynastic and radical politics since the 1850s. Foreign influence, intervention, expertise and example had also featured in Iranians' experience for over a century, but had extended and intensified from the 1960s. While it is important to grasp the qualitative shift in the material circumstances of many Iranians during the 1960s and 1970s, it is also important not to sever them from their antecedents.

That shift involved complex relationships with older elements of material life in Iran. If migration and seasonal wage earning transformed household economies in Iranian cities or villages, such economies and their gendered divisions of labour still provided a crucial framework for material life. The role of women in the expansion of carpet production in some rural areas, the decline of their contribution to domestic food processing in others, and their growing participation in areas of urban wage labour from domestic work to white-collar jobs, demonstrated just such a blend of significant change and persistent structures. The continuing importance of the *bazar* in wholesale and retail activity, the adaptation of the *bazaris* to new opportunities, and their clashes with state regulation or entrepreneurs in the 'new' sector, is another complex instance. The outcomes of land reform in the Iranian countryside were likewise complex with radical redistribution of ownership (peasant sharecroppers becoming proprietors) and the ending of old cultivation teams (*buneh*) co-existing with older patterns of widespread landlessness, absentee landlordism and subsistence agriculture.[24] In each case, the dense proximity of contrasting, sometimes conflicting, patterns of work and relationships is as significant as the disruptive introduction of new elements. Qashqa'i women buying imported fabrics in the Shiraz *bazar* to make 'traditional' clothing, or migrants to cities maintaining contact with their villages of origin and forming associations with others from their region, while adapting to factory or street labour, lived such discontinuities and proximities as everyday experiences.

The impact of modern bureaucracies, market forces and changed patterns of work and survival overlaid and clashed with the continuing influence of existing relations and divisions of labour (gendered, communal, familial) rather than removing it. Villagers in Khuzestan made their own adaptations of established work patterns and family obligations in the aftermath of land reform, using the opportunities and accepting the constraints of state and market power. Village 'headmen' (*kadkhodas*) might now be agents of government rather than landlord authority, but still came from those regarded as having familial and personal qualifications for the position on the basis of past experience.[25] In the squatter settlements of Tehran and Tabriz, the help provided by relatives and migrants from the same area for those seeking jobs, social support or marriage partners, contrasted with the harsh experiences of wage labour, street conditions, poverty and modern officialdom in migrants' daily lives.

Patterns of work and life expressed not just confrontations of 'old' and 'new', but complex genealogies and blends of material and social change. The effects of global dependency on imported capital, technology and market forces were visible in the 'screwdriver' industries which drew in skilled and semi-skilled labour to produce cars and consumer durables under foreign licence. The drive to capitalistic entrepreneurial development, begun before the Second World War, shaped concentrations of production more rapidly from the 1960s, characterised by ties to state patronage, high profits and inherited advantages.[26] Increases in modern manufacturing output and employment did not involve general enlargement or concentration of production. In 1977, between 68 and 72 per cent of workers in manufacturing worked in units with fewer than ten employees, some 244,000 of the total of 250,000 manufacturing establishments. Small-scale commodity production, whether of established crafts or newer goods, was significant for industrial output and non-oil exports, with 'traditional' industrial goods (notably carpets) being some 35 per cent of the former and 28 per cent of the latter. Older manufactures, adapted to new demands and possibilities, held their place in material life, contributing to its layered complexity.[27]

This was the context for the ambivalent experience of *bazar* communities. The accelerated growth of modern commerce, finance and manufacturing challenged older established forms, notably in imports and private sector credit. Small-scale production, much of it located in the *bazar*, employed declining numbers of workers and created limited added value, despite its *quantitative* dominance in the manufacturing sector. The expansion of banks, chain retail outlets and modern urban shopping areas, established alternatives to *bazar* food retailing and money-lending, just as imported and factory-made goods competed with local craft products. The share of domestic trade in GDP fell from over 9 per cent in 1963–64 to under 6 per cent in 1977–78. However, rather than displacing *bazar* activity altogether, more complex processes of competition and adaptation appeared. Continued and growing international demand for a 'traditional' product (carpets) stimulated new entrepreneurial activity, subordinating rural producers to urban contractors, and provincial *bazar* businessmen to Tehran exporters, while sustaining an old craft industry. In the 1970s, *bazar* merchants still controlled about 66 per cent of retail and 75 per cent of wholesale trading, but only 30 per cent of imports and 15 per cent of private sector credit.

This complexity was expressed in the patterns of urban commercial and productive activity in which modern street-based and *bazar*-based workshops and retail outlets co-existed. Bonine's work on Yazd shows important shared structural characteristics and comparable responses to change in both locations as well as significant divergences between them. New investors in shops, using capital earned working abroad, opened premises in both areas. Weavers who turned to textile trading, and former tailors now retailing factory-made garments, similarly operated from both *bazar* and modern street outlets. Kin, occupation and local links influenced the patterns of shop location on modern avenues as well as *bazars* since access to networks of customers, family and fellow traders was a key material factor for both. New opportunities created by foreign demand for Iranian carpets, and domestic affluence increasing demand for carpets and jewellery, assisted entrepreneurship in *bazar* as well as street locations, although there were significant differences and competition between the older and newer sectors. In Yazd by the 1970s, street outlets dominated trade in general, outnumbering *bazar* outlets by ten to one, and selling the majority of 'modern' products like personal goods (e.g. toiletries), non-food household provisions or personal services. This paralleled the emergence of industrial, financial and wholesale entrepreneurs, rooted in modern textile factories, trucking businesses, and banks linked to Tehran and thence to national and international trade and production. An uneasy combination of responsive resilience to economic change and external intervention was well attested in the *bazar* sector of urban economies more generally.[28]

In the quarter-century before the Shah's overthrow, Iranian society was marked by diverse and sometimes discordant material trends. These can be set in the analytical frameworks of dependency, despotism and underdevelopment, emphasising the state-driven nature of economic change, the dominant role of foreign capital, oil and strategy-led links to the wider world, and the uneven growth of prosperity and productivity across Iranian society. The stalled development of agriculture and consequent outflow of migrants to populate underskilled and underemployed urban industries and settlements lacking services or infrastructures has to be set beside the growth of new propertied, educated and affluent groups. Various forms of rural and urban poverty and deprivation remained endemic, whether calculated in terms of spending capacity, housing and health conditions, or malnourishment; for the urban poor, their share of household expenditure actually declined between 1960 and 1974.[29] Within this overall picture of material change and inequality, of structural dependency and state economic intervention, other elements also played a significant role. Changed entrepreneurial and productive activity took place *within* existing frameworks – pastoral groupings, *bazar* structures, village communities – in which Iranians combined responses to new influences and immediate circumstances with resources and repertoires embedded in their history and developed patterns of adaptive resilience.

These patterns shaped more than just the practicalities of work, production and exchange. Historic distinctions of gender, class, generation and location continued to have key roles while being reconfigured by newly influential market forces, state intervention, increased formal education, and the growth of communication and migration. These influences were themselves shaped by existing gendered divisions of power and productive labour, historic patterns of family and collective activity, and the structures of class difference. Patterns of male migration, of female paid employment, and of ambivalent responses to new state medical and educational provision, expressed the openness of Iranians to new opportunities, their support for established family, community and gender arrangements, and their capacity for creative syntheses.[30]

Where was the material position of religious specialists, their activities and their institutions located in this complex context? What impact did the processes of globalisation, state economic intervention and social change have on the assets, opportunities and resources available to religious specialists? Like others they faced the interventionist and controlling efforts of the second Pahlavi autocracy, whether attempts to control *vaqf* properties and endowments, or continued assertion of a supervisory role over the definition of *'ulama* status and rights. The increase in state-sponsored secular bureaucracies, technocrats, lawyers and teachers, intensified the professional marginalisation of the *'ulama* begun under Reza Shah. The accommodations with the state achieved by *'ulama* leaders like Shaikh 'Abd ul-Karim Ha'eri Yazdi in the 1930s, and Ayatollah Sayyid Muhammad Husein Burujerdi in the 1950s produced a certain professionalisation of the *'ulama*, explored in Chapter 3, but the *entente* (or stand-off?) between *'ulama* and state power had material consequences. It defined and protected a clear, but restricted, niche of professional expertise and legitimacy which *'ulama* continued to use to gain and redistribute financial resources (using *khums* and *zakat*), and to manage their own professional formation. This supported a growing number of students who went on to provide religious services in both urban and rural communities.

The 1960s land reforms had distinctive effects on religious specialists. Those who were landholders in their own right faced the same situation as non-*'ulama* counterparts, with similar chances to manipulate or avoid land redistribution, receive compensation and continue as absentee landlords. In areas like Azerbaijan, or around Isfahan, where extensive *'ulama* landholding dated back to nineteenth-century acquisitions, this was a significant phenomenon.[31] More importantly, the extensive lands (some 10–15 per cent, or 40,000 properties) designated as religious endowments for support for mosques, shrines and *madraseh* education, or welfare for the needy (*vaqf i-'amm*), were excluded from the 1962 reform provisions. Land designated as personal endowments, usually trusts, for the endower's family (*vaqf-i-khass*) was treated like privately owned land. However, 1963 additions to the 1962 law required the leasing of *vaqf-i-'amm* land on ninety-nine-year leases to its cultivators, and among the peasants with recognised cultivation rights (*nasaq*) were 172,000 (some 8–9 per cent of the total) who received such leases by 1971. Interviews in rural communities in the 1970s suggested that the five-yearly rent reviews provided for in the leases produced conflict between cultivators and *vaqf* administrators seeking to maintain or raise the flow of income from *vaqf* land.[32]

Stagnation or decline in *vaqf* support for religious specialists and their activities was caused mainly by the encroachments and appropriations of *vaqf* property by state-appointed *vaqf* administrators. Revenues were also appropriated as 'salaries' or 'gifts', and land sold off to relatives and government officials in pursuit of patronage and influence.[33] Appropriations of *vaqf* income had occurred under earlier dynasties, and now contributed to the embattled and defensive stance of the religious establishment in the 1960s and 1970s and their anxieties for their material security. So too did the weakening of *'ulama* ties to landed patrons who commanded reduced resources, or were less likely to use them for religious purposes. The fact that only 10–12 per cent of villages supported a resident *mulla* in the 1970s suggests that rural change did not enable many communities to expand religious activities, which were subsidised from other sources.[34] Existing material connections between religious specialists and rural society were not ended by changes in landholding and agriculture after 1962, but did experience restructuring and instability.

More significant contributions to *'ulama* income (some $30 million annually plus alms, according to 1972 US government estimates) and to their social support came from elsewhere. Evidence from the 1970s shows that the major shrine at Qum derived less than a third of its income from endowments and just over 11 per cent from *vaqf* land.[35] Other material support for religion included labour and materials provided by villagers to construct mosques, payments to *mullas* and *rawzeh-khwans,* and regular transmission of the 'Imam's share' (*sahm i-imam*, half of the *khums*) from urban and rural communities to leading *'ulama*. Donations from pious groups and individuals provided important contributions to the upkeep of *madraseh* education, and the welfare efforts of the *'ulama*, underpinning a variety of social networks linking *mullas* to predominantly urban patrons and partners.

At the core of this pattern was continuing *bazari* support for religious activities, people and institutions dating back to the nineteenth century. As shown above, the *bazar* section of the economy adapted to the changes of the 1960s and 1970s. Pious and propertied *bazaris* had the means to continue funding religious associations and publications, as well as *madraseh* students and teachers and *'ulama* philanthropy. *Bazari* money supported activities ranging from the contentious efforts of innovative groups like those involved in the Huseiniyeh Ershad (where reformist *mullas* and religious intellectuals set out their ideas in the 1960s), and *hay'ats* (religious associations) set up by and for new urban migrants, to traditional *rawzehs* and welfare work. Patronage and money from merchants and entrepreneurs continued to maintain Muharram rituals, and senior *'ulama*'s initiatives to expand religious services or construct clinics and libraries. They linked religious specialists of all ranks with *bazaris* on the one hand, and communities of women, male activists, urban migrants and poor people on the other.[36]

This historic pattern of *bazari* patronage of religious activities, of *'ulama,* and of 'lay' religious groups was sustained by *bazar* prosperity in the 1960s and 1970s, and also extended to propertied and influential groups outside the *bazar*.

Just as 'new' street-based urban economic life co-existed with, and sometimes drew on, the *bazar* economy, so traders, officials and entrepreneurs in the 'new' urban sectors funded *mullas, hay'ats* and Muharram rituals. This might reflect the *bazari* origins or connections of these 'new' patrons, or acknowledge how support for religion conferred status and respectability, just as government patronage and the ability to 'fix' links with the bureaucracy aided material success. It allowed patrons to select and control relations with chosen *'ulama* and thereby manage consensus and contain incipient dissidence. For *bazaris*, who also chose among *mullas* with different views, support for religious aims and interests sprang less from short-term conformism than from persisting solidarities and continuities of patriarchal kinship and work. It expressed a strongly rooted, but now challenged, cultural identity, as they faced new rivals and material forces, and was a relatively low-risk political gesture of independence from, if not opposition to, the dominant secular autocratic order.

The diversification of the urban economy and the tensions between *bazar*, state and new economic interests from the 1960s did not undermine historically constituted links of *bazar* and *'ulama*, although creating a different context for them. Stripped of judicial and educational roles since the 1930s, *'ulama* continued to find material means and opportunities within that relationship, enabling them to sustain and refigure their specialised forms of teaching and scholarship, and roles as community leaders. They provided a continuing flow of *madraseh*-educated preachers and local religious leaders to urban, and some rural, communities. The physical closeness of *bazar* trade and production to religious institutions survived the 'modernising' intrusions of the state and new entrepreneurs, while now under challenge. In the 1960s and 1970s the spread of modern workplaces and service and retail outlets around such spaces and along the 1930s avenues which cut through existing *bazars* in Yazd, Kermanshah, Shiraz, Semnan or even Qum altered urban space without wholly obliterating old connections. However, the demolition of the area around the great shrine at Mashad (including *madrasehs* and *bazar* areas) at government command in 1975, and similar grandiose plans for Qum and Tehran, indicated threatening possibilities for terminal confrontation between the *bazar*/religious nexus and the power of a dictatorial state. It coincided significantly with a harsh government campaign against *bazaris* as 'profiteers'.[37]

The established marital and familial links connecting *bazaris* and religious specialists changed during the 1960s and 1970s. The diversification of career opportunities for educated Iranians in that period, competition between 'secular' and 'religious' outlooks, and the effects of support, opposition or acquiescence to the regime on job prospects, introduced different patterns. A partial survey of *madraseh* students in Qum in the mid-1970s showed the largest group coming from rural families, with *mulla* and *bazari* families in second and third places, perhaps indicating that for bright rural boys there were fewer routes to secular professional advancement.[38] At the apex of the religious establishment, the occupational genealogies of four *ayatollahs* show both the predominance of religious occupations in their families and a decline in the *bazari* element, which was more prominent in current and preceding generations than in younger ones (forty-six compared to twelve). By contrast, the number of religious occupations in the current and younger generations exceeded those in the older generations (seventy-five compared to thirty). This suggests relatively open access to senior ranks of the *'ulama* but also a growing tendency for that access to be consolidated within families. The emergence of a new trend in these families with younger generations in 'modern' professions not entered by their forebears (twenty-four compared with seven) is suggestive in another way. It indicates that even in *'ulama* families, 'modern' professional work was now an option, and that by the 1970s two or three generations of 'modern' secular professionals (lawyers, academics, doctors, bureaucrats, engineers) had *mulla* and/or *bazar* grandfathers, cousins or uncles.[39] This process can be read in contrasting ways: on the one hand it marked the decline of the more pervasive role of religious professionals; on the other it was sufficiently recent to preserve material connections of work or family between established religious specialists and their secular counterparts.

The theme of material compromise and competition over religious activities and institutions was also visible in *mulla* philanthropy. Historically, the provision of welfare for the needy had nurtured links between *'ulama*, those with the means to give to charity, and the poor. In the 1960s and 1970s the continued flow of *zakat*, *khums* and other donations to the *'ulama* allowed them to continue as sponsors of clinics, hospitals or housing projects, and as distributors of funds to the needy. Contest and emulation both among leading *'ulama* and between *'ulama* and the state were significant features of these activities. The building of hospitals in Qum, for example, involved interactions between *'ulama* and state bureaucracy and legislation, as well as among those *'ulama*.[40] The growth of more organised distribution of welfare for the poor in Shiraz in the 1960s manifested new elements, replacing older systems of personalised giving with a structure of organised donations and disbursements of funds using 'modern' bureaucratic procedures. 'Discreet' styles of *mulla* benevolence were displaced by more hierarchical, judgemental procedures whereby the scrutinising and stigmatising of petitioners were rationalised as good and careful practices. *'Ulama* philanthropy was a source of pride and anti-government point-scoring in a climate of growing regime pressure on the religious establishment, just as government officials denigrated and restricted *'ulama* initiatives, a competitive relationship offset by negotiations over duplication of facilities or mutual support.[41] Another interesting shift in patterns of that philanthropy in the

1960s and 1970s was the role of the *tullab* sent by senior *'ulama* rather than resident *mullas*, associating charitable work with these activists rather than local incumbents. As with the role of the new *hay'ats*, existing traditions, linking *mulla* benevolence, *bazar* resources and the needs of the poor, changed with changing circumstances.[42]

These trends shaped the survival of a viable material base for religious specialists, religious institutions and religious activities through the 1970s. The interventionist policy of the state challenged and constrained the material autonomy of the religious establishment, but also supported some 40 per cent of *tullab* and 80 per cent of *madrasehs* in the early 1970s.[43] The flow of funds from *bazaris* sustained established *'ulama* teaching and philanthropy, and newer activities like the expansion of urban *hay'ats*, innovative teaching and publications, and religious activity in rural areas. It supplemented the declining income of the some 40,000 *vaqfs* which survived into the 1960s. Economic expansion in the 1960s and 1970s supported tens of thousands of *'ulama*, *tullab* and lesser religious practitioners, able continue their functions despite government repression and regulation.[44] Ritual, charitable and educational work no longer connected religious specialists to the whole spectrum of social groups, as new elites and secularised workers lost interest in, or commitment to, what they had to offer. However, growing pilgrim numbers, consumption of religious publications and the expansion of new urban religiosity indicate new interests in religious activity. The material base of religion rested not just on the commitment of established communities, but on support from new groupings emerging from the changes of the period.

Had religious specialists and institutions been *more* materially damaged by those changes, their story might be told just as one of 'decline'. Had they been *less* damaged by them and by the Pahlavi regime, they might have been less concerned to defend and manoeuvre against such threats. In fact, while a sense of political and cultural confrontation loomed large for many *mullas*, the work of preserving insecure but important *material* relationships and activities was also significant. Although their freedom to manoeuvre had been curtailed by state power, the *'ulama* retained sufficient institutional and material autonomy to protect their interests and roles. When other crises developed in Iran during the 1970s, as at the time of the 1891 Tobacco Protest and the 1905–11 constitutionalist movement, sections of the *'ulama* were to use this capacity to historic effect.

THREE

A story of distinctive institutions and vested interests

While the 'social' presence of religious activities, religious world-views and religious specialists in Iran has been supported by their material relationships and their cultural roles in the communities within which they existed, it has also relied on the professional and institutional organisation of religious specialists. Studies of the role of 'religion' in the history of Iran from the nineteenth century have tracked the institutional and professional frameworks which sustained 'religious' ideologies and politics, and the challenges and problems faced by 'organised religion'. The narrative here addresses these questions and sets them alongside others. It seeks to balance an account of the adaptability, difficulties and survival of organised religious hierarchies and institutions with a view of their relationship to 'informal', less structured, aspects of religious experience, discourse and practice. It considers the shifting interaction between the corporate vested interests of the *'ulama/ruhani* 'class' and their collective or institutional responsibilities and links to others. It acknowledges the influential role of institutional and professional structures and of the collective organisation and self-identification of sections of the *'ulama*, but also considers their limited contingent character, depicting them in a complex *range* of religious practice and discourse, rather than as the sole/central feature.

The emergence of professionals who interpret, transmit and apply the rituals, texts, traditions and thought that constitute a particular religion is a widely found phenomenon, embracing Hindu *pandits*, Calvinist ministers, Jewish rabbis, as well as the 'learned men' and spiritual leaders of Islam. Sociologists might emphasise a comparative and analytical approach to this aspect of religion, while historians often focus on narratives of particular places and periods, and specific priestly/clerical/spiritual specialists. Historically and anthropologically informed interpretations have compared the religious education and scholarship of Iranian *'ulama* with Judaic *yeshivas* or medieval European cathedral schools and universities.[1] This strategy can demystify the history of Shi'a Islam in Iran by examining differences and similarities to other traditions, placing it on the terrain of shared, if diverse, human reality and comparative understanding rather than depicting it as incomprehensibly 'other'.

The history of religious professionals in Iran has several layers. Its base is the evolution of the interpretation and practice of Islamic *shari'a* law and its links to scholarship and education on the one hand, and to government and administration on the other. These underpinned the role of 'learned men' (*'ulama*, singular *'alim*) in judicial practice in the community, in intellectual life and in relation to rulers and bureaucracies. Their position was further strengthened by use of patronage and kinship links to create and maintain hereditary, familial and collective solidarity among *'ulama* lineages and ties to wealthy powerful elites and rulers. These influences entwined with the growth of formal education in legal, textual, philosophical and critical skills in forming Islamic scholars, legal experts and literate administrators. The expanding world of scholarship included theology and jurisprudence, speculative philosophy and mysticism, and varieties of orthodox and dissident thought, while learned *fuqaha* (*shari'a* jurists) and officials worked with other military or civilian officers of various regimes. By the twelfth Christian/sixth Islamic century, there were informal study networks centred on eminent scholars, and endowed colleges (*madrasehs*) providing organised courses of study. Patronage by rulers, local elites or sectional groups opened routes to employment and spiritual and intellectual influence in urban centres whose growing size and affluence created opportunities and constituencies for religious professionals.

Another layer was contributed by the development of Shi'a communities who, in addition to their commitment to a particular succession of 'legitimate' leaders of the Muslim community, created their own distinctive intellectual and legal traditions. Shi'a belief and practice stemmed from the contest for leadership of the Muslim community after the death of Muhammad, in which the following/faction (*shi'a*) of 'Ali, Muhammad's nephew and son-in-law, and his sons was prominent. These claims and their defeat, notably the killing of 'Ali's second son Husein and his followers at Karbala in 61AH/680AD, led some Muslims to commit themselves to 'Ali and his descendants as rightful leaders (*Imams*) of the community. This commitment became a focus for groups who identified themselves as Shi'a, as a theological position with learned exponents, and as an expression of passionate spiritual loyalty, and sometimes political action, as well as quietist religious practice.

Until the sixteenth century, Shi'a communities, with their own men of learning, were scattered across what are now Iran, Iraq and Syria/Lebanon. They co-existed with majority Sunni communities with whom they both conflicted and interacted, influencing the development of religious thought and legal practices. Strands of rationalist philosophy and styles of legal analysis crossed from Sunni to Shi'a learning, just as Shi'a messianism influenced non-Shi'a millenarian movements. This interaction was favoured by a number of developments among early Shi'a; the need to protect themselves from 'orthodox' enemies encouraged the practice of *taqiyeh* (tactical concealment of Shi'a beliefs to protect and preserve them); with the end of direct personal authority and leadership in the Shi'a community after the disappearance of the six-year-old Twelfth Imam in 260AH/873–74AD, the community, especially its learned leaders, supported the quietist preservation of Shi'a tradition and practice rather than confrontational politics; the ability of prominent Shi'a *'ulama* and scholars to gain patronage from elites outside the Shi'a community encouraged strategies of accommodation.

One significant feature of Shi'a adjustment to the ending of the living presence and authority of descendants of 'Ali as their *Imams* was the emergence of *'ulama* authority as interpreters of the will and spiritual authority of the Hidden Imam. Shi'a religious experts developed the concept of the 'concealment' (*ghaibat*) of the Twelfth Imam in order to sustain belief in the role of a living guide/exemplar for Shi'a believers (the Imam), and to distance themselves from those who took political action in the name of claimants to the imamate. By depicting the Twelfth Imam as 'concealed' (living but inaccessible), they maintained a living exemplar without risking political dissension and political confrontation. This left the question of how the Hidden Imam's will would be known to believers, which was answered by the establishment of a distinctive role for the *'ulama* as the collective 'deputies' or 'agents' of his spiritual authority, and of legitimate practice. They built on their scholarly development of distinctive Shi'a juridical and theological traditions, and strengthened concepts of the imamate. They drew on the practice of using 'agents' or 'representatives' (*wukala*, singular *wakil*) to circulate information on the will of the Imams among the scattered Shi'a communities of the Fertile Crescent and Iran, and to collect the *khums* and *zakat* from those communities. By establishing Shi'a legal traditions, philosophy and arguments for *ijtehad* (use of reason and jurisprudence in judgments on religious law), Shi'a *'ulama* created a professional tradition and identity based in scholarly networks and centres.

These developments were part of a spectrum of religious expression and organisation emerging in Shi'a groups. These included the establishment and patronage of popular rituals commemorating the virtues and suffering of 'Ali and Husein, messianic movements looking for the return of the Hidden Imam, or supporting claimants to the imamate, and groups of practitioners of mystical Islam (*sufis*). The growing institutionalisation of *vaqf* bequests and their trustees, of urban brotherhoods celebrating 'Ali as the embodiment of *futuwwa* (manly virtues), and the positioning of Shi'a *sayyids* (claiming descent from Muhammad) as notables and authority figures, expanded Shi'a communities and practices. This introduced important new features, establishing a dynamic in which religious specialists incorporated or accommodated other practices, but also sought to control and attack them, defining themselves against competing sources of authority. The evolution of 'Twelver' Shi'a doctrines and *'ulama* (acknowledging twelve designated Imams) involved rejection or manipulation of messianic ideas of the Imam's return, and of mystical knowledge of the spiritual domain. It involved *'ulama* negotiation with popular aspects of religion, using expertise and authority to recognise, modify or condemn them, and becoming patrons in order to retain authority.

Layered into the history of Shi'a religious professionals were dynamic relationships with other religious practitioners, the growth of specialist legal and theological education and the texts which transmitted them, and the entry of *'ulama* into bureaucratic, judicial and communal roles. The shared identity of these men came from acquired skills, the ability to use them to claim authority and communal support, and their definition of their particular authority by distinguishing it from 'ignorant' and uncanonical expressions of faith. They took a leading role in defining the character of Imami/Twelver Shi'ism through theological and communal activity, and began to establish arguments that Shi'a believers should look to the *ijtehad* of learned men to resolve questions of law and conduct. These initiatives confirmed the core of Shi'a *'ulama* as sources of legal and educational services, and as exponents of distinctive Shi'a beliefs and identity. The concept of believers' duty of 'imitation'/*taqlid* (following the opinions of a learned jurist) was broadened by the sixteenth century into arguments for the general competency of *mujtaheds* (those who exercise *ijtehad*). To the role of *'ulama* as guardians and teachers of Shi'a thought and tradition was added authority to interpret them for believers, an authority based in Shi'a tradition itself independent from external control.

The growth of this corporate professionalism based in jurisprudence and rationalist scholarship has been opposed to mystical, speculative and messianic aspects of Shi'ism, but was arguably the product of *'ulama* ability to *engage* with such trends through adaptation and interaction as well as opposition. The actual experience of religious specialists was of complex alliances and antagonisms and of alternative institutions, whether Sufi brotherhoods, state bureaucracies or urban guilds. Their influence and professional identity or authority was grounded in legal and theological learning, but also in piety and intimacy with the will of the Imams, which might be manifest to an *'alim* in dreams and visions. The holiness of such men was demonstrated by the ability to perform miracles or have visions as well as by learned rulings. These claims to spiritual as well as legal and scholarly leadership indicate that in addition to being sources of learned authority, the *'ulama* claimed respect for piety and spiritual qualities.

By the establishment of the Shi'a Muslim Safavid dynasty as rulers in Iran after 1500, there were many layers of professional and institutional expression of Shi'a religious practice, much of which was not located in Iran, nor specific to the learned experts, nor grounded solely in formal law and theology. Most centres of Shi'a learning and scholarship were outside what became the Safavid domains. Existing Shi'a practice was strongly flavoured with the emotive, messianic, popular and mystical devotion of Sufi groups, the cultures of tribes and communities focused on the return and manifestation of the Imam, and the legacy of the various *ghuluww* ('extreme') traditions and networks in the movement under Safavid leadership. When in 1501 Shah Isma'il Safavi proclaimed Shi'ism as the religion of his new regime, he combined the prestige of a notable lineage, the military power of a conqueror, the authority of a Sufi *pir* over his followers, and the charisma of a 'Shadow of God' for his warrior/devotees.

The development of Shi'a *'ulama* in Iran involved accommodation and self-definition in relation to the ruling regime, to folk-based and 'extremist' variants of Shi'ism, and to existing vested interests. The period from 1500 to 1700 saw the 'Iranianisation' of Shi'ism with growing numbers of Twelver Shi'a among Iranians (whether Farsi-, Turki- or Arab-speaking) and of Iranians in the major Shi'a centres of Najaf and Karbala, as well as the 'Shi'ification' of Iran. Biographical surveys of famous Shi'a *'ulama* suggest that some 30 per cent of those dying c. 1590–1690 were of Iranian origin, while figures for the following century place some 70 per cent in that category. Arjomand described the period of Safavid rule (1501–1722) as one when Twelver Shi'ism became a 'national' rather than 'sectarian' religion. [2]

The starting point for this process was the Safavid policy of establishing Twelver Shi'ism as the official and dominant form of religious practice in their domains. This was a more complex matter than the 'importation' of Twelver *'ulama* and their traditions and practice into the Safavid territories. It was a process whereby 'extreme' Shi'a activities were constrained, co-opted under elite patronage, and if necessary repressed, and where the regime sought to strengthen stability and royal authority by varied means, allying itself with established elites and interests. This involved the strategic use of incoming *'ulama* alongside existing religious notables, and manipulation of the charismatic authority of the Safavid rulers and associated popular religious traditions rather than the imposition of learned Twelver views. By the seventeenth century, there were growing numbers of Twelver *'ulama* in key positions as *mujtaheds* and mosque leaders, forming some 20 per cent of the elite of learned experts, religious administrators, scholars, *qazis* (magistrates), *sayyid* notables and shrine trustees, compared with some 5 per cent a century earlier.[3] Access to royal patronage protected them from rivals and opened posts in the hierarchy, notably those of *shaikh al-Islam* (chief religious dignitary in major towns) and *pish-namaz* (leaders of worship) in prominent mosques. They contested rivals, whether Sufi movements or positions taken up by other scholars. They built family connections with one another and with other elites, strengthened arguments for the authority and role of *mujtaheds*, and became dominant teachers of the religious sciences. These developments built on established tradition among Shi'a *'ulama*, linking Qur'anic injunctions to 'command the good and forbid the evil', the role of *'ulama* leaders as intermediaries of the Hidden Imam, the exercise of *ijtehad*, and the duty of believers to follow it. Reliance on living *mujtaheds* and the acceptance of *ikhtilaf* (divergent opinion) among them promoted pluralism, the need for *'ulama* expertise, and an ability to respond flexibly to circumstances. It is significant that this assertion of professional authority was supported by Safavid shahs but did not depend on it, allowing the *'ulama* to define their collective position autonomously through Shi'a doctrine and practice.

There was another strand to their advance as they mobilised a range of beliefs and needs which were important to Shi'a believers. Leading scholars and authors produced works in Persian, reaching wider literate audiences than the Arabic used by religious specialists. They dealt not just with questions of law and conduct, but with hopes and fears surrounding salvation and damnation, and the importance of prayer and of visits to shrines *(ziyarat)*. They took an interest in the 'para-religious' practices of charm writing and the use of the Qur'an to divine the best course of action, which were undertaken by *mullas* for ordinary believers. Their anti-Sufi strategies included persecution, polemic and the counter-promotion of devotion to the Imams and their descendants through Muharram rituals or shrine visits, which *mullas* supported in exchange for recognition and rewards. As sources of guidance for popular religiosity as well as for legal and doctrinal matters, the *'ulama* consolidated a distinctive authority based on willingness to recognise that religiosity, and on defining themselves as a religious elite guiding the *'awamm* (common people).

This pre-modern history of the institutional and professional aspects of religion in Iran presents a genealogy of resources which would develop in the era of modernity. The legacy of professional practice and ideology was complex and many-sided rather than a monolithic body of 'tradition'. The emergence of religious specialists as office-holders, legal experts, educators, scholars and notables, and its ideological grounding in roles as intermediaries and interpreters of sacred material, judicial issues and right conduct depended on pluralism, polyvalence and adaptability. This sat somewhat paradoxically with their advocacy of a doctrinaire rationalist orthodoxy which led Arjomand to label leading Twelver *'ulama* 'the dogmatic party'.[4] Actually, that party built its institutional and ideological presence not just on dominance over rival tendencies, but on its credibility in urban communities, on links to royal patronage, and on alliances with notables, which established a range of social and political relationships, skills and niches buttressing their role as custodians of 'orthodoxy'.

It has been argued that these achievements dissipated in the decades from the 1720s to the 1790s which saw the end of the Safavid dynasty and a period of war-lord conflict as various leaders sought to establish stable bases of power, as happened briefly under Nadir Shah Afshar (c. 1736–47) and Karim Khan Zand (c. 1750–79). Those decades of military confrontations and arbitrary exactions, with their resulting disruption of security in everyday life and of material and cultural resources, are often depicted as an unhappy interregnum between periods of dynastic, and hence communal, material and cultural stability. Although there is truth in this view, it discounts the capacity of particular groups and communities to sustain themselves, adapt or survive out of reach of disruptive events and forces.

For religious specialists and religious institutions, the disappearance of organised royal support for Twelver *'ulama*, the disruption of life in major Iranian centres, and the hostility (in Nadir Shah's case) or indifference (in Karim Khan's case) to the *'ulama* as an interest group, had an obvious impact. The seizure of *vaqfs* by Nadir Shah and the decline of patronage for learning and scholarship broke up or diminished many institutional bases and opportunities. In consequence, their activity declined, or in some cases relocated as *'ulama* from Iran settled in Iraq or India. The interventions of militarised nomadic forces and their leaders put pressure on the urban communities, whose energies were directed to survival strategies in which religious specialists might not figure very prominently. It has also been argued that divisions and contradictions between various sections of *'ulama* opinion and practice undermined professional cohesion and creativity.[5]

Such a picture is incomplete and misleading in several ways. There is evidence that the unstable conditions of the eighteenth century, while putting pressures on religious specialists and their institutions also allowed them opportunities. Recent studies have shown continuities in scholarship and teaching in centres like Isfahan, and patronage and material support from the rapidly changing sequence of rulers and would-be rulers. They also illustrate the wide spectrum of learned debates on ethics, doctrine and judicial authority among the *'ulama*, in Iran and the Shi'a shrine centres of Iraq. What was later depicted as binary conflict between the 'traditionalist' (*Akhbari*) and 'juristic' (*'Usuli*) versions of authority (described below), like 'conflict' between 'orthodoxy' and mystical or speculative approaches to religion, can be seen in less dualistic ways, with changes and overlaps of view among the learned.[6]

Most significantly, the absence of stable centralised government, on which many *'ulama* had relied, and the social uncertainty associated with political instability, made it necessary for them to secure new bases of patronage and security. This took several forms: religious experts built up communities in the shrine cities of Iraq, with their traditions of learning and sanctity as burial places for the Imams, forming a professional centre which supported Iranian *'ulama* from then on; in urban centres in Iran; *'ulama* made links to those with local resources, status and power, and began to acquire or expand their own resources; by the end of the century, Twelver *'ulama* were consolidating an 'orthodoxy' that buttressed the arguments for the authority of *mujtaheds* with clearer opposition to rival tendencies; this did not preclude the pragmatic pursuit of alliances in particular local settings, as when the *'ulama* of Kerman, who attacked the popular Sufi missionaries who arrived in the 1790s, also acquiesced in the rule of a local governor, whose wealth came from leadership of dissident Isma'ilis, as a guarantor of law and order.[7]

The challenge of uncertain political and material conditions in the period from the 1720s to the 1790s, when the new Qajar dynasty created stable authority, evoked varied and creative *'ulama* responses, influencing the developments of the modern period. Sharper ideological and professional identities, and new alliances and patron–client networks, repositioned the *'ulama* as they established themselves as an influential group during the nineteenth century. First, we can consider the form and content of the professional activities and self-definition of the *'ulama*, through legal expertise, scholarship and learning, and pious and ritual activities. Second, we can look at the relationships created among the religious specialists, and between religious specialists and communities or government in Iran.

During the nineteenth century, the professional formation of religious specialists and their visible collective identity took increasingly stable and organised forms. As established *'ulama* mobilised resources from the new Qajar rulers, notables and the *bazar* community, they were able to attract and support growing numbers of students who went on to hold religious offices. The foundation or revival of *madrasehs*, the growth of structured religious study and increased recognition of the practice of *ijazeh* (the granting of permission by a teacher to a student to teach the field they had studied, or a statement of their ability to exercise *ijtehad*) established a framework of professional development for aspiring *'ulama*. The effective propagation of *'Usuli* arguments for the duty of pious Shi'a to seek and follow the legal and doctrinal judgments of a chosen living *mujtahed* created a growing need for such *mujtaheds* in urban centres. By the end of the nineteenth century, *mujtaheds* numbered some hundreds, compared with perhaps a tenth of that figure at the beginning.[8] There was cross-fertilisation between the growth of professional opportunity and training, the arguments supporting them, and the communal and personal relationships created by religious specialists.

The growing number of students who studied and gained qualifications in Iranian *madrasehs* or at the apex of the scholarly/doctrinal system in the shrine cities of Iraq came to occupy a number of positions, mainly in urban centres. As teachers in schools and *madrasehs,* as recognised experts on legal questions, and as holders of judicial and ritual posts in the gift of the government, they had a presence and status defined by learning and authority. Whereas, formerly, notables of *sayyid* descent with hereditary status, office and patronage, had been significant rivals to the Twelver *'ulama*, by the nineteenth century the *'ulama* were dominant. Their contribution to professional life in Iran, their roles as dispensers of resources and services, and their collective identity, were publicly recognised, for example. This reflected the position of *'ulama* with wealth and property who were involved in landholding or commerce, and marked their religious professional identity as a specific segment in the local establishment. Student–teacher and patron–client relationships likewise linked members of the *'ulama* through the transmission of expertise and learning, as well as socially and personally.[9]

One expression of professional identity was the expanded use of 'orthodox' *mujtaheds*' exercise of *takfir* – the act of declaring opponents *kafir*/infidel or heretical. These powers were used against *sufis* in Kerman in the 1790s, Kermanshah in the early 1800s, in Gilan in 1819–20 and Tehran in the reigns of Fath 'Ali Shah (1797–1834) and the pro-*sufi* Muhammad Shah (1834–48).[10] While this did not eliminate *sufi* interests and beliefs, it sharpened ideas or boundaries of orthodoxy and the *'ulama*'s power to establish them. Similarly, the growing collective role of the *'ulama* was grounded in successful advocacy of '*Usuli*' arguments for active learned interpretation of doctrine and tradition to reach legal and ethical judgments followed by ordinary believers. This opposed '*Akhbari*' arguments for acceptance of the 'traditions' reporting the views of the Prophet and the Imams as the sole basis for such judgments. The debates dated back to Safavid times, with Akhbari views achieving some dominance in the eighteenth century. The response to this, led by Aqa Muhammad Baqir Behebahani (revered as the founder/'renewer' of contemporary Shi'ism), combined doctrinal arguments for the use of deduction and reason with emphasis on the need for a specialised cadre of experts defined by learning and skill. Such cadres could claim religious authority in both legal and moral spheres, and hence leadership and material support in the community.[11]

The pattern set by early nineteenth-century confrontations between Twelver *'ulama* and *sufi* and Akhbari rivals continued with the reaction of the 'orthodox' to the heterodox Shaikhi tendency from the 1820s and its fully dissident and ultimately separatist Babi and Baha'i offspring from the 1840s. Shaikhi thought – named from its originator Shaikh Ahmad Ahsa'i – revived speculative, occult and intuitive traditions in Shi'a thought and emphasised the role of the charismatic guide (the 'Perfect Shi'a') as intermediary between the Hidden Imam and believers. It appealed to the spiritual and messianic aspects of Shi'ism less emphasised in the legal and rational approach of 'orthodox' *'ulama*. While its reliance on Twelver tradition and its intellectual quality aroused interest among some *'ulama*, Shaikhism was also treated as a challenge and condemned by senior *mujtaheds*, threatened by a rival for patronage and popular following. The even sharper confrontation of the Babi movement's messianic announcement of a new religious dispensation superseding Shi'a traditions, produced even stronger responses from the religious establishment. As with Shaikhism, the combination of a challenge to doctrinal and legal authority with the emergence of a social base for Babi–Baha'i views, and Babi armed uprisings, fused issues of social power, right belief and political order which that establishment could not ignore. The collective identity and authority of 'orthodox' *'ulama* was consolidated by condemnation of dissident or heterodox alternatives, and their confinement within the practices of concealment, of intellectual study circles or cautious nonconformity. Just as the giving and taking of *ijazehs* recognising learned authority for *ijtehad* were links in a professional network, persecution of the 'unorthodox' as unacceptable 'Others' affirmed shared 'orthodox' identity and practice.[12]

To understand the religious specialists solely in terms of their opposition to and distinction from alternatives would be to underestimate the ways in which 'orthodoxy' emerged within a *spectrum* of influences, its flexibility and complexity, the limits of *'ulama* authority and dominance, and the unclear boundaries of 'professional' and 'orthodox' identity or authority. Shi'a *'ulama* drew on diverse resources inherited from the centuries of their history. The centrality of judicial expertise and authority to their development and identity should not obscure elements of asceticism and pious contemplation, willingness to work with the popular practices of divination or mourning for the Imams, or wider scholarly and literary activity. The reputations of major *mujtaheds* rested on visionary experiences, on command of broad scholarly knowledge, and even on poetry writing. Nineteenth-century writers on the *'ulama* used biographical accounts of networks of learned men, and of miracles, piety and *kalam* (speculative theology), as well as arguments for *ijtehad* going back to Safavid times.

The professional position of religious specialists, while resting on their role and self-presentation as arbiters of orthodoxy, also benefited from their pluralism and the limiting of outright exclusion and demonisation of 'unorthodox' Others. Persecution of Sufis and heretics went along with strategies for containing them, and acceptance of a degree of co-existence. The Shaikhi and *sufi* communities of Kerman in the 1870s were listed by a local author as variants of Shi'ism alongside the 'orthodox' in recognition of diversity as a normal state of affairs, albeit broken by episodes of conflict. Shaikhi circles in Tabriz and Yazd, the revival of Sufism, and the acceptance among the learned men of 'freethinking', dissident individuals with possible Babi/Baha'i tendencies, bear witness to this tendency.[13] They can be seen as symptoms and causes of the rather unstructured character of religious specialists as a group. Although the *'ulama* are depicted as practising and defending 'proper' Twelver Shi'ism, the reality was diverse and fluid, encompassing continued interest in Sufi, esoteric or Akhbari ideas, as well as accommodation with newer dissident trends.

The emergence of the Babi movement in the 1840s as an explicitly radical (and anti-*'ulama*) alternative, proclaiming a revolutionary and messianic revelation and a break with the Shi'a past, did meet open confrontation and condemnation from the religious leadership, leaving the term 'Babi' as a lasting term of abuse for heresy, innovation and unbelief. However, it is notable that Shi'a leaders moved cautiously and gradually to outright condemnation, acting in conjunction with secular authorities, and that senior *'ulama* were divided from lower-ranking *mullas* and *tullab*, numbers of whom were attracted to the new movement. Following a period of confrontation and persecution and the expulsion of prominent Babis from Iran in the 1850s, the continuation of the movement rested on the use of *taqiyeh* (concealment) by sympathisers, which preserved overlaps between members of the *'ulama* and Babi or their successor Baha'i and Azali groups. In the 1880s Baha'i assemblies included *mullas*, and antagonism to Babis and Baha'is as heretics did not prevent interaction between Shi'a and alternative views.[14] The drive to monopolise and define conformity/'orthodoxy' co-existed with pragmatic adaptability and shifting ideological boundaries, rather than establishing binary oppositions between 'permissive' and 'dogmatic' versions of belief and practice.

This influenced the development of ideas and practices of leadership stimulated by the expansion of networks of *'ulama* holding office in Iranian communities, by the need to manage such networks, and to deal with government, with those whose money and support sustained the *'ulama*, and with charity and patronage. The *'ulama* leadership needed to adapt to the new roles of former students and associates, to a ruling dynasty with whom they established partnerships, and to the merchant and notable circles who were sources of support. Although there were matters of principle and ideology at stake in defining leadership within the *'ulama*, it also raised material and political issues.[15]

The ability to recognise and adapt to this situation underpinned the emergence of certain individuals as recognised 'leaders' of the learned Shi'a and of believers in general. The notion of *riyasat*/leadership, that is management of the networks of individuals and resources, and representing religious interests, played an increasing role among the *'ulama*, seen in biographies of the period. At times this had a collegial flavour when *'ulama* and believers recognised 'leaders' for particular centres, or cultural groups (Turki- or Arab-speaking *mullas* and communities). At other times, a single prominent *mujtahed* achieved recognition across groups and communities, as with Shaikh Murtaza Ansari in the mid-nineteenth century and Mirza Hasan Shirazi in the late nineteenth century. The leadership of the former rested on his learning and management of the 'Imam's share', while that of the latter rested on student networks and merchant support. In both cases the ability to attract and make judicious use of funds for religious institutions, activities and students played a central role.[16]

These variables created a visible hierarchy of leaders, *mujtaheds*, lesser-ranking *'ulama*, and students rather than a highly structured organisation of religious experts. It was supported by assertions of professional identity and the authority to identify 'right' belief and conduct, and by professional practices, including formal declarations of competence (*ijazeh*) or heresy (*takfir*), the expansion of *madraseh* education, the use of funds from believers, and consensus about leadership. This has been called a 'hierocracy', but it is arguable that the importance of pluralism, the traditions of *ikhtilaf* among *mujtaheds*, and constant shifts in the cultural and political environment, kept the 'hierarchical' element fluid and partial. Confronted with the emergence of Babism, opposition to western competition among Iranian merchants, or the changing attitudes of rulers and government officials, a degree of adaptability was both a practical response and a defining characteristic of the *'ulama*.

The professional position of the *'ulama* was sustained through personal relationships with one another, and with the governments and communities with whom they lived and worked, as well as through organisation. Granted the limited character of the hierarchy, it is not surprising that *'ulama* solidarity relied extensively on personal networks. Student circles around leading scholar/teachers formed ties to one another and to their teacher which persisted as they took up legal and scholarly posts, carrying with them the affiliations, rivalries, ideas and texts which had shaped their training. Thus pupils of Behebahani and his followers spread *'Usuli* views, just as the pupils of Ansari, or the Shaikhi leaders Ahsa'i and Rashti carried their teachers' ideas into the communities where they established themselves. Combined with the use of the *ijaza* and methods of debate, question and answer in religious study, they personalised the professional and intellectual development of the *'ulama* through peer, patron–protégé and teacher–student relationships. Reputation, rivalry, respect, influence and patronage were as central to the professional lives of *mullas* as organised learning and authority.

This was reinforced by intermarriage and family connection. At the highest level there were prominent *mujtaheds* and holders of high offices who traced lineages to the seventeenth century or earlier. The nineteenth-century *imam jom'ehs* (chief prayer leaders) of Tehran, the *shaikh al-Islams* (chief judicial officers) of Isfahan, and leading *mujtaheds* of Kermanshah could all show descent from the Majlisi family who had been Safavid religious leaders. Other leading scholars and *mujtaheds*, such as the descendants of Behbehani, and Bahr al 'Ulum (major early protagonists of 'Usulism) intermarried and had sons who pursued religious careers and intermarried with other clans of *'ulama* and *sayyids* (descendants of Muhammad) such as the Tabataba'is. *'Ulama* influence was consolidated by the intermarriage of new entrants into existing *'ulama* families and the establishment of hereditary claims to religious posts. The shared outlook and interests created through religious training and probation were strengthened by kinship links, although cross-cut by professional rivalry or religious differences. The kin network of Mirza Hasan Shirazi, recognised leader of Shi'a *'ulama* and believers from the 1880s to his death in 1895, included links to *mujtaheds* in Kerman who taught and held the post of *imam jom'eh* for two generations, and to the founder of the Babi movement.

Another significant feature of the relationships among the *'ulama* was the all-male character of their training and profession. Its significance lies less in the defining fact of women's exclusion from *madraseh* education and religious office (although individual women, usually in *'ulama* or notable families, wrote, studied and gained religious reputations) than in the distinctive relationships and identities associated with single-sex institutions. Studies of such institutions – schools, colleges, military bodies, religious organisations – show how their gendered character shapes the formation of their members. In single-sex settings, daily life, work and relationships among all-female or all-male groups give distinctive strength and flavour to ideas and practices of male or female identity and solidarity. Those identities and solidarities are, of course, influenced by all the social settings from which entrants to armies, colleges or professions come, but in forming single-sex groups these institutions combine the distinctive experiences of sex/gender with their own aims and activities. People's sense of themselves as male or female is defined, confirmed and even sharpened as they undergo military training, formal education, religious initiation or professional development in single-sex settings. The resulting 'old-boy' networks, regimental loyalties or attachment to single-sex religious, legal and educational institutions, combine professional and occupational self-definition with sex/gender solidarity.

Thus the study-circle, *madraseh* and professional networks of *mullas* and *mujtaheds*, which were all-male associations and institutions, gave a particular spin to the versions of masculinity available in Iranian society. Collegial/ brotherly and fatherly/patron relationships were one facet of that experience; the role of gendered language in which females or feminine references are 'deviant', 'outside' or 'other' was another. The political and ideological positions on women taken up by the religious establishment illustrate the power of religious institutions and values in forming opinion, and their grounding in the exclusively masculine character of their profession.

One particular feature of the *madraseh* experience was the bringing together of *young* men to undertake formative training at the same time as the equally complex and challenging process of development into adult males. Learning to manage sexuality and purity was a profoundly personal concern and a professional religious issue, figuring in the doctrinal concerns, rules for behaviour and textual discussions of purity and pollution. The semi-concealed but persistent interest in *irfan* (mystical knowledge), and the importance given to asceticism in religious practice, expressed intensely relevant responses to the personal challenge of self-control in sexual matters faced by adolescent males, as well as core concerns of the faith. The shared experience of negotiating a difficult part of the life-cycle in both personal and professional terms played its role in developing a shared identity, not to be trivialised by sexual voyeurism. Relative neglect of gender and sexuality in studies of the *'ulama* should not obscure an appreciation of their formative professional and institutional influence.

Depictions of organisation and relationships among religious specialists reveal only part of their professional position in the nineteenth century. *'Ulama* success in creating authoritative positions as definers, defenders and dispensers of moral, legal and doctrinal leadership and 'orthodoxy' rested on the relationships they developed with others as well as on self-development and self-definition as a professional and vested interest. The growth of a body of professionals with a common educational background, supportive occupational and family networks, and a clear ideological outlook was buttressed by the alliances they formed with the new dynastic regime, urban communities and local elites. As already shown, they integrated themselves with the *bazar* economy and craft and commercial groups. The more privileged propertied and wealthy sections of the *'ulama* became significant players in urban life, joining the networks of notables in roles that became increasingly normal and regular. Their legal expertise and authority provided judicial and regulating machinery for commerce and entrepreneurship through the legal registration of contracts and property, the management of trusts and the guardianship of orphans, minors and those deemed incompetent. Those who acquired property, wealth and hereditary claims to leading posts in mosques, courts and *madrasehs* joined local elites, wielding social and political influence that supported their professional roles and stimulated competition among rivals for such advantages. Intermarriage into landed, official and merchant families consolidated the place of senior *'ulama* in the propertied and ruling establishment, just as family links between lower-ranking *mullas*, traders and lesser landowners or bureaucrats embedded them in their communities.

The social position of *'ulama* patricians combined professional expertise and solidarity with connections to fellow notables, buttressed by their following among students, and those who attended their mosques and courts, or accepted their spiritual leadership, and by the physical backing of urban toughs. Vahid Behbehani's use of *mir-ghazabs* (strongmen/executioners) to intimidate Akhbari rivals prefigured similar practices by leading *'ulama* in Isfahan, Kerman, Tabriz or Qazvin. The mobilisation of *lutis* and their strong-arm tactics aided the pursuit of personal and professional conflicts, whether competition among *mujtaheds*, *'ulama* manipulation of secular authorities, or support for anti-Babi, anti-*sufi*, and anti-Jewish protests. In such protests and conflicts, the professional and spiritual strength of the *'ulama* was underpinned by their confrontational methods, their ability to bring supporters on to the streets, and their consequent leverage on government and community. The capacity of *mullas* to invoke shared authority was a collective and an individual asset. Although sometimes divided by personal or sectional differences and rivalries, *'ulama* could and did assert collective status and authority, grounded in history, ideology and their position in their communities.

'Ulama use of a collective approach was particularly visible when they perceived core interests and concerns to be in danger. When the doctrinal and spiritual explorations of Sayyid 'Ali Muhammad, the Bab, turned to criticism, and ultimately rejection, of established forms of *'ulama* authority and special-ist knowledge, they responded by allying with secular authorities to repress his movement as subversive and heretical. Although doctrinal heterodoxy and esoteric speculation could be accommodated within the flexibility and plural-ism of Shi'a practice, Babi challenges to the authority of *mujtaheds* struck at central features of that practice and at the vested interests of leading *'ulama*. While some lesser-ranking *mullas* and seminarians were inspired by the radical rethinking of revelation within Babism, the religious establishment was more likely to feel threatened. Although it moved cautiously and in tandem with government policy towards frontal condemnation of Babism, it is significant that both Shaikhi-oriented and orthodox *mujtaheds* contributed to its final expulsion from acceptable practice. Babism's challenge to *ijtehad*, and the expertise enshrined in the *madrasehs*, confronted leading *'ulama* with threats to their authority and identity as guardians, interpreters and transmitters of law, belief and tradition. As Amanat notes, this institutional challenge came at a time when the cohesion and confidence of the Shi'a establishment may have been weakened by the passing of a generation of strong leaders, leaving their successors somewhat defensive.[17]

The pursuit of shared interests also reflected the reliance of religious spe-cialists on merchant and *bazari* supporters. Just as the increasingly organised collection and use of *zakat*, *khums* and the 'Imam's share' for the upkeep of *mullas* and *tullab* provided material security for the *'ulama*, so the con-cerns of the urban communities who made these contributions influenced their politics. *'Ulama* protests over European competition, and government grants of concessions and privileges to European entrepreneurs, culminating in their significant entry into the Tobacco Concession protests of 1891, are key examples. Historians differ in their interpretations of merchant leverage on 'ulama, and of 'ulama influence on public opinion or government, and of the differences among leading individuals.[18] Nevertheless, contemporary perceptions of 'ulama involvement, and the use of the authority of Mirza Muhammad Hasan Shirazi as acknowledged leader (ra'is) and marja'-ai-taqlid (source of religious emulation) to mobilise opposition to the Concession, gave it cohesive character and ideological authority.

Whatever the balance of initiative or influence among merchants, 'ulama and other opponents of the Tobacco Concession, the episode shows the 'ulama's position within significant alliances which affected their outlook and activities. It is worth noting that leading mullas in Mashad, where the main source of posts and patronage was the royally supervised shrine rather than the commercial community, were more inclined to back the Shah's policy. This may indicate prudent calculation, but it also draws attention to the shifting, varied and contested position of religious leaders and specialists. The establishment of clear patterns of doctrine and professional development was offset by the looseness and informality of professional structures. The advantages of pluralism and heterodoxy were offset by division and rivalry. The construction of key alliances with the dynasty, local elites and bazaris gave mullas security and status while exposing them to the pressures and demands of their allies.

Observers often emphasised the high degree of autonomy, independent legitimacy and political influence which allowed 'ulama to act as both vested interest and as leaders and advocates for broader movements and issues. They noted the 'ulama's independent sources of revenue, their cultural and moral centrality in community life, and their contribution to the ideological underpinning of royal power and political order. However, the constraints and limitations upon mullas cannot be ignored. They relied to a significant extent on the patronage and support of those with other sources of power and revenue, whether from commerce, politics or landholding. They had to accommodate to the autonomous role of popular religious practice and culture, and of non-religious claims to authority within nomadic groups, or patriarchal households and lineages. They could not rely on strongly centralised cohesive systems of authority and organisation of their own ideologies and activities, as might be seen, for example, in the Roman Catholic Church after the Counter Reformation.

Nineteenth-century Iranian 'ulama faced dilemmas, to which they sometimes responded collectively but often managed in varied individual ways. In the later decades of the century, new influences modifed the existing challenges to their professional and institutional position. Sections of the elite explored new approaches to education and administration, whether from opportunistic desire to strengthen their position and resist external pressures, or from interest in new forms of law, knowledge, military organisation and government. Just as that elite had deployed many resources independent of 'ulama support in the past, so efforts to pressure and reform government in the era of modernity drew on 'modern' approaches used by Russians, Ottomans, western Europeans or Egyptians. Explicit attempts to restrict *shari'a* jurisdiction, protective *bast*, or *'ulama* influence, met relatively successful resistance, but advocacy of new, secular, options by a new generation of intellectuals signalled change. The appearance of new forms of learning and intellectual authority outside Shi'a traditions, and of Iranians educated and interested in modern, foreign, secular subjects posed qualitatively different challenges from those of Akhbarism in the eighteenth century or Babi/Baha'i movements in the nineteenth. Added to attempts to introduce secular styles of government and administration, the first secular schools, and first modernist critiques of religion and *mullas*, they prefigured new paradigms of power, knowledge and authority. Condemnations of new and/or imported influences by religious writers like Muhammad Karim Khan Kermani suggest that some *'ulama* recognised this. Such denunciations can be seen as evidence of ignorance and prejudice, but also of the *'ulama*'s sense of threat from influences outside their grasp or control, and consequent angry rebuff to such influences.

The external challenge of these new developments intersected with existing divisions between *'ulama* leaders and dissident, junior, or less advantaged, *mullas*. There were ideological differences over responses to modernist agendas, and material and political tension between *'ulama* with resources, status and privileges and those who lacked influence and patronage. There were convergences between reformist interests stimulated by contact with western secular thinking and what Mangol Bayat has called the 'socialisation' and 'politicisation' of religious dissent among Iranian Shi'a after 1840.[19] Growing debate on justice, good government and social well-being drew on either or both of these traditions. From the perspective of the *'ulama*, these debates opened up various alternatives, and the differing responses of individuals or groups reinforced the lack of cohesion and consistency. While some *mullas* emphasised the threats posed by secular political and social thinking, others sought to establish common ground or mutual interests between new ideas and Shi'a traditions, both orthodox and dissident. These responses were influenced by the networks of kinship, rivalry, patronage and sectional interest linking senior *mullas* to colleagues, juniors and students, giving a material and opportunistic flavour to political and intellectual divisions.

This was manifest in the changing arguments and relations among leading *mujtaheds* in Tehran between the 1890s and 1910s, in networks of reformist *mullas* described in sources such as Nazem al-Islam, and the entwining of local and wider politics in centres like Kerman or Tabriz.[20] Their place in narratives of political change in Iran is considered elsewhere, but they indicate *'ulama* divisions over challenges to their status and authority in these decades, which, although limited in scale, foreshadowed situations they faced during the next century. Three elements are worth identifying. First, there were signs of open confrontation between the *'ulama* and critics of their roles, authority and influence. Second, some *'ulama* developed adaptive reformist approaches to critics. Third, these positions intersected with the local circumstances, and interests of particular *mullas*. While *'ulama* had an influential position as independent specialists and as allies of other groups in their communities, they had no coherent or consistent response either to the growing tensions between their interests and those of government, or to new ideas about law and learning.

The institutional and professional fortunes of the *'ulama* had their own course through the period of constitutional upheaval and the rule of Reza Shah Pahlavi. In the 'constitutional era' (1905–11), battles over the status of *shari'a* law in the Constitution, attempts to develop new systems of judicial administration, and the expansion of secular learning, literature and education indicated change in the *'ulama*'s dominance in those areas.[21] In the case of law and education, change was central to the agendas of secularist or anti-clerical reformers who wrote on or actually implemented new forms of government in a modernist vein. The changed political and cultural climate in urban communities in Iran after 1900 resulted in greater opportunity and growing audiences for advocacy of modernist reforms in law and education. The establishment of a representative National Assembly (Majlis) and associated elections, party politics and a political press created new terrains for these debates. However, the critiques of *'ulama* dominance, which were forcefully put by radicals and modernisers, should not be confused with substantive change. The years from the Constitutional Revolution to the accession of Reza Shah Pahlavi in 1925 were a period of heated advocacy for change, and equally heated defence, of the *'ulama*'s established position, which in itself altered little.

Actual change came under the Pahlavi regime, centred on a ruler whose main objectives, beyond the maintenance of his own power, were state building and authoritarian modernisation. These agendas included the creation of secular legal and education systems, with direct consequences for the professional position of *mullas* in these areas. The erosion of their dominance between the mid-1920s and the deposing of Reza Shah in 1941 was a process rather than an event. The reduction of the jurisdiction and activities of *shari'a* courts and the *'ulama* who worked in them took place in a series of steps. The drafting and establishment of a secular Civil Code (1926–28) created a legal framework requiring different professional skills and knowledge, and based on different principles and traditions, mainly western European. The 1931–32 legislation, which gave the state control of referrals to *shari'a* courts, removed their rights to sentence, confined their jurisdiction to marriage, divorce and trusteeship, and ended *'ulama* registration of legal documents, directly assaulted their legal functions. The 1936 requirement that those appointed as judges in the courts should have modern secular legal qualifications completed the process. Quite apart from loss of income and employment, these developments eroded the professional status and identity of those 'ulama accustomed to being legal experts and authorities.

In the field of education and learning, 'ulama also faced the emergence of new, secular and state-controlled alternatives to their roles as teachers and scholars. State schools with a secular curriculum were the predominant form of schooling, teaching some 72 per cent of all school pupils in the mid-1920s and over 89 per cent by the early 1940s.[22] Although the *maktabs* ('traditional' elementary schools with *mulla* teachers) increased their absolute numbers of pupils during the 1930s, their decline in a period of reduced state control in the 1940s shows their weakened appeal. Despite the limited expansion and defects of education under Reza Shah's rule, such as it was, the new provision marginalised its predecessor and the role of religious specialists in the school system.[23]

The situation with advanced education and scholarly activity was more complex. The growing prestige and use of 'modern' knowledge (secular, scientific, technical), and of professional training in law, medicine, engineering and their acquisition by established elites and new aspirants, reshaped learning and expertise. As modern higher education became a key asset for entry into government, professional employment or new business and financial institutions, the old pattern and prestige of religious study and of traditional bureaucratic or professional training were eroded. New forms and centres of professional authority and expertise, and the success and influence of practitioners of 'modern' skills and knowledge, shifted the balance in the traditional partnership of secular and religious authority. They also fed the process whereby religious learning and education became more specialised and potentially marginalised activities.

Suggestive, if imprecise, figures indicating a fall in the number of *tullab* from around 5,500 to around 3,000 between the late 1920s and the mid-1940s show declining prospects for those with religious qualifications, and the attractions of other forms of education and training.[24] Paradoxically, this took place as leading Shi'a 'ulama reconstituted their activities in the revived *hawzeh-yi-'ilmi* ('reservoir'/centre of learning) in the city of Qum. In the 1920s, the arrival of the *mujtahed* Shaikh 'Abd al-Karim Ha'eri Yazdi, accompanied by other senior 'ulama, at the request of those already reviving *madrasehs* there, signalled a capacity for new professional initiatives among leading 'ulama and their supporters. By the later 1940s, Qum was the centre where one-third of the officially recorded religious students in Iran were being educated, and the gathering there of senior 'ulama offered a new professional focus. Undermined by government encroachments in the fields of law and education, and the management of the *vaqf* endowments that supported their activities, the *'ulama* sustained an independent, if defensive, position. Clashes of interest and ideology between state policies and the collective interests of the *'ulama* actually stimulated greater cohesion, and more self-conscious pursuit of protection, and thus *'ulama* politicisation.

The obvious manifestations of this politicisation were the strategic use both of quietist refusal to become involved in unhelpful confrontations, and discreet use of opportunities to establish political protection for their professional concerns. Ha'eri Yazdi was noted for maintaining caution and distance towards politics and government, emphasising the priority of preserving the professional activities of the *'ulama*, and perhaps the importance of establishing separation between *'ulama* and the state. In 1924–25, senior *mujtaheds* played a significant, although not consistent, role in the contest over a possible republic, which involved the ambitions of Reza Khan, Majlis politics, and popular and *'ulama* protests. The role of political *mullas*, such as the Majlis deputy Sayyid Hasan Mudarris who challenged the 'unconstitutional' ambitions of Reza Pahlavi using backing from Tehran *bazaris* and wider religious influence, was accompanied by other manoeuvres. Reza Khan's initiation of contact with the newly established *mujtahed* circle in Qum, and Shi'a *mujtaheds* from Iraq who had 'withdrawn' there as part of their anti-British campaign was, from his perspective, a tactical manoeuvre. Blocked in attempts to gain support for his plan to replace the Qajar Shahs with a republic, he needed to consolidate his position by other means and dissociate himself from the unpopularity and protest it had provoked. The newly established *hawza* leaders had an opportunity to protect their specific interests, to maintain a stake in regime politics, and to respond to their *bazar* constituency, which Mudarris mobilised in the anti-republican cause. Significantly, the proclamation issued by leading *mujtaheds* after meeting Reza Pahlavi, confirming that on their advice he would not back republicanism, was addressed to notables, merchants and the people generally.[25] Divisions among the *mujtaheds* and the desire to protect professional interests and political connections were reflected in its cautious wording.

There were other moments in the period of Reza Pahlavi's rule when combinations of caution, political pressure and indirect opposition were expressed in the institutional practices of the religious leadership. In 1927 and 1928, protests over conscription led by *mullas* took place, although Reza Shah had modified the 1925 conscription bill in response to *'ulama* concerns, perhaps a partial trade-off for earlier co-operation.[26] There were tensions between the manoeuvrings of leading *'ulama* who petitioned the government and the role of others who vocalised, and even instigated, the grievances of those confronting conscription. The exemption of *'ulama* and *tullab* who met the criteria set by the law defined their specific identity and status while subjecting them to the secular state, codifying both their subordination and recognition of a distinct 'religious' grouping. Similar dynamics can be seen in the conflicts over state-led attempts at dress reform in the 1920s for men and 1930s for women. Aggressive government enforcement of the 1928 law requiring *mullas* and *tullab* to prove their right to exemption from the requirement to wear European dress provoked public protest, and direct criticism from the 'quietist' Ha'eri Yazdi. It is noteworthy that Ha'eri Yazdi's opposition took the form not of a *fatwa* (a legal ruling), but a *political* communication by telegram.[27] The government's 1936 campaign to end 'veiling' and segregation practices among that significant proportion of women in Iran who followed them, met official and unofficial *'ulama* opposition as well as general protest. Preaching against the government is alleged to have had covert backing from senior *'ulama,* and violent government responses to large-scale protests in Mashad opposition to the Shah's family in Qum staged the issue as a head-on confrontation which lived on in the 'memories' of the contending parties.[28]

These cases illustrate the tensions and loyalties that fostered *'ulama* solidarity against repugnant policies, if muted by the political calculations of senior *'ulama,* or divisions between activists and *politiques*. On the one side, the historic benefits of responding, even giving direction, to grievances in the Shi'a Muslim community, and their own ideological opposition to the regime, impelled preachers and other religious specialists to align themselves with protest. On the other, the equally important need to defend the position of religious institutions and specialists favoured a more cautious approach. In the context of state attacks on the *'ulama,* and the growth of secular anti-clerical opinions, such defensive reactions make sense, marking a shift in the consciousness of religious specialists. While that consciousness continued to rest on established relationships between *'ulama, bazaris* and urban communities, it was now reinforced by new pressures to defend themselves. Embattled with government intervention and the rise of alternative professional and cultural communities and values, they needed to act and think differently, creating tension with their role as defenders of established belief and practice. The ability of *bazari* funders to stop Ha'eri Yazdi's plans to send students abroad with threats to withdraw funds indicates how restrictive this role could be.[29]

The removal of Reza Shah in 1941, the foreign occupation of Iran in the first half of 1940s and the nationalist, oil and Cold War politics of the late 1940s and early 1950s changed the political context of religious institutions. For the first Pahlavi shah, as for Qajar predecessors and the reformers of the constitutionalist era, links between *din*/religion and *doulat*/government were significant, but in the 1941–53 period governments had other priorities. Reduced state intervention, and the removal of political repression, allowed the free and vigorous expression of diverse and conflicting views and campaigns over religious institutions. Those involved in core religious institutions and activities considered and acted upon the experiences of previous years. Both committed Muslims, and more secularised sections of society, had opportunities to press their views about organised religion. While not a time of specific corporate and institutional change in Shi'a Islam, the 1941–53 era revealed the changes of earlier decades in clearer form and indicated key issues for the future.

One option for those in charge of religious institutions was to continue and consolidate their embattled but recognised relationships with state and society. The preservation and confirmation of the centrality of Qum as the professional and organisational focus and powerhouse for Iranian *'ulama* and believers was an obvious feature of the 1940s and 1950s. The role of Ha'eri Yazdi, who died in 1936, was maintained first by a group of *ayatollahs* (top-ranking *'ulama*) and then by Ayatollah Burujerdi whose leadership was recognised from his arrival in Qum in 1944 until his death in 1961. He supported the tendency to act defensively to maintain the autonomy and status of organized *madraseh* education, and the representation of religious interests by recognised senior *'ulama*.[30] Rather than seeing this solely as a manifestation of 'conservatism' or 'quietism', it can also be understood as institutional redefinition using political tactics and organisational control. This had two aspects: in relation to the state Burujerdi and others sought recognition not as one of the 'twin pillars', but as one among several established interests bargaining with government and the Shah; in relation to the *'ulama*'s intellectual and educational roles there was recognition of the specific, as opposed to universal, character of *madraseh* scholarship and education as distinctively *ruhani*/spiritual. Acknowledgement of a relativised position in the public arena went with confirmation of a limited but recognised collective identity. Photographs of government figures beside *ayatollahs*, exchanges of visits and compliments, and the use of lobbying and *fatwas* were features of a protective politics. Control of *madraseh* curricula and administration of the '*imam*'s share' sustained a degree of professional autonomy.

However, challenges to *'ulama* interests in the period stimulated other responses. Ideological pressures from secularist and leftist critics of religion, now with larger, more receptive audiences in the changed urban communities and open political culture of the time, challenged the confidence of believers and specialists. For the first time there were tens of thousands of Iranians who had experienced secular education. Leftists, nationalists and labour activists were recruiting and polemicising in Iranian towns, and secular language and arguments spread in printed and radio formats. The obverse of the *'ulama*'s protection of religious knowledge and education, so central to their collective identity and interests, was the problem of co-existence with other potentially hostile views. One response to this problem was covert sponsorship of militants committed to attacking those they identified as enemies of Islam. The links of the Feda'iyin i-Islam to political *'ulama* like Ayatollah Kashani used his patronage and connections as well as his political authority, and the assassinations associated with the organisation were legitimised by accounts of the endorsement of Ayatollah Qummi, who had backed militant preaching in the 1930s. In this sense, the intellectual polemic of a Qum *'alim* like the young Khomeini against the vehemently anti-Shi'a Ahmad Kasravi mirrored the physical violence of the Feda'iyan who killed him.[31]

Another of Khomeini's targets in his 1940s text *The Unveiling of Secrets*, Shari'at-i-Sangalaji, represented another development. In addition to *'ulama* repudiation of anti-Shi'a and secular ideas, there were also efforts to explore the possibilities and desirability of change in Shi'ism. Sangalaji (died 1944) used writing, study networks and preaching to critique the *fiqh*-centred approach of the religious establishment and beliefs which distracted from the core message of the faith, emphasising instead the centrality of the Qur'an. Sayyid Mahmud Taleqani opened up consideration of the contemporary relevance of religion and of the Qur'an in controversial organised discussion sessions.[32] They used the authority, learning and inherited opportunities that went with their *'ulama* position, but explicitly developed concerned and thinking lay constituencies and critical reflection on existing practices. Other devout educated Shi'a pursued similar objectives, ranging from the Muslim student and professional associations, which challenged leftist counterparts in the 1940s, to discussion and propaganda groups founded by Muhammad Taqi Shari'ati in Mashad and Muhammad Nakhshab in Tehran. Such initiatives, aimed to oppose communistic influences, expressed the convictions of their initiators that religious commitment was compatible with socially progressive and patriotic politics, and often aligned with nationalist and Mussadeqist ideas.[33] Their significance lay in the fact that they scoped Shi'a Muslim views beyond repudiation of 'modern' developments and drew non-*mulla* believers into debating future Shi'a practice and ideas.

These were significant developments in the stance of active Shi'a towards the changes of the preceding decades. They engaged with those changes, and looked for modes of adaptation and mutual acceptance, as well as creative challenges to the appeal of secular ideas and organisations. They reached out in particular to the graduates of 'modern' schools and colleges, whose outlook embraced both religious belief and the views and aspirations encountered in that education and its associated urban setting. They also pressed at, if not challenging, familiar boundaries of institutional and professional authority in defining and disseminating Shi'a Islam. Over the nineteenth century, *'ulama*, trained and legitimated within structured institutions and practices, had dominated religious structures and activities. Ideas about change tended to come from the dissident or marginal, whether ambitious activists like 'al Afghani' or the mystically and critically inclined. In the 1940s and 1950s the urgency of social and cultural change and the existence of new, educated, politically aware groups encouraged non-*ulama* influence in religious thought and debate. Discussions of 'Ali's sermons and the Qur'an, like the desire to equip believers with means to counter the appeal of leftist and secular thought, put religious innovation on to the agenda. While not diminishing the power of existing institutions, it foreshadowed a new dynamic between *ulama* authority, wider involvement in Shi'a Islam, and the encounters of Shi'a Muslims with new ideas.

Religious institutions emerged from the period of political upheaval of the 1940s with new features as well as confirmed commitment to established practice and interests. The latter was supported by an *entente* with secular power which the religious elite, like their predecessors, were willing and able to negotiate. Nevertheless, the sharp questions about 'modern' life and thought faced by the devout opened up debate and dissension on the essentials and needs of the faith going beyond the defensive strategies of the *ulama* establishment. Unlike the comparable conditions underpinning the success of Christian Democrat movements in Europe in the 1940s and 1950s (or 'social Catholicism' or evangelical and Lutheran reformism in the nineteenth century), circumstances in Iran did not yet favour fast growth in these trends. What did emerge was the definition of religious activity and institutions as a set of 'modern' interests to be defended or reformed like others, and glimpses of new opportunities to connect religious ideas to the social and political world.

Trends of professional self-defence amid conflicting interests, of tension over change within existing practice and belief, and of the role of non-*ulama* believers, continued to shape the period after the overthrow of Mussadeq in 1953. As in the 1930s, religious specialists and institutions faced a controlling authoritarian government that might court *ulama* support but also sought to contain them in an allotted sphere. Continued and increasing state intervention in *vaqf* management, censorship and policing the activities of *ulama* and *tullab* fed an atmosphere in which organised religion seemed embattled. While the precise degree of conflict is hard to estimate, the rhetoric and culture of active state opposition to religious specialists and institutions, increasing after the mid-1960s, was undoubtedly part of their experience. Those who studied in *madrasehs* felt themselves to be, and often were, at a disadvantage in the increasing competition for jobs requiring educational qualifications which preoccupied school or college graduates in the 1960s and 1970s. Suggestions that the state's own 'religious corps' rather than *ulama* might provide religious education in Iranian communities, or that mosques, *madrasehs* and endowments might be obliterated by urban redevelopment (as in Mashad in the 1970s) reinforced this picture.

In this situation, religious leaders and *ulama* confronted difficult questions.

Was their best strategy to use the familiar mixture of discreet negotiation and explicit criticism to defend religious specialists and institutions? Should they meet growing criticisms of their irrelevance to a young, potentially more secular, populace by reasserting established paradigms, or by adaptation and innovation? Could the Shi'a Muslim establishment be reconfigured to rebalance the contributions of *'ulama* and other believers to the direction as well as to the practice of the faith? The response to such questions produced a set of tentative and multifaceted initiatives, retreats and negotiations with the revived autocracy, a changed social constituency, and continuation of debates inherited from the 1940s. While members of the religious establishment increasingly perceived the state as their enemy, there was no consensus as to how to deal with that situation. When discussion of land reform policy began in the late 1950s, the leading *mujtahed* Ayatollah Burujerdi, long associated with non-confrontational, 'non-political' strategies, combined public protest invoking the *shari'a*, with private negotiation to protect *'ulama* interests. When the force of reform proposals and religious opposition to government intensified in the early 1960s, a spectrum of *'ulama* protest from the manoeuvrings of Burujerdi to the vehement condemnations of Khomeini opposed the Shah's programme.[34] Equally significantly, many *'ulama* kept a range of options open. Just as Khomeini was ambiguous in his responses to requests to attack or support the radical Shi'a thinker 'Ali Shari'ati, so members of the *'ulama* leadership who did not openly support Khomeini's intransigence, maintained contact with him after his exile in 1964.[35] Retrospectively, analysts have identified tendencies or factions within the religious establishment, but at the time choices were arguably not so clear.

The same held true for the debate on how far the emphasis, content and practice of Shi'a Islam could or should be adapted to changing social and cultural circumstances. By the 1960s, initiatives dating to the 1940s which sought to reconnect Shi'a Islam to modern urban constituencies (professionals, educated youth), and to reassess the forms and priorities of religious practice, were generating controversy and innovation among *'ulama* and other believers. Concern with authority and organisation within the Shi'a establishment, and with the form and content of knowledge and belief, were central issues. Circles of concerned *'ulama* and believers raised questions about the role of spiritual leadership, and especially of the *marja' yi-taqlid* (source for emulation) which sharpened after the death of Ayatollah Burujerdi in 1961. Issues discussed included the possibility of collective leadership, review of the *madraseh* curriculum, and specialisation/division of labour within religious learning and expertise (an idea canvassed by Ha'eri Yazdi in the 1930s). More generally, Shi'a Muslims were concerned about how to engage with contemporary problems and experiences. They debated how to address young urbanised Iranians from the second or third generation who had been exposed to 'secular' education and to radio, television and cinema. They examined possible stances towards a repressive regime with limited legitimacy which was increasingly less interested in negotiation with the religious establishment. Legacies of religious support for Mussadeqist politics, of pragmatic manoeuvre, and of condemnation of a 'godless' government backed by foreigners, were used and tested in debates over religious modernisation.

As Fischer and Akhavi have observed, the initiatives of groups like those around Taleqani, Bazargan and the Huseiniyeh Ershad (a purpose-built centre for religious debate and education founded in 1963 and closed down by the government in 1972) stimulated controversy but little change in the religious establishment.[36] None the less, there were initiatives among leading *mujtaheds* in Qum aimed at greater outreach and at adapting *madraseh* education. They established new publications, centres for 'missionary' contact, and new curricula in the 1960s and 1970s, suggesting some willingness to experiment with change. However, they did not pursue the review and restructuring of *mujtahed* authority, religious knowledge, or lay–*'ulama* relations advocated by some religious 'modernisers'.

One way to see this is to pose the 'conservative' outlook of the religious establishment against the 'modern' or 'creative' innovations of the 'Monthly Talk' association of the early 1960s, or the Huseiniyeh Ershad group. Attention can be drawn to the way in which 'modern' initiatives were led by non-*mullas* or lower-ranking *'ulama* and how this drew defensive and self-interested responses from senior *'ulama*. The modernisers' emphasis on re-establishing links between religious world-views and a changing society, and demonstrating their 'relevance' to contemporary circumstances, represented a clear challenge to the religious establishment. Moreover, like nineteenth-century Sufis, Shaikhis or Babi activists, charismatic and popular preachers and intellectuals like Taleqani and 'Ali Shari'ati became powerful *alternative* poles of attraction and potential rivals to that establishment.

However, this would be only a partial analysis. Resistance to change, to competition, and to challenges to existing hierarchies did shape the responses of religious leaders to modernist ideas and activities, but they also drew on more positive resources. As seen in Chapter 2, established religious networks still had access to material resources and social connections. If the lecturers at Huseiniyeh Ershad and religious circles like that of Bazargan and his Liberation Movement reached out to students and professionals, *mullas* had links to a whole range of urban clients and supporters and also connected to new constituencies. While *bazari* resources did go to modernist and activist innovators, they also flowed to established *'ulama* recipients, maintaining old relationships between urban entrepreneurs, the religious establishment and philanthropy or ritual. As new migrants established themselves in Tehran, the flourishing of *hay'ats* (religious associations based on origin, occupation, location) was supported by 'traditional' *mullas* and *rawzeh-khwans* through recitation, preaching, patronage and philanthropy.[37] By the 1970s, *'ulama* resources allowed Ayatollah Milani in Mashad to send *tullab* into Khorasani villages and Qum *marja's* to appoint preachers and village *mullas*. Such visitors or appointees might not be welcomed uncritically in rural communities, and anthropologists like Loeffler and Goodell found evidence of tension and suspicion, but they also show how established religious specialists extended activities into new areas.[38] If the religious establishment was partly characterised by caution and suspicion towards innovation, it was far from incapable of new initiatives.

The emergence of new partnerships of *'ulama* and other Shi'a in projects to redefine or re-energise religious commitment complemented and competed with existing practices. While the political and ideological elements of renewal in Shi'a Islam are part of the stories of ideas, images and movements told in later chapters, they had implications for religious interests and institutions. If an understanding of the meaning and relevance of Shi'a Islam could be acquired through independent reading and discussion, or be provided by speakers and writers not trained in the *madraseh* system, the role of that system as the key institution in disseminating and legitimating the faith was under question. If learned and creative interpretations of the faith could be provided by those who neither saw themselves, nor were seen, as *'ulama*, then the position of *mulla* scholars and jurisconsults might be challenged. That such 'non-traditional experts', texts and activities were a real 'alternative' is shown by their evident appeal for numbers of educated urban youth, and some religious specialists. The thousands who attended the Huseiniyeh Ershad to hear 'Ali Shari'ati and others explore 'modern' Shi'a social and spiritual agendas, and the circulation of perhaps two million copies of Shari'ati's works from its 1972 closure to 1977 indicate their attraction.[39] They connected with the oppositional work of the Muslim students' associations formed by Iranian students abroad, a network also not controlled by *'ulama*.

These innovative, and much discussed, developments, their appeal to specific social groups, and the degree to which they could be contained or appropriated by the religious establishment should be placed in context. The very intellectual qualities that gave the reformist thinkers appeal restricted their access or relevance to wider constituencies of less educated pious urban migrants, or rural settlements. While some of their vocabulary and imagery entered the broader streams of activism in the opposition politics of 1977–81, their developed critiques of Shi'a institutions and practices reached only specific audiences. The constraints placed on religious reformers by government repression, and their uneasy relations with *'ulama* associates or critics, further limited the impact of their work. While reformers were committed to developing diagnoses of the problems of existing religious institutions and criticising their deficiencies, they shared anxieties about the embattled situation of religious belief and practice with less critical Shi'a Muslims. They therefore tended to look for allies and supporters *within* 'established' religious circles even while challenging the establishment to change. Conversely, while members of the *'ulama* might resent and resist challenges, and criticise the views of reformers such as Shari'ati, they were also aware of their own vulnerability and the need to consider changes in their practices. This led to a spectrum of overlapping interactions between reformers and leading *'ulama*. These ranged from mutual condemnation (Shari'ati's opposition of good ''Alid' Shi'ism to *mulla*-dominated debilitating 'Safavid' Shi'ism, and attacks on his work by senior *mujtaheds*) to the politically nuanced refusal of the exiled Khomeini to condemn Shari'ati and the attempts of *bazaris* and *'ulama* to broker accommodation between Shari'ati and his critics.[40]

The movement of *'ulama* between various options again illustrates the fluid, personalised and pragmatic responses of religious specialists to circumstances in the 1960s and 1970s. The group of *'ulama* and 'lay' Shi'a intellectuals associated with the debates and positions developed in the *Goftar-I-Mah* (Monthly Talk) publications and the essays on the future of the *marja'* function in the early 1960s evolved in various directions. Some became associated with the Khomeini regime in 1979, some with the Liberation Movement's Shi'a Muslim modernism, while others remained scholars and teachers.[41] Shari'ati may have attracted condemnation from some senior *mujtaheds* and well-known preachers, but he worked with others, and was read and quoted by *tullab* studying in the 'traditional' *madraseh* system as well as other young Iranians. A leading *'alim* like Morteza Mutahhari, who taught at Tehran University in the 1960s and played an important role in the *Goftar-I-Mah* group and at Huseiniyeh Ershad and could be seen as a 'moderniser', was also a defender of established viewpoints against Shari'ati's critiques and joined Khomeini's government in 1979. Condemnation of modernisers (and the Shah's regime) did not so much clash with concerns about the religious reform, or personal rivalries (as with Mutahhari and Shari'ati), as entwine with them. *Bazari* funding went to Huseiniyeh Ershad, popular *hay'ats*, the anti-Baha'i Hojjatiyeh organisations, and established *'ulama*. Patterns of pluralism, and flexibility, long embedded in religious practice in Iran, were as real as the differences and controversies argued out in the 1960s and 1970s.

As will be seen in Chapter 5, the ideological role of gender and sexual themes was a significant feature of contests over religion and the institutions and interests of religious specialists. Shifts in gender relations, in secular education, dress codes, and the wider social participation of women, raised issues for those whose authority and learning supported old-established practices. So too did the increasing flow of alternative images of gender and sexual roles and relations available to growing numbers of Iranians through imported media. It is noteworthy that co-education, co-sociability and female veiling, as well as theories about the differences between and roles of men and women, which combined religion and 'modern' scientific rationality, were central themes in debates on change, resistance and tradition in Shi'ism.[42] Attacks on women's suffrage in 'ulama opposition to the Shah in 1963–64, or on Shari'ati for allowing unveiled females to attend his lectures, like initiatives in Qum to provide religious schooling for girls, gendered the politics of reform, opposition and 'ulama interests. As will be seen, this area of social and moral practice became a symbolically charged issue, but also a terrain on which Shi'a intellectuals of varying views staked rival claims to authority. Yeganeh and Keddie have shown the clear differences among those claims, although it is also clear that the tradition of masculine pronouncements on gender questions was not abandoned in any of these views.[43] As with contests over female veiling in the 1930s, this gendered public discourse, grounded in masculist institutions of intellectual and religious authority, centred on male reformers, 'ulama and commentators rather than on women's views and preferences.

The whole complex and unstable spectrum of challenge and defence within and around the institutions and vested interests of religion from the 1950s to the 1970s was linked to politics. With a repressive and increasingly impervious regime and a legacy of previous controversy over religious involvement in politics, the organisation and conduct of religious worship, education and activism were bound up with difficult choices about the relations of religious interests to state power. 'Ulama pursued varied strategies to preserve and adapt their roles as preachers, educators and intellectuals, each with implications for their political relationships with government bureaucrats, security services and censors. The concerns of active Shi'a with education and the exercise of moral and cultural influence confronted them with the social and cultural changes now reshaping Iranian communities. From migration to cities to the spread of modern media, new lifestyles and secular education, these changes had to be addressed by those speaking for religion, whether critically or adaptively, if they were to sustain influence and authority. Religious leaders tapped into and gave voice to doubts and difficulties about the socio-cultural change experienced by many Iranians, and made their contribution to the changing cultural environment. These were profoundly *political* activities since they fed into contests over the shape and direction of society and culture in families and communities as well as in intellectual and political circles. Sexual morality and the consumption of popular culture were crucial in these contests and religious interventions. The degree to which state power and social change could be managed or resisted, and what forms adaptation, opposition or disengagement might take, were political choices for *'ulama* leaders, pious Shi'a, and the whole range of specialists, activists and intellectuals.

By the 1970s, religious institutions and established interests had been politicised and in turn increased politicisation. This happened through *'ulama* involvement with 'new' initiatives, their use of established techniques of defensive management, their withdrawal into familiar areas of work, or active resistance to authority and 'unacceptable' change. Having argued that individuals or groupings combined or moved between these approaches, and that there were few fixed or monolithic positions, it is important to recognise the pervasive atmosphere of confrontation with an intrusive regime and with large socio-cultural changes. When sections of the religious establishment had questioned government policies or incipient changes in Iranian communities prior to the Constitutional Revolution, it was within a context of institutional and cultural authority, and a restricted sphere of debate. In the years before the anti-Shah movement of the late 1970s, similar questions emerged in a very different context. The modern state power of the Pahlavi regime, with its large resources, posed a more politically and materially substantial threat to religious institutions, than had the Qajar state. State power and resources also contributed to social changes which challenged existing religious practices and institutions. Having previously left the core bases of religious autonomy and effectiveness in the *bazars* and urban communities of Iran largely intact, allowing religious interests to continue and even regroup, government attacks on *'ulama* and *bazaris* in the mid-1970s sharpened confrontation with those interests. They provided the contingent context for *'ulama* resistance, one that was also historically familiar.

Confronted with loss of role and status in the short term, and a longer-term erosion of their social and cultural positions in Iranian communities, defenders of religion were not without institutional as well as ideological and material resources. The historic networks linking *'ulama* of all ranks to religious leaders and to believers still existed in the patronage and personal connections that underpinned the rebuilding of religious education and authority in the 1920s, and were strengthened in the 1950s and 1960s. They also adapted to reach out to new groups of urban migrants, and to raise tentative questions of intellectual and organisational reform. Some *'ulama* (like their forebears in the constitutional era) worked in suspicious tandem with 'dissident' Shi'a thinkers, such as Shari'ati, while at times attacking them. Like their forebears, they nurtured links to popular constituencies and their practices, whether through 'traditional' preaching, philanthropy and *rawzeh* rituals, or via the newer media of radio and tape transmission. Pressured by state intervention, by the growth of social environments where they had little status or power, and by secular or anti-clerical viewpoints, those defending the interests and institutions of Shi'a Islam in Iran mobilised resources from both past and present to maintain them.

PART TWO
The 'religious' and the 'political'

Introduction

The starting point for this exploration of religion, culture and politics in Iran during this period is the questioning posed by the dominance of religious interests, ideas, images and leadership within the large and diverse coalition of Iranians who openly opposed the Shah during 1977–79. While giving due weight to the specific short-term circumstances which favoured such dominance in that period of protest and of the overthrow of the regime (as discussed in Chapter 6), this section of the text will also focus on long-established features of Iranians' political interests, beliefs and experiences that contributed to the developments of 1977–81. Three approaches will be offered: first, we will consider the political *issues* taken up by Iranians in the era of modernity and their religious aspects; second, we will look at the *ideas* and *images* used by Iranians to express political interests and aspirations; third, we will examine the kinds of political *movements* created and supported by Iranians in this period. This will provide a historical and flexible view of how 'religious' features of 'politics' and 'political' features of 'religion' were created and used by Iranians from the 1870s to the 1970s.

Just as the question of the most relevant and helpful uses of the terms 'religion' or 'religious' has been discussed, so it is helpful to examine what concepts of 'politics' and the 'political' will help to make sense of that history. It will be useful to clarify what activities, ideas or institutions can appropriately be considered 'political'. The aim is to use the term in ways which are *clear*, in that they identify something specific, and also *flexible*, in that they do justice to the diversity of human situations and activities. We can begin with a general proposition that 'politics' is a *means* whereby particular people deal with issues that arise among them either as individuals or as groups. Politics is thus a question of *relationships* on the one hand and *conflict* on the other. Emphasis on relationships situates 'politics' in the interactions of actual human beings in their social contexts, be that a marriage relationship or the mobilisation of thousands in campaigns or elections, rather than emphasising impersonal structures and ideas. Emphasis on conflict is not an assertion that hostility is the main motivator of politics, but a recognition that human societies contain individuals and groups with different and potentially incompatible aims and interests arising from the variations and inequities in their power, abilities, resources and influence, and hence experiences and outlooks. People create 'political' activity, thought or institutions in pursuit of such aims and interests, and the study of 'politics' should focus on that creativity.

This combination of a broad approach with a clear focus on people's chosen responses to their diverse and unequal circumstances as the stuff of politics allows us both to capture specific aspects of the past and to do justice to their varied forms of expression. Such forms range from conciliatory alliance-making to aggressive physical confrontation, from emotive communal rituals to carefully thought-out programmes and theories, and from small-scale personal transactions in households to large-scale national and international campaigning or organisation. Nevertheless, they share the distinctive characteristics of conscious human intervention in response to perceived differences, deficiencies or inequities in their lives.

This framework or starting point for using the terms 'political' or 'politics' has been made deliberately general in order to avoid the constraints which limit their use to an unjustifiably narrow range of phenomena. Two examples illustrate the point. Conventional definitions of 'politics', canonised by scholarly work from the eighteenth century onwards, have located it in a so-called 'public' sphere of state power, citizenship and nation-making. This has been explicitly contrasted to the 'domestic' sphere of family and household affairs, and the 'private', if social, interests of economic life focused around property, production and commerce. This contrast is neither an accurate description of links or overlaps between these supposedly distinct spheres, nor intellectually consistent, since religion, education and morality are placed in *both* spheres, but has influenced scholarly and 'common sense' thinking about 'politics'. It is assumed that 'politics' takes place in 'public' places (streets, parliaments, royal courts, offices), and is communicated through the *publication* of pamphlets, newspapers or petitions, or through 'public' speaking and activity. Its subject matter is defined as issues of 'public' interest, whether law and order, foreign policy, social reform or the financing of such activities.

These restrictive views and definitions have been effectively challenged by investigations and analysis of the 'politics' of family, personal, marital and household life. Building on an interest in power and gender, this scholarship has drawn attention to experiences and activities in those settings which are 'political' in the senses already described. It has shown how issues of power, resources, knowledge and influence, and perceptions of difference and inequality in those areas, are important in the allegedly 'private' settings of marriage, kinship, household and parenthood. It has also shown that intimate and personal issues like sexual desire and behaviour, childbirth and rights to bodily autonomy and independence are matters for political debate, social regulation, campaigning activity and conflicts over power, choice and control. Understanding of the complex and varied forms and locations for political ideas and activities has been enhanced by work on issues as diverse as the relationship of sixteenth- and seventeenth-century witch-hunts to views of childbirth and female sexuality, and modern concerns with adolescent sexual behaviour, medically assisted conception, or pornography.

The impact of gender-aware scholarship combines with other important scholarly work which explores and explains broader versions of 'politics'. That work challenges a second well-established view of 'politics' which links it predominantly to 'government' – that is, the formation, maintenance and control of state power. Such a restrictive view generalises from specific experiences, notably in Europe over the last four centuries. Its limitations have been revealed through studies of medieval European societies, of societies in the Indian subcontinent and the Middle East, and of less privileged or powerful groups, whether slaves, peasants, artisans or networks of women. The 'politics' practised by eighteenth-century Indian landholders, sixteenth-century French peasants, nineteenth-century radicals or former slaves in the USA dealt with power, difference, self-interest and aspiration in a *range* of ways among which state power and 'government' might figure little or not at all. Studies of rural communities, of religious sects, of family life, of urban neighbourhoods and workplaces show ample evidence of 'political' life as defined above. Contests over authority in a village or religious group, arguments over decisions or problems in a community, and the enforcement of or resistance to rules and customs within it, shape or are shaped by people's involvements in the relationships and institutions around them and in the daily life of a church, a family, a workers' association or a village.

These approaches have directed investigations of 'politics' to a wider and more varied range of activities, institutions, ideas and relationships than older conventions and enriched our understanding of what the term might usefully mean. The discussion of 'politics' in the following chapters draws on these approaches to explore how Iranians experienced, perceived and responded to the difference, power and change in their lives, and the extent to which religious elements influenced their 'political' ideas and actions.

FOUR
The life, death and afterlife of political issues

Encountering change: a story of reform and resistance

'There is no such thing as modernity in general. There are only national societies each of which becomes modern in its own fashion.' (Jeffrey Herf)

As Iranians' encounters with the world underwent qualitative changes over the period discussed in this book, questions of how to understand and deal with those encounters emerged as a new kind of political issue. Rulers and elites had long been able to deal innovatively with external and internal challenges, whether imperial rivalry with the Ottoman state, the consolidation of various forms of dynastic rule, or competition among religious and propertied factions. Residents in rural, urban or nomadic communities adapted to and influenced new developments, from the establishment of new communal Shi'a practices under Safavid rule, to invasion and external disruption by the Afghans in the eighteenth century, and new power negotiations among elites and the incoming Qajar rulers in the nineteenth.[1] Members of the *ulama* modified and transformed their expert traditions and social relations, as shown in Chapter 3, just as pastoralists or traders evolved responses to European demands for wool, silk and carpets, and artisans developed new designs for new markets. In these senses Iranians were active practitioners of 'change' not just as a reactive and pragmatic response to circumstances, but as a creative, even innovative, activity.

These points are reminders that initiatives and notions of reform cannot be simplistically associated with the 'modern' era examined here. Just as fifteenth-century Ottoman sultans established their 'New Troops'/Janissaries, and seventeenth-century Russian tsars and nobles constructed a 'new' peasant serfdom, so sixteenth- and seventeenth-century Iranian rulers and *ulama* created, and were conscious of creating, new religious and administrative practices.

In the 1840s and 1850s the Babi movement used indigenous modes of revelation and inspiration to press its visionary case for a new spiritual and social dispensation, demonstrating the continuing power of this approach to change. Other reform projects of the period show the impact of different influences. Amir Kabir, chief minister of Nasir al-Din Shah from 1848 to 1851, who suppressed the Babi movement, was mainly concerned to reform the government's military, financial and administrative procedures. Like an earlier 'reformer', the Qajar prince 'Abbas Mirza in the 1820s, he responded to the assertive power of the tsarist empire on Iran's northern borders and to the example of state-led reform in that empire.

What distinguishes such initiatives from later concerns with 'reform' was their pragmatic and contingent character. The later decades of the century saw qualitative shifts in contacts between Iranians and a wider world with resulting changes in their cultural repertoires and in their perceptions of the aims and content of the changes they might want to make. As described in Chapter 1, the material involvement of the Russians and British in Iran intensified, as did their strategic concern with it as an unstable 'buffer state' between their respective expanding empires in Central Asia and India. European diplomatic and business visitors to Iran were supplemented by missionaries (American in north-western Iran, British in the south), telegraph staff (following Iranian linking with the Indo-European telegraph system in the 1860s), and military and technical 'experts'. The growth of Iranian communities in Istanbul and Bombay, the maintenance of links with Iranians living under Russian rule in the Caucasus, and the movements of migrant workers between Iran and Russia brought particular groups of Iranians into contact with a wider range of experiences and ideas. Merchants, migrant workers, intellectuals and government officials had the opportunity to compare and contrast work, culture, politics and education as practised in Iran, the Ottoman Empire, India, the Caucasus and Egypt. Few in number, these Iranians played significant roles in setting new agendas for change.

These agendas involved specific grievances about foreign competition and interference, but also new perceptions of 'progress' and 'reform'. Two elements in the emerging discourse are significant. First, advocates of these projects increasingly imagined some kind of *systemic* transformation as much as specific changes. Second, they made more extended comparisons between the 'deficiencies' or weaknesses of Iranian government, education, and law and systems elsewhere. This shift in the rhetorical register reified reform as the 'answer' to Iranian problems, but focused attention on identifying some key to change, that, if introduced into Iran, would have the desired generally transforming results. For some writers, this key was rational knowledge, for others law, and for yet others education. In each instance, while specific proposals might be included, the main thrust of the argument celebrated the reforming power of 'the law', or railways, or 'education' to effect some wholesale change in the fabric and outlook of Iranian society, or made general appeals to 'reason' and 'science'. For Mustashar al-Douleh in the 1860s it was railways, and later his 'one word', the law, echoed by Malkom Khan's celebration of *qanun* (law), the title of his reforming journal. Writers like 'Abd al-Rahim Talebof.[2] Talebof

117

and others like Zein al-Abedin Marageh'i (both from merchant backgrounds and resident outside Iran) argued that education and the printed word would renew and strengthen Iranians generally. They expressed the conviction that the introduction of modern education, or legal frameworks for trade and property, or organised administrative structures, would open routes to prosperity, and to international respect and safety for Iran.[3]

Three features of these early explorations of reform were to be significant over the next century. Most obvious of all was the way in which they placed government and the state at the centre of their arguments. This emphasis arose partly from the fact that the early advocates of reform from lobbyists like Malkom Khan and Behbehani to those with significant responsibilities such as Mustashar al-Douleh, Mushir al-Douleh and 'Ali Khan Garusi were often diplomats and other officials of the Qajar government.[4] It was also influenced by their interest in the active reforms of the Ottomans, Russians and French Second Empire which they observed in the 1850s and 1860s, where ruling regimes were driving through major changes in law, administration, education and economic policy.

These advocates, drawn from the small educated and office-holding sections of Iranian society, translated actual experiences of conflict with indifferent or resistant vested interests and supporters of established custom into rhetorical emphasis on their own special role. The discourse of reform was also a discourse of *reformers* – those with knowledge and commitment to explaining, designing and proselytising on behalf of change which set them apart from ignorant, self-interested, conservative 'others'. From this was to emerge the notion of the enlightened thinker, an early version of which was put forward by the radical thinker Mirza Aqa Khan Kermani, who had moved from a dissident and Babi backgound to admiration for French Enlightenment ideals. Speaking of those who enlighten others and attack superstition, he proclaimed, 'If ten learned men and philosophers emerge in a nation they can be more beneficial to that nation than ten million ignorant and deprived people.'[5] By the time of the Constitutional Revolution, terms like *munavvar al-ouqul*, *munavvar al-fekr*, *rawshan-fekr*, combining Arabic and Persian terms for reason, thought and enlightenment, came into use to describe reforming intellectuals. They designated a new kind of learned and activist group, differentiating themselves both from older groups of 'men of the pen' and thinkers and from the majority of Iranians embedded in familiar ways of thinking and acting politically.[6]

One important feature of their 'difference' was access to and enthusiasm for ideas and practices developed in societies outside Iran, whether French rationalism, or Ottoman reform. The power of European productive technology, the efficacy of European social and political practice, the benefits of rational and scientific approaches, like the success of recent reforms in the Tsarist and

Ottoman Empires, were critically compared to Iranian failures in those areas, or, worse yet, refusal to see the disparities. As one early reforming office holder put it, 'we believe we have reached the highest degree of progress and have nothing to worry about'.[7] This enthusiasm was entwined with sharp concern about the compatibility of imported/foreign innovations with indigenous Iranian cultures and practices, expressed in arguments for the compatibility of such changes with Islamic principles and beliefs. In his *Yek Kalameh*, an appeal for legal reforms, Mirza Yusuf Khan Mustashar al-Douleh combines support for the French legal principles with arguments that they 'confirm the *shari'a* of Islam', commenting to a fellow reformer that he had found proofs and precedents in the Qur'an and *hadith* which supported 'progress and civilisation'. The advocate of educational reform 'Abd al-Rahim Talebof argued that replacemnt of existing school curricula could be 'the best guarantor of the range of influence of the religion of Islam'.[8]

More generally, advocates of radical change in Iranian institutions saw their adoption not as remaking Iranians and their society as clones of European or Ottoman versions, but as reviving and protecting distinctively Iranian interests, and a 'national' identity which they themselves were energetically imagining. The discourse of reform was entwined with discourses of nation and patriotism, as these writer-activists constructed and disseminated notions of 'Iranian' identity and history.[9] Tensions between ideas that the renewal of 'Iran' demanded the use of imported insights, techniques or institutions, and ideas of a distinctive and valuable indigenous culture emerging among reformers in the late nineteenth century became central to cultural politics and political culture during the twentieth. Ongoing debate about the links, or lack of them, between 'modernisation', 'reform' and Europeanisation or westernisation featured in both.

As the early initiatives and arguments of reformers became frustrated by the indifference and resistance of the governing establishment, the idea of constitutional as well as administrative or educational reform began to be put forward. The wish to direct or contain monarch and government if progressive aims were to be achieved, led modernisers to add ideas of consultative or representative government to their depictions of transformation. This fed the protests over misgovernment, oppression and threats to *'ulama* and *bazari* interests which led to the grant of a constitution in 1906. In that 'moment', groups of reformers were able to play the role of enlightened leaders, guiding others on to the path of progress as they used the mass occupation of the British legation grounds to advocate constitutional solutions to the protesters' grievances. The establishment of the Constitution and the Majlis (national assembly) focused attention on the parties, elections and public politics associated with them, and the attempts by Shah, ruling elites and foreign interests to undo them between 1906 and 1911. In reformers' political activity and thought, the defence and advancement of

'Iranian' progress, security and autonomy became bound up with the fate of these 'modern' institutions.

In the 'constitutional era', understandings of 'reform' as either alien or indigenous were intensified by controversies over the role of *shari'a* law and Muslim identity within the new polity and its institutions. While some constitutionalists argued that they were compatible with and even enjoined by Muslim precepts and practice, others differentiated the modern agenda of the new system from religious and despotic predecessors, leading yet others to denounce it as godless and heretical. The first group were exemplified by the senior *mujtaheds* who worked with the Majlis and developed arguments linking Shi'a ideas and representative government.[10] The second emerged in the radical, sometimes religiously dissident, sometimes anti-clerical or secular, support for constitutionalism from preachers like Sayyid Jamal al-din Isfahani 'Va'iz' ('the preacher') or Hasan Taqizadeh, both of whom played prominent roles in the struggles to establish and then maintain the constitution. The third emerged among members of the *'ulama* who opposed secularist elements in the pro-constitutional coalition (described in Chapter 6), and among members of established elites who distrusted the social radicalism of some of those elements.[11] While cross-cut by short-term or opportunistic alliances, and personal links and rivalries, they shaped reform discourses in which relationships to indigenous cultures and religious traditions, and issues of 'moderate', as opposed to 'radical', change, were defined and contested. The extent to which peasant interests should influence land reform, the rights of non-Muslims or women as citizens, or the role of *shari'a* law and popular access to justice were issues through which these different perspectives took political form.[12]

The centres of reform politics in this period were the Majlis and the political community in Tehran and similar public politics in the *anjumans* (local councils) and on the streets of other urban centres. The role of the Majlis as national representative assembly, with its elections, debates and political parties, and its symbolic significance as the great reform won by the politicised sections of the nation, now expected to implement the hopes and aims of its supporters, gave it an iconic significance in Iranians' views of change. It was the place where the 'national' drama of winning freedom from foreign interference and progress for the 'nation' was played out, and the institution whose survival against royalist counter-coups in 1907 and 1908 and foreign pressure from 1907 to 1911 promised a better future as seen by those Iranians who formed that particular political public. The failure of the Majlis actually to implement lasting substantive reforms sat paradoxically alongside its foundational political role representing hopes for change.

Experience and debate from the 1890s to the 1920s established three trajectories for reforming thought and practice. Most obvious was the powerful association of reform with state power as both a means to change and the key set of institutions to be changed. The need for trained and organised administrative cadres, for a structured legal system, and for oversight of national interests and prosperity all featured on the agendas of the reforming intelligentsia who emerged over the period. The unavoidable realities of great power intervention in Iran highlighted the importance of military and administrative effectiveness, and the state finance needed to support them. Between 1911 and 1921, civil strife, local and regional conflict, and foreign invasion, revealed the inability of the governments which replaced the Qajar autocracy to assert or manage central control, or law and order, emphasising the need to reform state power.

The statist approach to reform fostered in these conditions underpinned the claims of the first Pahlavi Shah to be a reformer as well as a patriot and effective centralising ruler. Support for his rule among reformers expressed appreciation of his ability to assert law and order, and to drive through policies of central reform and authority, although some looked more like rhetorical display than substantive change. His rule embedded notions of progress spreading from centres of state power to recipients through the agency of a modernised governing elite wearing suits and studying abroad, or acquiring modernising ideas and images through the expanding state education system and applying them at more modest levels. An ethos of authority backing technical and organisational modernisation, legitimised in nationalistic language, gave the greed, dynastic self-interest, and repressive tendencies of the regime a reforming aspect. Military and political crushing of regional dissidence and of political opposition were presented as the removal of obstacles to progress, claims which were not wholly unconvincing to those who had experienced the frustrations and setbacks of preceding decades.[13]

Like his father, Muhammad Reza Pahlavi combined practical and rhetorical elements in his state-led reforms. The publicity associated with land reform and the so-called White Revolution of the 1960s, and the proclaiming of the 'Great Society' in the 1970s staged the regime both for international audiences and for its subjects. Where Reza Shah had left key areas of economic activity untouched, his son's reform programme, described earlier, was more directly interventionist. This reflected the greater resources (notably oil money) at his disposal and a different political climate, in which state-led modernisation programmes, and the range of 'development studies' that accompanied them, were the characteristic mode of governance in the post-1945, postcolonial world, both 'communist' and 'non-communist'.

Nevertheless, this trend to shape reform through command and control, which could appeal to enthusiastic reformers as well as ambitious shahs, was not the only legacy of the earlier period. Both before 1905 and during the constitutional era, reformers nurtured projects for change concerned with the rights of subjects, the rule of law, and programmes for social justice and the protection of the subordinate and unprivileged from the predations of the powerful.[14] Newspapers like *Sur i-Israfil* (*The trumpet of Israfil*) proclaimed ideas of emancipation underpinning Iranian law, and Nazem al-Islam, a participant in and early historian of the events of 1906–10, spoke of how 'justice and national sovereignty must come about through ... the poor and oppressed people'.[15] The Constitution itself was the symbolic institution upholding those possibilities. The discourses and practices that posed the 'people's' (*melli*) interests against those of government (*doulat*) will be explored in the next section of this chapter, but it is important to note here the extent to which they shaped discussions and programmes of reform and views of desirable, or undesirable, change.

Views that society needed to change through the redistribution of power if not of material wealth were explored in journals, discussion circles, radical *anjumans*, and party political or labour organisations which developed between 1905 and the 1920s. They drew on Iranian experiences of and links to the radical nationalist, social democratic and anti-clerical politics and journalism of cities in Russian-ruled areas of the Caucasus. In Tabriz, Tehran and Gilan, Iranians campaigned on the oppression of peasants and the poor, formed socialist cells and urban workers' associations and worked with the Democrat Party.[16] These initiatives were small-scale and had limited impact, but established a political repertoire referred to by succeeding generations of political activists for whom they embodied aspirations to social justice, participatory politics and popular rights.

These elements of concern with social injustice, political rights and 'Muslim traditions' persisted in the leftist and democratic traditions which were largely submerged by the conformist, statist and repressive Reza Pahlavi regime. Censorship closed down political debate, parties and unions were banned, and radicals and dissidents imprisoned.[17] While this repression restricted such views of reform to very small groups, it also endowed the radical tradition with an aura of struggle and persecution, confirming the value of its particular stance on change. Advocacy and organisation in this tradition expanded in the open political situation which developed after the abdication of Reza Shah in 1941, following the British/Russian occupation of Iran. It found expression in the leftist movements around the communist Tudeh (Masses) Party and in the democratic/patriotic politics of the coalition underpinning the National Front.

The period from 1941 to the overthrow of the National Front government led by Muhammad Mussadeq in 1953 saw the development of new relationships between statist and redistributive views of reform. The revival of the Majlis, elections, party politics and the press took place in a public sphere much enlarged by urban growth and the effects of Reza Pahlavi's modernising policies described in Chapter 1. Although this politics was still dominated by the discourses of those whose forebears had launched debates and campaigns on reform half a century earlier, they now addressed different constituencies (modern wage workers, professionals and high school students as well as artisans and *bazar* traders). Moreover, the composition of the intelligentsia had changed with the expansion of education and modern white-collar work. The immediate exigencies of foreign occupation, Cold War politics, and the new importance of control of the oil industry, dominated national politics, and for the first time there were discussions about social questions such as land reform which went beyond rhetoric. Nevertheless, the contests for power between Majlis, government ministers, the Shah, and great power interests kept questions of the state and constitution at the forefront of the reform agenda.

Both state-centred and people-centred approaches to reform became increasingly secular over the first half of the twentieth century. Reza Shah's policies, the democratic and social justice initiatives of the early twentieth century, and the leftist and National Front politics of the 1940s and early 1950s emphasised material improvement, political institutions and social relations. Such objectives were to be reached through the application of expertise, modern technologies and rational/scientific knowledge, producing sharper distinctions between those Iranians with access to and contact with modern literacy, technology or skills, and those without them. For reformers this produced tensions between the confidence and enthusiasm of those who knew best what would be good for society, and anxiety about the distance between themselves and those whose lives they believed they could improve. In the Iranian case the presence of a spectrum of political views of reform informed by religion still challenged reformers as it had done at the start of the twentieth century, albeit in conditions where the secularisation of parts of political culture had changed the terms of engagement.

The issue of religion was part of the ever-open question of what kind of 'indigenous' approaches to reform might be combined with 'universal' ('western'?) elements in programmes of reform. The flavour of this combination in a period of populist nationalism and secular reformism in the 1940s and 1950s differed from that in the era of third worldist anti-imperialism in the 1960s and 1970s. It is important to distinguish between polemical characterisations of religious outlooks as 'essentially reactionary' or of reform politics as 'essentially secular' and the complex interactions and slippages which in fact took place.

In order to understand this more fully, it is worth examining the story of religious approaches to reform. While Shi'a, like other Muslims, rejected the notion of *bid'at* (heretical innovation), this can be contrasted with Shi'a traditions of valuing *tajjadod* (renewal). The achievements of leading *mujtaheds* like Vahid Behbehani in establishing the dominance of Usulism at the end of the eighteenth century, or of Mirza Hasan Shirazi as *ra'is* (leader) of the Shi'a in the late nineteenth century, were recognised by entitling them *Mujaddid* (renewer). In their ability to resist but co-exist with heterodox, mystical, millenarian or dissident Muslim practice, 'orthodox' Shi'a demonstrated a creativity and flexibility which enabled them to adapt if not reform. As shown in Chapter 3, even in the case of the Babi movement there was a zone of indeterminacy which included discreet accommodation as well as outright persecution. Among Shi'a thinkers there were those like 'Afghani' who argued for Muslim political renewal through reform, and were drawn to pan-Islamic politics with limited appeal to Iranian Shi'a. There were also those like Tabataba'i and Na'ini at the turn of the twentieth century who engaged with issues of constitutional reform.[18] In the same period, the tradition of anti-establishment Shi'a thought identified by Bayat linked dissident thinkers and preachers with Azali Babi and secular liberal, radical and nationalist trends in reform politics.[19]

These examples suggest the unfixed and polyvalent potential of Shi'a Muslim views and commitments. Thus, during the constitutional movement, the Shaikhi community of Tabriz identified with the constitutionalist cause, whereas the Shaikhi community of Kerman was anti-constitutional.[20] This difference may be explained by local conditions and rivalries, but suggests that religious outlook was not predictive in any simple sense. While many *'ulama* distanced themselves from constitutional politics or explicitly opposed it, some chose to acquire and practise the skills of representative parliamentary politics. Sayyed Hasan Mudarris in the 1920s and Abu'l Qasim Kashani in the 1940s went beyond tactical accommodation to new political forms, becoming effective exponents of new syntheses of piety, nationalism and activism.[21] They might not expound the same reforms as non-*mulla* counterparts, and remained socially conservative, but they did embrace other kinds of political change, whether defence of the Majlis or popular nationalist campaigning.

Nevertheless, religious politics/political religion between the 1920s and the 1960s was deeply influenced by the pressures of state-led secularisation and the expansion of non-religious education and culture. This produced a politics of defensive resistance and embattled negotiation, described in Chapters 3 and 6, in which involvement in reform could be seen as problematic. The resistance to Ha'iri's reform proposals in the 1930s, and to proposals for change in the curriculum and leadership of the religious establishment in the early 1960s, are cases in point. However, the challenge of secular education and the spread of leftist thought among young educated Iranians from the 1930s produced some reformist responses. Mehdi Bazargan and the Liberation Movement of Iran sought to combine acceptance of modern scientific thought and technology with equally active pious support for Muslim interests in the modern Iranian polity. Supporters of such views participated in Mussadeq's National Front coalition in the 1940s and its successor bodies in the 1950s and 1960s defining themselves as a distinct strand within this liberal national grouping. The more explicitly radical God-Worshipping Socialists promoted patriotic pious commitment to social justice as a Muslim alternative to leftist and secular nationalism. 'Ulama like Taleqani and Mutahhari encouraged committed Muslims to respond creatively to a new social and cultural environment and to reach out to disaffected youth.

All of these initiatives, which at times overlapped and co-operated, expressed the desire to provide answers to the questions about the compatibility of Shi'ism with modern reform which were also questions about the role of 'indigenous' versus 'imported' values and practices. The association of change with both the threats and the positive example of western states and societies had embedded that issue in the politics of reform in Iran since the later nineteenth century. The politics of 'national' autonomy and self-assertion, the politics of cultural authenticity, and the politics of progress and strengthening, converged as well as conflicted, producing hybrid and inconsistent approaches to reform among pious Iranians. It is significant that their doubts and difficulties were as much about reform within the domain of religious practice as about changes in other spheres of life.

The most high-profile and appealing of the hybrids to emerge from this contested terrain was that associated with the work of 'Ali Shari'ati. Its explicitly political dimensions and contribution to the anti-Shah movement of the 1970s are examined in Chapter 6. Here the question to consider is whether his work should indeed be considered as a 'reform movement' as Akhavi argues.[22] At the heart of the texts and lectures produced by Shari'ati was a set of paradoxes. His formative experiences in his father's Mussadeqist and activist Shi'a politics and the activism of Iranian students abroad in the 1960s grounded his work in traditions of activist polemic. His exposure to Fanonist cultural analyses of colonial domination and resistance and third worldist anti-colonialism in France gave him a global context for his Iranian nationalism. His strong Shi'a commitment and intellectual activity enabled him to argue for a renewal of the faith and a redefinition (he would have said rediscovery) of its purposes, but as a non-'alim to do so outside the conventions of formal religious training.

Shari'ati offered more suggestions about how Shi'a practice might be reformed through new educational programmes and emphasis on the activity of pious intellectuals rather than religious specialists, than proposals for reform in other spheres. In many ways, his concern to 'rediscover' the 'Shi'ism of 'Ali' (and oppose it to the Shi'ism of the 'ulama establishment), and his invocation of an early Muslim figure, Abu Zarr, as an image of commitment to the oppressed, mobilised Shi'a ideals for political activism rather than offering a developed reform programme. His achievement was to ally Shi'a beliefs with enthusiasm for change and struggle, and project familiar and newly dynamic Shi'a images of martyrdom into the world of frustration experienced by the college and high school graduates who were his initial constituency. He offered the political and emotional stimulus of envisaging change as possible and desirable, and a vision of personal and collective renewal through what he called 'the return to self/selfhood', which encouraged people to imagine reform, if not proposing anything very specific. His life and writing provided models of religious commitment as culturally modern, socially relevant and politically active, powerfully acting out more tentative initiatives by other religious reformers.

It is instructive to compare his trajectory with that of Khomeini, who also refigured relationships between religion and change. His reworking of the arguments for the 'guardianship of the jurist' (*velayat i-faqih*), and appropriation of populist and politically appealing concepts like that of the 'oppressed' (*mustaz'afin*) can be seen as ideologically innovative as well as opportunistic.[23] His reliance on the familiar and respected skills and authority of *'ulama* training and on his rank and status as an *ayatollah* can be contrasted with Shari'ati's use of his non-specialist status. He combined defensive arguments for the preservation of Islam with radical alternatives (the Islamic Republic) which challenged older approaches to the relations of religion and the state, whether notions of the twin pillars of order, or of distrust and bargaining. As with Shari'ati, it is arguable that this was more about seeking a viable political strategy than creating a programme of reform, although of course the Islamic Republic did indeed 're-form' important aspects of culture and society in Iran.

Both Shari'ati and Khomeini were responding to the entrenchment of secular influences and institutions in Iranian culture, society and politics, and the actual or implied challenges which that produced for Iranian Muslims. The 'reactionary *mulla*' image used by Muhammad Reza Pahlavi as well as by some leftists and liberal reformers told at most part of the story, just as the association of reform with secular ideas and policies ignored resistance to change on grounds of material self-interest or secular ideological conviction (like anti-communism).

Most significantly, these stories have been told entirely from the perspective of policy-makers, intellectuals and government. As ethnographic work from the 1970s shows, cultivators, nomads, wage workers and the urban poor had their own ways of creating, resisting or managing change. This might take the form of social and economic initiatives among Khuzestan and Boir Ahmad peasants following land reform, the 'quiet encroachments' of squatters and street people in Tehran in the 1970s, or the renegotiation of pastoral practices among nomads.[24] These were creative activities, not just coping strategies, and were underpinned by clear views about change and innovation as well as achieving actual changes.

The point is not to establish inconsistency or duplicity but to appreciate the multiple locations from which people imagined, enacted or resisted change.

A story of *doulat* and *mellat*: issues of state and people

Iranian history in the era of modernity, like that of other societies, has been partly shaped by new questions about the relations between governments and those over whom they rule. New enlarged military ambitions and needs among rulers, new forms of wealth and economic activity in society, and new thinking on power, law and finance among both rulers and subjects, were features of 'modern' approaches to the making and implementing of policy in these areas, whether in eighteenth-century colonial North America, nineteenth-century France or twentieth-century India. Whether seen as a remote, unpredictable and hostile force, or as a potential source of protection, prosperity and justice, *doulat* (the state) became the object of new debates and demands in which established values and material interests influenced, and were in turn influenced by, new concerns.

The *doulat* of the Qajar dynasty has been characterised in a number of ways. After their initial conquest of power, Qajar rulers established authority and legitimacy through their use of the royal clan and management of its rivalries, through the creation of a limited bureaucracy, and through cultivating and on occasion intimidating powerful interest groups. They made rapprochements with sections of the *'ulama*, and existing office and landholding elites, and challenged 'tribal' leaders whom they saw as over-mighty subjects, deploying patronage and force to control if not wholly subordinate them. Military and diplomatic setbacks in the first half of the nineteenth century showed the external limitations on their power and effectiveness, but their creation of alliances and compromises and their refurbishment and propagation of traditional symbols and codes of royal authority and legitimacy gave their internal rule form and substance. It is notable that these codes and symbols derived from traditions linking monarchy to the upholding of religion, as well as from traditions of tribal military leadership, and non or pre-Islamic Iranian notions of kingship. In the honorifics of ruling shahs, titles like 'shadow of god' (*zill-allah*), and 'shield (or refuge) of Islam' (*Islam-panah*) sat alongside the ancient Iranian title of *shahanshah* (king of kings), the Turco-Mongol title *Khaqan* (paramount Khan or commander) and allusions to royal military prowess, glory and care for justice. During the nineteenth century, increasingly elaborate use of titles, or court display and ceremonial, and of the distribution of honorifics, gifts and patronage by the shah show the importance of these supports and symbols of power. The regime also made use of the arbitrary power and patronage that allowed shahs to dismiss, advance, expropriate, manipulate and physically destroy ministers, favourites and members of their kin and court circles, a power that was a historically recognised, if much criticised, prerogative.

The assets, symbols and prerogatives of *doulat* offset its distance and lack of direct power over its subjects. The shah was remote from ordinary villagers, urban workers or nomadic pastoralists by virtue of geographical distance, disparity in wealth and resources, and the attributes of wealth and hierarchy, and because the core activities of 'government' (law and order, taxation, administration) were not exercised by a central regime. The localised exercise of these functions was not so much the distribution of power from the centre as a consequence of the shah's *lack* of power. The dynasty, court and royal clan had to deal with powerful elites wielding control over landed, pastoral and commercial wealth and *independent* authority, coercion and patronage based on family and clan support, on regional networks of co-operation and competition, and on inherited resources or legal military and administrative office. Major land- or office holders and 'tribal' leaders, or senior *'ulama* and merchant-entrepreneurs all wielded varying degrees and forms of *autonomous* power and bargained with the Qajar regime on this basis. Images of 'despotism' purveyed by foreign observers of the period, or of royal supremacy proclaimed by supporters of the shah, should be set beside the constraints and compromises forced upon rulers faced with these effective and deeply rooted alternative sources of power and influence.

Both royal government and the autonomous elites with and through whom it brokered dominance made demands on the subject populace (*ra'iya*) for resources and control. They dealt not with an undifferentiated mass of individuals but with a range of relatively self-sufficient, self-regulating and distinct groups whose subordination to the powerful was shaped by self-reliance, by hierarchies within groups, and by the mix of force and manipulation used by the powerful to impose their demands. One feature of this relationship was the ability of the powerful to coerce money, labour, obedience or fighting men from subordinate groups. Others included bargaining between representatives of dominant and subordinate groups, the custom and practice of collective responsibility for meeting the demands of the powerful, and traditions of self-regulation and group solidarity as defences and constraints on the intrusion of those demands. The responses of villages to landlord/official demands for rents and taxes, of nomad encampments to levies of money, flocks and men by 'tribal' leaders, or of guilds of urban craftsmen and traders to the requirements of taxation or policing town streets, combined elements of negotiation and resistance with manipulation and acquiescence.[25]

While the rhetoric and ideology of government were hierarchical and absolute, its practice depended on bargaining and manoeuvring with others who wielded power. Control of the subject population was constrained in a number of ways. This is *not* to argue that the status and legitimacy of the Qajar monarchy was unreal, but that its reality was personalised (around the shah, royal clan and court), ideological (that is, highly reliant on rituals, words and images) and conditional (constantly negotiated with other wielders of power and authority). The ideal of a contractual connection between monarch and subjects, which Abbas Amanat argues was a real element in the *doulat–ra'iya* relationship, should be seen in the context of these realities.[26] Three features stand out in the politics of that relationship: first, the grip of the monarchy on the independent holders of power, and on the relatively self-reliant communities of Iran was provisional; second, the arbitrary, remote and unpredictable experience of monarchical power by subject people is recorded in literature, popular lore and anecdote; third, the influence of ideas and beliefs about legitimacy, hierarchy and authority are easier to track in the written record than are popular doubts or criticisms of them. Perceptions of the real limitations on Qajar 'despotism' and its hold on subjects and intermediaries should be balanced with an appreciation of the shah's capacity to manoeuvre within those limitations, and the durability of notions of *doulat* as a remote, capricious but enduring political reality.

By the last third of the nineteenth century, the Qajar *doulat* confronted new pressures which destabilised some of its sustaining conventions and relationships. This generated new practical demands and expectations, and new thinking on the issue of relations between *doulat* and what was coming to be called the 'people' (*mellat*). New external material and political pressures challenged royal government to adapt, if only to sustain its traditional place in the system of power and resource sharing. The depreciation of the monetary worth of state revenue was a product of international currency movements and global commodity flows and prices. Means were sought to sustain lavish and increasing expenditure on the royal court, its elite pensioners and its ventures into extravagant foreign travel. The prices of office and favours were raised, attempts to levy revenue intensified, and the use of foreign loans and sale of commercial concessions expanded.[27] From the start of Nasir al-din-Shah's reign (1848), royal ministers and officials periodically advocated schemes for more effective collection of taxes and the better functioning of civil administration and military organisation. However, such schemes foundered on the strength of the vested interests opposing them, the capacity of factional rivalries in court and government to block initiatives, and the shah's short-lived and fluctuating interest in or support for reform. Additional pressure on court and government came from the jockeying of British and Russian diplomats to secure political or commercial advantage, influence policy and resist each other's influence.

Just as the conduct of the Qajar state was modified by these new circumstances, so they had a combined and uneven impact on various Iranian groups and communities, with visible political results. The impact of external commercial influences which increased the role of foreign markets for particular Iranian products, and of foreign imports, created material pressures, opportunities and differences among Iranians, which found various political expressions. The grievances of merchants over concessions and preferential treatment given to foreigners, the demands of landlords on cultivators in areas of commercialising agriculture, declining opportunities for urban craftsmen, and sharper pressures and fluctuations in standards of living for the poor were all sources of political protest as well as of material inequity and competition. As the government sought to stave off its own financial problems by raising the price of offices and favours, the elite recipients of those offices and favours aimed to pass on increased costs to those from whom they exacted revenue, as they did with pressures to pass on more taxation to the state. Growing groups of entrepreneurs and property owners, who acquired advantageous positions in foreign trade, finance, commercial production or middleman activities, had political concerns, as they pursued their interests in purposive and self-conscious ways, arguing with government, competitors or rivals. Significantly, this pursuit of material interest involved demanding state protection against foreign competition, which while voicing old-established expectations of rulers, also set up new expectations that the ruler should act effectively against a qualitatively different threat or danger. By implication, and sometimes explicitly, they sought not just traditional favours from the state but substantive *change*.

Arguments that the state needed to change in character, rather than merely modify policy or reallocate favours among contending interests and factions, were expressed by well-established sections of Iranian society (merchants and officials), and by a new group of self-conscious 'reformers' and 'modern' intellectuals. It was this group that created, disseminated and campaigned for new approaches to the state and its role. They were impelled by the contrast they saw between the material prosperity, technical innovation, and cultural and political progress achieved in France, Russia or Ottoman Turkey and their absence in Iran, and their sense of Iranian vulnerability to actual or potential threats of foreign intervention. They associated these problems with the reform of the state, and thought that the transformation of state power was crucial to the advancement of 'progress', and to successful resistance to foreign involvement in Iran. Their thinking on these questions contributed to the development of new nationalist responses to the encounter of Iranians with European power, discussed in the next section. However, it is equally significant that they addressed the question of state power, and reconstituted older Iranian views of monarchy as charged with the protection and welfare of its subjects in new forms influenced by reformist thinking in Turkey and Egypt, and by European ideas and examples. They began to make innovative uses of the established concept of a *mellat*, conventionally used to designate a 'community' defined by religion (Christian or Zoroastrian as well as Shi'a or Sunni), by cultural features such as language or history (Ottomans) or both (Armenians, Kurds). In new usages influenced by nineteenth-century interests in representative and constitutional forms of government, the term *mellat* came to express ideas of a nation or citizenry.[28]

For some, notably those in government employment, the emphasis was on the creation of 'modern' efficient systems of administration, taxation and military organisation based on rational, controlling, consistent and centralising practice rather than personalised, arbitrary, decentralised and patronage-based forms of power. Others argued that the rule of law and the spread of 'modern' education and scientific knowledge were the key task of the state if the defence and prosperity of Iranians were to be assured, and their relationship to the state reformed. As attempts to work for reform within government, or to influence it from without, were tried and failed between the 1870s and 1890s, these explorations of new forms of state power took on the character of *challenges* to the existing regime and demands for some alternative. These included establishing the rule of law and consultative or deliberative institutions to check royal absolutism, calls to create a 'party of humanity' to promote change, and appeals to the *mellat* generally to transform itself and take up political responsibility and agency.

This represented the first attempt, albeit by a small atypical group, to put discussion about the relationship of state and people on to the political agenda, linking it to practical concerns about material prosperity, and introducing new ideas and examples into the existing repertoire of thought, policy and argument on these matters. Later generations of political activists and writers, not to mention historians, have tended to give undue attention to a group with whom they have found it easy to identify, but none the less their endeavours did have some impact. On the one hand, they reinforced trends towards making the state the source and means of modernisation and centralisation, which were to be pursued by democrats, autocratic rulers and governing elites through the twentieth century. On the other hand, they stimulated interest in new ways for people to influence and constrain the arbitrary unaccountable power of rulers, interests that were also taken up enthusiastically after 1900. More immediately, these initiatives fed the many-sided opposition to the Qajar regime evolving in the 1890s, and more forcible in the Constitutional Revolution of 1906–11, whose very name signals how, for some Iranians at least, political activism and transformation embraced the relations of state and people.

If new players and new interests in the politics of that relationship prefigured change, their influence gained greater potency by association with religiously based approaches to the state, the ruler and government. The Qajar regime had established itself on the basis both of direct patronage and bargaining with elite sections of the *'ulama*, and of more general use of religious themes and symbols in constructing or asserting its legitimacy.[29] The stability and credibility of the monarchy partly rested on such material and cultural relationships, but equally on the ability of monarchs to deal with the autonomous power of religious elites and institutions, grounded in their independent sources of finance, authority and patronage described earlier. Monarchs also dealt with religiously flavoured assumptions and expectations of Iranians in general when manoeuvring among the vested interests and communities whose consent or at least acquiescence sustained the regime.

These important religious factors enabling the Qajar state to maintain sufficient support or acquiescence were paralleled by the conduct and attitudes of religious specialists and believers toward the state, which varied as well as having some common themes. While some 'ulama combined acceptance of royal favours, jobs and patronage with general support (as members of the 'respectable' establishment) for government as guarantor of the law and order ordained by religious precept, others used those precepts to criticise the failures or exactions of an increasingly pressured government. 'Ulama also presented themselves in contemporary accounts as spokesmen and protectors of local or popular interests, with the autonomous status and responsibility to rebuke rulers for 'oppression' or 'injustice'. The image or practice of this role gave later generations of 'ulama useful credibility with client groups and can be contrasted with the way in which they were also seen as part of the 'establishment'.

Some historians see these divisions as expressing a horizontal 'class' divide between more and less wealthy, privileged or well-born 'ulama. Others associate them with specific intellectual, sectarian traditions which modified, dissented from, or even rejected, 'orthodox' Shi'ism and flourished in particular communities or networks within the rich patchwork of heterodox groups and traditions typical of nineteenth-century Iran. Others emphasise the context of competing personal, family and group rivalries in urban centres, or around court, capital city and government, which shaped individual choices of political outlook and changes of view.[30] This illustrates two points of more general importance: first, the religious thinking and activity of various individuals and groups in the political arena was shaped by material and cultural complexities; second, those with a religious outlook were able and willing to discuss the structure, functions and policies of the state.

While intellectual and cultural expressions of religious views of politics are considered in Chapter 5, religious influences on the state–people relationship as a political *issue* are the concern here. The key contributory elements were established religious expectations that (a) royal government would protect the Shi'a faith and *shari'a*; (b) government would care for justice and the well-being of its subjects; (c) it would hear and respond to the admonitions of the 'ulama with their recognised legitimate claims to 'command the good and forbid the evil', and hence pronounce on government success or failure. Both high- and low-ranking 'ulama made alliances with or demands on government over the political and spiritual challenge of the Babi movement in the mid-nineteenth century, and some led or joined opposition to royal concessions and failures in the face of foreign political, commercial and military intrusions. As Nasir al-din Shah's capacity to manage such interventions, and those who held them, more or less successfully gave way to a perceived decline in the monarch's ability to fulfil his proper functions, or his willingness to keep religious interests close to royal government, new approaches emerged. Traditional criticisms of the shah were supplemented by more specific concerns about how the state might be *altered* to remedy its defects, posing the question whether its existing form was adequate to its aims.

As the state's perceived inability to meet religious demands, expectations and vested interests raised questions about the need or desirability of changing its form, they shaped and were shaped by the divisions referred to earlier. Some of these were differences of opinion and judgement about the potential harm or benefit of reform for religious interests and institutions, and whether it was a threat to them in principle. Some expressed the ambitions and rivalries of particular individuals or groupings, with opposing parties taking up opposing positions. Senior *mujtaheds* faced choices between giving their authority to challenges to the shah (as in concession protests in 1872 and 1891), or standing by the regime. For lower-ranking *'ulama*, and believers generally, local loyalties and patronage networks and sectional beliefs and interests were important considerations. Among urban traders and producers in particular, grievances about the failure of government, as they saw it, to protect their interests from foreign competition had a religious and cultural as well as practical economic character.

During the 1890s, reformers with more secular approaches to the modernisation of government and the creation of a legal and constitutional framework for the monarchy recognised overlapping, if not identical, interests with the *'ulama* (as well as their material and cultural power) and advocated political alliances on that basis. So in a similar fashion did those seeking to strengthen the regime against its opponents. While the 'secular' element may have dominated this alliance as the constitutional crisis developed into the confrontation of 1906, as they also dominated new ideological developments, the presence and influence of a religious element cannot be ignored. For religious office holders, and *'ulama* protective of their status, the shah's attempts to stake independent claims as a patron and exemplar of piety through supporting *ta'zieh* and public devotion to 'Ali represented a challenge, as did attempts to modify the boundaries between royal and *shari'a* jurisdictions. Material concerns over competition, insecurity and European influence in the *bazar* economy, to which many *mullas* were connected, questioned the state's ability to meet its sacred task of protecting the welfare and faith of its subjects.

In the era of change, protest and uncertainty between the emergence of a 'constitutional' movement in 1905–06 and the consolidation of a new regime in the 1920s the personal rule of the Qajars, and the structures of government more generally, were openly and forcefully confronted, tested and ultimately replaced. Leaving analysis of the movements for separate discussion, it should be noted here that the issue of who controlled the state and how its power was to be expressed and organised became an immediate preoccupation. Political demands evolved from arguments for 'consultation', the 'rule of law', or a 'house of justice' in the 1890s to successful proposals for constitutional monarchy with a representative body embodied in the grant of the Fundamental Law and calling of a national assembly (the Majlis) in 1906–07. This was followed by nationwide elections, the formation of active political organisations in Tehran and other cities, and the enactment, though not enforcement, of reform in taxation and state land grants (*tuyul*), all of which placed government on a new footing for communities, classes and vested interests across Iran. This loosening of the tradition of royal government (including abdications in 1909 and 1925 and a change of dynasty in 1925) contrasted with the continuing power of landlords, *'ulama*, merchants and the bureaucratic and tribal elites, grounded in established networks and power bases, and also the new Majlis. These developments fostered conscious and widespread concern over what tasks or initiatives should be undertaken by central government and its relationship with the old intermediary powers and with the subject populace.

In the years after 1906, the telegraph, the press and the politics of *anjumans* (local councils or political associations) disseminated information, rumour and debate, and stimulated action by those who saw opportunities to make new demands on government. Peasants, carpet weavers, urban street gangs and other unprivileged groups took action in pursuit of interests or rights which they could now associate with the reforming and constitutional character of government, drawing on publicity and support from political activists and writers with their own agendas.[31] This period marks the entry of different issues on to the existing terrain of *doulat–mellat* relations.

As will be shown in Chapter 6, the coalition that achieved the changes of 1906–07 and staved off the counter-attack of the shah and his supporters in 1908–09 broke up as its members pursued divergent aims and conflicting vested interests. One area of dissension was precisely over the shape and responsibility of the state itself. Those who wished the state to act as defender of order, property and social hierarchy clashed with those who envisaged it as a representative and defender of collective 'national' or 'popular' interests, and of the unprivileged. Another important area of conflict was over the established position of religious law, and its specialist exponents under the new constitution, and even over whether representative government and democracy were compatible

134

with Islam. This was a matter not just of a confrontation between 'secular' and 'religious' views and interests, but of a *range* of initiatives and responses to the challenge of reframing religious institutions or values or *'ulama* in a changing political and constitutional environment. The manoeuvrings of leading *mujtaheds* around the Majlis, court and government in Tehran, the clashes over how far Shi'ism and Shi'ites should be privileged in the Constitution, the emergence of pro- and anti-clerical protests and *anjumans*, and the rivalries of religious political leaders and their followers were all part of this process.

The historic options of the *'ulama* had been to be clients of the state, to use their autonomous power and influence to shape its conduct, and to disregard it and rely on autonomous sources of status, wealth and authority in the community to meet their political needs or aspirations. In the 'constitutional' period, they confronted possibilities that a reformed state would not be a patron, might not respond to their pressure, and might even challenge their independent power and resources. They also had opportunities to argue for the inclusion of their interests and those of religious Iranians more generally in the framework of the state and to influence political decisions and debates. While members of the *'ulama* could and did deploy traditional political resources, they also made new responses to changing circumstances, forming new alliances and engaging in new debates, and deploying new methods of communication and propaganda in pursuit of their aims. The leading defender of established religious interests against constitutionalist reformers, Shaikh Fazlullah Nuri, was willing to use the 'modern' means of pamphleteering as well as traditional factional manoeuvres and loyalties.[32] Whether through conviction or opportunism, or both, *mullas* found themselves addressing familiar questions of relations between religion and the state on a new basis, balancing innovation against the maintenance of tradition.

By the outbreak of the First World War, idealistic projects for transforming the state were blocked by the dissensions within the coalition which had launched them, by the ability of established elites to resist and to adapt to political change, and by powerful opposition from Russia and Britain which had their own agendas in Iran. Equally importantly, the opening of gaps between an emergent 'political nation' (both 'new' and 'old') and the Iranian populace at large once more separated the concerns of *doulat* and *mellat*. This can be attributed to the overtly 'secular' emphasis of that 'political nation' and its focus on central government which seemed irrelevant, even inimical, to the concerns of peasants, *bazaris*, and the urban poor, or to the unwillingness or inability of advocates of democracy and justice to address and respect the interests of the unprivileged.

The creation of a new type of monarchical state (and new dynasty) in the 1920s was the product of all these tendencies. Reza Khan (Reza Shah from 1925) was a recognisable 'man on horseback', using his position as a 'modern' military commander, and manipulating political forces in Tehran and great power interests to serve his forceful personal ambition and seize control of government. His success in consolidating that control and establishing a lasting autocracy also built on the hopes of the 'political nation' for strong modernising government and Iranian self-assertion against foreign interests, and took advantage of the vacuum in 'national' politics created by factionalism. His increasingly dictatorial regime used military force and repressive measures but also gained acceptance, and sometimes support, by addressing the fears and aspirations of many important groups. The imposition of law and order and established property rights satisfied the possessing classes, while the vigorous pursuit of 'modernisation' of law, education and administration pleased reformers, as did the use of assertive nationalistic rhetoric and imagery combined with a centralising of government power.

This centralising modernising autocracy produced a new relationship between state and people. Whereas the Qajar regime had maintained legitimate authority by accommodating and managing various autonomous centres of power, the new Pahlavi regime cut down and neutralised them. Independent regional and tribal forces were crushed militarily, traditional magnates politically sidelined (though their material interests were protected), rival politicians and organisations manipulated and removed by death, imprisonment and suppression. When Reza Shah co-opted allies and assistance from among the old elites and the more recent generation of reforming politicians, he controlled and disposed of them at will. His modernising initiatives, however partial in their actual effect, were driven by his will and authority and forced on the subject populace not through independent intermediaries or by winning consent, but through whatever coercive and bureaucratic power he could mobilise. It is significant that two of the 'modern' institutions that developed most rapidly during Reza Shah's rule were a more up-to-date army and a reorganised bureaucracy reaching out from the centre of government into the provinces and centres of settlement via improved and extended road and communications systems. Whether through more effectively exacted taxation, state regulation of dress, the forcible settlement of nomads or the state takeover of the *'ulama*'s traditional roles in law and education, *doulat* now had a direct and interventionist impact on its subjects, with or without their consent.

While there is debate over the real and lasting impact of Reza Shah's dictatorial and interventionist regime on communities in Iran, especially in comparison with that of his son, there is general agreement about its secularising character. One main effect of Reza Shah's transformation of government was to reduce the *'ulama*'s role and power as shown earlier. In this climate, *'ulama* were more likely to withdraw from politics than look for favours or patronage, although on occasion they also opposed the regime. It is significant that protests over the 1935 decree on men's headgear and women's unveiling combined specifically religious condemnation by *mullas* with expressions of more general popular dissent, drawing on the historic tradition whereby Iranians expressed their grievances through *'ulama* who claimed their role as spokespersons on communal issues. In the 1930s, the assault on dress regulation was combined with resentment at high prices, tax burdens and state control of trade in key foodstuffs. It suggested that despite the advance of secularisation there were still religious aspects to the relationship between state and people, and political consequences for the state's indifference to the religious views and interests of its subjects.

The longer-term effects of state secularisation policies were somewhat complex. Although reformers might welcome such policies as 'progress', the question of how far Shi'ism was a constituent element of state and nation remained unresolved, as was clear from its resurgence following Reza Shah's departure in 1941. His dictatorship and its confrontational approach did not so much eliminate the 'religious' factor in the equations of people, government and politics as add a new dimension and reinforce old contradictions. The intensified enmity of 'state' and 'religion' might encourage political quietism among the pious, but also reinforced the contribution and relevance of religion to political opposition. Similarly, the modernising policies of Reza Shah's government attracted support from reformers, while its repressive, corrupt and dictatorial character aroused their hostility, or forced them into political quietism. Reza Shah's dictatorship superimposed itself upon the new politics of state and people rather than eliminating them, and its modernising and centralising achievements increased the separation of this 'new' politics from many of the Iranian people to whom the regime and its critics so often referred and whom they sought to influence. Its legacy to disillusioned reformers, *'ulama* and many ordinary Iranians, was the unmet challenge of making positive relationships between state and people.

The period from Reza Shah's removal in 1941 to his son's emergence as an autocratic ruler in 1953 saw the working out of this legacy. Paradoxically, foreign intervention and occupation between 1941 and 1946 created conditions for more open politics with the end of repressive restrictions and the appearance of a freer press, Majlis elections, and opportunities to organise, debate and campaign politically. For some Iranians at least, this was an opportunity to address issues submerged during Reza Shah's reign, notably constitutional questions about Shah, Majlis and government, and their concern for popular material needs, and foreign threats to national and religious interests. The politics of these questions played out through changing links between the class of educated and committed activists (a political intelligentsia) and wider constituencies, and through differences between urban residents with new kinds of 'modern' education and employment, and rural settlements. We should also note forms of modern class politics with the organisation and activity of trades' unions of oil workers and urban wage workers combining employment grievances with political demands on the state, and demands on the state from regional and ethnic groups.[33]

Although these varied forms of politics emphasised oil politics, foreign intervention and social grievances, each issue also raised key questions about the relations of state and people. As seen below, 'national' confrontation with foreign military occupation, foreign economic interests and foreign political interference, took centre-stage for many Iranians in this period. Historic indigenous views of government as guardian of the 'protected domains' and newer identifications of the state as representative of the 'nation'/'people' placed these matters squarely among the state's responsibilities, and among popular expectations of the state. Demands and campaigns over democracy, threats to religion, and constitutionalism were strengthened and flavoured by nationalistic considerations, discussed below.

It was the ownership and control of oil in Iran which was now seen as the most central and prominent of the 'national' issues that the state was expected to resolve. British ownership and exploitation of the major oilfields in Iran had been the object of government concern since the 1920s, supplemented by the emergence of American and Soviet interest in concessions for further oil exploration and exploitation in the 1940s. Success in negotiations over payments, control and eventually nationalisation of the British company, as well as in rebutting other demands, became a test of the patriotism and effectiveness of the governments that followed Reza Shah. The achievement of greater Majlis influence over oil negotiations, the manipulation of Majlis, court and foreign interests by ministers eager to sustain their position by success in these endeavours, the power of urban crowds and oilfield workers to make oil issues the centre of their pressure on governments were all elements in this process. Above all they underpinned the emergence of a coalition of politicians with popular backing, taking the name National Front, and linking the prime political objective of gaining control of the oil industry to constitutional reform and the containment of royal and elite power in government and society. The mythic power of the memory (both negative and positive) of Muhammad Mussadeq, the National Front leader, has drawn strength precisely from his linking of the oil nationalisation issue to confrontation with royal power and state corruption, and advocacy of constitutional democratic bonds between *doulat* and *mellat*.

Mussadeq's appeal to the people/nation both as a practical source of mass political support on the streets and as a key theme and symbol in his political language touched on the social as well as national interests which brought Iranians into politics and shaped their demands on the state. The disruptions and hardships of occupation and inflation in the 1940s, added to social changes among new groups of workers in oilfields, towns and white-collar jobs since the 1920s, gave new force and shape to their historic demands for social justice and material support from their rulers. There was also increased use of modern political languages challenging oppression and poverty in liberal or leftist terms, especially by those growing groups of urban Iranians able and willing to use literacy and modern education in their politics. The revival of Majlis, street and party politics and debate provided opportunities for the needs of 'the masses', or 'workers' or 'exploited people' to figure among the concerns of political activists alongside concerns with reform, nationalism and the constitutional conflicts of Shah, government and Majlis.

Political contests over royal autocracy and representative government entwined with the opposition between defenders of social order and material privilege and various populist, liberal, religious and leftist critics and with conflicts over how the Iranian state should deal with foreign intervention. In 1942, protest over food prices and inflation influenced the attempts of the government of Ahmad Qavam to control both the Shah and the British. In 1944, strikes and riots in Isfahan produced sharp realignments in regional and national politics as magnates and political parties confronted challenges to social order. In 1946, the twists and turns of another government led by Qavam embraced manipulation of trade union politics and tribal and ethnic conflicts in attempts to contain the power of the Shah, Great Britain and the Soviet Union. Above all, in the period from the establishment of the National Front in 1949 to its overthrow in 1953, popular grievances and hopes for material prosperity and social justice influenced the street and parliamentary politics of oil nationalisation and constitutional government.

Questions of social justice and class difference divided 'progressives' from 'reactionaries' or religious believers from those with secular views, and stimulated different approaches to the state by different religious Iranians. Each group linked their loyalties and actions to nationalistic and constitutional demands in the name of Iran and/or Islam. Members of the *'ulama* were involved in crucial decisions about direct participation in politics, acceptable alliances, and what issues to pursue with Shah and government outside their own interests and rivalries. As in the 'constitutional' era, they had to consider the dangers and opportunities involved in joining their interests to those of others; as in Reza Shah's time they faced choices between confrontation or compromise with government power and its secularist policies. Although secularisation, and the withdrawal of senior *'ulama* from direct political activism, are understandably emphasised by historians of this period, other trends are also worth noting.

The career of Ayatollah Kashani (Sayyid Abu'l Qasim Kashani) illustrates another significant aspect of 'religion-in-politics'. Kashani's ability to mobilise a popular following, to play a role alongside secular groupings in the National Front, and to criticise governments, Majlis and even the Shah in the name of patriotic, anti-western Islam certainly differentiated him from 'non-activist' *'ulama*. It also represented an attractive variant of religious politics/political religion which on occasion gained tactical or explicit backing from that leadership, whether from a sense of *'ulama* solidarity, or sympathy for his forceful combination of nationalism and anti-communism in populist religious politics.[34]

The issue of gender roles and women's rights was a familiar political marker for the activist Kashani, and quietist *'ulama* leaders in the 1940s and 1950s, as it had been in the reign of Reza Shah and again after 1953. It was a topic which delimited boundaries between religious and secular views of modernity, and the proper sphere or limit of state intervention, and was the focus of contests between *mellat* and *doulat* over that limit and over democratic constraints on government. Reza Shah's legislative and administrative attempts to impose the 'unveiling' of women met with both *'ulama* and popular resistance in the 1930s, and posed dilemmas for modernist reformers who saw the policy as 'enlightened', but disliked its autocratic implementation. The end of his rule enabled official toleration of re-emergent veiling and allowed the whole question of women's public status and political rights to become an item in the manoeuvres of male political groups and government ministers. Prime Ministers placated religious opinion by formalising the acceptance of veiling (Soheili in 1943), or 'progressive' views by proposing voting rights for women (Qavam in 1946). Communists and women's organisations pushed women's suffrage on to the Majlis agenda, as in 1944, just as religious and 'traditional' elements in the National Front coalition forced abandonment of the issue in 1949 and 1952–53. Trafficking over these issues indicates that they were considered expendable and negotiable in pursuit of more important aims, and that they mattered enough to figure in political bargaining. It is also significant that women's rights issues concerned the public and governmental spheres of legislation and police regulation. The reappearance of those concerns in confrontations between religious interests and royal autocracy in the 1960s suggests that for the political nation at least they carried continuing significance.

The re-established royal autocracy which emerged from the overthrow of Mussadeq's government in 1953 established full political control over the following decade. Building military and foreign support from the late 1940s, Reza Shah's son Muhammad Reza Pahlavi reinstated a regime which placated or manipulated particular groups but crushed independent political life and opposition whether tribal, religious, leftist or just critical, using the army, secret police and bans on political organisation and discussion as appropriate. Like his father he pursued authoritarian modernising and centralising policies, albeit in different forms and circumstances. Once again the relationship between *doulat* and *mellat* was characterised by the separation of state and political nation and forceful government intervention in the lives of its subjects. To an extent unknown before the 1960s, the state remodelled the economic and social experience of Iranians, as described in earlier chapters. This had several consequences for relationships between Iranians and the state, opening opportunities for some, while for others its bureaucratic or repressive interference, corruption and misjudged initiatives suppressed or frustrated their aspirations. The visible and widespread presence of government, initiating and manipulating socio-economic change, made it the obvious target for distrust, criticism and avoidance by subjects lacking access to its favours but unable to avoid its interference and mistakes.

Two other factors were perhaps even more significant. Reduction in infant mortality from the 1960s dramatically shifted the age balance of the population, so that by the 1970s half the population was under sixteen and two-thirds under thirty, creating a generation of subjects without direct experience of the political traditions of earlier generations. The cumulative effects of land reform, the decline of nomadism, and the growth of migrant labour and long-term migration, as well as the regime's expansion of its own administrative systems, reduced or removed many of the old networks of localised patronage and authority which had survived Reza Shah's rule. The mesh of intermediary powers which had both oppressed and buffered unprivileged communities were deprived of political expression, as were parties, unions, professional bodies, or interest- and issue-based organisations. So long as global circumstances, government policies and local conditions offered opportunities for at least some Iranians, they passively endured or actively avoided and manipulated *doulat*'s intrusions, rather than questioning them. When the situation altered in the 1970s there would be greater willingness to respond to, if not to initiate such critical questioning, not least because government policies and favouring of foreign interests and a few close supporters were such obvious targets.

Whereas in the past the political rhetoric of government failure did not match the lived experience of many Iranians, by the late 1970s rhetoric and experience were more closely connected. The historic power of this rhetoric of *doulat*'s failure in obligation and responsibility towards the *mellat* gained new resonance in a period when more Iranians experienced changes and disruptions in which the government could be directly implicated. The direct experience of rural communities, buffeted by the failures of state agricultural policy, like that of *bazaris* and urban wage workers confronting competition, deprivation and inequality as well as government repression, encouraged oppositional politics. Moreover, the opposition politics of 1977–79 spread more widely across classes and communities than the popular politics of 1941–53 or the brief revival of 1963.

Historians differ on whether to emphasise the specific mistakes of the Shah's regime and their disruptive consequences between 1977 and 1979, or the influence of long-standing hostilities to that regime as illegitimate, repressive and unconcerned with welfare or social justice. In any case, the growth of opposition to the Shah shifted from sectional grievances to promotion of programmes and slogans, raising once again the issue of the transformation of state power. From advocacy of human rights to demands for a constitutional monarchy or an Islamic republic, opponents of the regime sought not only particular concessions, but the construction of constraints on, or alternatives to, the Pahlavi autocracy. Since the state had taken a more interventionist and unconstrained role in the material lives and the political management of Iranians, it now faced greater expectations and criticism from a broad range of its subjects. Religious, leftist and liberal opposition references to the constitutionalist politics of 1905–11 or the Mussadeq period indicated how the 'crisis' of 1977–79 had become a frontal encounter of *mellat* and *doulat*, coloured by the myth/ 'memory' of those earlier encounters.

The establishment of an Islamic republic was the outcome so manifestly different from either that of the 1906 Constitution or the rule of the two Pahlavi shahs. Equally striking, if less emphasised, is the fact that this achievement, the dominance of religious elements within it, and the role of Ayatollah Khomeini as focus of both resistance and outcome, involved a *range* of political groupings and interests. In 1979–81 religious populists allied with the revived National Front and other anti-Shah groups of leftist or liberal persuasions to establish a regime in which eventually all but one Islamist strand of politics were rejected or subordinated, and in which *'ulama* took on the actual direction of government. The caution which many *'ulama* had exercised with respect to politics in earlier periods, whether from opportunism or quietist beliefs, clearly differed from their prominence in the developments of 1977–81. Their contribution, and the broader backing for their role, and in particular for the placing of *doulat* under the 'guidance' or guardianship of a religious jurist (the *velayat i-faqih*), in the person of Khomeini, placed government on a new basis, embedding a new variant of religious influence and authority at its centre. It recast earlier formulations of religious legitimation, using populist support and modern strategies for ideological and organisational dominance in a one-party (rather than twin-pillared) state in very modern postcolonial style, including appeals to cultural nationalism and economic autarchy.

This recasting of *doulat* and its relationship to the Iranian *mellat*, now ideologised as *mustaz'afin* (the deprived/oppressed), had both negative and positive origins. In practical terms, the Shah's success in fragmenting, repressing or placating many leftist, patriotic and reformist opponents, whether politicians, labour organisations or students and intellectuals, left religious specialists and institutions among the few surviving focuses for oppositional activity. Compared to the exiled and underground clusters of activists who tried to sustain radical politics, mosques, *'ulama* and centres of religious study had secure, if contested, spaces for such activity. In political terms, the Shah's disempowerment of religious specialists, their institutions, and their influence posed greater challenges than ever before to policies of quietism or opportunistic manipulation by *'ulama* and their supporters, although these remained preferred options for many before the late 1970s. In ideological terms, both *'ulama* and Shi'a believers proved able not just to survive but to revive during the 1960s and 1970s, and in particular to offer newly effective contributions to debates on *doulat–mellat* relations.

There were three main strands of religious discourse on this issue, whose intellectual and ideological specificities are discussed in Chapter 5. Here it is significant that, in addition to their piety, patriotism and oppositional fervour, they all made ideals of the *mellat* central, and offered visions of a *doulat* fit for the people's needs. They gave renewed creativity and relevance to specifically religious critiques of the state. The fluid and overlapping character of these discourses, and the generality of their language and aims, facilitated practical collaboration among varied and potentially hostile groups within anti-Shah politics, ranging from religious students and *bazaris* to university graduates, wage workers and pious professionals and intellectuals. Interestingly, use of the term 'oppressed'/*mustaz'afin* to designate the 'people' in whose name activists argued and struggled migrated from a 1960s translation of Franz Fanon's *Wretched of the Earth* by 'Ali Shari'ati into the language of Muslim leftists by the early 1970s and into Khomeinist propaganda during that decade.

The establishment of an Islamic Republic dominated by a form of Muslim populism, different from the radical laicised version envisaged by Shari'ati's followers or the liberal version supported by those of Bazargan, was underpinned by ideological factors, as well as the astute political moves of its protagonists. Among those factors was an appealing, because vague yet relevant, vision of a *doulat* which was counterposed to the *taghut* (godless tyranny) of the Shah. As a vehicle for moral regeneration, for national cultural authenticity, and for a new bargain between the state and different social groups, the notion of an Islamic Republic offered a variant of the *mellat–doulat* relationship able to appeal to significant numbers of Iranians. Its proponents addressed the conflict of *mellat* and *doulat* in a form which was, momentarily, more attractive than alternatives, while also organising ruthlessly against those alternatives. It seemed to meet aspirations for a form of government expressing popular needs and values, and breaking with past regimes' corruption and elitism. Such aspirations were rooted in recent experience, but also in longer stories of Iranian relations with their rulers over the preceding century, and their responses to that history in innovative religious as well as reforming, nationalist or revolutionary terms.

A story of nation and nationalism: the politics of identity, solidarity and difference

> There is no such thing as a people ... it is wholly artificial and made, like all other legal fictions, by common agreement. (Edmund Burke)

'Iran' and the 'Iranian nation' have been major issues for political action and debate among Iranians in modern times. Previously shaped by dynastic, communal, familial, occupational and local attachments and concerns, the period 1870–1980 saw the politics of nation and nationalism develop first among an intellectual and reforming minority and then among other sections of the population. This account tracks that development and the diversification of nation-centred politics, looking at its 'modernity', comparing it with nationalistic traditions elsewhere, and considering its religious aspects. The 'national' question was a contested, complex and unstable issue, cross-cut by other influences which converged and conflicted with it, shifting its content and purposes over time as circumstances and interest groups shaped and reshaped its form.

For those Iranians whose encounters with modernity in the later nineteenth century led them to advocate 'national' themes and aims in politics, there were older resources to draw on alongside contemporary experiences, influences and circumstances. Records and remembrances of periods of dynastic rule, controlling various regions of 'Iran' and their resources, sustained some notion of an 'Iran' which was more than the sum of its regions. The appeal and credibility of successful monarchical regimes (itself a strong influence) could be associated with the protection and management of 'Iran' and victorious warfare against 'outsiders' (Ottoman, Afghan, Russian, Turcoman) in written histories and oral traditions. General, if far from universal, use of the Persian language maintained shared literate and oral traditions of poetry, legend and folklore which crossed social and geographical distances and contributed to ideas of *iraniyyat* ('Iranianness'). The commitment of rulers since the sixteenth century to sponsoring Shi'a Islam, and their use of Shi'a rhetoric and propaganda, established associations between state, Shi'ism and collective 'Iranian' identity. By the nineteenth century, differentiation of Sunni Arabs, Turks and Afghans from Shi'a Iranians had political as well as religious meanings.[35]

However, too much should not be made of such influences. For most Iranians, the legacies and practicalities of communal organisation and activity, shared religious practice and of hierarchical distinctions, conflicts and patronage networks, as well as linguistic and cultural diversity, were more significant bases for political commitment. They constituted the political reality of many nineteenth-century Iranians, and the starting point for examining the transformations which added a 'national' dimension to political life in Iran.

A number of influences encouraged the use of new concepts of 'the nation' as an object of political concern. Iranians' encounters with new ideas, facilitated by travel and print culture, regime attempts to defend itself through reform, foreign pressures and challenges to Shi'a thought, played a role in changing notions of *iraniyyat*. During the nineteenth century, 'nation' and nationalism became political themes attracting the creative energy of statesmen, intellectuals, political activists and government officials in Europe, the Americas and parts of Asia. The core constituents of nationalist politics – the making of territorial, constitutional and institutional demands on the state by asserting the political needs of those claiming common identity and interests on the basis of shared laws, language, customs, history or religion – emerged earlier in western Europe and North America. During the nineteenth century, they were adapted and adopted in Latin America, eastern and south-eastern Europe, India and the Ottoman Empire. Demands for 'independence' and self-government in the name of a 'people' or 'nation' used models of political assertion against the unjustified power of rulers and old elites, and ideas of 'nation' created through accounts of the history and culture of particular 'peoples'. This gained particular force when nationalists challenged the power of 'outsiders' over 'their people', defining a politics of 'national' solidarity and resistance to an 'alien' dominating Other. With the expansion of European dominance beyond Europe, that challenge politicised economic competition between non-European and European entrepreneurs, the insecurities of rulers and elites, the grievances of the poor, and the aspirations of indigenous professionals and intellectuals. The interpretation of such experiences as political and oppositional to 'foreigners' redefined custom, language, history or religion, in 'national' terms.

The growth of nationalist projects in Iran was led by Iranians who encountered such projects outside Iran in the course of work, travel or study. Most important were the Ottoman and Tsarist Empires, especially the Caucasian and Azeri areas of the latter, with their established Shi'a, Persian and Azeri-speaking communities, and Istanbul and the Russian centres (Petersburg, Tiflis, Moscow) where Iranians engaged in trade and diplomacy. In both Tsarist and Ottoman Empires there were nationalist movements, ideas and programmes to interest Iranian visitors or residents. Government action to modernise state power in the interests of ruling dynasties and elites justified such policies in new, quasi-nationalist terms. Critics and reformers wishing to change or challenge state power also appealed to the need to defend indigenous interests against 'foreign' intervention, or to claims of 'national' groups and their rights against Ottoman or Tsarist rule. Both official and oppositional approaches to state reform combined modern and secular views of rational, effective and improving government exemplified in Europe, with strong cultural and religious reactions *against* European influence and criticisms. The defence or assertion of Islam was associated with projects to renew, reform or strengthen political and social institutions the better to resist external intervention, modernise government or establish new states.

In the Caucasus and Istanbul, Iranians encountered new movements of reform or revolution (Ottomanist, Russian, Muslim, social democrat) and 'ethnic' assertion (Turkish, Arab, Armenian, Azeri). Political debate and writing among those groups, and among Iranians outside Iran, stimulated Iranian concerns with 'nationalist' issues, as did French, British or German contacts in Istanbul, Petersburg, Tiflis or Trabzond as well as London, Paris or Berlin. It is not surprising that early expressions of nationalistic ideas and programmes by Iranians tended to come from those like Husein Khan Mushir ad-Douleh, Iranian ambassador in Istanbul 1858–69, reforming minister in Iran 1870–80, who commented enthusiastically on the *tanzimat* (Ottoman government reform programme) of the 1860s and introduced notions of *vatan* (nation/fatherland) and *vatan-parasti* (patriotism) into his arguments for reform in Iran.[36] Persian-writing intellectuals of Iranian origin like Fath 'Ali Akhundzadeh (1812–78) or 'Abd al-Rahim Talibzadeh/Talibof (1834–1911) living in the Caucasus used personal experiences and foreign texts in political and satirical writing designed to 'awaken' Iranians to their country's problems and needs. Polemicists and campaigners like Mirza Malkom Khan (1833–1908), Jamal al-Din Asadabadi known as 'Afghani' (1838/9–97) or Mirza Aqa Kermani (1853–96) undertook political writing and activity from Cairo and Istanbul to Paris and London.[37]

Many of these publicists and reformers put considerable political and intellectual effort into influencing Iranian government policy. Their identification of the nation and its interests with strong government and modernisation, and of government with national protection and prosperity, flowed from encounters with nationalist thinking in the Middle East and Europe, and perceptions of pressures on the government of Iran. In the later nineteenth century, the need of dynastic rulers in Iran to work to sustain somewhat conditional authority over the powerful vested interests around them, at court, in the regions of Iran, or beyond its borders, was affected by new demands. The presence of expansionist imperial powers (Russia and Britain) with direct strategic interests in Iran, and economic and cultural challenges described earlier, became issues for government and its subjects. The response of government was one of resistance and deflection, but the need to deal with new pressures and challenges, whether military–diplomatic confrontation from assertive foreign powers, or subjects using the modern media to exert influence, had its own effects.

Both dynasty and central government became the focus of hope and criticism among those seeking to transform the nation by transforming the state. The politics of reform was entwined with career and faction politics in government circles and with the association of state and nation, which reformers put on the political agenda. Established views of the monarch as champion of the 'protected domains' changed as the Shah manoeuvred British and Russian diplomats and concession hunters and confronted the administrative, military and financial weaknesses of his regime in the face of their pressure. As demands for educational and legal reform, economic development or new administrative systems began to be couched in terms of benefit to 'the nation', the government too deployed that language. The Shah's decree creating a consultative council in 1881 claimed it would help to 'bring to light and realise whatever the government intends and has in mind for the progress of the kingdom and nation', echoing references in earlier proclamations.[38] Rebuffing the reforming polemic of Malkom Khan, the Shah's powerful son Zill al-Sultan contrasted interest in 'honour and patriotism' with personal interests.[39] While far from espousing the nationalism of the reforming intelligentsia, the Shah and his officials reflected and resisted that frame of reference. Tentative attempts at reform, and use of the language of *mellat* as well as the monarchical language of *doulat*, maintained the possibility that the government might transform the nation. Lack of continuing commitment to reform exposed it to growing challenge and sharper nationalist critiques by reformers attacking its corruption and betrayal of the *mellat*.

In their different ways, reformers and government increasingly focused on the challenge of European power and intervention. For government this was a matter of calculation and improvisation in dealings with European diplomats or concession seekers, interwoven with rivalries within the Qajar court and bureaucracy. For reformers the pressures of European interests on Iranian merchants and the state provoked resistance to and criticism of Europeans and discussion of how to replicate their achievements.[40] They developed political images of 'Iranians' as an identifiable community facing common problems and external enemies, comparing European achievements and predatory intentions with Iranian vulnerability and unwillingness to reform, and issuing clarion calls for Iranians to equip themselves to change. The influx of western commodities, European attempts to manipulate central and local politics, Iranian lack of interest in how to resist them and advance their own interests, were their key themes. While their arguments were most directly relevant to the educated, commercial, politically interested urban classes, they spoke of a larger 'national community'. As hopes and projects for reform foundered on lack of interest, rivalries and opposition in royal and government circles, some reforming nationalists shifted into an oppositional mode.

Turning to confrontational and propagandistic activity to support their aims and ideas, some advocates of reform focused on concepts of the nation with religious elements. These already featured in the thinking of patriotic reformers, whether Afghani's lifelong interest in renewing Muslim thought, government and culture as part of resistance to European power, or Mustashar al-Douleh's work *One Word/Yek Kalameh* (subtitled *Spirit of Islam/Ruh-i-Islam*) arguing the convergence of Islamic tradition and principle and the proper rule of law (the 'one word' of the title). By the 1890s, reformers were making links between Iranians' 'national' identity and interests and their Muslim/Shi'a loyalties, and between national revival and the well-being of Islam in Iran. Whether from the opportunistic desire to build alliances with *'ulama* and pious Iranians who opposed foreign infidel influences, or to emphasise their own Muslim cultural attachments, they now linked nationalist and reforming politics to religious concerns.[41]

The 'imagined community' of Iranians which featured in the writings and politics of critics and reformers found active expression in the 'Tobacco Protest' of 1890–91. Opposition to the Shah's grant to Europeans of the right to exploit Iranian tobacco production mobilised the material interests of producers, merchants and consumers, the political hostility of 'patriots' to foreign influence and the venality of the ruler who allowed it, and religious authority and popular feeling against an 'ungodly' concession. It was a moment of 'national' politics in that protests, riots and demonstrations took place in many places in Iran, linked by postal or telegraph communication, and in the sense that some participants saw it as a movement of the nation/people (*mellat*). It saw the first 'national' alliances between a politicised intelligentsia, religious specialists and grassroots protest, moved by specific material grievances and cultural and political concerns.[42] The ability of reform-minded critics to work with the defensive politics of *'ulama*, and popular opposition to the tobacco concession, is evidence of a convergence of specific interests, and of a new potential for 'national' politics.

The influence of religious elements in the politics of 'nation' and 'Iranian' identity had several sources. The distinctive and dominant role of Shi'a Islam in Iran created institutional, ideological and popular associations between state and *'ulama* support for Shi'ism, and the political identities of shah, *'ulama*, and communities as Shi'a. In the nineteenth century, religious identity and its political influence jostled with those shaped by hierarchy and community, but acquired new meanings as Iranians faced the growing visibility and influence of Europeans. Hostility to European commercial competition, and reactions to European visitors, missionary initiatives and political influence, all contributed to their responses. While some Iranians saw 'modern' European practices or ideas as resources which Iranians could appropriate for their own 'national' objectives, for many they seemed irrelevant, or threatening. They clashed with popular and *'ulama* commitment to religious world-views and practices. Some '*ulama* saw threats to the stability of government and the socio-cultural order in which they were key players and beneficiaries. Others had broader anxieties based on encounters with Europeans and on rumours and stories about them. The hostile or uncomprehending stance of Europeans towards Iranian beliefs and practices, and the real or imagined threats to decency, orthodoxy and cultural integrity which many Iranians saw in foreign alternatives caused suspicion and antagonism.

A strong, if ambivalent, relationship emerged between 'Islam in danger' and 'Iran in danger' in which ideas of religious and 'national' solidarity entwined. For leading activists in the Tobacco Protest and the 1905 Constitutional Movement, this was expressed in tactical decisions to gain support for their causes by linking them to the influence and status of religious values and their professional custodians, the '*ulama*. This calculated initiative was set in the context of material and cultural confrontation, where migrant workers, bureaucrats, merchants and intellectuals grappled with dislocations and alternatives to established patterns of life, work and thought. A widespread sense of shared ownership of a religiously flavoured culture, based in specific communities but common to many, shaped appeals to the classic combination of cultural/historical solidarity and resistance to 'alien' influences so characteristic of many nationalisms.

Similar developments in areas of the Middle East, India and Central Asia familiar to Iranian merchants, intellectuals, pilgrims or migrant workers are directly relevant to this story. Reforming politics in Istanbul, anti-imperial nationalisms in Bombay, Cairo and Alexandria, modernising and ethnic politics among Azeris, Armenians or Central Asians under tsarist or Ottoman rule, were noted by such Iranians. When dissident ideas and their propagators fell foul of the Iranian authorities, Iranian political thinkers and activists found themselves living and working outside Iran in contact with like-minded residents in the places where they were active. Famously, the Iranian activist Jamal al-Din Asadabadi (known as 'al Afghani') operated, like other Iranian activists and propagandists, in Cairo, Istanbul and Paris as well as in Afghanistan, India and Iran.

In the 1880s and 1890s, radical thinkers like those producing the newspaper *Akhtar*, the elite dissident intellectual Shaikh al-Rais, and other pan-Islamists and religio-political dissidents made use of opportunities to be found in Istanbul, with its 20,000 or so Iranian expatriates, and the currents of political reform, cross-cultural confrontation and nationalism there.[43] In the Caucasus, Iranian reformers and nationalists wrote, debated and joined organisations whose political ideas and energies entered the Iranian constitutional movement bringing in the thinking and activities emerging in that area. In Baku, Tiflis or Erevan, Russians, Azeris, Armenians, Georgians and Central Asians as well as Iranians formed diverse groups and movements – social democratic, Pan-Islamic, ethnic

149

nationalist, patriotic reformist. Ideas of patriotism, of historically and culturally based common identities, and of links between 'progress', 'national' autonomy and resistance to foreign intervention, were developed and carried to areas under Ottoman or Qajar rule.[44]

This patriotic mélange used varied but overlapping cultural material and metaphors. The notion of the physical territory of Iran (*Iran-zamin*/soil of Iran), sustained by references to stories of pre-Islamic and Safavid empires, flavoured a political rhetoric of ancient identity ('natural'/age-old boundaries and territories of 'Iran') and current vulnerability (recent foreign attacks on or conquests of the 'ancestral' domains). This was linked to critiques of rulers' failures to defend the 'protected domains' or nurture their material prosperity.[45] This *physical* construction of 'Iran' shifted into *physiological* images of Iran as a 'body' wounded and bleeding from the attacks of enemies, or an erotic and familial body of a mother/beloved to be desired, protected and objectified.[46] Old traditions and mythologies combined with newly acquired archaeological, descriptive and historical material in narratives of cultural identity and continuity based on ideas of an 'Iranian' civilisation and of a 'national' language (Farsi), whose promotion was a patriotic task for nationalists like Malkam Khan and Akhundzadeh. These historicised, physically imagined and politicised narratives shifted the concept of *mellat* from older meanings of a cultural/religious community to a powerful new designation of citizens/'people' of the national homeland (*vatan*) of Iran. Ideas of nation and people were attached to language, poetry and religion, mobilising Firdausi's epic tales, Shi'a Muslim tradition, and notions of ethnicity which distinguished 'Iranians' from Arabs, Turks or Afghans, using historical and cultural attributes to construct an essentialised 'Iranian' identity. Above all, writers/activists endowed the idea of nation and patriotism with emotive and spiritual force. Malkom Khan's *Qanun* refers to 'our most holy/sacred land', and the journal *Akhtar*, produced by Iranians in Istanbul, proclaimed '*Vatan* is both your beginning and your end ... so he who loves his *vatan* loves himself.'[47] Such inspiring visions disregarded the actual cultural diversity of nineteenth-century Iran, and, like elements in European nationalist thought, developed racialised xenophobic versions of ethnic essentialism.

A number of points should be noted about Iranian nationalist ideas and claims to 'Iranian' identity in this period. First, they flourished primarily among numerically small and socially distinctive groups of Iranians. Nationalism was created and disseminated among town-dwelling, educated, literate groups of merchants, intellectuals (religious or secular), entrepreneurs and members of the bureaucratic class. Whatever might be said about the *mellat* (people) of Iran, nationalism did not yet have a broad following. Second, nationalist views were not uniform or coherent, but encompassed tensions and contradictions among different concepts of 'national' identity, and 'national' goals and interests.

Emerging from the linguistically diverse communities of Iran, nationalists like Akhundzadeh and Talibof, who used Azeri Turkish as well as Persian, emphasised attachment to the 'soil' or 'honour' of Iran rather than cultural unity, and argued that love of country could co-exist with local and regional loyalties.[48] The turn to 'nation' as the focus of their politics side-stepped issues of social and cultural diversity.

There were similar ambiguities in the positioning of religion within nationalistic thinking and activity. Attachment to Shi'ite Islam, with its distinctive place in Iranian communities, and useful role in alliances with politically minded 'ulama, co-existed with tensions over modernist and secularist critiques of conventional religious practice and of mullas. The appeal of 'Islam in danger' as a nationalist slogan clashed with views that national emancipation should involve reform of religion and its role in law, education and government. While Iranian nationalists might share pan-Islamist hostility to European cultural threats and colonial expansionism, the defence of Islam was more problematic, and their uneasiness is reflected in conflicting or coded references to religion, modernisation and secularism in their writings. Although Shi'ism was sometimes foregrounded in Iranian 'national' identity, for many activists it required reform for it to further 'national' progress, liberty or self-strengthening. For some it provoked anti-'ulama secular visions of the 'national' future.

Nationalists also had ambiguous and contradictory visions of the relationship of 'state', 'nation' and 'people'. Merchants seeking government support against foreign competition in the language of 'national' well-being reminded government of its duty to care for the 'well-protected domains'. Officials and those wanting government posts advocated reform and modernising government for patriotic purposes as well as self-interest. Those less attached to governing circles, or disillusioned with the possibility of reform, used ideas of nation-as-people to challenge despotism, oppression, backwardness and injustice in the name of an Iranian 'nation' or 'people'. A few expressed patriotism in terms of radical class-based and populist critiques of the state and its oppressive role, drawn from contacts with socio-democratic and other revolutionary groups in the Russian-ruled Caucasus. It is notable that, as elsewhere, developing notions of 'love of country' and 'Iranian identity' included visible contradictions between inclusive emancipatory visions of a vatan of free, prosperous, empowered Iranians and an exclusionary, power-centred, emphasis on the need for forceful means to attain 'national'/patriotic ends. From this early stage in Iranian nationalist thinking and activity, a centralist focus on state power pulled against a democratic focus on people, creating slippages and unresolved tensions.

Another persistent and contested theme in the story of Iranian nationalism involved women and gender. This took three major forms: the symbolic use of gendered and sexual images to signify 'national' problems and aspirations; debate on women and gender policies; and the casting of women as inspiring angels of the 'national' cause and the onset of modernity in Iran. In respect of the first theme, patriots like Mirza Aqa Kermani lamented the Arabo/Islamic subjugation of Iran with metaphors of the rape, sale and theft of Iranian women symbolising national defeat and humiliation.[49] From a religious perspective, the threat of European influence to Iran/Islam in the nineteenth century could be expressed by a modernist reformer, or an aristocrat Shaikhi *mujtahed*, in terms of the 'corruption' of women's behaviour.[50] In a parallel image, Malkom Khan described the failure of Iranians to change their government and society and their consequent weakness and subordination as a loss of 'manliness', reflecting and confirming the gendering of 'reform' and 'politics' as *masculine* concerns. Calls to action by various patriots and reformers made regular reference to defending the 'honour' of Iran, and the fulfilment of tasks or roles convention-ally regarded as masculine – the warrior saviour, the professional expert, the protective father/brother/husband.[51]

When patriot/reformers proposed specific programmes, they also opened up a second theme of reform policies for gender relations and women's lives. Issues of marriage, and of women's access to education, presented as part of 'modernisation' and visions of 'national' self-strengthening and revival, were the most discussed issues. Reform was needed to reconstitute women as 'modern' wives and mothers of patriotic and progressive male citizens. 'Patriotic' pro-grammes criticised institutions like polygamous and 'enforced' marriage, and the segregation or 'veiling' of women and their exclusion from education. In raising these issues nationalist writers and activists opened up contests between visions of 'national' tradition and honour rooted in religious authority or convention, and those which mobilised modernist images of patriotic renewal.

If national honour and autonomy were figured as male loss of dominion over 'their' women, and national renewal included policies on gender and women's issues, the gendered flavour of constructions of the 'nation' was strengthened by symbolic uses of female images to inspire nationalist activity. For Mirza Malkom Khan, women were the 'angels of humanity' who would teach 'manliness' to Iranian men.[52] For others the protection of women from dishonour was part of their image of patriotic commitment, as notions of families or individual males defending honour converged with ideas of the violated honour of the nation or people. Calls to patriotic activism could be framed in terms of long-established patterns of male responsibility/authority over womenfolk and kin, reinforcing a new message (love of country) in familiar gender/patriarchal terms. They accompanied arguments for women's rights as fellow members of the nation, or for women's role supporting male patriots of the current and future generations, in the discussion of women's access to education.[53]

These themes, the concern of restricted literate and politically conscious circles in the 1890s, found more extended expression and significant expansion in the 'constitutional' era. If writers and propagandists of the earlier period initiated the agendas followed in later periods, it was the press and politicians of the early twentieth century who elaborated, contested and disseminated them. For the first time views of 'the nation' were shaped in an arena of political activism embracing the politics of the street and of representative institutions, a satirical and polemical press, and the competition of political factions, parties and interest groups for power in central government and local settings. Conflicts between sectional and party views and intervention by foreign powers in the new political arena further politicised the concept of the 'Iranian nation' as an increasingly powerful trope. Support for 'the nation', however, was far from universal and it is important to consider the divergences between those for whom nationalism was a mobilising force and those politicised by communal, religious and material interests and grievances. The politics of the 'nation' was characterised by new energy and participants, but also by new divisiveness and contention.[54]

The political activism of 1905–11 involved urban traders, artisans and entrepreneurs, *'ulama*, intellectuals and less privileged groups. It expressed highly localised grievances and rivalries, ambitions for power in central government, and large-scale and radical projects of social and political reform, and was rooted in the immediate impact of indigenous and external pressures on the lives of the Iranians who participated in the protests, elections, organisations and civil conflicts of the period. Most significant for the history of ideas of the 'nation' in Iranian politics was the newly prominent role of a reforming, sometimes radical, intelligentsia on the forms and language in which goals and grievances were expressed and pursued. They linked ideals of the 'Iranian nation', and its needs and characteristics to critiques of oppression, zeal for modernisation, hostility to foreign influence, and the defence of religion. It was they who focused the guild representatives, *mullas* and *tullab*, merchants and activist participants in the 1906 occupation of the British embassy grounds on the demand for a constitutional body as the means to these ends. They made and won the case for a body which was to be consultative, representative, and also *melli*, that is 'of the nation/people'.

The establishment of the Majlis (assembly), and the emergence of elections, political associations (notably the pro-constitutional *anjumans*), and conflict between various political interests, created new arenas for political activism. As the regime mobilised opposition to radical change, and supporters of change organised themselves to confront opponents and rivals, the role of pamphlets, newspapers, leaflets and oratory as well as assemblies, demonstrations and confrontations in streets, mosques and committee rooms became increasingly prominent. These settings were the forcing house of activism and argument. Ideas and images, which had previously operated mainly in literary and semi-private discourse, were now used for large-scale political mobilisation in streets and public gatherings, and in manoeuvrings for power and influence in Majlis and government. As a badge of political identity and credibility, a standpoint legitimating the pursuit of political goals, or an ideal colouring political aspirations from Islamic modernisation to social democratic radicalism, the concept of the nation acquired a many-sided presence and usefulness. By the time of the second Majlis, established after the defeat of the Shah's anti-constitutional moves in 1909, the so-called 'Moderate' party could attack the prominent constitutionalist Taqizadeh for supporting views 'in conflict with the Muslim characteristics of *the nation*' (my emphasis), showing that this language was used for a range of purposes.[55]

The theme of nation/people/patriotism gained further force and relevance from the interventions by the British and Russian governments in political developments in Iran. The involvement of foreign diplomats with Iranian political groups and politicians, the issue of foreign loans and the leverage they gave, the presence of foreign experts and advisers and their relationships to Iranian clients, patrons and employees, fed the politics of 'national' resistance to foreign interference. They also provided a divisive element as individuals or groups sought foreign support or accused others of doing so. Embattled and exiled constitutional radicals appealed to European liberals and social democrats, while elite politicians sought advice and money from Russian or British embassies, and women activists contacted British suffragists, just as the Majlis hired an American financial adviser, and the Shah used Russian troops. Politically active Iranians contested the use of British and Russian influence in Iran as a bargaining chip in their imperial and European rivalries. The 1907 Anglo-Russian agreement on spheres of influence in Iran, their backing of the Shah against constitutionalists, support of factions or individuals, and ultimately military intervention, were realities with which those activists had to deal. Interventions by Russian troops and British diplomats brought 'patriots' on to the streets, into political gatherings, and even armed conflict, shaping the foundation myth of twentieth-century Iranian politics. 'Patriotism' and skill in resisting or manipulating foreign pressure were now important parts of the political repertoire, whether passionate opponents of Russian attacks in 1908–09 and 1911, or career politicians and party groupings seeking to influence or enter government.

These developments fostered diverse uses of ideas of the 'Iranian nation' rather than a single 'nationalist' tradition. Active constitutionalists associated their achievements with the freedom and progress of Iran, threatened by internal unpatriotic enemies and foreign intervention. The emergent political establishment used the 'national' issue in their pursuit and use of power and influence. Specific communities attached 'patriotic' language to concerns for women's rights, resistance to landlords or foreign competition, or loyalty to local leaders and associates. Even the anti-constitutional arguments of Fazlullah Nuri advocated Islamic government as overcoming heresy, religious diversity and apostasy in 'our Iran'.[56] Here were potential conflicts among alternative visions of 'the nation'. Versions centred on defence of Shi'a traditions and identity, like those linking 'national' honour and autonomy with masculine honour and authority, clashed with those emphasising patriotic solidarity and parity between men and women. Populist and socially egalitarian patriotism conflicted with support for state power and social order as guarantors of 'national' safety and unity.

Varied and conflicting versions of 'the nation', like other political issues of the constitutional era, were entwined with religious themes. Religion was both a connecting thread and a source of tension in the new political practices and languages now coming into use. On the one hand, the drama of debate and decision-making in the Majlis combined depictions of nation-as-Muslim with nation-as-Iranian. Reacting to attacks by tribes and troops from across the Ottoman border in August 1907, Majlis members are described as showing 'zeal of Islam and fervour for Iran combined'.[57] In the contests over constitutional amendments in the same year, the radical *anjuman* in Tabriz argued that the 'rights of the nation' and protection of the *shari'a* were compatible. The radical journalist Dehkhoda spoke of political struggle 'with the pages of *Sur i-Israfil* (a constitutionalist newspaper) in one hand and the Qur'an in the other'.[58] This trend sat alongside anti-clerical and anti-elite denunciations of leading *'ulama* and even *mullas* in general, as unpatriotic traitors to national/popular (*melli*) interests. Less religious, more democratic, and culturally 'authentic' versions of 'the nation' were posed *against* the Shi'a Muslim version. By 1910 the social democrat Rasulzadeh invoked an 'Iranian' community where Muslim and non-Muslim children played together as fellow Iranians, explicitly rejecting religious definitions.[59] Growing reference to 'the nation' created complex meanings and unresolved conflicts.

The effects of a decade of constitutionalist views of 'the nation' involved both exclusion and inclusion. For an expanded class of educated and politicised Iranians, the term moved from the pages of small-circulation texts into public argument, partisan organisation and manoeuvre in government or street politics. This enlarged constituency created a more extended and sophisticated repertoire combining old and new elements in images of national honour as sexual honour, of defence of religion as defence of the nation, of popular challenges to oppression and autocracy as patriotic politics, and of links between national unity and prosperity. However, the very character of these views of the nation reveals their limitations. The defence of religion, and contests over male power and female subordination, over social inequity, and over democracy, reform and religious or linguistic diversity could marginalise, undermine or minimise any 'national' focus. The realities of social and cultural division, and their associated loyalties and conflicts, ensured that the 'national community' would remain largely 'imagined', notwithstanding the power of such imaginings.

Within the lived, remembered and imagined experience of constitutional politics in the foundation story of the 'Iranian nation', two themes were important for the future. From the earliest discussions on nationalism it was associated with reform, whether legal, educational, commercial or administrative. In the constitutional era this view was promoted by activists, for whom the achievement of the constitution and the Majlis was the opportunity to create institutional guarantees of justice and equity in law, taxation and administration. The implementation of such reforms also gave established office-holding elites, especially those with a modern education, a role and rationale in the new political environment. It was also relevant to popular critiques of oppression and injustice and expectations that the new *melli* (national/people's) Majlis would address their concerns by reforming and controlling the agents of government. It might even connect with the patriotism of heterodox or dissident religious thinkers concerned with the duty of social comment and judgement which was part of both religious tradition and the challenge of modernity.

Even more striking in the development of nationalist ideas and politics was the emphasis on government, as the growth of political life and energy in Tehran and other urban centres focused the attention of a newly active political class on Majlis, shah and ministers. For idealistic campaigners and the intelligentsia, the creation of representative institutions and new political leverage on government offered the opportunity to use them for liberal, modernising, democratic objectives, and to remake law and administration. Such assumptions placed considerable, perhaps unrealistic, expectations on new and fragile political structures, keeping political attention upon them. The enthusiasm of some for closer alignment of 'people/nation' and state, and the interventionism of government officials or those with influence in support of state modernising policies, strengthened this identification of 'state' with 'nation'.

Iranian nationalists who put such emphasis on the state and on modernisation had French, Egyptian, German, Japanese, Italian or Turkish counterparts. Their preoccupations reflect nationalists' need to adapt to their circumstances, in the Iranian case the manoeuvrings of the ruling establishment, the new political arenas of press, party and Majlis, older popular and religious constituencies, and Russian and British intervention. The strengthening and/or reform of the state, its public accountability and credibility, and its ability to resist external encroachments thus became 'patriotic' themes constructing the political nation, and linking present difficulties to future hopes. The requirements in the new electoral laws that Majlis deputies be both Persian speakers and able to read and write Persian, and the religious provisions in the supplementary Fundamental Laws (introduced after successful *'ulama* lobbying), institutionalised links of 'nation', state, language and religion which were central in such discourses.[60]

There are other parallels between the nationalism emerging in Iranian politics and contemporary developments elsewhere. While the rhetoric of sacrifice, blood and martyrdom tapped Shi'a Muslim discourses on the first Shi'a imams' stance for justice and right against tyranny and evil, described earlier, they were also tropes among European, Indian and Egyptian nationalists. Images of the nation as a female body, erotic and maternal, providing an object of desire or source of nourishment (mother's milk), whose honour and safety demanded the vigilant protection and passionate commitment of 'her' patriotic sons/lovers are another instance. Depictions of Marianne, Mother India, Cathleen na Houlihan, or the *matka Polska*, flourished in French, Indian, Irish and Polish nationalist discourses, just as Iranian references to the soil, honour, past glories and historic identity of the 'nation' are paralleled in other nationalisms.[61] Early Iranian nationalism had its distinctive character but shared significant cultural elements with such traditions. Iranian nationalists, like others, involved themselves in self-definition and representation as part of the politics of reform, state power, culture and material life, typical of the politics of modernity. Like Indian, Egyptian or Chinese counterparts, they had ambivalent relationships to European colonial dominance combining 'national' self-assertion against foreign power with appropriation of European models.

For all their vitality, the discourses of nationalism developed in the constitutional period were fragile and limited. By 1911 (when the second Majlis closed) constitutional politics was fractured by the reassertion of elite and vested interests, foreign intervention, and factional divisions along moderate/radical, religious/secular, regional, communal and personal lines. The impact of Russian, Turkish and British invasions during the First World War, movements for land, ethnic rights and political autonomy in various parts of Iran, and the inability of establishment leaders or political factions to constitute an effective government, showed the obstacles facing nationalism. On the one hand, both 'old' and 'new' politicians used nationalist ideas, images and arguments in attempts to sustain a 'Government of National Resistance', the patriotic exhortations of exiles like those publishing the journal *Kaveh* in Berlin, or the aristocrat minister Nusrat al-Douleh's appeals to 'national' boundaries and identity in dealings with the British Foreign Office.[62] On the other hand, such initiatives came from restricted groups of politically aware and involved participants in journalism, party politics and government, and the link between nationalist aspirations and the representative government meant to deliver them was broken by government 'failure'.

These contradictions help to explain how the Pahlavi autocracy which ended the Qajar dynasty and representative government was able to mobilise parts of the nationalist agenda and discourse in support of Reza Khan (who took the family name Pahlavi in 1925) from his 1921 coup onwards. The coup was the product of Reza's ambition and position in the Cossack Brigade, interacting with the interests of career politicians, office holders and British diplomats, and with reactions to foreign invasion, insecurity and tribal or regional self-assertion.[63] Those events challenged the viability of central government, the effectiveness of its rule, and its ability to resist external interference. In the years before the coup, the decline in law and order, the number of separatist movements, and the British attempt to impose a quasi-protectorate through the 1919 Anglo-Persian Agreement, were material threats to central government. As core functions of government disintegrated amid competition among elite families, Majlis and party politicians and office holders, so its role as historic protector and agent/custodian of 'national' interests came into question.

Reza Khan, the self-made soldier from Mazanderan, fitted a recognisable role of military strongman, bringing the troops he commanded into Tehran to force order and decisiveness in government, and gradually defeating rivals and separatists by force and political manoeuvre. His military seizure of power and subsequent reform and expansion of the army sustained his passage from commander of Cossack troops to Sardar-i-Sepah (Commander of the Army), war minister, prime minister and eventually Shah. However, his progress was not just a matter of using military force.[64] The rise of Reza Shah was supported by notables and politicians who saw him as a useful partner in their attempts to stabilise government, and by reformers and activists attracted by his ability to express his ambitions in nationalistic forms. The authoritarian regime he created was underpinned in part by the credibility of a government which sustained law and order, drove through some social and administrative change, and framed these activities in the rhetoric of national glory and improvement.

This support for the Shah from sections of the patriotic activist intelligentsia of the constitutional era arose from their perception that his aim of strengthening, modernising and centralising state power matched their own patriotic enthusiasm for legal, educational and administrative reforms which would build 'national' status and effectiveness. The well-established nationalistic emphasis on the state and on national achievement requiring a centralised, even authoritarian, drive for change from an enlightened minority dovetailed with the Shah's own ambitions. Even before the arrival of Reza Khan, the military twist given to patriotism by experiences of counter-revolution, invasion, world war, foreign occupation, and regional uprisings between 1908 and 1920, encouraged explicit links between nationalist aspirations and belief in the role of an army in salvaging them. Political speeches and journalism in that period picked up this theme speaking of a 'national *jihad*', and the country's need for 'organised armies (to) ... protect its honour and rights'.[65] Diplomatic struggles over the admission of an Iranian delegation to the Versailles negotiations, and the 1919 Anglo-Persian Treaty, intensified awareness of 'national' integrity and international standing, and their connection to lack of forceful leadership and military effectiveness. In this context, the willingness of nationalists to regard the rise of Reza Khan/Shah with optimism responded to immediate circumstances, and established concerns for the well-being of the 'nation'.[66]

Desire to assert state control over the territories of the 'nation' meant that many of the political classes saw Reza Khan/Shah's defeat of regional movements in Khorasan, Gilan, Khuzestan and Kurdistan as patriotic achievements as much as the imposition of order. Since concerns for territorial integrity and military encroachment had featured in the 'national question' throughout the nineteenth century, the successful use of force and diplomacy against such movements was welcomed by patriots. There were other significant ways in which the new regime was seen to pursue a patriotic agenda. The creation of an effective army was accompanied by alterations in state and society which had long been part of that agenda. The programme of legal, educational and administrative reorganisation was supported by nationalistically minded Iranians, who themselves shaped it by implementing the relevant reforms. By backing such a programme, the regime attracted the active involvement of such Iranians who contributed experience and ideas developed among nationalists over preceding decades. The educationist Isa Sadiq, the historian, judicial official and language reformer Kasravi, the politician and writer Taqizadeh, were among many Iranians influenced by nationalism who joined the regime's work, endowing it with 'national' images and traditions.[67] Nationalism became official and official policy became nationalistic.

However, by legitimising certain kinds of nationalism as official practice and ideology, the regime emphasised some aspects of the tradition at the expense of others, neglecting or suppressing whole areas of the earlier nationalist repertoire. Three features worth noting in official Pahlavi nationalism were conformism, secularism and authoritarianism. In pursuit of conformity the government rejected linguistic, cultural and religious diversity, reflecting nationalist traditions associating 'national' identity with the use of Persian as the 'national' language, and assertions of 'shared' culture going back to Kermani and Akhundzadeh.[68] It suppressed linguistic diversity in schools and the press, renamed towns and regions in 'Persian' style, and attempted to remove 'imported' Turcic or Arabic words from Farsi. Government attacks on tribal groups and attempts to impose 'modern' dress codes, demonstrated its association of central power with 'national' identity.

If the nationalism of the regime was marked by the drive to undermine communal, localised cultural diversity, it was also characterised by explicit secularism. Reza Shah combined hostility to organised religion and personal religious indifference with a shrewdly pragmatic sense of how to manage and negotiate relationships with the *'ulama*. However, the culture and rhetoric of the regime was clearly distanced from religion, and the nationalistic images and ideas it selected and fostered were drawn from *non*-religious sources looking to both past and future. One strand of nationalism pointed to the progressive modernising achievements of government enabling Iranians to take pride in reaching parity with 'advanced nations'. This confirmed and fulfilled patriotic aspirations going back to the 1870s. The other strand of nationalism constructed the 'nation' through images of its non- or pre-Islamic history. Reza Shah's choice of the family name Pahlavi (the name of a pre-Islamic Iranian language) symbolised this trend. This discourse entered school textbooks where rulers and heroes of the pre-Islamic past were offered as images of past glory, and national identity was presented as the product of geography and language rather than religion, just as buildings in styles drawn from pre-Islamic architecture proclaimed it on urban streets. This use of a version of national identity founded on past dynastic glory, loyalty to land and ruler, and use of Farsi was no mere creation of official propagandists but drew on non-religious imaginings of 'the nation' going back to Mirza Aqa Kermani. The association of present and future 'national' fulfilment with secular progress and the inspiration of past achievements was fuelled by contemporary desires to strengthen a nation under threat, and criticisms of *mullas* and religion as obstacles to that process. The climate of the regime favoured such associations, and its use of state power, secular history, military success and territorial acquisition marginalised religious or democratic versions of patriotism.

The contested character of official nationalism grew clearer as the reign progressed, and the links between the Shah and the patriot reformers who initially supported him were broken by his dismissal, exile, imprisonment and even murder of leading figures, and his wider intimidation and disregard for independent, let alone critical, views. As his rule became more repressive, arbitrary and personally acquisitive, distance opened up between the prescriptive enthusiasm of those wanting progress in the interests of the 'nation' and the dictatorial practice of the regime. The government staked nationalistic claims through a series of initiatives, some substantial, like the expansion of transport and education, some symbolic, like ending foreign capitulations, and some ineffective, like attempts to control dress and language. These claims were increasingly weakened by the visible gap between government and society, manifest in the limits to what the former could impose on the latter, and in active and passive resistance to its power.

Both in its achievements and its confrontations with the political classes, popular religious and communal attachments, and the *'ulama*, Reza Pahlavi's rule was a period in which the idea of the 'nation' and contests over that notion were further embedded in the Iranian polity. It reinforced contradictions between state claims to patriotism, the focus on the 'nation' among political activists, and the relative isolation of such activists from the majority of Iranians mainly concerned with workplace and communal issues, and survival in the face of poverty, state coercion and elite power. It confirmed that the nature of the state and its promotion of territorial integrity, social reform and containment of 'foreign' interests were continuing nationalist themes. It demonstrated how an authoritarian regime could use patriotic rhetoric in partnerships with established elites and new cadres of supporters. Its capacity to do this owed much to the legacies of late nineteenth- and early twentieth-century Iranian politics, and is comparable to developments elsewhere. The period between the First and Second World Wars was one in which ambitious *arriviste* leaders used nationalist, often militarised, agendas to seize and hold power in the successor states of the Habsburg, Ottoman and tsarist Empires, as did Pilsudski in Poland, Ataturk in Turkey, or Horthy in Hungary. Like Reza Shah, the Chinese Kuomintang and Japanese governments in the 1930s deployed nationalistic rhetoric to support state power and modernisation, co-opting or coercing old elites and new cadres to their projects. As in Italy under Mussolini, or Argentina under Peron, populist, or corporatist, rhetoric, flagship projects and cults of the leader distinguished the new ruler from old aristocratic or dynastic regimes and factional politics. These points relate the story of nationalism in Iran to stories elsewhere in which visions and programmes for the 'nation' faced disruptions to the stability of existing states through invasion and the break-up of dynasties or party politics.

The period between the removal of Reza Shah in 1941 and the coup which assured the autocratic power of his son in 1953 is often seen as a high-water mark of nationalist politics in Iran. A time of open political activism, conflict and organisation provided opportunities for debate and mobilisation around nationalist images and programmes on a public and extended scale. While these features gave the years from 1941 to 1953 a particular character, nationalist thinking and politics in those years were rooted in the preceding period. The nationalisms of the constitutional era and of Reza Shah's reign provided later nationalist politics with resources to use and patterns to reject. Thus Reza Shah's forceful association of his regime with nationalist aims and images stimulated those who opposed this version of nationalism to reassert the identification of the 'nation' with popular and constitutional interests. Opposition to autocracy, which was central to politics after 1941, was linked to the struggle for national independence and progress.

Similarly, questions of how far the 'nation' would be secular and uniform, or should acknowledge cultural diversity and Shi'a Muslim identity, which preoccupied officials and reformers in earlier decades, remained on the political agenda after Reza Shah's departure. The challenges of Kurdish and Azeri separatism, and of leftist, religious and constitutional arguments about 'national' interests in the 1940s and 1950s were partly responses to experiences in the 1920s and 1930s. Reza Shah's dictatorial efforts to impose conformity and statist 'national' institutions, and to control and repress constituencies which might contest his version of the nation, informed the politics of the 1941–53 period as did the legacy of earlier debates. The nationalist flavour of the material and cultural changes made during the 1920s and 1930s, together with the frustrations and contradictions of the government presiding over them, bequeathed a distinctive legacy.

Whatever the influence of past experiences, the place of the 'nation' as a key political issue for Iranians in the 1941–53 period was shaped by new and powerful factors. The twin impact of foreign invasion with the removal of Reza Shah, and consequent liberating of political life, put the issue of nationalism in the forefront of political awareness and opened up the political arena to electoral politics, ideological debate and street protest. Iranians were brought into the course of the Second World War by the British/Soviet invasion of 1941, supplemented by an American presence from 1942, which in turn segued into Iranian involvement in the developing Cold War confrontation of the USSR with the Americans and British. The presence of large numbers of foreign troops, intelligence and technical staff, backed by extended diplomatic activity, confronted Iranians with huge material disruptions (notably inflation and food shortages) and overt and covert intervention in Iranian politics.[69] Claims for autonomy in Azerbaijan and Kurdistan raised further questions about the character of the 'nation'. These challenges were reinforced by the growing contest over Iranian oil resources, controlled, exploited and exported by the Anglo Iranian Oil Company (AIOC), with UK government backing, while Soviet and American interests also sought oil concessions. The revelation of discussions on such concessions in late 1944 provoked early manifestations of 'Cold War' rivalries, and Iranian sensitivities to foreign control of a major indigenous resource. Public protest and Majlis decisions against clandestine discussion of oil concessions put the issue into the mainstream of politics.[70]

Although nationalist views of the oil issue had surfaced during Reza Shah's renegotiation of the AIOC contract in 1932–33, it was in the 1940s and 1950s that they mobilised political action and symbolised 'national' independence. They connected a range of concerns and political traditions with varied versions of the 'national' interest. In the oilfields, the material concerns of workers, organised by the communist Tudeh Party, combined with anti-imperialism and class politics. For a wide spectrum of patriotic, liberal and left groups and their varied urban supporters, foreign control of the oil industry became the paradigmatic affront to national autonomy. To patriotic and religious *bazaris* and other pious Shi'a Muslims, infidel control of oil challenged their religio-national identity. Resistance to foreign oil interests and ultimately the nationalisation of Iranian oil became the focus for constitutional and democratic concerns, identified as 'national' and 'popular' issues by press and politicians, and testing the effectiveness of representative government.

The inescapable pressure of foreign interests, intensified by the circumstances of world war, the Cold War and the new petro-driven world economy, was a formative factor in nationalist politics in 1940s Iran, recalling earlier experiences. The role and image of Muhammad Mussadeq, representing unswerving resistance to such interests as opposition leader and then prime minister leading the attack on AIOC, were living links between the two eras, embodying 'national' politics. He represented a constitutional tradition which posed 'nation', 'people' and representative government against foreign and monarchical challenges to 'national' institutions and well-being. Patriotic deputies warned that the Shah's expansion of the army in the late 1940s threatened constitutional liberties, and his convening of a Constituent Assembly to increase royal powers in 1949 apparently confirmed such predictions.[71] Protests about electoral manipulation in 1947 and 1949 linked parliamentarians, students, *bazaris* and anti-court politicians in support of constitutional processes as guarantees of national autonomy. Mussadeq's declaration, when presenting his first cabinet to the Majlis in May 1951, that the new government would have only two goals – implementation of the oil nationalisation law and revision of the electoral law – indicates the link of constitutional and oil issues as main planks of the significantly named National Front.

There were important contradictions and conflicts within the nationalisms of the period. For the Tudeh Party, whose leftist ideals and Soviet affiliations entangled their 'patriotic' politics with desires to build class activism, please their Russian patrons, or deal with the aspirations of Azeri and Kurdish allies, as for pious National Front supporters balancing commitment to Shi'ism with support for Mussadeq, nationalist politics were neither pure nor simple. In a world of contested elections, political debate and street and workplace mobilisation, the patriotic themes which had preoccupied intellectuals and elites in the 1920s and 1930s now entered popular political discourse. Images and rhetorics of the nation, further explored in Chapter 5, became embedded in urban politics from parliamentary debates and intellectual *dowrehs* (discussion groups) to street activism and party or religious propaganda. As Majlis, street and court politics concentrated on oil nationalisation, the role of the monarch and foreign intervention, the implications of Mussadeq's rise and fall for stories of the Iranian nation entered the realm of mythic narrative and martyrdom for his sympathisers, and disaster for his critics.

'The nation' had shifted from being a preoccupation of reformers and governments to being an emotive icon projected in leaflets, sermons, radio broadcasts and appeals to the electorate. In addition to being something to be controlled or improved, it was now an object of attachment and emotional meaning. From the 1940s, Iranian nationalisms supplemented enthusiasm for modernisation with passionate commitment to emancipation from 'imperialist' foreign control. This reflected the legacy of leftist and constitutionalist thinking, and the wish of anti-Pahlavi activists to distinguish their patriotism from that claimed by the regime. Like his father, Muhammad Reza Pahlavi associated his rule with nationalistic rhetoric and the modernising policies described in Chapter 1, and like him drew reformers, including former opponents of the regime, into the cadres who implemented them. By linking their critique of the Shah's tyranny to its dependence on United States' support, those who opposed the Shah after 1953 expressed their politics in terms which resonated with Iranian political traditions and also spoke to the new world of US hegemony outside the Soviet bloc.

This new politics linked 'the nation' to aspirations for social justice, material progress, and an end to 'despotism' but also had important cultural aspects. While leftists emphasised anti-imperialist discourses of nationalism, some opposition activists focused on the threats posed by American influence and 'western' ideas and technologies to national *cultural* identity. They used traditions of celebration of the 'Iranian' past and of a distinctly 'Iranian' culture established by nationalists over previous decades. They also drew on recent critiques of western cultural imperialism among 'third world' anti-colonial nationalist intellectuals and activists like Franz Fanon whose work was translated into Persian by opposition activists who identified themselves as progressive, nationalist and Shi'a Muslim. One strand in this critique was a debate on political disempowerment and social alienation which placed false understanding of 'the west', and the damaging consequences of 'western' culture and technology, as the core problems faced by modern Iranians.[72] Ideas in this vein fuelled attacks on the regime for its unpatriotic association with western *cultural* influence as well as reliance on US armaments and money.

Concern with 'indigenous' Iranian culture and identity led back to concern with the place of Shi'ism in that culture or identity. If Shi'a beliefs and practices were part of an 'authentic' inheritance undermined by a century of intellectual denigration and half a century of anti-religious state reform, then their celebration and revival was a patriotic as well as a pious project. Enthusiasm for Shi'ism expressed not so much attachment to 'tradition' but contemporary experiences of American power, new anti-colonial ideas, and commitment to regenerating the 'national' and 'popular' politics derailed after 1953. By the early 1960s, activists were arguing that to turn to Shi'a Iranian culture was to open political communication with 'the people' rather than cultural nostalgia.[73] As these ideas spread, Shi'a imaginings of the 'nation' had a new contemporary appeal. They played to familiar xenophobia, and associations of 'Islam' with 'Iran' going back to the rhetoric of Mudarris and Kashani, expressing new views which gave cultural spin to the politics of autonomy. The National Freedom Movement of Iran, founded in 1961, declared itself Muslim and Mussadeqist, and in 1963 anti-Shah protestors used the slogan 'Mussadeq our national leader, Khomeini our religious leader', linking the iconic nationalist leader to religion and *ulama* protest. Just as late nineteenth-century nationalists used images of history and religion in emotively appealing and intellectually attractive depictions of 'the nation', so their descendants used anti-imperialist cultural critique to refigure the connections of Shi'a Islam to *iraniyyat*.

Not that this was an uncontentious process. If earlier Iranian defenders of Islam steered a tricky course in relation to pan-Islamist anti-colonialism, exponents of Shi'a Islam as part of the 'Iranian spirit' in the 1960s and 1970s faced the challenge of adopting/adapting global anti-imperialist arguments. Faced with the Palestinian issue, armed struggle in Algeria, and the tussles of Nasserite 'Arab' nationalism with great power interests, 'Muslim unity' in the face of those interests might combine radical and religious appeal more effectively than more precise focus on a Shi'a/Iranian nation; and religious radicals in this period sought to combine the two. In speeches and proclamations between 1963 and 1971, Ayatollah Khomeini spoke of 'the Muslim nation, whether in Iran or abroad', 'the Iranian nation' needing the support of fellow Muslims, and the experience of subjugation to imperialism common to different 'Muslim peoples'.[74] Pious supporters of National Front or leftist politics, Muslim Student Associations in Iran and abroad, and intellectuals such as Shari'ati, overlapped patriotic calls to liberate the Iranian nation from despotism and American control with comparisons between the Iranian situation and that of Algerians or Palestinians.

This reopened the question of whether activists committed to the liberation of Iran and to Shi'a Islam identified with a potentially *non*-national, non-Shi'a Muslim *umma*/community as well as or instead of the 'nation'. It was the potential slippage between these identifications which allowed supporters of Khomeini, Islamic leftists, and members of the Freedom movement to deploy ambiguous messages. Many in the anti-Shah movement in 1978–79 expressed precisely such mixed views of an 'Iranian nation', a 'Muslim *umma*', and Shi'a/Iranian 'people'. The 'honour of the Iranian people' evoked by a Qazvin factory worker, and the taking of their destiny 'into their own hands' imagined by a Tehran clerk, sat alongside affirmations of Muslim unity and identity and references to 'Ali and Hussein, linked by anti-imperialist rhetoric directed at infidel/American influence in Iran.[75] The slogan 'Liberty, independence, Islamic Republic' used in 1978–79 expressed the persuasive if unstable connections between legacies of nationalistic thinking and the associations of Shi'ism with anti-imperialism. For many Iranians the contest was between more or less religious variants of nationalistic discourse rather than between support for nationalism or hostility to it.

As with religious discourses and practices, a key feature of nationalisms in Iran has been their polyvalence. They entwined with desires for secularist modernisation, and the assertion of the religious character of 'national identity'. They interacted with concerns for familial and sexual honour, and with symbolic and actual concerns over women's claims as members of the 'nation'. They flavoured challenges to political exclusion, social inequity and foreign influence, and buttressed establishment and authoritarian politics. They combined with enthusiasm for western ideas and technologies for national ends in the 1920s, and with opposition to western cultural corruption and neo-colonial power in the 1970s. In the period under discussion, Iranian nationalisms developed symbolic and emotive power as well as a rich cultural repertoire of ideas and images drawn from images of the Iranian past, of religious traditions and modern intellectual and popular discourses of identity, freedom and authenticity.

FIVE
A story of language, symbol and discourse

'It's not what you say, but the way that you say it' is a clichéd popular comment on the power of language and representation in human affairs. Of course politics – defined in this text as the conscious pursuit of aims and interests in response to changing circumstances and the unequal distribution of power, resources, influence and opportunity – concerns substantive issues. These include contests over material assets, conflicts of interests within or between households, factions, communities or classes, or the use of governmental power or control. However, since people make conscious and deliberate choices when they become politically active on such issues, they use thought, perception, language, meaning and communication. Political activity involves persuading, inspiring, intimidating, negotiating and manipulating, all activities involving culture and communication, as well as political organisation and material and physical support.

The most obvious cultural and communicative aspect of politics is the use of argument, theory and ideology to demonstrate the reasons, feelings and beliefs underpinning political choices and actions. Speech and writing of every kind are typical means used for this, but verbal forms are only one means of doing so. The thoughts, beliefs and emotions which inform politics can be expressed in ritual, ceremony, visual representation, and the use of symbols and images. Since politics deals with human hopes, fears, values and desires as well as material interests and practical policy, political culture and communication address the former as well as the latter.

Thus, when examining relationships between 'religion' and 'politics' it is important to consider the full range of forms that communicate political meanings. In addition to examining *what* is expressed by political activity (vested interests, fears, aspirations, grievances), it is important to examine *how* activity is expressed in order to understand connections and tensions between religious and other elements in the political history of modern Iran. Effective advocacy or organisation for particular causes or interests requires the creation of effective links with potential supporters using ideas, symbols, references or images relevant to their situations. It follows that images, ideas, symbols and language can themselves be subjects of political action as groups or individuals as groups or individuals seek to create, control, challenge or communicate them. This reflects the central importance of the 'how' as well as the 'what' of political expression.

This is directly relevant to the central concerns of this text – relationships between the 'political' and the 'religious' in the modern history of Iran. Writing on this subject has often been attracted to the tempting clarity and apparent empirical force of a dualistic approach using binary oppositions between 'religious' and 'secular' or 'traditional' and 'modern'. It is notable that this scholarly choice reflects the outlook of Iranian activists who over the last century positioned themselves for or against 'religion', *mullas* and 'tradition', using these binaries to make judgements as much as for analysis. Thus other binaries – good/bad, desirable/undesirable, right/wrong, reactionary/progressive – became attached to the dualistic opposition of 'religious' to 'secular'.

The difficulty with this approach is that it is limiting. There has certainly been direct opposition between advocates of 'religious' or 'clerical' ideals and interests and advocates of 'secular' or 'anti-clerical' positions in the modern history of Iran. However, this is only part of the picture, since Iranians have made and followed a much more diverse range of options. They range from the convergent or alliance politics pursued by some constitutionalists in the first decade of the twentieth century to the nationalist politics of the 1940s, and the hybrid patterns of opposition to the second Pahlavi shah in the 1960s and 1970s. The existence of this range of options suggests that depictions of opposed monoliths of 'secular' and 'religious' politics does not do justice to Iranians' experience of politics in the modern period. As already shown, the presence of religious influences in many parts of Iranian society reached beyond the institutions of worship, ritual, law and education into everyday cultures. Those influences interacted with many others, including the growth of modern 'secular' education and the continuing influence of non- or anti-religious features of community life and work, gendered and familial power relations, and workplace, urban and party politics.

What, then, was the repertoire of religious resources on which Iranians drew in order to express their politics in the period under discussion? By the nineteenth century, Shi'a Islamic traditions in Iran, whether in 'official', heterodox or dissident forms, had generated a range of images and concepts rooted in the core beliefs, rituals and narratives of the faith, which also had 'political' potential. First, as with other religious traditions, religious elements fed into discourses of legitimacy, hierarchy, order and authority. Second, there was a parallel influence on the expression of dissidence, resistance to tyranny or injustice, struggle and suffering for ideals or causes, and visionary millennial aspirations. Third, and in contrast to either of those perspectives, religious elements could also express the political choice of acceptance and quietism. Fourth, religious traditions shaped widely held views of community and morality expressing the politics of gender, kinship or collective solidarity, competition and assertion. While religious resources shaped political activism and dealings with political power, they also provided norms, ideals or languages regulating life in households, workplaces or communities. They sustained political activity in those everyday settings as well as the organisation and expression of wider political movements and institutions.

By the later nineteenth century, religious idioms flavoured Iranians' political sense of order and power in government and community. In Shi'a Islam, images of divine authority, conveyed through reference to an all-powerful God, to the unique prophetic role of Muhammad, and the leadership of the imams 'Ali and Husein, also coloured perceptions of temporal power and authority. At the apex of formal politics the status, mission, authority and legitimacy of the Qajar monarchs was expressed in partly religious terms. Traditional Iranian political theory emphasised that the well-being of the state and its subjects (the word *doulat* conveying combined meanings of 'government' and 'well-being') rested on the twin pillars of monarchy and faith upholding social and political order. Ruling dynasties in Iran since the sixteenth century had linked commitment to Shi'a Islam with royal legitimacy.

As the Qajars established themselves from the 1790s, they too claimed a spiritual mandate in various symbolic and discursive forms. The first Qajar shah, Agha Muhammad, bore a sword called 'the sword of the Twelfth Imam' worn by him when visiting the shrine of the eighth imam at Mashad, and part of the coronation regalia of his successors, who adopted titles like 'Shadow of God' and 'Refuge of Islam'.[1] In the reign of Fath 'Ali Shah (ruled 1797–1834) the capital city of the dynasty, Tehran, became known as the 'seat of *Khilafat*' (sacred custodianship of Shi'ism) as well as the 'abode of the *Saltanat*' (monarchy). Nasir al-din Shah (ruled 1848–96) deployed images of 'Ali who, as the chosen successor of Muhammad, symbolised sacred sovereignty and godly rule as well as warrior valour in defence of the faith. A specially commissioned icon-like medallion portraying 'Ali, painted on the Shah's orders and worn by him, figures in his portraits, and was said to be a focus for his daily prayers.[2]

Celebration of the Shah's role as 'sultan of the Shi'ites' and of his commitment to the lineage of 'Ali featured in court and metropolitan art and literature. The Shah's use of the image of 'Ali and regular pilgrimages to major Shi'a shrines were part of his presentation of the intertwined honour of faith, dynasty and nation, like the acknowledgement of the role of religion in governance through the involvement of leading *'ulama* in court ceremonies and royal activity. This was in part a pragmatic tactic for consolidating the mutually beneficial alliance of state and *'ulama*, but it also sustained a wider framework of belief and ideology.[3]

Religious elements in the depiction of order and authority went beyond court and monarchy. For those with power, property and privilege in various centres of nineteenth-century Iran, relationships with subordinate groups entwined religious notions of authority, obedience and social order with other cultural and ideological elements. People who participated in riots, protests and similar challenges to authority were described in terms suggesting *moral* failings (wicked ones) as well as dissidence (insurgents), social inferiority (riff-raff, 'common' people) and criminality (rogues, ruffians). The term *luti*, which incorporated ideas of popular morality, decency and protectiveness, was often used at moments of popular disorder to stigmatise the violent, *immoral* and unrespectable character of protesters.[4] Such associations figured in the perceptions of subordinate as well as dominant groups in nineteenth-century Iran. The use of the Muharram gatherings by ordinary Iranians to petition the authorities to pardon and release prisoners is one example. A religious occasion commemorating Husein's martyrdom, and religious symbols of his suffering and commitment, were mobilised to seek concessions from those who reinforced their legitimacy by responding on such occasions.[5] Likewise the use of mosques, shrines and the houses of *'ulama* as refuges for protesting peasants, contending notables or urban rioters, linked the religious character of particular places and persons to political negotiation with the powerful, and to protection from the coercive use of power. Appeals to the protective legitimacy and status of religious specialists and institutions were understood by the powerful.[6] The combination of spiritual and social prestige attached to religious specialists in their localities, and the respect expected from all ranks towards mosques and shrines, allowed those in authority to manage dissent within a mutually recognised framework.

If the use of religious imagery and ideas in the politics of court and local government gave spiritual and moral force to the exercise of power in those arenas, it also flavoured intimate forms of patriarchal power in gendered and familial settings. Male privilege in kin groups and households, upheld by custom and material advantage, was also sustained by a repertoire of religious language and symbols. Control of sexual conduct and gender difference or hierarchy was expressed in images combining familial and communal concerns about honour and female purity with the authority of prescriptions attributed to the Qur'an, to *hadith* (religious tradition) or to Imam 'Ali. Notions of impurity and pollution often had meanings which were simultaneously religious (Muslim beliefs and practices around cleanliness), sexual (in relation to female sexuality and childbearing), and expressive of general beliefs in unseen forces and dangers in the natural environment. Dress codes for women, and gender segregation or inequities, were grounded in the power relations between genders and generations in families and communities, and in the power of religious ideology and language, varying according to rank or location. Religious and customary codes of propriety and female subordination differed significantly for working women in villages, towns or nomad encampment, the 'modest' but educated daughters of *'ulama*, or women of varied backgrounds trading or exchanging religious ideas in elite *anderuns*.

Relationships between the gendered, the erotic and the religious in discourses of politics and power were important signifiers of order and disorder, loyalty and opposition. When Nasir al-din Shah was defending his effectiveness and autonomy in the face of British and Russian pressures in the 1850s, themes of honour, religion and sexual propriety surfaced in his dealings with the British ambassador, Murray, and personal exchanges with his chief minister. In 1855 a tussle over the appointment of a former member of the Shah's household (and husband to a sister of one of his wives) to the ambassador's staff engaged these discursive elements and contributed to the outbreak of military conflict between Iranians and British in 1856. The Shah's dream of the prophet Muhammad encouraging him to challenge British power, like the emphasis on the sexual reputation of Mirza Hashem Khan's wife and his closeness to the royal household, were personal signifiers of a public struggle ending in the breach of diplomatic relations. The prospect of Murray having contact with the segregated sphere of the royal *anderun*, let alone the rumours about the sexual conduct of Hashem Khan's wife with Murray and his predecessors, entwined the personal and sexual domain with public and diplomatic self-assertion. 'They wish to take from us our power and authority, even over our own family and special wife,' wrote the Shah, as he and Murray invoked *mujtaheds'* views to legitimate their control over Parvin (Hashem's wife) in their contest for political dominance, and 'the preservation of the dignity of throne'.[7] Territorial, diplomatic and strategic threats to dynastic autonomy and dominance were played out on the terrain of the monarch's personal patriarchal authority and *namus*/sexual honour.

The emotive and moral impact of evocations of desire and control, corruption and purity contributed to the language of politics, whether the manoeuvring of Shah and ministers, or the responses of local notables to the dissident Babi movement. Another moral and emotive force came from the association of order, government and royal authority with symbols of Shi'a identity and solidarity which were at their most publicly potent in the annual Muharram commemorations. Qajar rulers and leading *'ulama* became patrons and supporters of the *ta'ziyeh* dramas representing the massacre/martyrdom of Husein, his family and followers by opponents. From an elite viewpoint, this provided identification with a powerful tradition separate from the legal and doctrinal authority of the *'ulama*, and hence an independent source of religiously grounded legitimacy. Patronage of *ta'ziyeh* gave ceremonial expression to links between religious and

171

secular authority, the twin pillars of order mutually guaranteeing each other, and the well-being of state, faith and community.

However, *ta'ziyeh* and the other rituals associated with Husein and Muharram also fed another repertoire of political language and discourse. The commemoration of Husein's martyrdom in *rawzehs*, processions and *ta'ziyeh* performances affirmed a narrative or paradigm with potent political meanings. The story of Husein's battle against opponents of his claim to rightful succession as leader of the Muslim community was also a story of the struggle for justice and virtue against tyranny and evil. His death in pursuit of these goals provided a paradigm of resistance to oppression and wrong conduct, and suffering in a righteous cause. Accounts of the killing of Husein's close kin, and his surviving daughter's defiance of their conqueror, added a story of familial loyalty, suffering and devotion to the political discourse of struggle and the religious image of martyrdom. Warrior, political leader, martyr, blessed head of a 'holy family', the narrative of Husein and his fate was a reservoir of political images for various uses, and a powerful resource for dissidents and protesters.

The power of the 'Karbala paradigm'[8] lay in its evocation of emotional and moral meanings and images of courage, virtue and suffering, and its ability to legitimise protest against the established order, just as naming Husein's enemies Shimr and Yazid invoked symbols of tyranny and evil. Regular commemoration of Husein's deeds and death in sermons and rituals facilitated the translation of shared religious ideals into collective political activism. This translation was enacted at many political moments and contrasting modes between the 1850s and the 1970s. The combination of communal ownership of the Karbala narrative with its powerful rhetoric of tragedy, nobility and spiritual glory made it a crucial political resource for protesters and critics. Each repetition of the narrative reinforced images of the destruction of legitimate rule (the defeat of Husein's claim as rightful successor to the caliphate), of family (the slaughter of most of his male kin and mistreatment of his female kin), of community (the killing of Husein's supporters), and of humanity itself (the cruel immoral acts of Husein's opponents). Use of these discourses extended well beyond the intense ten-day period of processions and *ta'ziyeh* enactments in Muharram. Images and meanings of the story were reproduced through the year in *rawzehs*, proverbs, sermons and slogans, crossing social hierarchies, everyday lives and diverse communities. They could be a parable, a source of models for how to live, and a marker of shared belief and identity. As persistent images of justice and right denied by the abusive exercise of power, they underpinned quietist withdrawal from the political domain or oppositional stances towards rulers and government.

This paradigm, like other elements of Shi'a religious language and practice, fed the politics of community as well as that of disassociation or dissidence from established power. Through Muharram rituals, *lutis*, women, notables, villagers or craft groups established and enacted collective identities and interests and created cultural resources for their political expression. Incursions into mosques and shrines and the taking of *bast* (sanctuary) in such places in pursuit of traders', peasants', women's or artisans' grievances over taxation, food supply, prices or misgovernment, claimed religious sanction for political protest.[9] Such claims were useful tactics to mobilise both *'ulama* support and the moral and ideological force of religious discourse. Demands for 'justice' or 'proper' treatment were reinforced by reference to the religious connotations of these objectives, established by the presence of protesters in village shrines or urban mosques.

Another view of these connections is provided by accounts of the role of the *'ulama* as advocates and defenders of 'justice' on behalf of those with grievances. Nineteenth-century biographies of leading *'ulama* by authors such as Tunakabuni, Khonsari and Aqa Bozorg Tehrani gave instances of their support for those suffering 'injustice' in order to establish images of their political as well as social and spiritual authority. Tunakabuni's accounts of rebukes by Mulla Ahmad Naraqi or Akhund Mulla Husein to the Shah for tolerating 'oppressive' government in their respective cities of Kashan and Yazd are examples, supported by other non-*'ulama* accounts.[10] In Qazvin in 1857, the *imam jom'eh* was bastinadoed for supporting protests against tax exactions, just as in Tehran in 1861 women protesting bread shortages and grain hoarding forced the *imam jom'eh* to seek the Shah's assurance that bread would be distributed and hoarders punished. Senior *'ulama* responded to public pressure, initiated action, and posed their authority against officials in the name of popular interest.[11] Such accounts affirmed the autonomous political roles of *'ulama* and gave it ideological grounding. They also legitimised critiques of official misconduct and the assertion of collective grievances in religious and moral terms. Shi'a vocabulary expressed not only the forms of political authority and negotiation but also the possibility of challenge to those with power.

These instances show how the emotive and legitimising power of religious language and ritual were mobilised for diverse political ends. If rulers and courtiers used Shi'a motifs to bolster the mystique of monarchy, urban crowds invoked them in support of demands on government. If groups of women or peasants sought the protection of religious sites in pursuit of political interests, governments allied with senior *'ulama* to disseminate the rhetoric of *jihad* (sacred struggle) to win support for war with Russia in defence of the 'protected lands of Islam/Iran'.[12] Elite political pressures and popular political protests both used religious discourses of faith, justice and morality. Muharram rituals were occasions for the assertion of elite authority, communal solidarity, public pressure on government, or conditional acceptance of established hierarchies

173

and power relations. Supporters of law and order, of opposition to 'unjust' conduct, or of withdrawal from 'political' arenas (itself a political stance) all drew on Shi'ism's storehouse of symbolic figures, evocative images, sacred rituals and religious language.

The rise and disintegration of the Babi movement in the mid-nineteenth century illustrated these connections. The development of Babism, and its successor Azali and Baha'i groups, into religious traditions outside Shi'ism had political implications. The language of community and martyrdom used by the Babis expressed growing social separation as well as religious rupture, while their opponents labelled them as both enemies of religion and a danger to the polity. The public parading and execution of the Bab in Tabriz in 1850, like the elaborately brutal killings of Babis after the failed attempt on the Shah's life in 1852, combined religious condemnation, group participation and public display of official vengeance to show that these were political as well as spiritual outcasts. In later political conflicts the term 'Babi' was used to stigmatise political opponents as simultaneously godless and subversive, and anti-Babi riots mobilised popular loyalties in support of urban elite conflicts. If, as Amanat and Cole argue, Babism and its successors expressed distinctive responses to modern situations in Iran as well as older dissident and visionary traditions, they left an important legacy of ideas and images to their successors.[13]

Forty years after the Bab's execution, another political upheaval which spread across Iran illustrates a new stage in the entwining of religious with political expression. In March 1890 a British entrepreneur was granted a monopoly concession over the production, sale and export of the tobacco grown in Iran. Materially, it affected hundreds of thousands of cultivators, processors, traders, and hundreds of thousands of smokers of this mass consumer product who used almost half of the 9.4 million kilo annual tobacco crop, the rest being a valuable export. Culturally, the arrival of officials to manage the Regie, as the concession was known, confronted Iranians with impending searches of their property, breaching conventions of gendered privacy, and non-Muslim handling of a product for intimate use by Muslims, with its associations of pollution. Politically, the Regie was the latest example of the central government's willingness to seek short-term advantage by granting commercial and diplomatic favours to Europeans. Foreign encroachments in Iranian trade and finance, described in Chapter 1, were seen as threats to newly conceived 'national interests' and offensive to the religio-cultural sensibilities.

Protest among merchants, 'ulama, intellectuals and urban activists following the announcement of the concession and the arrival of Regie officials brought several discourses into play. Merchant objections emphasised communal and proto-nationalist distinctions between 'Iranian' and 'foreign' interests. The reformist intelligenstia whose writings raised opposition to the Regie used the language of patriotism and modernisation to attack the government's surrender to foreign demands as evidence for the need to reform the regime if not actually change it.[14] Significantly, this discursive use of the 'nation'/people/community (*mellat*) alongside notions of the Shi'a community, and the close links of *bazaris* and *'ulama*, provided ready-made cultural resources and material connections to support protest. It allowed a turn to languages and ideas that tapped popular response, enabling commercial and intellectual campaigners to go beyond the lobbying of court and elite circles which had hitherto confined them. The casting of the anti-Regie movement in forms combining religious, patriotic and commercial discourses encouraged this turn to broad-based activism.

Depictions of concessions to foreigners as handing Muslim well-being to unbelievers, and of anti-Regie protest as *jihad* (struggle for the faith) appealed to beliefs linking different sections of the community. Leaflets and journalism spoke of the 'the officials of the government of Islam' failing to protect religion and the 'Islamic nation', of 'Muslim lambs ... being devoured by European wolves', and of those who 'have yielded the path of the Muslims to infidels'. A merchant refusing to trade tobacco with the Regie claimed he had sold it to God.[15] Mosques and pulpits became centres of opposition to the concession as merchants and reformers drew *'ulama* into campaigning, using their influence to mobilise the ability of religious leaders to reach popular constituencies. Starting with denunciations of concessions to foreigners, followed by arguments that the Regie contravened the *shari'a*, the campaign culminated in the issue of a *fatwa* (juridical ruling) in the name of Mirza Hasan Shirazi, the recognised 'supreme exemplar' for all Shi'a, stating, 'Today the use of *tunbaku* or tobacco in any form is reckoned as war against the Imam of the Age' (the hidden Twelfth Imam).[16] This launched a wholesale boycott of tobacco across Iran. 'Immediately [after the issue of the *fatwa*] with perfect accord all the tobacco merchants closed their shops, all the water pipes have been put aside, and no-one smokes any more, neither in town, nor in the entourage of the Shah, nor even in his *anderun*.'[17] Religious ideas and images transformed the pressure of specific interest groups into broad-based protest.

Bazaris, political activists, *'ulama* and popular opposition converged in demonstrations, preaching, leafleting and occupations of prominent buildings including mosques in Tehran, Shiraz, Tabriz, Mashhad, Qazvin and Isfahan. Research suggests that there were three crucial *non*-religious influences behind it: commercial classes concerned at foreign competition, reformers seeking governmental change, and Russian diplomatic pressure against a concession to British interests.[18] However, the connective tissue linking *bazaris* to *'ulama*, and their identification with Shi'a Islam, and its capacity to define foreigner/ unbeliever 'Others' and provide moral authority for political action, gave their actions emotive power and a popular base.

175

Whereas the Babi movement had proclaimed radical religious renewal encompassing political activism and social change, the anti-Regie campaign had political and material objectives expressed in partly religious terms and used religious resources against the concession. This shift expressed significant changes in the political climate as the internal and external difficulties of the Qajar regime increased. Writers and critics now deployed ideas of nation and reform which blended traditions of dissident thinking developed in Iran with those encountered elsewhere. Combinations of religious with modernising and patriotic references were often the preferred means for communicating their political aspirations. This convergence of religious thinking with modern concerns was partly the product of rational political calculations by reformers seeking access to constituencies influenced by Shi'a loyalties and images, and by *'ulama* attentive to *bazari* supporters. However, it also embodied overlaps between ideas of patriotic struggle for reform and national autonomy, ideas of godly struggle in righteous causes, and of Shi'a identity as constitutive of 'national' identity. Parading bodies of those killed in anti-Regie demonstrations, and invoking *jihad* and the Hidden Imam, expressed the relevance of rituals of martyrdom and struggle in contemporary political culture as well as the calculations of merchants, *'ulama* and activists.

These complexities are exemplified in the career of the reformist intellectual Sayyid Jamal al-Din known as 'al Afghani' (1839–97), who played a significant role in the movement against the Tobacco Concession. An Iranian with a 'traditional' religious education, he became a passionate advocate of Muslim renewal through reform in Muslim communities, polities and intellectual life in order for Muslims to better resist European encroachments. He developed arguments on the weaknesses of rulers, the shortcomings of the *'ulama* and ways to mobilise ruling elites, reformers and public opinion for change. However opportunistic his activities, they were serious attempts to generate modern political thinking and action *within* a critical relationship to Muslim history and belief. He was committed to a political agenda which neither mechanically imitated 'western' ideas and practices, nor rejected reform as 'un-Islamic'. Chameleon-like he wore the coat, tie, collar and fez of the modern Middle Eastern reformer when in Paris, appearing elsewhere in 'Nogai' dress, or more often a robe and the black turban of a *Sayyid* (one claiming descent from the family of Muhammad). In some contexts he emphasised rationalist sceptical views of Islam, in others used Qur'anic examples, Shaikhi theosophy, or other religious language.[19]

Jamal al-Din's varied and unstable presentation of himself and his ideas and images of reform and anti-imperialism expressed the rich and contradictory nature of the cultures of reform and nationalism in communities where Islam was influential. Defence of 'Islam' against external enemies and internal corruption or stagnation was a key trope for both reformers and conservatives expressing idealistic or self-interested concerns with Qajar government conduct, the economic plight of Iranians, and the needs of their communities for protection or change. As already shown, Shi'a Islam was an established component in discourses of shared identity and subject–ruler relations. However, it jostled with other ways of discussing reform, patriotism or government, creating hybrid, shifting political vocabularies and also potential competition within them, although direct confrontation was often side-stepped. For every Mirza Aqa Khan Kermani, an aggressively secular nationalist reformer, there were many more for whom patriotic commitment and tropes of Shi'a martyrdom, symbiotic invocations of Islam and Iran, and equations between political, religious and material progress and well-being were useful discourses.

The politics of the constitutionalist movement, recounted in Chapter 6, developed from the difficulties and discontents of the years following the anti-Regie movement. Here, language, symbol and ritual are discussed as part of the quantitative and qualitative changes in political life, with political networks, societies and parties linked to a growing print and popular political culture which shaped political upheavals between 1905 and 1911. These included struggles for the grant of a constitution (1905–06), controversy over its religious content (1907), a royalist anti-constitutional coup (1908) and its reversal by a pro-constitutional coalition (1909), and the disintegration of that coalition by 1911 under the pressures of its own divisions and dissensions, elite manoeuvrings, and British and Russian intervention. The discussion maps interactions between older and newer forms of political expression and between 'religious' and other elements in political language, symbol and ideology. As newly vocal political classes sought to influence government elites and institutions, and wider political constituencies, they used a whole spectrum of resources for political communication. Their success in stamping their agendas on political culture enabled them to establish myths and perceptions of the period as the disjunctive foundational episode of twentieth-century Iranian history, and the *caesura* between 'old' and 'new' in that history. As with constructions of other revolutions by participants and successors, such myths shaped historical writing on the period, which retains the label 'constitutional revolution' created by its protagonists.

The developments of 1905–11 were the product of a conditional, unstable but often effective alliance of cultures and ideologies as well as social groups and vested interests.[20] Ambitious senior *mujtaheds*, idealistic *'ulama*, modernising intellectuals, discontented merchants and urban protesters all had material, personal and opportunistic reasons to challenge the Qajar court and government, and to seek support for that challenge in streets, mosques and *bazars*. To this end, rituals of *bast* and mourning for dead protesters, of traditional manipulation and negotiation, and invocations of the Shi'a community, mixed with polemics on patriotism and reform, on government injustice and corruption, and on democracy and the rule of law. Popular slogans of 'Islam in danger' and 'government oppression', like appeals to communal loyalties by preachers and *mujtaheds*, combined with tropes of male honour and familial morality, and of subjects bringing grievances to their rulers. It is no surprise that images of the Karbala conflict, and its hero and villain, Husein and Yazid, fuelled the songs and leaflets challenging the government.[21] As in the anti-Regie protests, political discontent with government found expression in the symbolic languages and rituals of Shi'a tradition.

These phenomena were no mere survivals of old modes of political expression. Just as protesters learned the political and practical efficacy of occupying foreign embassy premises or telegraph offices as well as mosques, or *'ulama* houses, so *mullas* and other activists used modern technologies of telegraph and leaflet as well as sermons and *fatwas*. Old tropes of 'Islam in danger' were linked to the new confrontations of modernity. Already in the tobacco protests the established authority of a senior *mujtahed*'s *fatwa* had been transmitted and confirmed via the new power of telegraph links between the shrine cities of Iraq, Tehran and Iranian urban centres. In the constitutionalist era, political societies, *'ulama*, and protesters made regular and extensive use of this medium, as well as of *shab-namehs* (illicitly posted leaflets) and sermons. The opening up of politics with the grant of a constitution encouraged an explosion of print culture with an indigenous political press offering news, analysis and polemic to increasingly politicised constituencies of readers and audiences. Contested policies, elections and causes found expression in journals, cartoons, leaflets and the correspondence columns of the press, creating and sustaining languages and narratives that shaped political ideologies, organisations and cultures.

Older forms of communication could be used for new purposes. The 14,000 merchant, *'ulama*, artisan and *tullab* participants in the *bast* at the British legation summer quarters outside Tehran in July and August 1906, whose pressure achieved the grant of a constitution with a representative assembly, underwent an intensive development of ideas and arguments on the issue. Reformers and activists from both 'religious' and 'secular' backgrounds expounded and debated the meaning of these institutions, while negotiating with government representatives, *bazaris* and the senior *'ulama* who had 'emigrated' from Tehran as part of the campaign for changes in government. Ideas of a 'consultative assembly', 'house of justice', or 'fundamental laws' which had been canvassed among leading *'ulama*, and secularising reformers in the 1890s, now fused in the heat of political controversy and manoeuvre. Demands for reform in the period preceding the *bast* included arguments from a senior *mujtahed* Sayyid Muhammad Tabataba'i expressing 'traditional' concerns that government fulfil its responsibilities to its subjects, ideas of political accountability and representation current in Iranian reforming circles, and Muslim reformist thinking from authors like Kawakibi.[22] In speeches, letters and conversations with supporters he projected concern for the strength and safety of Iran/Shi'a Islam alongside aspirations for constitutional law and government, modelling a process which drew others into support for constitutional change.

Within this process, other languages and images also contended for support and authority. The actual shape of the fundamental laws and constitution granted in 1906 drew on knowledge of the Belgian constitution acquired by modernising reformers. Similarly, Iranians brought languages and images of radical populism and social democracy emerging in the Russian-ruled Caucasus regions from those regions into the political associations, activities and publications of Tabriz, Tehran and other cities. Where Afghani and Kermani in the 1890s tentatively considered drawing 'the people' into their activism, the real and imagined presence of 'the people' was now central to political discourse. The dissemination of newspaper and pamphlet material via resale and reading aloud, like the use of *shab-namehs*, and the publication of telegrams, speeches and sermons, provided the material basis on which visions of 'people', 'nation' or 'government' were projected to the very 'people' addressed in political texts.[23]

In these texts the various available languages cross-fertilised and clashed with one another. Satirists combined popular idioms with new ideas of non-Iranian origin. Newspapers like *Musavat* (Equality) and *Sur i-Israfil* (*Trumpet of Israfil*, angel of the Resurrection) argued constitutionalist and radical views in terms which linked them to 'good/true' religion, fending off accusations of heresy/secularism from anti-constitutional *'ulama*, while developing anti-clerical positions.[24] Preaching by leaders such as Tabataba'i or heterodox dissidents such as Sayyid Jamal-al-din Va'ez evoked the need for constitutional change and political renewal in terms of Muslim needs and their traditional duty to remedy injustice.[25] In the *bast* of 1906 the chanting of *rawzehs* combined with discussions of a representative assembly that was to be national (*melli*) rather than Islamic.

Nevertheless, the arguments over whether the new Majlis was *melli* (of the people) or *Islami* (of Islam) indicated developing conflicts among ideas and images as well as vested interests. Battles over the incorporation of Shi'a Muslim checks in the constitution and the role of *shari'a* law shaped a battle of discourses of inclusion, reform and state power. In these discourses conflicting notions of people/nation, law/government, progress/tradition shaped immediate partisan definitions of 'patriot', 'heretic', 'reactionary' or 'freedom lover', but also political cultures and confrontations which lasted through the twentieth century. The tactic of denouncing opponents as Babis/heretics/infidels used old conventions of conflict to sharpen new contests over religion and its place in

179

the emergent politics of reformers, government and Majlis, and over issues of social change and justice, such as land redistribution.[26] From discontented peasants and artisans to internationally linked social democrats and Shi'a leaders, these contests were central to self-presentation, self-definition and concomitant definitions of opposed 'others'. They emphasised divisions between 'religious' and 'non-religious' approaches to political issues, while also signifying the continued importance of religious discourse for *all* approaches.

Two other fields of discourse developed within constitutionalist and anti-constitutionalist politics. Most obvious were the pervasive images of patriotism and nationalism in forms ranging from the religious images of those who saw the Iranian *mellat* as Shi'a Muslim to liberal and leftist visions of a free, just, equitable society. Like counterparts in Europe, the Ottoman Empire and India, this discourse mobilised historical narrative as a new and successful literary form, with popular variants, alongside racialised notions of blood descent. The racialisation of notions of 'Iranianness' goes back to writers like Kermani using the term *jins* as well as *mellat* to designate the collectivity of 'Iranians' and the Arabophobia in the writing of Kermani and Akhundzadeh.[27] References to the inherent inherited nobility and conquering tradition 'ingrained in Iranian blood', and appeals to 'brothers of the Iranian race' sat beside evocations of pre-Islamic rulers, epic heroes and seventeenth-century conquests. Combined with advocacy of hegemony for the Persian language and territorial images of 'Iran', these tropes of blood, history, culture and soil fused with visions of modernity and state-building in a potent legacy for future political use.[28] This rhetoric embraced emotive, mythic and religious aspirations, alongside modernising rationalist reform agendas.

The other discourse which gained impetus in the constitutionalist era centred on gender and sexuality. The personification of 'Iran' as an injured, virtuous, desirable mother/beloved whose patriot sons/lovers would defend her purity like epic male heroes, or cure her ills as modernising male professionals, had already brought gendered images of politics and rationalism into oppositional reformist language. Writers like Malkom Khan invoked 'manliness' as the quality that (male) Iranians needed to change existing institutions, and envisaged foreign intervention as the 'rape' of 'Iran' or Iranian women and a threat to established Iranian/Islamic gender norms. As political confrontation and armed conflict intensified between 1905 and 1911, these tropes were increasingly frequently used, in the debates around the 'daughters of Quchan' analysed by Najmabadi, and in journalism, cartoons and *shab-namehs*.[29] Supporters of constitutionalism and of patriotic resistance to the Shah and foreigners developed images of a male citizenry reforming, defending and loving a mother/beloved figure's honour and well-being. *'Ulama* critics of the constitutional movement equated modernising reforms with 'prostitution' and with the breakdown of conventions of male/female difference and hierarchy seen as underpinning social order.[30] Regular reference to love, honour, purity and corruption in the languages of political argument reinforced the gendering and sexualisation of political culture.

Further complexity was introduced by women's political activism and their contributions to the debates on citizenship, nationhood and political agency, which challenged, troubled and energised political culture. Responses by male colleagues and commentators struggled between tropes of heroic sisterly participation, vulnerable femininity or subversive women's agency. If 'Iran' was to be renewed, what might that mean for its women inhabitants/citizens? Was the 'new' Iranian woman to be a product of controlling male agendas or mere symbol of change, or shaped by her own agency as a partner in reforming and progressive projects? Were the *zan-ha* of the nation/*mellat* its active participant 'women' or its dependent 'wives' (*zan* having both meanings)? Debate on veiling, marriage and women's education, attacks on girls' schools and women reformers, and the recording and subsequent erasure of Majlis debates on women's rights staged powerful discourses on the symbolic values and meanings underlying these issues.[31] Languages and images of masculinity, femininity and sexuality crossed political constituencies, with tropes of sexuality, gender difference and gender power relations shaping the political culture of nationalists, *mullas*, leftists and modernisers.

By the time that divisions among constitutionalists, conflicts between court, Majlis, government and political activists, and confrontations with British and Russian intervention had fractured movements for change after 1911, Iranian political vocabularies, rituals and symbols had been changed and directed to new ends. The 'Karbala paradigm' of martyrdom which brought protesters out in 1905–06, and traditions of *bast*-taking, leafleting, and elite manoeuvring were now associated with party and *anjuman* organisation, journalistic debate, cartoons and satire, and of political lobbying and activism. The anti-constitutionalist *mujtahed* Fazlullah Nuri used printing press and telegram to buttress his traditional power to withdraw services and issue authoritative opinions, and his control of *tullab* and clients. Social democrats combined egalitarian ideals and arguments emerging in Europe and Asia with familiar Iranian poetry, *shari'a* tradition and ideals of religious struggle, describing their activists by using indigenous terms like *mujahed* and *fida'i* alongside leftist, rhetoric, analysis and propaganda. Conservative politicians and elite statesmen deployed vocabularies of modernisation and patriotism alongside older bureaucratic and manipulative skills to secure places in the changing political order. Idealistic reformers reconfigured ideas of popular rights and representation familiar to European radicals, and of state-led social engineering used by Bonapartist, Ottoman or Bismarckian nationalists, within the framework of 'Iranian' cultures and patriotism. New political repertoires and cultural resources entered Iranian political life, shaping struggles around the constitution, agendas for change and foreign intervention.

While the period 1905–11 established political discourses on trajectories which continued throughout the twentieth century, these discourses were neither stable nor clear. Sharp conflicts between radicals and establishment interests, 'ulama and secularists, or the powerless and the powerful, created languages that opposed desirable ideals ('true' religion, national salvation, freedom/progress) to the unacceptable 'other' (godlessness, subordination, tyranny, reaction). Like material conflicts over religion, socio-economic reform, and Russian and British interference in Iranian politics, these languages constructed oppositions and alternatives that coloured subsequent Iranian politics and culture. Conversely, partisan activists seeking broad support, 'ulama or officials defending their changing position, or radicals attached both to indigenous dissident traditions and to new visions and ideas, found eclecticism and hybridity more useful. Protesters in streets, fields and bazars also juggled new views of their desires with old and valued forms of political thought and action.

Changes in political cultures during the constitutional struggles contributed to the rise and development of Reza Shah's regime, which took advantage of the failure of both establishment elites and aspiring activists to sustain effective government. To the former he seemed to offer the promise of re-establishing the law and order threatened by dissident movements in various regions of Iran in the decade after 1911. To the latter he appeared to hold out the possibility of assertive state-led reform and modernisation and 'national' strengthening in the face of external pressure. Reza Khan's use of plot and force in the 1921 coup d'etat which made him war minister, and his move to become prime minister in 1923 and first shah of a new Pahlavi dynasty in 1925, signalled not just the momentary success of military power but a militarisation of politics. In addition to the material factors of his political skill and ruthlessness, the power vacuum created by the stalemated exhaustion of the political elite, and the collusion of British interests, his use of cultural resources should not be ignored. His ability to manoeuvre in and out of alliances as he constructed and then consolidated his regime was also the ability to deploy language, ritual and symbol to powerful political effect.[32]

While accounts of the political culture of the 'Reza Shah era' (1921–41) are often written in terms of repression, long-term developments in that culture were quite complex. Building on the discourses of nation and modernity, which Iranians had been constructing over two generations, the new regime contributed its own authoritarian and controlling rhetoric which meant repression or censorship. Famously, Reza Khan's proclamation the day after his coup is said to have begun with the words 'I command', and the springboard for the regime was the reform, centralisation and mobilisation of a new military force which was to remain at its core. As part of centralising reforms described elsewhere, the regime assumed a 'command and control' style of government which, whatever its success, was a distinct shift in political process and culture.

These developments characterised political culture as well as regime policy. As Kashani-Sabet argues, the breakdown of constitutionalist politics into civil conflict, foreign military intervention and localised armed struggles contributed to 'the growing militarization of Iran's political culture' from 1910, reinforced by the consequences of the outbreak of international conflict in 1914.[33] The language of *jihad* (sacred struggle), now attached to discourses of nationalism, and of armed resistance to foreign threats to 'national' borders and to gendered 'Iranian' honour, was accompanied by glorification of historic military successes and demands for military improvements. When Reza Khan spoke of the army as 'the supreme means of the prosperity of the country' in his post-coup declaration, he echoed the patriotic view that 'we consider the basis of all reforms ... the existence of full military encampments and organised armies', stating that the army should be respected as 'the supreme means of the prosperity of the country'.[34] The linking of images of military command and order to ideals of modernity and of 'national' interest became symbolically as well as materially central to the character and credibility of the regime. The use of uniforms, patterns of regimentation and inspection in schools, workshops or hospitals, and attempts to regulate dress codes, whether effective or not, disseminated a new culture of control and uniformity. [35]

Whatever the rationale of the regime for such policies, their impact in the wider political community was reinforced by other discourses. The association of state power with modernity went back to earlier fascination with tsarist and Ottoman achievements, and beliefs that government and reform were mutually dependent. The forceful rhetoric and practice of the new regime's assault on legal, administrative and educational reform, and its self-promotion as the executive arm of a modernising project, had cultural as well as practical results. State support for a growing modern professional/administrative/educated stratum, and their reciprocal support for state policy, encouraged the embedding of modernist discourse as the hegemonic mode for public discussion. From the Shah's viewpoint, the discourse of modernisation supported alliances and legitimations useful to his regime, and consolidated the dominance of languages of modernity in Iranian political culture. The significant shift in the Reza Shah era was the separation of ideas of freedom and democracy from the 'official' version of that language.[36]

Militarisation and centralisation were legitimised as necessary to the strengthening and progress of the 'nation' through territorial unity. Beyond that the language of *vatan* (fatherland), *mellat–melli* (nation–national), and 'Iran' was now the rhetoric of government policy, propaganda and school books, as well as journalistic and intellectual discussion. Official sponsorship of this rhetoric built on the dissemination of patriotic and nationalistic ideas and images during the constitutionalist era, appropriating discourses which had supported struggle and change to shape images of the Pahlavi regime, and enabling the Shah to create links with groups to whom nationalism was important. As primary and secondary schools were established in Iranian towns, officially sponsored nationalistic discourse in the curriculum and textbooks shaped the political culture of the next generations of Iranians.[37] It went with public use of nationalist imagery in official buildings and publicity, and marked the emergent dominance of visions of centralised standardised 'national' needs and interests over older sectional alternatives.

One prominent feature of the 'national'-minded political culture of the 1920s and 1930s was its increasing secularism. This is often seen as a characterising feature of Reza Pahlavi's regime, and histories of the period emphasise the antagonism and conflict between the regime (and its modernising allies) and protagonists of religious interests and institutions.[38] Certainly there was much emphasis on non- or pre-Islamic aspects of the national past, from the promotion of Firdausi (author of a well-known epic poem using pre-Islamic legends) to replicating figures from the pre-Islamic palace of Persepolis on the new national bank building. The 'twin pillars' of religious and monarchical order underpinning the ideology of Qajar government and the 'religious–radical' alliance of constitutionalist politics were displaced by a statist unipolar image of power and change. Democratic, leftist and constitutionalist critics of the regime emphasised the importance of a central state (albeit a different one) for the benefit of people and society in Iran as much as did government rhetoric. In both cases the language of opposition to 'reaction' or 'backwardness' involved attacks on the 'superstition' or 'corruption' associated with traditional religious practices and practitioners.

The fact that 'secular' critiques of 'religion' emphasised practice and practitioners, rather than 'Islam' as such, suggests that binary conflict was not the only cultural dynamic. The Shah manipulated the symbols and representatives of Shi'a Islam, sometimes accepting gifts from Qum *mujtaheds*, or leading Muharram processions, and sometimes attacking and humiliating *'ulama*. The use of *shari'a* approaches to personal law in the new secular law codes had ideological significance as well as being politically opportune. In manoeuvrings with the *'ulama* over conscription laws in the 1920s, Reza Shah made undertakings 'to preserve the greatness of Islam and the *'ulama* leadership' in their tasks of 'carrying out their convictions and intentions as well as in distributing the sacred religious texts'.[39] This opportunistic and unfulfilled commitment was an interesting rhetorical acknowledgement of *'ulama* roles for political purposes. The need for an anti-religious autocrat like Reza Pahlavi to recognise their political interests suggests the importance of ideological balancing acts as well as confrontational culture politics.[40]

Another way to see religious language, image and ritual in politics in this period is to examine religious responses in the political arena more directly. Between the 1890s and the 1920s, *'ulama* and others used religious discourses in debates on constitutional change and 'national' interests, matching their engagement in Majlis and political associations with political argument. One effect of the increasing centralisation and autocracy of the regime was to restrict spaces and opportunities to engage in such debates. The decline of the *'ulama* presence in the Majlis during the 1930s, like the arrest and internal exile of the leading political *mulla* Sayyid Hasan Mudarris in 1929, signalled a political decline matching the institutional attacks on the *'ulama* which was a signature regime policy.[41] For senior *'ulama*, the regime's confrontational politics stimulated a return to the political culture of manoeuvre and negotiation well established in their repertoire. Conflicts over republicanism in 1924–25, or over conscription in 1926–27 illustrate the durability of this style of political engagement.

Nor did some *mullas* wholly abandon campaigning approaches to state power developed in the nineteenth century. The intersection of popular concern with the influence of preachers, overtly or covertly supported by their seniors, was clearly at work in the protests over state regulation of dress codes. Attacks on women who abandoned 'traditional' veiling conventions accompanied *'ulama* preaching and protest in significant public opposition to unveiling, and repressive official responses, on streets and in shrines and mosques.[42] The ability of *'ulama* to mobilise popular protests and choreograph telegrams defending their views showed the continued importance of this kind of activism. In the repressive climate of the 1930s, this tradition might not surface often or effectively, but remained within the political repertoire.

Political aspects of religious ideology between the 1920s and the 1940s were complex. In the constitutional era a spectrum of languages around Shi'a Islam, political change and socio-cultural modernity was deployed by *'ulama* and intellectuals with religious backgrounds. For some the defence and well-being of Islam were the criteria for acceptance or rejection of constitutional change, while for others education and gender relations were test issues and symbols in their engagement with modernity. *'Ulama* withdrawal from the political arena from the 1920s was not just rejection of secularism, but a position within a repertoire of political possibilities and religious thinking. Their defensiveness and anger flavoured the language of opposition alongside assertions of Shi'a Islam as central to virtue, order and identity. When the leading *mujtahed* 'Abd al-Karim Ha'eri Yazdi, famed for his cautious and defensive approach to politics, protested directly about steps 'openly contradictory ... to the law of Islam', he combined traditions of remonstrance with those of confrontation.[43]

Defensive responses, whether public or discreet, were not the only elements in the repertoire of discourse on religion and politics. It included traditions like that of 'al-Afghani' advocating Muslim realignment to modernity, or *mujtaheds* such as Tabataba'I and Na'ini whose writings provided endorsement for constitutionalism, or the preachers, activists and writers who brought religious discourse into constitutional and nationalist politics. On the activist side the careers of 'political *mullas*' such as Sayyid Hasan Mudarris and Abu'l Qasim Kashani bridged the clerical involvement of constitutionalist times and developments in the 1920s. Until his suppression, Mudarris was an effective exponent of a pragmatic party politics whereby *'ulama* adapted to and defended the gains of the constitutional era in alliance with secular politicians. Kashani, who was to be more prominent in the 1940s, appears in the 1920s as active in anti-British politics in Iraq, and supported Reza Khan/Shah, whom Mudarris opposed.[44] The visibility of such individuals showed the ongoing possibility of *'ulama* participation in 'modern' politics, which, while curtailed by more aggressive secularism and repression in the 1930s, embodied ongoing experiments with the politics of religion in modern settings.

Such experiments took various cultural forms. Within religious practice and institutions themselves even limited discussion of the need for reform provoked ideological controversy and had political edge. The career of an *'alim* like Mirza Reza Quli 'Shari'at Sangalaji', combining writing and proselytising on reformist issues, relationships with Reza Shah and participation in modern intellectual life in Tehran is an example.[45] He wrote critiques of Shi'a practice within Shi'a reforming tradition, and had contacts with the leader of Reza Shah's programme of legal secularisation. His calls for rigorous and purified forms of Shi'a Islam grounded in the Qur'an and monotheism provoked debate and condemnation. His preaching and discussion meetings parallel initiatives by thoughtful *mullas* like Sayyid Abu'l Hasan Taleqani in Tehran, and the contacts formed by Muhammad Taqi Shari'ati as a school teacher in Mashad. They could also be compared to the work of the ex-*'alim* 'Ali Akbar Hakamizadeh whose critical writings were published in the 1930s, and who like Sangalaji was attacked by Ruhollah Khomeini in his 1940s text *The Unveiling of Secrets*.[46] The fact that the production of this text was supported by Tehran *bazar* merchants, as others supported Taleqani, or challenged Ha'eri Yazdi's ideas of reform, indicates the diversity of discourse and opinion. State repression meant that the reform of Shi'ism and its alignment with 'modern' circumstances explored in these initiatives also involved hostility to 'despotism'.[47]

These developments, limited as they were, form part of the story of religion in the politics of modernity, and of the terms, concepts and politico-cultural practices which emerged in the Reza Shah era. In the 1940s and 1950s they developed further, with the radical religious thinker 'Ali Shari'ati listing Sangalaji among the authors he used as a student activist, and Mahmud Taleqani developing the tradition of debate on Islam in the modern world started by his father.[48] The experiences of Iranians growing up in the 1930s, influenced by both religious backgrounds and encounters with modern and secular ideas and education, shaped their later political ideas and practices.

Another significant aspect of political culture was its forceful consolidation of gendered languages and representations of 'nation' and 'modernity'. Building on the images of male patriotism evolved in the constitutionalist era, and increasingly militarised by the 1920s, official ideas of manly discipline and modern skills mobilised for the benefit and progress of 'Iran' flourished under the first Pahlavi Shah. Celebrations of warrior heroes and rulers of the past in school textbooks and government rhetoric, like references to honour and brotherhood in the depiction of Iranian ethnic identity, projected distinctive masculine images.[49] Equally interesting was the reconstitution of discourses of femininity in which women's roles as home-makers and mothers were reconfigured as modern and patriotic, and new codes of honour and chastity projected by male intellectuals and reformers. Again school textbooks used languages with new visions of women's 'national'/social responsibilities in which modern education, maternal breastfeeding and 'scientific' housewifery would produce a different version of Iranian womanhood.[50] Political projections of femininity in the Reza Khan/Shah era advocated statist morality and interventionism. Quite apart from the significance of this for the history of heterosexuality and gender roles and relations in Iran generally, it embedded discourses of gender, virtue and honour in the public perception and rhetoric of government, politicians and intellectuals.[51] The official symbolism of educational and dress reform policies linked with the intellectual and emotional authority of gendered versions of 'nation' and 'progress' to reinforce and disseminate the enactment of 'modern' and 'national' ideas in gendered language, image and performance.

While the political culture of the 1920s and 1930s was dominated by an authoritarian and restrictive as well as modernising and centralising state, it encompassed critical and oppositional elements. Alongside versions of patriotism and progress promoted by the regime, discourses of resistance, or alternative versions of these tropes, maintained a presence among 'ulama and leftists. Political languages of family, honour, community, piety hierarchy and cultural diversity, rooted in communities where the impact of the state was limited, survived to have a future role. The explosion of political activity in the period between the removal of Reza Shah in 1941 and the overthrow of prime minister Mussadeq in 1953 drew on existing ideological resources while transforming and adding to them. This period was one when an open politics of party and electoral activity, and ideological journalism was able to flourish as it had from 1905 to 1925.[52] This open politics established cultural tropes and symbols which reverberated through subsequent generations. Out of the experiences of that time myths and images of the national struggle against foreigners, of masses and leaders united in movements for social justice and equity, and of the confrontation between a despotic Shah and the people, became established politico-cultural currency.

For the first time the leftist languages used by small groups of activists in the constitutional era and intellectuals in the Reza Shah period were tried out in the larger arena of the Tudeh (= masses) Party and associates and sympathisers from trade unionists to school teachers. Activists and writers coined a language which combined constitutional (anti-despotic), nationalistic (anti-imperialist) and socialist (anti-elite) ideas, aimed at broad constituencies of wage workers, professionals and small producers. They embedded a body of language and image in the wider political culture through publications, mass mobilisation and organised political networks. Terms like 'oppression' and 'social progress', the culture of labour organisation, and slogans and ideals promulgated by party and union branches and occupational or local organisations, entered the experience of many urban groups.[53] The coalition of parties around the National Front likewise deployed press and local politics to spread visions of national autonomy, opposition to dictatorship, and the struggle for oil nationalisation. Carefully argued ideas of 'negative equilibrium' aimed at educated nationalists were buttressed by accessible media versions of the drama of 'Iranian' confrontation with external enemies and the 'people's' challenge to 'despotism'.[54] While leftists and nationalists drew on the legacy of preceding decades, the scale and extent of their activities in a relatively open political culture allowed them to explore new purposes and new constituencies.

Equally innovative in this period were reshaped linkages of religious and political language. Earlier tentative moves towards Shi'a Muslim modernism blossomed into coherent if embattled visions of the relationships between Islam, human progress and political change. The writing and preaching of Mehdi Bazargan (pious Shi'a, scientifically trained) and Mahmud Taleqani (*madraseh*-trained preacher and theologian) sought to respond creatively to the advance of secularist and anti-clerical views and to the Shi'a Muslim establishment's reluctance to adapt to changing circumstances. In addition to exploring the links between their faith, democratic government, nationalism and social reform, they advocated and modelled rationality, political commitment and social responsibility in Shi'a Muslim practice.[55] The development of these themes in the 1950s and 1960s drew on the activities and publications of discussion groups, organisations of students and engineers in the 1940s.

Two themes predominated in the new discourses. First, religious commitment was identified with political activism, particularly against the foreign intervention threatening Islamo-Iranian interests. Second, there was an emphasis on rethinking religious belief and understanding as a creative modern alternative both to secularist views and to unreflective religious traditionalism. Significantly, these tropes were often deployed in non-mosque settings by non-'ulama activists, whether Muhammad Shari'ati's discussion groups and school texts in Mashad, or Muslim student societies and professional and *bazari* networks in Tehran.

The opening up of innovative discourse on religion, politics and society to new constituencies took enthusiasts like Shari'ati and Bazargan among school students, *bazaris* and professionals, and Taleqani into radio broadcasting.[56] The urgent need to challenge leftist and nationalist recruitment of young Iranians to secular ideas, and the conflicts around the National Front and oil nationalisation, with their associated threats of repression, gave force to their activities and to their language and style. Drama, conspiracy, confrontation were intrinsic to their vocabulary and presentation, as was emotional as well as intellectual commitment to the contemporary 'relevance' of Islam, which could take uncompromisingly activist forms.[57] Another strand of innovative politico-religious discourse in the 1940s was provided by the mass politics around Ayatollah Abu'l Qasim Kashani, and the Feda'iyan-i-Islam, a campaigning group involved in the assassination of several major figures, but with a programme, publications and an ideology.[58] That ideology and language trumpeted opposition to 'anti-Islamic' aspects of society and politics, while their activism mirrored that of less religious, or less hard-line organisations. Their language exalted 'tradition' but their party programme, their use of electoral campaigns and demonstrations, and their internationalist support for the Palestinians and oil nationalisation, mark their involvement in modern political discourses of populism and anti-colonialism.

It is not surprising that they were associated with the political activity of Kashani, whose activist history went back to anti-British campaigns in Iraq at the end of the First World War and Majlis politics in Iran in the 1920s. His ability to mobilise large public demonstrations and to play a role in Majlis and party manoeuvrings enabled him to influence the nationalist movement of the 1940s.[59] His popularity rested partly on his anti-secularist stance, but increasingly on forceful exposition of anti-foreign, anti-imperialist politics and of support for Muslim unity in the tradition of 'Afghani'. When referring to the collectivity of 'Iranians' he was more likely to use the nationalist term *mellat* than the Islamic term *ummat*. He spoke of the 'sacred and national struggle' against the British, established his own *bazar*-based faction the Mujahedin-i-Islam (a name with constitutionalist and religious associations), and joined the National Front coalition.[60]

However, the innovative aspects of political culture in this period were driven by tensions and conflicts in the political arena as much as convergences of interests, ideas or aspirations. The impact of two decades of secularism in urban communities affected politico-religious discourse, whether modernist or conservative, in the 1940s. Divisive class and ethnic interests cut across languages of national unity and centralised policy-making. Political cultures of antagonism were fed by the immediacy of the Allied occupation of 1941–46, the oil nationalisation battle, and conflicts over Azeri and Kurdish separatism, as well as by fears of repression among leftists and constitutionalists, or of social revolution among propertied elites. Established tropes of martyrdom in the fight for a 'good' cause, and of the opposition of tyrannical ruler to patriotic/democratic 'people', combined with new dramatisations. Combative and militarised language ('enemy', battle', 'glorious') emphasised highly coloured adversarial images of the aims and ideals of political activists, reinforcing narratives of struggle, victory and defeat as preferred representations of politics. This imagery combined with strikes, demonstrations and physical conflicts to establish a dramatic approach to politics, whether leftist, religious or nationalist. A politics of struggle expressed the challenge of new political actors to the 'old' politics of manoeuvre and compromise.

As in other periods of Iranian history, it is important to draw attention to the unstable and shifting meanings of key political concepts. Ja'afar Pishevari, the veteran leftist leader of the Azeri separatist movement of 1945–46, deployed the languages of his communist background ('the government of the country should be the government of the masses'), of Azeri identity ('Azerbaijan must maintain its distinctiveness') and of sacred struggle (*jihad*) against Tehran centralism.[61] Religious language co-existed with a range of others, so that Mussadeq referred to his patriotism as 'the creed of the Lord of Martyrs' (Husein), and the Tudeh Party commemorated the death of a forebear with a religious service, and paid tribute to the *'alim* Mudarris.[62] Conversely, *'ulama* and committed Muslims like Taleqani, Shari'ati and Bazargan conjoined piety, patriotism, social concern and opposition to despotism. The energy and the frustrations of political culture from 1941 to 1953 were creatively expressed in the hybrid, overlapping images and languages of those active at that time.

Whatever the legacy of ideas and images from the 1941–53 period, it is arguable that its most potent resource (for good or ill) was a set of myths to be redeployed in subsequent decades. Most obvious of these was the mythic narrative of a cross-class struggle for national autonomy associated with Mussadeq, whose name and blessing were invoked by various opposition movements in the 1950s and 1960s. Alongside it stood myths of the efforts and/or 'betrayals' of leftists, notably the Tudeh Party, which coloured the initiatives of younger generations of radicals. As they made recollections of the 1941–53 era into historical or polemic narratives, former activists constructed stories of the 'divided' social structures and cultures of Iran, contrasting 'modern/progressive' elements with their 'reactionary/traditional' opposites. As Iranians lived with the reimposition of the Shah's autocratic power and the role of foreign influence, their views of the preceding period emphasised the malign role of foreigners, and fused into conspiracy theories about British, Russian, American (and later Israeli) ability to manipulate Iranian politics. This conspiracy view, which included critiques of Soviet control of the Tudeh Party by the non-communist left, and anti-semitic and anti-Baha'i images of Baha'is and Jews as 'Zionist agents', was powerful across a wide spectrum of political groupings and outlooks. Along with the iconic figure of Mussadeq and conflicting versions of his overthrow, it reinforced experiences and beliefs remembered, revisited and reconfigured after 1953.

Debates on Iranian political cultures from 1953 to 1978 have focused on questions of change and continuity as well as on the sources for the apparently hegemonic role of religious discourses in the 1977–81 upheavals that established the Islamic Republic. The reimposition of autocracy, with its cycles of repression and relative permissiveness and ultimate drift to overweening 'sultanism', was the overarching framework in which political cultures were shaped. In the 1960s and 1970s, material shifts, changes in education and migration, and cultural as well as physical communication established new socio-cultural arenas, possibilities and challenges. Rather than opposing 'continuity' to 'change', or 'religious' to 'non-religious' political discourse, this account explores Iranian political cultures of the period in terms of colliding and/or converging discourses within overlapping and competing milieux.

For those with political experience of the 1940s and the Mussadeq premiership, one response was to promote a political culture of resistance and reaffirmation. Through the 1960s the founding and refounding of 'National Fronts' and references to Mussadeq by groups opposing the Shah affirmed the symbolic importance of maintaining links between the ideals of the 1940s and 1950s and current attempts to intervene in Iranian politics. When Mehdi Bazargan, modernising Muslim, lay intellectual and National Front activist, outlined the key principles of the newly founded Liberation/Freedom Movement of Iran in 1961, he identified the movement as 'Musaddeqist' as well as Muslim, Iranian and constitutionalist.[63] The image of struggle against foreign intervention in Iran, reinforced by American backing for the Shah after 1953, was buttressed by reference to the National Front era, by the leftist tradition of anti-imperialism, and by religious hostility to non-Muslim influence. The shift from public commemoration of Mussadeq in the period of the Shah's overthrow in 1979 to his 'unpersoning' and vilification by 1981, signalled the shift away from this political culture of reaffirmation to reinvention and then rejection of a 'secular' icon.[64]

The Pahlavi regime's success in containing and repressing exponents of patriotic, constitutionalist and reformist politics drove that tradition into clandestine forms and exile. Left/liberal political culture was largely kept alive by intellectuals and students operating in the shadow of censorship and punishment inside Iran, and by groups of exiles and students abroad. They continued the tropes of resistance to despotism in the name of the *mellat*, of the quest for social justice, and desire for freedom from 'external' (now seen as American) intervention in 'Iranian' affairs. These ideals, and images of a *mellat*-centred, autonomous Iran where all would benefit from progress and prosperity, fuelled the opposition culture of the 1960s and 1970s. Additionally, the traditions and discourses of resistance inherited from the political experiences ending in 1953 were overlaid with conflict and debate over what was to be learned from that experience. These debates fuelled both the preservation and adaptation of the political cultures of the previous generation. The rhetoric of despotism, injustice and exploitation, and images of the Iranian *mellat* challenging Pahlavi rule and foreign interference in Iran continued to figure prominently in the oppositional literature of the 1960s and 1970s.

Changes in the international scene, and contact with other political traditions and experiences by Iranians abroad encouraged new developments in Iranian oppositional political culture. Anti-colonial movements, especially in Algeria, the impact of Nasser's style of nationalism, and the evolution of the Israeli–Palestinian conflict were stimuli for new images of anti-colonial nationalism and struggle in Iranian oppositional writing. They provided new and contemporary hero/martyr figures alongside the increasingly remote Iranian figures of the 1940s and 1950s. They also fuelled the ideal of armed struggle as an expression of committed resistance and leadership. They inspired guerrilla activity which embodied the emotional force of dramatic action in the image of heroic warriors for good causes across the world, and Iranian/Shi'a tropes of martyrdom. Growing numbers of Iranian students studying abroad in the 1960s and 1970s were able to cross-reference their existing ideas and beliefs with those they encountered in European or American settings. The images of Iranian culture and identity developed as a committed Shi'a Muslim by 'Ali Shari'ati were rooted both in the traditions of religious Mussadeqism which shaped his own and his father's experience and in the intellectual and cultural resources he acquired during his sojourn in France.[65]

Although inspirational tropes of struggle and liberation inherited from past experience and developed in the 1960s and 1970s did survive, they did so in difficult conditions, and their effects were limited in several ways. Government repression restricted the production and dissemination of oppositional ideas and images. Leftist, nationalist and reformist oppositional cultures were cut off from the constituencies who supported them in the 1940s and 1950s. At that period the ideals of nationalism, social justice and democracy going back to the constitutionalist era had involved wider groups of Iranians. After 1953 the regime's suppression and harassment of political parties, unions and other forms of civil association that had supported that involvement left custody of the political cultures of the preceding period with educated urban groups, notably intellectuals, professionals and students.

Discourses of leftist or nationalist politics became predominantly assets for an oppositional intelligentsia expressed in terms relevant to them. Largely deprived of opportunities to describe, debate or disseminate such discourses in Iranian settings, leftist pamphleteers, organisers, theorists, and later guerrillas, often did so in terms derived from the discourses of international marxisms, socialisms and communisms. Their analyses of Iranian society, of international capital, and of possible revolutionary strategies, fortified their existence as underground and émigré organisations with small committed networks of clandestine supporters undertaking high-profile armed actions. Their focus on these activities sidestepped the question of how larger sections of Iranian society might be mobilised, although this limitation was offset by the increase in the pool of better-educated young Iranians among whom leftist groups might recruit. The political cultures of underground and émigré Iranian leftist groups, like other such organisations, combined idealistic visions of the needs/interests of the masses/people with the elitist confidence of isolated, clever, dedicated and intensely involved activists

While the makers and spokespersons of leftist ideologies drew on international resources, fleshing out rhetorics of imperialism, exploitation and the struggle against them, they were less engaged with new discourses of identity and ethnic politics. Well versed in thoughtful analyses of material interests and social structures in Iran, they concerned themselves less with cultural developments. They used populist anti-colonial versions of nationalism as the protest of exploited peoples against tyranny or international capitalism, but were less attuned to emergent 'nativist' depictions of the 'essential' and 'authentic' characteristics of the 'nation'. These ideals and depictions of the 'Iranian' nation/people/community came to play transformative roles in Iranian cultures and politics from the 1960s, as new expressions of cultural nationalism influenced politically concerned Iranians. Developments in the rhetoric and imagery of cultural nationalism created significant new relations between 'religious' and other elements in the political cultures of discontent and resistance in that period.

The anti-western discourses of the 1960s and 1970s differed in flavour and content from older versions and appealed to new constituencies. Older hostility predominantly used a language of *defence* of established custom, religion and community against alien or ungodly alternatives intruding on Iranians from outside. It had expressed the views of those who saw the need to protect existing relationships, institutions or hierarchies from such intrusions. Newer reactions to 'the west' used languages of *analysis* and *critique*, and focused on the common stake of all Iranians in 'their' culture. They used a wide repertoire of 'modern' thinking (existentialist, third worldist, anti-colonialist) in addition to images of Iranian belief and custom, to celebrate 'indigenous' Iranian culture. Where modernisers of earlier generations used ideas of 'backwardness' to depict the problems faced by Iranians, and their traditionalist critics used images of an alien/infidel threat, the new exponents of cultural authenticity used what came to be the signature term in their oppositional discourse – *gharb-zadegi*. Its most literal meaning might be 'west-struckness', but its significance is better conveyed by the term 'west-toxication' with its suggestion of a combination of disturbing attraction and poisoning or damage (as with the English word 'intoxication').

New critiques of 'the west' argued that indigenous cultural resources served *contemporary* needs better than 'imported' equivalents, and indeed opposed indigenous traditions which did not serve those needs. The discourse of cultural authenticity offered a credible alternative both to uncritical enthusiasm for western practices or ideas, and to the mere perpetuation of 'tradition', envisaging an active quest for authenticity in the present, not passive contemplation of the past. Above all, the new cultural nationalism opened up spaces for religion, and was a profoundly *political* analysis supporting resistance to the Pahlavi regime. Its exemplary figures were the author of the iconic text *Gharb-zadegi*, Jalal Al i-Ahmad, and 'Ali Shari'ati.

The character and complexity of these discourses of anti-westernism have been extensively explored as a body of thought. Their origins in literary innovations in the 1920s and 1930s, in the desire to configure religious modernity in order to resist colonial incursions going back to 'Afghani', and in Iranian cultural thought from the 1940s, have been traced. So too have their diverse modes of expression which drew on Islamic modernism, German and French philosophy, post-war third worldist analyses of culture, and Iranian discourses of 'nation' and modernisation established over several generations.[66] Discussion of these discourses has also assumed that there were connections between these specialised writings for limited audiences and broader oppositional ideas with their populist versions of religiously flavoured anti-American nationalism. The juxtaposition in many accounts of the 1977–81 revolution of descriptions of the careers and ideas of intellectuals like 'Ali Shari'ati and Jalal Al i-Ahmad (populariser of the notion of *gharb-zadegi* among his educated readership) with the broader discontents and popular religiosity of mass politics in those years is interesting. This can partly be explained in terms of a contingent coming together of different strands of protest and opposition, but also had cultural aspects.

While the wider groupings of Iranians who joined the upheavals of 1977–81 might have had no direct access to Shari'ati's ideas, they, like those who did have that access, lived the multifarious and sometimes discordant cultural experiences in Iranian society in the 1960s and 1970s. It was a society in which literacy reached only just over 40 per cent in the 1970s but where radios, televisions, and cassette tapes spread contemporary cultural messages to diverse audiences, including those in rural communities. It was a society in which many educated people had absorbed modern ideas of progress, but were also aware of ties to cultural and personal resources which they perceived as indigenous and 'Iranian'. It was a society in which migrants from small towns and villages were suddenly negotiating the material and cultural demands of large cities as they sought work and social survival. It was a society in which there were contests over the possible/desirable/unacceptable roles of Shi'a Islam as a socio-cultural norm, as a set of outdated beliefs and practices, as a body of truth to be exhumed, or as a vital marker of 'national'/popular authenticity and political commitment. The conflicted and complex awareness of many Iranians made them receptive to ideas and images which *politicised* their experiences.

In the 1970s, choices and differences were understood and dealt with personally and locally, as with poor women from south Tehran studied by Bauer who combined concern with female dress codes with ideas of gender equity, women's disadvantages and TV watching. While they addressed such matters pragmatically, they also conceptualised them as disjunctions between their circumstances and those of the materially privileged and educated, between individual aspiration and communal constraint, and between convention and innovation.[67] These women also demonstrated their grasp of issues which intellectuals discussed in literary, philosophical or polemical terms, and their own intellectual agency. Similarly, the unemployed worker turned street vendor who invoked the ideal of unified (*tawhidi*) ideals and society in the months after the Shah's overthrow picked up a theme from Shari'ati offering an inspiring alternative to the discordant unequal society and culture of Pahlavi times.[68] These instances are not 'evidence' of direct links between unprivileged Iranians and the work of writers who critiqued the role of 'western', 'foreign' elements in contemporary Iranian life, but *are* glimpses of convergent concerns and perceptions with a political edge. They added to the resources drawn on by participants in the 1977–81 revolution as they created that revolution in the name of the overthrow of 'corruption' and 'injustice'.

It is in this context that we should consider the role of Shari'ati's ideas and the upsurge of politicised religious discourse among the young educated activists who provided ideological and organisational leadership in the neighbourhoods and workplaces where protests, strikes and demonstrations emerged to unseat the regime. Shari'ati (1933–77) was a teacher, writer and activist who gained fame as a radical innovator in religious thought and exponent of committed progressive Islam. He grew up in traditions of pious Mussadeqist patriotism and anti-despotism and acquired political insights through immersion in both Iranian and French progressive intellectual culture.[69] He propagated discourses of dissidence and opposition to Pahlavi rule, of egalitarian activist Shi'a Islam, and of its (re)discovery as an *indigenous* inheritance supporting resistance to corrupt, alien/alienating and repressive aspects of contemporary Iranian culture. The passion and appeal of Shari'ati's lectures and writings derived from the eclectic use of diverse elements and repeated images.

These images combined familiarity, innovation and multiple meanings. The centrality of the Karbala paradigm and the figures of 'Ali and Husein in Shari'ati's work invoked familiar ideals, while reconfiguring their suffering as active and political like modern heroes of social and political struggle. His appropriation of the less familiar Abu Zarr, a figure from early Muslim history known for ascetic renunciation, was a more innovative move to assert the socially egalitarian agenda of Islam. His controversial critiques of *'ulama*-led religion as denying the call of Shi'ism to commitment and struggle for change tapped into well-established anti-*'ulama* views. His attractive argument that Islam was to be grasped and interpreted by intelligent believers rather than a limited group of specialists, appealed directly to a new generation of college-educated young Iranians from pious backgrounds who were rooted in both cultures.

He combined emotive ideas of Islam as a religion of struggle and social justice owned by committed believers, rather than the *'ulama*, with leftist discourses of anti-imperialism and anti-despotism from the 1940s and 1950s, and third worldist ideas of the 1960s. Thus the sermons of 'Ali and the Karbala narrative cohabited with the languages of contemporary protest politics, and a rich repertoire of mystical and poetic references characteristic of certain kinds of Iranian cultural discourse. He offered a synthesis of social and political analysis and polemic familiar in 'secular' thought from Marx to Fanon with his vision of Shi'a Islam as the paradigm for all those struggling and suffering in their search for the 'justice and equality of classes and races'.[70] As he put it towards the end of his life, he had a mission to show Muslims that Islam was revolutionary, and to persuade non-religious revolutionaries to rejoin their fellow Iranian Muslims.[71] This mission was expressed in a discourse of search for selfhood and authenticity, which in Shari'ati's view came through commitment to struggle for a better society, and to Shi'a Islam as its authentic expression. His passionate exposition of these themes, use of familiar images, an iconoclasm attractive to youthful audiences, and ability to appeal to diverse viewpoints linked him to the varied cultural worlds of his hearers and readers. The number of these grew as tapes and clandestine printings of his inspirational lectures were disseminated beyond the few thousands who heard him at Huseiniyeh Ershad in the late 1960s and early 1970s.

The intellectual content and coherence of Shari'ati's work have been much debated in recent scholarship, but both his work and his life contributed to the repertoire of resources used by the activists of the late 1970s.[72] His visions of personal and shared commitment, at once deeply religious, socially radical and assertive of Iranians' 'indigenous' selves, might not stand up to scholarly or theological scrutiny, but expressed the needs of those he addressed as *roshan-fekran* (enlightened and pious intelligentsia). They allowed many in the Iranian opposition, damaged and disillusioned by experiences in the 1950s and 1960s, to regenerate and restructure their thinking. Shari'ati's contentious calling to account of 'traditional' secular leftism and *mulla*-led religion had an attractive edge for young activists distancing themselves from the 'failures' of the preceding generation. Tropes of martyrdom converged with the turn to armed struggle of the leftist Muslim Mujahedin groups who also developed an ideology combining leftist radicalism with commitment to Shi'a Islam in the late 1960s. Syntheses of religion and political radicalism addressed embattled activists' desire to reach wider constituencies. His explorations of Iranian Shi'a selfhood touched the susceptibilities of those troubled by tensions between commitment to 'modern' aims and values, suspicion of the Americanised modes of modernisation pushed by the regime, and desires for 'indigenous' alternatives. The polyvalence of Shari'ati's concerns and language made them influential.

Shari'ati's revival of the old slogan 'Every month Muharram, every day 'Ashura, every place Karbala', in a speech following the execution of activist friends and students in early 1972, encapsulated the image of politicised, combative Shi'a Islam. It reconfigured the image and narrative of Husein's martyrdom as signifiers of political opposition which characterised the rhetoric of many participants in the 1977–81 revolution. The new politicised view saw his martyrdom as an active deed of resistance in his battle against unjust tyrannical authority, marking a shift also seen in other settings.[73] A controversial study of Husein published in the early 1970s by a Qum *mujtahed* also argued that Husein's actions and death were revolutionary sacrifices rather than just saintly fulfilment of divine fate. In his 1970 lectures on *Velayat-i-faqih: hokumat-i-Islam (The guardianship of the jurist: Islamic government)*, Ayatollah Khomeini argued, in a clear reference to the illegitimacy of the Pahlavi regime, that Husein had raised his revolt against the principle of hereditary kingship – a political and activist reading of the Karbala story. By 1978 stories about the activism and social consciousness of Ali and Husein were appearing in pronouncements by Khomeini and Muslim Students' Associations and retailed to foreigners.[74] During the 1970s the reformed Karbala paradigm and Shi'a icons, which had of course been deployed in earlier moments of high political activity in 1905–11 or 1951–53, entered the culture of politically aware Iranians.[75]

It was the convergence of the iconoclastic and activist Islam spreading among young educated Iranians, with the increasingly vocal oppositional rhetoric used by *'ulama* and *tullab* among groups with whom they worked, that fed growing political protest. At the same time that Shari'ati and leftist Muslims were evolving new readings of Shi'a Islam, sections of the Shi'a 'establishment' were also developing new discourses. *'Ulama* and *tullab* who had joined protests over the Shah's reforms in 1962–64 responded to the suppression of their activities, the exile of Khomeini, and the increasingly hostile stance of government, with their own hostile and defensive discourse. In addition to condemning the regime as illegitimate and oppressive, *'ulama* heightened their indictments of corruption and immorality, blaming them both on the Shah and on foreign/godless influences. Such rhetoric expressed the anxieties of conventionally pious urban audiences through the sermons and religious gatherings which brought them together with the *'ulama*. Concerns among the urban poor about policing gender and sexual conventions or about conflicting principles for dealing with daily difficulties in new settings, and shared anxieties about 'threats' to religion, linked *mulla* and believer constituencies. The language of populist religion appearing in the 1970s contained seeds of the rhetoric of 'corruption' and 'justice' which figured in the popular discourses of the revolution. It expressed familiar tropes which acquired new force in changed circumstances, where the intransigent stance of Khomeini gave religious resistance to the regime a revolutionary image, focus and force.

Just as the activist version of Husein shifted 'traditional' representations of his story, so the discontents to which 'religious' and 'secular' languages of opposition gave voice after 1953 can be distinguished from the languages of protest emerging after 1977. Khomeini's direct calls for the overthrow of the monarchy were accompanied by a clear shift to use of populist terms like *mustaz'afin* (oppressed) or *mellat-i-mustaz'ef* (oppressed nation/people) and even *tabaqeh* (class) which *'ulama* had previously avoided due to their leftist associations. This facilitated convergences between the ideals of religiously flavoured opposition and those leftist traditions. Imprecise but powerfully appealing concepts of *haqq* (justice) and oppression spread through the vocabulary of participants in the strikes and demonstrations of 1978 and 1979. Similarly, the language of struggle and martyrdom claimed by leftist groups since the 1960s and by those steeped in the Karbala narrative brought terms like *shahid* (martyr) and *enqelab* (revolution) together with the labelling of the Shah as 'Yazid of the age'.[76]

The ideologies and convictions of those who participated in the 1977–81 revolution can be seen as a set of overlapping, sometimes competing, sometimes mutually reinforcing images and languages. Languages of anti-despotic and patriotic politics inherited from the politics of the 1940s and 1950s, of anti-imperialist and revolutionary armed struggle developed in the 1960s and 1970s, jostled with the modernist, radical and popular applications of Shi'ism to political commitment and activism. The charisma of Khomeini, uncompromising denouncer of the Shah's oppressive, ungodly, illegal regime, of the guerrilla groups sacrificing themselves to confront the government, and of Shari'ati the passionate communicator of contemporary, radical religious visions for struggle, were available to inspire various protesters. If Khomeini's religion seemed alien to leftist activists, his uncompromising stance and anti-Americanism echoed their own commitment; if Shari'ati's intellectual version of radical patriotic Shi'ism used language meant for *roshan-fekran*, it could be translated into terms used by young activists and workers without their educational privileges.[77] A young woman supporter of Khomeini used the language of devotion to Islam to enable her to resist her father's restrictive rules in the name of the faith, recalling women who reworked the gendered traditions of Christianity in their challenges to the restrictive treatment of women.[78]

While this transformative expansion of religious tropes of martyrdom, justice and opposition to ungodly tyranny and imperialism was the striking feature of political ideas and images in the late 1970s, those who were dissociated from them should not be forgotten. Most obviously, members of rural communities whose culture was shaped by self-managed religious practice and for whom scepticism about external interference had limited rapport with the new activist forms of politicised religion and religious politics. The distanced views reported by Goodell and Friedl, or critics of the revolution interviewed by the researchers for Vieille and Khosrokhavar may not be typical, but do indicate some need to modify sweeping accounts of nationwide mobilisation.[79] Like studies of urban squatters and street politics, examinations of village political cultures in Iran reveal dynamics and aspirations located in that environment as much as in the larger context of national politics or international forces.

The discussion in this chapter began by postulating intimate connections between the form and content of political expression. As the pamphlet and the airwaves replaced the political cultures of nineteenth-century bread riots and *bast*-taking, and Iranians organised themselves in both old and new ways, so their images and ideas shifted and persisted. The continued 'plasticity of informal politics'[80] in village networks, vested interest groups, and urban *dowrehs* entwined with the new presence of political parties, state education and new ideologies. Inherited repertoires of the 'Karbala paradigm' or just rule were rethought and redirected, and newer notions of nationhood, citizenship or class contended with embedded views of gender, community and religious affiliation. The new culture of the street demonstration could be adapted by village women in the late 1970s to combine desire for participation with established codes of modesty, just as images of sexual honour were mobilised for nationalistic or xenophobic and anti-colonial purposes from the 1870s to the 1970s.

The story of ideas and images in Iran over that period is best told as one of flexibility, negotiation and creativity rather than 'continuity' and 'change'. This has the advantage of emphasising the *agency* of Iranians in their own political cultures, whether or not they were innovators. The story of ideas and images is also one of a series of ruptures rather than a smooth linear narrative. The Qajar regime's loss of acceptability at the start of the twentieth century, like the withdrawal of consent from its Pahlavi successor in the 1970s, involved sharp accelerations and redirections of thought as well as action. The intensity of political mobilisations and innovations in the 1940s and early 1950s, like that of the 1905–11 and 1977–81 periods, contrast with periods of adaptation or withdrawal.

The continued presence of religious features in Iranians' politico-cultural repertoires has involved remaking and reconfiguring ideas and images rather than the 'survival' of 'old' elements in 'new' settings. It has involved creative engagement with new possibilities, as with 'Afghani', Na'ini and the constitutionalists at the start of this period, or Shari'ati, Bazargan and the Mujahedin in its latter part, and creative resistance to such possibilities by Nuri, Mudarris or Khomeini. In this sense 'conservative' positions were as much 'made', and therefore contemporary, as were 'radical' ones. It is this 'making' of local, national or trans-national ideals and arguments which is at the core of the story of language, image and discourse.

SIX

A story of movements and struggles: convergence, conflict and cohabitation

Historians often struggle to express their sense of how past events and developments are simultaneously contingent and historically rooted. The human choices and actions which create political movements need to be understood both as immediate responses to the circumstances of a particular time, and as formed within cultural material and political environments and resources inherited from the past. This is especially the case with episodes of upheaval and dramatic change which surprise and disturb contemporaries and commentators. In Iranian history, the Constitutional Movement of 1905–11, the rise and fall of Mussadeqist nationalism, and the overthrow of the second Pahlavi shah are cases in point. The accounts of these movements given here will seek to do justice to their immediately contingent and to their historically rooted features, and to the tensions between them. The aim is to convey the fluid and unpredictable relationships between 'religious' and other elements in political activity in Iran since the later nineteenth century.

The very concept of movement is associated with dynamism, creativity and immediacy, and, in periods of high political activity and change, such themes are especially relevant. Flagging processes of convergence, conflict and cohabitation as themes for this chapter draws attention to the fluidity and diversity within major political movements and suggests that they be seen in terms of shifting complexities and co-existing contradictions. The concept of convergence addresses the processes whereby differing interests, experiences or motives come together for particular purposes or within particular campaigns and organisations. The concept of conflict conveys how divergence and opposition between people's interests or viewpoints contribute to the shape of political movements, and define their interests or viewpoints. The concept of cohabitation indicates that in addition to conflict or convergence, political involvement and interests involve uneasy co-existence as well as close links or actual opposition. The history of political movements can be traced through the composition and recomposition of alliances or coalitions, in which the convergences, conflicts or cohabitation of people's varied experiences and aspirations take actual form.

The first period of high political activity of the modern period in Iran had its early manifestation in the Tobacco Protest of 1891 and developed into the

Constitutional Movements of 1905–11. The aim here is to discuss the interaction of contingent circumstances and established patterns between the 1890s and the First World War in terms of cohabitation, conflict and convergence and of the shifting alliances of people and interests. Participants in the Tobacco Protest and Constitutional Movements included familiar and established groups, interests and political agendas with unstable relationships to newer political players. The attention often paid to 'new' aspects of political activity in the 'constitutionalist' era highlights important issues, but does not do full justice to the role and influence of established social groups in pursuit of their ideals and interests and of established styles and forms of politics. There are three particularly significant instances. First, the role of members of the *'ulama*, the significance of their alliances with other interests and the use of political language and tactics with religious content are widely recognised as major features of the Constitutional Movement and opposition to it. Second, the widespread presence of various kinds of popular protest brought traditions of political action inherited from the past into modern settings. Third, as the crisis of the old regime evolved, sections of the ruling elite moved from reactive resistance to new challenges to adaptive involvement in constitutional politics. By considering each of these elements and looking at their interaction with innovative aspects of politics in the period, the outcomes of the Constitutional Movement can be explored without using an either/or model of 'progress' versus 'reaction'.

'Ulama relationships with *bazari* groups in the nineteenth century contributed to the shape and content of politics in the period 1890–1920. The growing reliance of *mullas* on the goodwill and material support of *bazaris* influenced *'ulama* pursuit of their own aims and grievances and brought some of them to join the political challenges to the Qajar regime which emerged in the *bazar*. The shared interests of *'ulama* and *bazaris* in social order and material security similarly led some to oppose radical and popular politics and to reject republican or anti-clerical movements. For both *mullas* and *bazaris*, the religious language of struggle for justice and good government, and newer concerns with 'Islam in danger' combined with defence of *'ulama* and religious interests in both 'pro-' and 'anti'-constitutionalist politics. In 1906 the closure of *bazars*, the withdrawal of senior *'ulama* with their followers and services from Tehran, and the mass use of the tradition of taking *bast* (sanctuary) echoed the campaign against the Tobacco Concession of 1891 and established patterns of pressure and activism.

In addition to the influences and interests of religious specialists, the politics of the constitutional era were also shaped by an inherited repertoire of protest in urban communities in Iran. Merchant, artisan and popular groups were accustomed to pursue grievances and gain leverage with the powerful by closing the *bazar*, thus withdrawing commercial, financial and retail services.

Groups and individuals used the tradition of taking *bast* in shrines, mosques or notables' houses to gain support from powerful persons in pursuit of their aims, or to avoid enemies or the authorities. Nor were the street politics of riot and demonstration new in the 'modern' era. Material distress over food and prices, or resistance to mistreatment by rulers had caused popular protests and confrontations with the powerful in earlier times. As shown in Chapters 4 and 5, significant new political aims, ideas and campaigns came into play in the first decades of the twentieth century, but, far from arriving on an empty scene, they entered an environment richly endowed with political practices and discourses.

The presence of establishment figures in constitutional politics as well as in resistance to that movement indicates again how historic forms and styles of notable politics were embedded in the politics of the period and not just set in opposition to them. Personal and factional networking in a Majlis filled with urban notables, *'ulama*, and land- or office holders was as much a feature of its political life as the emergence of new 'democrat', pro-*shari'a*, 'moderate' or 'social democratic' groups with their modern apparatus of ideology, campaigning and organisation. Members of the Qajar clan, of central and provincial elites, and of the propertied and religious classes, made new links with Majlis, royal court, office-holding and parliamentary politics, local *anjumans* and regional government.

The group involved in drafting the initial proclamation of a constitution, the electoral laws, and the 1906 constitution itself, included men who had held office under various Shahs, including those like Sani' al-Douleh who had married into the Shah's family, and members of notable tribal and bureaucratic families (Isma'il Afshar, Mumtaz al-Douleh, Vosuq al-Douleh, Qavam al-Saltaneh). Families of landowners or officials made up one-fifth of the first and second Majlis (1906–11), which also included members of prominent religious families, as well as less powerful or established *'ulama*. Notables established and joined *anjumans* both to express political affiliations and in the tradition of networking, patronage and factional organisation which were part and parcel of court and urban politics. Family or occupational links and rivalries shaped the life of the new institutions alongside programmes of reform and constitutionalism. At the extreme, the opportunism of Qajar princes like Farmanfarma and Zill al-Sultan led them to provide money and/or military support for proconstitutionalist groupings at moments they deemed tactically advantageous to them. The roles of factions, networks, rivalries and patronage were reframed in the new setting of debate, parliamentary manoeuvring and urban activism.

Much of the dynamic of political life in the 'constitutional' era came from historic practices and approaches, whether the mobilisation of urban support by religious leaders, the pursuit of popular discontents and communal interests, or notables' use of their tactical skills in competition and patronage. Nevertheless, the myths and narratives depicting the politics of the period as transformed and transformative are based on evidence of important and visible features of political activity, ideas and organisation. Those looking back at that period with views shaped by later contests over government, religion, nationalism and social change have positioned the 'constitutional' era as the foundation period for these issues. They constructed stories of the Constitutional Revolution in which chosen heroes, traitors and conflicts foreshadowed later developments. In doing so they have drawn attention to newly active groups, new political practices and organisation, and new ideologies and political programmes which emerged in the early twentieth century.

A starting point for discussion of this aspect of the period is those newly active groups. In Iranian towns the changing material circumstances of merchants and craft producers described earlier encouraged a more critical and politicised stance towards a government on whose support they could not rely. Iranians with merchant interests and backgrounds began to contribute to the arguments and debates about social reform and modernisation both directly and by sponsorship of political writing in journals. Writers with merchant experience or connections like Zein al-Abedin Maragheh'i and 'Abd al-Rahim Talebzadeh wrote texts calling for educational, legal and technological modernisation which circulated in merchant and reforming groups. Merchants in Istanbul and individual merchants (Haji Zein al-Abedin Taqiev in Baku, Haji Muhammed Husein Kazeruni in Isfahan, the Amin al-Zarbs, father and son, in Tehran) supported reformist publications and discussion groups seeking political influence through established networking activity, or by pressure to open up the political system in new ways.[1] Just as they made practical use of 'ulama influence during the Tobacco Protest, so they drew on the polemical and intellectual talents of radical thinkers, whether Shi'a dissidents or those with more secular approaches. They promoted arguments for the interests of commerce and manufacture, for state backing for entrepreneurs, and for reforms to support 'modern' economic growth.

Among the most visible makers of the new politics were those intellectuals with a self-conscious mission to propagate change through writing, organising and activism. From discussion, writing and preaching they went on to form campaigning organisations that played crucial roles in the movement challenging the government in 1905–06 and defending the Majlis constitution and 'national' interests thereafter. Some had Babi and Baha'i links, while others were independently minded critics of restrictive, hierarchical, fiqh-bound and illiberal aspects of conventional Shi'a practice. They used intellectual, cultural and ideological resources from their religious backgrounds and sometimes links with established religious leaders. They might be regarded as suspect, heretical and subversive, but with increasing confidence presented themselves as a new crusading force.[2] They shared a sense of mission and identity with others with more explicitly secular outlooks and agendas with whom they worked. As discussed earlier, travel, work and study outside Iran, and access to texts and ideas from elsewhere, had given certain Iranians the opportunity to experience, read about and debate an expanded range of political possibilities.

By the early twentieth century, this self-consciously progressive intelligentsia, including members of the office-holding elite, the offspring of commercial, *mulla* and bureaucratic families, and itinerant teachers and entrepreneurs, was consolidating its political forces. They established alliances with the dissatisfied leaders of the religious hierarchy, and with wider sections of radical opinion with religious outlooks, recognising that broad support for change was more likely to emerge through such alliances than through blatant advocacy of secular reform programmes. The coalition orchestrated the discontents over misgovernment, threats to merchant interests, and the intrusive role of Europeans, shifting protest in the direction of structural change in forms of government, notably by demanding a constitution and a representative assembly. Their organised groupings, writings and speeches, and direct participation in *basts*, assemblies and protests, as well as negotiations with leading *'ulama* and government representatives, ensured the entry of secular modern political aims and institutions into the ongoing tussles of government, vested interests and popular grievances. These aims and institutions were supported by modernist activists in the new Majlis, in the press and in parties, clubs and campaigns supporting constitutional government, 'national' progress and autonomy from foreign intervention.

In Iran, as in other parts of the world from Ireland to China and from Russia to Mexico, the nineteenth and early twentieth centuries saw the emergence of new politically active intelligentsias. They not only constructed ideologies and programmes for reform, nationalism and social progress, but increasingly participated in the day-to-day politics of elected assemblies, public protest and party political campaigning and organisation. Currents of modernity also contributed to the emergence of another politically aware group pursuing political interests in a number of forms – activist women – and of the associated politics of gender. Established traditions of female participation in urban politics, expressing grievances over food prices/supplies or religious issues, were supplemented by new forms and aims for women's politics developing in the new conditions of political debate, activity and innovation. The period of constitutionalist politics saw the emergence not only of a 'woman question' in the political arena, but of women's political organisations, women's political journalism, and women's campaigning initiatives. This can be seen as a *consequence* of that political situation and also as *contributing* to it. New interventions by women raising 'modern' issues played a significant part in reconstituting the politics of reform and nationalism in gendered ways around notions of the 'modern' patriotic roles and activities distinctively appropriate to men and women.[3]

It is difficult to identify the background of individual women whose words survive in newspaper correspondence or reports of speeches and meetings, since convention often led them to omit their names, referring to themselves as 'patriotic lady', using a father's or husband's name, or signing writings as a group. Nevertheless, such names and biographical details as are available show how particular women from elite, bureaucratic and some religious families founded pressure groups and women's *anjumans*, established girls' schools and undertook political journalism. Like early generations of French, British or American feminists, their families were often involved in reforming, dissident and innovative ideas and politics.[4] Such women were in a paradoxical situation. They used the advantages and support provided by their families, gaining access to debates on the role and treatment of women, but in taking up these opportunities moved towards autonomy as writers and activists on their own behalf, and also to more challenging expressions of female interests and demands. They set up schools, welfare activities and discussion groups for women, publicly supported constitutional and patriotic causes and took their views to wider audiences in the new press, simultaneously expressing and going beyond the ideas and practices of the men in their milieu. If Majlis deputies debated the compatibility of women's *anjumans* with the *shari'a*, women challenged constitutionalist *tullab* with the question, 'Do you also recognise us as human beings?' While male reformers discussed the evils of veiling and arranged marriage as damaging to 'proper' heterosexual gender roles, women like the upper-class campaigner Durrat al-Mu'ali critiqued established views of femininity, pinpointing the cultural shift she wanted to create. 'In our country there have always been numerous women who dominated men and indirectly determined the course of events. What distresses me is the fact that they have gained this influence through charm and allurement and felt no need for intelligence and rationality.'[5] Her views recall the insights of Mary Wollstonecraft in England or Hoda Sha'arawi in Egypt. Women's writing expressed new images and practices of commitment and participation.

These activities, limited as they were, posed uncomfortable challenges for defenders of established values and practices, and for male reformers with their own views about appropriate gender reforms and ideals. These were often less about female emancipation or self-determination than about hetero-normative remodelling of 'modern' masculinities and femininities around models of motherhood, male patriotic comradeship and authority, and reformed family relations.[6] Female and male activists opened 'modern' debates about gender roles and the gendering of patriotism and citizenship in which women's independent contributions interacted with reformers' agendas, contested established patterns, and scoped new roles and images. The new women's campaigns and polemics also cohabited with female activism based in established local loyalties and material interests and religious ideals. For women activists of later times these innovative developments foreshadowed their own concerns with women's political participation and women's rights and opportunities. For supporters of constitutional government, nationalism and modern reforms, the female presence in the foundation drama of 1905–11 confirmed the breadth of support for these causes and thus their potency and legitimacy 'even' among women (as put by several canonical accounts).[7] New interventions by women had an iconic significance.

If the women's associations, journals, campaigns and demonstrations were small-scale features of the Constitutional Movement, the role of crowd politics was more substantial and extensively recorded. Records of mass activity (*basts*, street protests, *bazar* closures, armed conflicts) show how sections of the urban, and sometimes rural, population were mobilised 'for' and 'against' constitutional government. Closer investigation of memoirs and other records reveals complex and shifting coalitions of participants (with local variations) who did not confine their demands to the reformist, nationalist and constitutionalist concerns of the intelligentsia. *Anjumans* and other pro-constitutional organisations involved quite specific sections of the urban population – traders, professionals, artisan/entrepreneurs and intellectuals, whether religious or secular. The urban underclass and groups followed links of patronage, material need and communal interest into both 'pro-' and 'anti-' constitutional activity depending on the influence of loyalties, leaders and circumstances.

Conventional wisdom about the crowd politics of the constitutional period is that they 'lacked' the 'modern' characteristics of 'class'-based or 'mass' politics. Analysts emphasise both the continuing power of 'old' communal, religious and patron–client discourses and values, and the multi-group character of the 'crowds'.[8] There is significant evidence of existing political forms and ideas being turned to new causes or ends, whether greater control of government and foreign interference, or schemes for social reform. This convergence of old and new political activity, although limited, signals the start of developments with considerable future importance, as did the acceptance by *lutis*, *mullas* and establishment reformers of the participation, influence and occasionally the leadership of an emergent modern intelligentsia, and even some of their ideas. While this was often a matter of contingent and opportunistic convenience, and the ability of apparently incompatible allies to see some compatibility in their diverse interests and outlooks, one effect, however unintended, was the entry of new elements in so-called 'traditional' political settings.

Among the most strikingly 'new' aspects of the Constitutional Movement were the innovative forms of political expression and organisation evolved in the early twentieth century. Modern styles of newspaper production and writing, modern organisation of political interests in committees and parties and the creation of new forms of representative government, reconfigured the arena of politics and contributed to the development of a new political class. To advocates of modernisation and nationalism these political forms were not only the means to pursue and defend their ideals, but powerful symbols and signifiers of progress and freedom in Iran. Threatened with closure in 1910, the editorial writer of the leftist journal *Iran-i-no* depicted the free press as central to the battle between progress and reaction, using French, Ottoman and Russian comparisons.[9] *Anjumans* in urban centres became the focus for organised constitutional and patriotic campaigning, surging into activity at moments of confrontation with opponents and legitimising themselves as agents of progress and of resistance to tyranny and foreign intervention.[10] The very existence of the Majlis and the Constitution came to be seen by modernisers as proof in itself of progress and freedom, whether imagined in liberal, nationalistic or socialistic terms. As the poet Asraf al-din Husseini Gilani put it:

> From the Constitution the country prospered;
> From oppression, the nation was liberated,

echoing the 'Letter from a Shirazi' in the journal *Majlis* in 1907, 'we Iranians have a consultative assembly. We will no longer hear the sarcasm and damnation of foreigners ... no longer will the sighs from the chest of the bereaving oppressed reach the heavens.'[11]

The new forms of political expression had more than symbolic or rhetorical importance. The writing and dissemination of newspapers created new producers and audiences with the appearance of full-time journalist/writers, political polemicists and popularisers, and urban readers (and hearers since newspapers were read aloud in workshops and coffee houses).[12] This supported new styles of opinion, debate and communication. The presentation and discussion of information, ideas, analysis and polemic took new forms in newspaper editorials, articles and letters to the press, supplementing established forms of preaching, discussion circles, oral transmission of news or rumour, and the semi-clandestine distribution of leaflets and posters (*shabnamehs*). The practical experience of organising *anjuman* activities, committees and meetings, or mobilising for demonstrations, stimulated new skills, new patterns of political behaviour, and new associations and loyalties. The evolution of Majlis politics, with public debates, committees, parties, programmes and factions, introduced participants to new modes of involvement with 'national' issues, and added new participants to the process of debating and influencing central government.

To the fore of this process were the questions of 'national' identity and independence from foreign intervention, and the relationship of religion to community interests and social change. As shown in Chapter 4, the opening up of political space for nationalist ideologies and ideals normalised references to *vatan*, *mellat* and to 'Iran' itself as meaningful terms for growing numbers of Iranians. In a situation where resentment of Belgian officials, British and Russian banks and foreign concessionaires had stimulated the 1905–06 upheavals, and Russian and British intervention influenced the course of constitutionalist politics, the practical concerns of political activists understandably focused on national strength and autonomy. Drawing on discourses of national unity and regeneration from Asian and European repertoires, they linked the reform and extension of state power to nationalist aims, setting supporters of such policies on a path of confrontation with supporters of customary religious and *shari'a* practices in law, education and administration. Containment of religious interests, and separation of 'religious' and 'secular' spheres and powers, came on to reforming agendas, provoking opposition from *'ulama* and their supporters alongside anti-clerical and secularist discourse and campaigning.

Such contests intensified as *mullas* led attacks on secular or girls' schools and were satirised as 'reactionary', 'corrupt' and superstitious, as political groups divided over whether the Constitution should be made *shari'a*-friendly, and as social protest and new ideas challenged established interests. Could religious views and loyalties embrace the provision of schooling for women, the evolution of partisan and electoral politics, and peasant or urban radicalism? Could the 'patriotism' invoked by old and new political players combine discourses of a Shi'a nation, a glorious past, and agendas for national progress based on modernisation of key institutions? Could the 'religious–radical alliance' of 1905–06 survive divisions and confrontations between supporters of the *mashruteh* (constitution) and advocates of the *shari'a*?

Yet oppositional depictions of 'old' and 'new' in the politics of this period do less than justice to its complexity or to the fact that many Iranians had more limited or contingent involvements in constitutional politics. It was the stimulus of immediate grievances over the distribution of office and power among elites, over professional and commercial problems among *'ulama* and merchants, or over oppressive taxes and administration among peasants and craftsmen, which timed and directed their participation in the events of 1905–11. In 1904–06 opposition to the Belgian customs administration, the exactions of provincial governors, and government mistreatment of senior *'ulama* and merchants provided impetus for the protests which activists then shaped into demands for a constitution. Similarly, the divisions among the reformers, activists and political groupings in the Majlis and *anjumans* from 1907 on, while fuelled by political and ideological differences between 'radicals' and 'moderates', or defenders and critics of established property rights, also expressed immediate concerns and grievances. Decisions by government ministers and office holders triggered discontent, creating political opportunities for protest, organised lobbying and manoeuvres by ambitious individuals. Such decisions and the opposition to them emerged from the developments of preceding decades. Idealism and opportunism, long-held interests and new aspirations entwined together.

Thus, the dramatic invocations of 'Iran' which featured in constitutionalist journalism and parliamentary speeches drew on both imported and recent versions of 'the nation' and on popular, mythical and literary constructions of past history and cultural identity.[13] The street protests and political debates of the period expressed both 'traditional' forms of popular pressure (*bast*, petition, procession, tax evasion) and a willingness to adopt and adapt more recent forms (strikes, party campaigns and organisation). Shaikh Fazlullah Nuri mobilised anti-constitutional opinion through 'modern' agitation as well as the established tools of political *'ulama*.[14] Clandestine and dissident groups, where *'ulama*, critics of government, religious dissidents and reformers campaigned for change, were fuelled by common, if short-lived, commitment to challenging a 'tyrannical' regime in the name of justice and progress as well as sectional interests. With artisan and *tullab* supporters and clients among the urban populace, they mobilised a multi-class alliance to which the diverse elements described here all contributed. Learned *mujtaheds* used established scholarly resources and new ideas to craft arguments for representative government within a Shi'a Muslim framework (as Baha'is and Sunnis did within their traditions).[15] Idealistic reformers invoking patriotism in support of legal, economic and educational change used religious and literary imagery as well as modern discourses of progress and national identity.

However, the overlapping agendas, interests and ideals of the multi-class alliance who produced and defended a constitutional framework for monarchy, reform and national self-strengthening did not unite the participant groups or their diverse aims and outlooks. Leading *'ulama*, concerned with challenges to their influence and threats to Shi'a Muslim practice and belief, tolerated but did not necessarily accept the ideas and approaches of dissident and secular activists and vice-versa. Pragmatic and uneasy relationships likewise emerged between regional and national activists or organisers and their urban followers, where the interest of the former in new forms of government had to co-exist with the interest of the latter in communal and material gains. The constitutionalist fighter Sattar Khan, horse-dealer and *luti*, with a base in a Shaikhi quarter of Tabriz and links to local government before 1906, as well as the constitutionalist *anjuman*, talked of proclaiming a republic if the Shah rejected 'laws, liberty and a constitution'. Yet amid the factional rivalries following the 1909 restoration of the Constitution, he was less concerned with these ideals than with his position as commander of the *mujahedin* (fighters), a matter of personal interest, 'traditional' responsibility, and attachment to his urban constituency. His alliance with the Moderate Party, like his 'chivalrous brigand' conduct during the siege of Tabriz, indicate how support for constitutionalism co-existed with very different aims and interests.[16]

Reformers, too, were uneasy cohabitants of liberal, statist and redistributive approaches to state power, social justice and the achievement of material and cultural progress. For some in the constitutionalist movement, the removal of tyranny and of the monopoly of state policy-making by a restricted elite were seen in terms drawn from French critiques of their *ancien régime*. Their main concerns were individual (male) rights, the separation of religious and state institutions, the equitable rule of law, and the rightful role of the Majlis, all written into the new Constitution, and argued in parliament, journalism and party politics thereafter.[17] This classically 'liberal' agenda sat beside inter- ventionist aspirations for reformed government as an agent of wider reforms through legislation and state policies for economic, educational and social development.

Newer approaches came from those who raised the challenging issues of gender roles and gender justice, and from those concerned with the inequities of the propertied and the poor, landlords and peasants, masters and wage workers. Influenced by contemporary social liberal and social democratic ideas, programmes of social justice and redistribution, and critiques of 'feudalism' and exploitation, Iranian leftists took up demands like the right to strike, land redistribution and the abolition of peasant obligations to landlords.[18] Inspired by social democratic and revolutionary groups and programmes in the Caucasus, and directly encouraged by such organisations, they began to establish comparable groups in Iran. Members of these groups saw the new political circumstances as opportunities to argue for social change, using the class-based views of the socialist tradition and socialist views on feudalism, nationalism and revolution. They connected these ideas and programmes to the expressions of peasant or worker grievances, including refusals to provide dues and obligations to landlords, disputes with silk merchants, and women's strikes emerging from older forms of *bazar* and rural protest.[19] Social democrat programmes quoted Sa'adi, the well-known thirteenth-century Shirazi poet, and referred to *shari'a* law, and socialist groups named themselves *mujahedin*, a term with religious connotations of 'fighters for the faith'. Leftist activists and writers made use of patriotic and religious references in order to connect their interests to the ideas and rhetoric of 'nation' and 'people' and to the defence of Islam.[20]

It is the many-layered hybridity of the Constitutional Movement which is significant. Uneven material developments affected disparate producers, traders and entrepreneurs, including carpet manufacturers and merchants linked to international markets, sharecropping subsistence cultivators, commercially orientated landlord/merchants, casual or service workers, and female weavers meeting household needs. There was comparable unevenness of political concerns, from traditional anxieties over food supplies, prices and exactions on peasants, to new competition and opportunity stemming from the presence of foreign interests. For bureaucrats, established practices of administration, and the manoeuvrings of court politics and its local variants, existed in an uneasy relationship with aspirations to create effective 'modern' forms of government inspired by awareness of practices elsewhere. For political activists, emotive calls to struggle and martyrdom based in Shi'a tradition and images of Islam in danger could be evoked alongside familiar protests over oppression and injustice, and new ideals of constitutional government, patriotic resistance to Russia and Britain, and populist, modernising and egalitarian programmes.

Thus, E. G. Browne's reported descriptions of the variegated crowds occupying the British legation in Gulhak in 1906, or resisting the Shah's attack on the Majlis in 1907 evoke the *dis*continuous, even incompatible, character of support for constitutionalism as well as unity of purpose or identity. The *wish* for unity is visible in Kasravi's evocation of the political atmosphere in Tabriz, Nazim al-Islam's description of Tehran and the language of journalism, Majlis speeches, and local propaganda.[21] The reality was a mosaic of shifting alliances, sectional interests and diverging visions of the future. Historians of various revolutions often note a sharp disparity between the capacity to converge, if not unite, in opposition to established regimes and the inability to agree on what should replace them. In Iran in 1905–06, the alliance that challenged Qajar absolutism converged around critiques of its arbitrariness, failures and weakness. In the following years, the concerns of the pious for the status of Islam, of reformers for social and political change, and of grassroots activists for their aspirations, could still converge momentarily in opposition to the Shah's coups of 1907 and 1908 or Russian intervention in 1911 and 1912, although with limited effect.

Closer examination of politics in a centre of activism like Tabriz, a centre at one remove from prominence like Kerman, and the capital Tehran, reveals the conflicts and discordance tugging against the politics of convergence. Conflicts between 'moderate' and 'radical', 'religious' and 'secular', 'lower' and 'higher' classes, or rival sects and individuals, were as real as the political activities in which they joined together, leaving traces in the records of activists and observers. The Tabriz Shaikhi *mujtahed* Thiqat al-Islam, commemorated as a constitutionalist 'martyr' after the Russians executed him in 1911, recorded his clashes with the secularising and leftist radicals of the Tabriz *anjuman* over their 'threats' to order and religion.[22] This clash over constitutionalist aims and tactics and for influence and leadership in the local movement shaped the confrontation between constitutionalists, royal opposition and Russian intervention in Tabriz. Similar cleavages among 'moderate' and 'radical' constitutionalists during the Shah's attacks on the Majlis in Tehran in 1908 were recorded by Nazem al-Islam Kermani and historicised by Kasravi.[23] They evolved in Majlis debates over the role of the *shari'a*, confrontations over social reform in the provinces, and the aftermath of an attempted royal coup in 1907. Localised versions of these divisions appeared not only in a centre of activism like Tabriz but also in quieter cities like Kerman where rifts between 'respectable' constitutionalism and a populist confrontational 'crowd element' were reported by the British consul.[24] Often cross-cut by personal, communal and contingent influences, a growing sense of polarities between 'moderation' and 'extremism', religion and reform, or haves and have-nots, became features of the constitutional movement.

While contests between those pursuing opposed interests were part of the very stuff of politics in this period, it is hard to make a tidy separation between conflicts, convergences and cohabitations. All the actors in this foundational period of modern Iranian politics created and experienced a mixture of these. Just as leading *'ulama* were found in both pro- and anti-constitutional groups, so modernising reformers were members of religious and social-democratic groups as well as more loosely defined patriotic, radical or interest-based associations. Similarly, street activists or guild organisations were mobilised by arguments for liberty, justice and constitutionalism, by appeals to martyrdom and religious conviction, and by the material concerns of their communities. Any assessment of the importance of reforming, religious or leftist or nationalist influences needs to take account of the *hybridity* of these categories for Iranians in the early twentieth century as well as their distinctive and antagonistic aspects. It can be seen that people held divergent or inconsistent aims and ideas, without seeing them as a hierarchy of 'real' or 'true', as opposed to 'assumed' or 'pretended', views. The very conditions that produced these oppositions were fluid and many-sided, with the divisions seeming clearer in retrospect than at the time. The point is not just that the traditions of leftist, Islamic or reformist politics took time to evolve from their beginnings in the constitutional era into later forms; the *mixed* character of political thought and practice in these years was a *constitutive* factor in the new political possibilities of the time.

The discourse and legacy of religious dissidence was more than a 'mask' or incubator for new critiques of government, social injustice and national weakness, but rather gave flavour and character to the politics and oratory of radical activists like the preacher Sayyid Jamal al-Din Isfahani, or the Azeri regional leader Shaikh Muhammed Khiabani. New versions of the concept of an Iranian 'nation' proclaimed across the political and social spectrum drew on indigenous religious and poetic resources, imported nationalistic ideas and images, and leftist theories of imperialism. Established skills and codes of good administration and negotiation, as well as self-interested or pragmatic considerations, flavoured the advocacy of state-centred reformist policies. The unstable alliance of discontented *'ulama*, reformers and *bazaris* combined opportunistic calculations by the parties involved, serious conflicts over the role of religion in a reformed polity, and the inspiring energy of shared endeavour and rhetoric. Just as the 1906 British embassy *bast* provided the opportunity for talks on European constitutions alongside *rawzehs*, so in the early 1920s politicians like Sayyid Hasan Mudarris spoke of the fusion of politics and religion.[25] The use of the 'Karbala paradigm', the entwining of appeals to Shi'a traditions with non-Shi'a constructions of an Iranian 'nation', and of the overlapping categories of 'people' and 'believers', all contributed to that 'fused' relationship.

This relationship co-existed with serious conflicts of interest and ideology around the role of religious practices and values in government, law and culture. The contests between constitutionalist reformers and activists and defenders of religious interests and a *shari'a*-based constitution (*mashruteh yi-mashru'a*), like those between critics and defenders of established property rights and social inequities, were none the less real for being polyvalent and unstable. Real confrontations between peasants and landlord representatives were politicised by radicals in the Majlis and the *anjumans*, just as accusations of lewdness and godlessness revealed the sharpness of divisions among more and less radical or secularising sections of the political nation, now manifest in protest, journalism and partisan organisation.

The historic 'moment' of the constitutional movement marked the emergence of new elements with hybrid features in Iranian political life, and became the foundational episode in the narrative of modern Iranian politics. It embedded new political projects and beginnings within older practices and ideas. Narratives of this movement of 'the people' gaining and defending a constitution and Majlis, containing and resisting 'tyranny' in the name of freedom, and seeking progress, justice and 'national' prosperity, had symbolic and ideological power for subsequent generations of politically aware Iranians. Later contests over the roles played by various protagonists (the liberal constitutionalist Taqizadeh, women activists, 'dissident' preachers, leftists influenced by Caucasian social democracy, the 'anti-constitutional' *mujtahed* Fazlullah Nuri)[26] show how ownership and interpretations of this foundational narrative themselves became political issues.

As will be shown, this symbolic legacy played its part in subsequent historic 'moments' of political upheaval around Mussadeqist nationalism in the 1940s and 1950s, and of opposition to Shah Muhammad Reza Pahlavi in the 1970s. However, the legacy of the 'constitutional' era was also material and practical. The democratic and reforming initiatives of 1905–11 opened the way not for parliamentary government and constitutional monarchy but for an authoritarian regime seeking to control and modernise various features of Iranian life using state power and nationalist rhetoric. The 'reform' and 'patriotic' agendas developed by critics and innovators among the intelligentsia, merchants and office holders from the later nineteenth century were appropriated by an ambitious army officer, Reza Khan, who seized power in 1921 and made himself first Pahlavi Shah in 1925. This outcome incorporated both recognition and rejection of the objectives of activists of the 1905–11 era.

In the context of the internal political divisions and Great Power pressures that engulfed constitutionalist politics between 1911 and 1921, the support for Reza Pahlavi among some of its protagonists is not surprising. His overt and effective support for a strong militarised state, for modernising administrative and educational reforms, and for nationalistic discourse, found resonance among supporters of 'national' self-strengthening and modernisation. His forceful pursuit of reforming policies and of opponents of such policies, whether separatist groups of ethnic Arabs and Kurds, or rivals for power among army officers, tribal leaders and political groups, was anti-democratic and oppressive, but also contrasted with the ineffectiveness of preceding governments. Thus, although his arbitrary and increasingly repressive rule became the object of hostility among sections of the intelligentsia and political classes, especially after his removal in 1941, there was some real convergence between parts of his agenda and their concerns.[27] The suspension of representative government and crushing of independent politics among Iranians was one feature of the period of Reza Khan/Shah's rule, which, together with the shift in the material and cultural circumstances of various groups in Iran, shaped the internal features of the historic 'moment' of the late 1940s and early 1950s.

The material and cultural shifts between the 1920s and the 1950s have been discussed in earlier chapters and had particular political significance for that 'moment'. It would be 'modern' wage workers in the oilfields, railways, mechanics' workshops and offices who joined the Tudeh ('Masses'/Communist) Party in disproportionate numbers as well as the unions able to organise the post-Reza Shah period. Wage workers reacted to swings in wages, living costs and job opportunities in this period, but their strikes and protests addressed 'political' issues as well as wages and conditions. The links between union activity, a classic feature of modern workplace relations, and organisations like the Tudeh, or supporters of Mussadeq's National Front, and other nationalist and activist groups, stimulated political mobilisation. It would be the newly established professionals with 'modern' education who were disproportionately active in political organisations, and as consumers and producers of political journalism and other political writing. Such was the role of this section of Iranian society in radical politics that anti-leftists used the term '*roshanfekr*' (literally 'one with enlightened thought'), previously used for modernisers or educated professionals, to label someone a communist fellow traveller.[28]

If the context for the nationalist and popular politics of the 1940s and 1950s was partly shaped by the presence of new social groupings and their relationships to established classes, it was also shaped by the state forms and political agendas of the preceding period. Both the constitutionalist era and the rule of Reza Shah placed state power and state-building high on those agendas. Hopes of a reformed, just and responsive government had fuelled the constitutionalist politics of intellectuals, street protesters and organised activists. The 'man on horseback', who took power when those hopes faded into faction and frustration, likewise linked his hold on power to the construction of an interventionist state clothed in the rhetoric, and sometimes practice, of modernisation. The encroachment of the state into civil society, via attempts to control or change law, economic activity, education and communally based authority, like the Shah's coercion or repression of rivals and critics, emphasised state powers.[29] These were based in an army which grew five-fold between 1926 and 1941 and civil service (90,000 by the 1940s), in a patronage system using the Shah's accumulated wealth, and in the reduction of the autonomous power of landed and tribal magnates, guild elders and senior 'ulama. Not surprisingly, the revival of politics in streets, parties and Majlis after 1941 saw attempts to reduce or reform the the state. Constitutional change, effective resistance to foreign interference, and the use of state power for social change, were issues taken up once more by leftist, religious patriotic and reforming activists.[30]

The 1940s and 1950s saw challenges and conflicts around the role and organisation of the state including separatist moves by Kurds, Azeris and tribal leaderships, revived contests over the relations of monarch, Majlis and ministers, and demands for government action against foreign influence. However, it was not only social change and state-building that set the context for political movements in the 1940s and 1950s. Just as the symbolic power and presentation of the political upheavals of 1905–11 focused on a 'constitutional' revolution, and those of the revolution of 1977–81 focused on its 'Islamic' character, so the identifying theme and symbol for politics in the 1940s and 1950s was nationalism. The symbolic and narrative role of nationalism in the politics of that period expressed its material and political significance for various participants. The 'nationalist/ national' theme drew on traditions stretching back to the nineteenth century, and on the greatly increased involvement of great powers in political and economic life in Iran more recently.[31] While these traditions had critiqued and adapted western models of nationalist images and ideology, nationalist concerns were now sharpened by more direct encounters between Iranians and foreigners.

Three elements need emphasis. First, the tentative venture into the commercial exploitation of oil resources in Iran by a British company before 1914 expanded dramatically during the inter-war period and the 1940s in conditions of unequal global power relations and imperial interests. The agreements under which the company extracted, refined and sold oil gave the Iranian government royalty payments representing between 5 per cent and 10 per cent of the company's income in the 1920s and about 11 per cent between 1933 and 1949.[32] The purchase of a controlling share in APOC by the British government in 1914 directly linked Iran to British global imperial concerns, sustained by a worldwide naval presence soon to be fuelled by oil. Such concerns already involved British diplomats, imperial strategists and to a lesser extent business interests in Iranian affairs, but after the First World War the growth of oil production gave them new edge in the context of commitments to mandates in Iraq and Palestine and nationalist challenges in India.

If oil from Iranian oilfields fuelled the British presence in Iran during the Second World War (taking from 27 per cent to 62 per cent of local sales in the four years 1942–45 compared with some 3–6 per cent in years before and after),[33] the presence of British troops, like those from the Soviet Union and the United States, signalled wider relations of power and dependency. Historically, the governments of the Russian and British Empires had intervened politically and sometimes militarily to protect territorial interests in India and Central Asia and wider rivalries as major powers in Europe and Asia. After the First World War the emergence of the Soviet regime and British opposition to it brought troops from both sides on to Iranian territory. The consolidation of British mandates in the Middle East as part of the post-war settlements brought the 1919 attempt to pressure the Iranian government to accept a treaty intended to tie Iran to British aspirations in the area. Hostile 'nationalistic' Iranian responses to this treaty, and British desire for an Iranian government with whom they could do business, paradoxically converged to support Reza Khan's rise to power. Although nationalist mythologies subsequently overemphasised the British role in Reza Khan's coup, his successful positioning of his regime as acceptable to them while not a client, marked the role of dependency and external influence in the construction of his regime.[34]

The events of the Second World War confirmed and reshaped Iranian ties to the unequal power relations of global politics, whether of empire, oil exploitation, anti-communism or military strategy. While the role of British interests in Reza Shah's rise combined with internal factors, his removal was explicitly and entirely the result of British and Soviet war aims against Germany following the German invasion of the Soviet Union in 1941. Reza Shah's pro-German stance during the 1930s was the product of growing Iranian commercial involvement with Germany, which by 1940–41 provided 42.6 per cent of Iranian imports and took 47.9 per cent of Iranian exports, and of his use of links with Germany to counterbalance British influence. The occupation of Iran by Soviet and British troops and the removal of Reza Shah were driven not by the strains and difficulties of the autocracy, but by the need of those powers to defend the southern flank of the Soviet Union, the oil resources of Baku and Iran, and Britain's informal empire in the Middle East. The arrival of American troops and advisers in 1942 as part of the anti-Hitler alliance further confirmed that foreign powers had the military, political and material ability to override and manage local interests and considerations in the interests of their war.

The foreign occupation of Iran in the 1940s is part of the longer history of 'great power' interventions in Iranian affairs, but by the mid-1940s a new element entered the calculations of those powers with the emergence of the Cold War. Soviet expansionism in Europe and Iran, the 1949 Chinese revolution and Korean War, nuclear proliferation, and the challenges of decolonisation and third world nationalism all shifted the concerns of great power policy-makers with significant consequences for Iran. The fact that American policy turned to global anti-communism meant that Iran's position in that worldwide power play was a continuous concern of that policy. By 1946, American military and diplomatic advisers saw the 'protection' of Iran from Soviet influence as central to the 'domino theory' of containment.[35] Manifestations of anti-colonial nationalism in the Middle East, Africa and Asia raised questions about whether the success of nationalist politics in Iran would favour Soviet influence, as in China. For British policy-makers, incipient decolonisation and changes in their wider 'informal' empire gave the protection of their Iranian interests more general importance. For both British and Americans, the material issue of access to oil, and the political importance of influence on Iranian governments for their larger imperial and international interests, locked their policies towards Iran into the wider Cold War conjuncture.[36]

For politicised Iranians, intensified British, Soviet and American intervention stimulated qualitative and quantitative growth in nationalism. Increasing numbers of Iranians across a spectrum of 'left' and 'right', 'religious' and 'secular', 'reforming' and 'traditional', used nationalist language and had nationalist aspirations. The open links of American and British diplomats to court and elite circles, Soviet intervention in Iranian ethnic politics in the Azeri and Kurdish regions and connection to the Tudeh Party, like the legacy of military and political intervention from the war period, were obvious targets for patriotic opposition. Above all, the question of ownership, control and exploitation of Iranian oil took political centre-stage for Iranians as for foreigners. Wresting oil from foreign control was a material issue, and a mark of national strength and autonomy. The emotive and symbolic significance of oil nationalisation was as important as its economic and political purposes, shaping the high moment of nationalist politics in this period.

The emergence of support for oil nationalisation in the politicised environment of urban Iran in the 1940s was more than the triumph of a single-issue movement. Rather, it represented the focus for a number of alliances and many-sided political aspirations. These ranged from the frustrated intentions of two generations of reforming politicians and administrators and the concerns of *bazaris* and *'ulama*, to the new enthusiasms of a younger intelligentsia and emergent white- and blue-collar workforces. The fact that a small number of professional politicians in the National Front, which led the politics of oil nationalisation from 1949, had such leverage over governments, Majlis and street politics, was evidence of skilful use of clan and alliance politics, and of the dynamic links between the agendas of the political elite and wider politics. Beyond the manoeuvring of ministers and political factions in Tehran over the oil issue in the 1940s, the political contest around oil mobilised other interests. Oil workers protesting wages and conditions imposed by their British employers, patriots opposed to the oil company as a state within the state making unjustified profits, reformers looking for leadership and progress from a government acting on behalf on the 'nation/people' rather than a corrupt elite, all treated the issue as the key to their goals. This diversity came from the mix of old and new elements in political life and culture in Iran, and the variety of participants in that life and culture.

The immediate context for the flourishing of a diverse and energetic political culture was the removal of the repressive restrictions of Reza Shah's regime on intellectual and political activity. Paradoxically this freer situation was the product of the very foreign intervention which became the object of political controversy, since it was the Soviet and British occupation of Iran that triggered the abdication and exile of Reza Shah. The growth of both press and political activity shows that in the urban areas Iranians took up such opportunities.[37] Political groups and ambitious and/or idealistic individuals took advantage of greater freedom to create and address constituencies among the intelligentsia, workers, *bazaris* and students. From debates among *mullas* and pious lay people on the desirability or direction of political activism, to the efforts of the Tudeh Party to recruit intellectuals and workers, propaganda and activism reached into the new urban constituencies. They built on limited but real growth in literacy in the preceding two decades, based on a seven-fold increase in school pupils (compared with a population increase of some one and a half times), plus some hundreds of thousands of adult pupils.[38] Combined with the movements of people into new forms of wage labour (white or blue collar) this formed a socio-cultural setting in which the dissemination of ideas on nationalism, imperialism, progress and justice beyond the narrow confines of a few intellectuals became possible.

The newly politicised sections of society, like those with longer histories of political involvement, like *bazaris* or intellectuals, now engaged with changing movements and ideologies in an environment significantly different from that of the constitutional era. Older invocations of nationalism, reform and freedom from oppression as calls to political activity now combined with more developed rhetorics on imperialism and social justice and with immediate issues of food shortages, oil concessions and labour disputes. In particular, the emergence of the Tudeh Party in the first half of the 1940s and of the National Front in the second half demonstrate the impact of both ideas and organisation on street politics, industrial relations and government itself via mass mobilisation.

In the case of the Tudeh Party, this is seen in the sheer range of activities and social groups with whom they established links. Union activity among wage workers, cultural work with intellectuals, alliances with journalists and ethnic separatists (a contentious matter for the Tudeh leadership), and contacts with students and peasants all figured in their work at various points during the 1940s. By 1946 they could mobilise tens of thousands of demonstrators in Tehran and strikers in the oilfields, had over 350,000 trade union affiliates, and considerable influence on local administration in some industrial centres.[39] Adopting an inclusive populist tone, rather than a narrower class approach, signalled by naming itself the party of the *Masses* of Iran, Tudeh activism in the early 1940s mobilised disproportionately large groups of wage workers and modern salary earners. By the later 1940s and early 1950s both the language and support of the Tudeh had a more emphatically class character, with its union affiliates surmounting repression to mount effective mass action over oil nationalisation and opposition to the Shah, as well as over wages and conditions. Over a decade it played an important part in the transformation of urban politics with the introduction of mass organised activism, and modern ideas of class and radical change on a more extended scale than in the past.

However, the politicisation of urban Iran would not have developed as it did in this period had the Tudeh been the only force at work. The party's ability to influence political activity and culture was limited by the way in which traditions of democratic centralism, clandestine organisation, Soviet sympathies and an ideology distant from those of many Iranians, shaped its policies and outlook. It made most headway with sections of the intelligentsia receptive to ideas of thoroughgoing change, and those wage workers in search of new approaches to labour relations. Tudeh activity can be contrasted with the role of the National Front which became a prime political influence from the late 1940s. While the Tudeh approach focused on particular target groups (intellectuals, wage earners, educated women) with ideas and policies appropriate to their views and interests, the National Front used general inclusive appeals to nationalism, democracy and progress. These were transmitted in various ways by the different member groups in the alliance which came together under the umbrella of these ideals, and in support of the National Front coalition of politicians. Despite the absence of the organised initiatives and structures of Tudeh activists, the coalition of those who supported the broad ideals and simple goals of the National Front had a powerful and persistent impact, with a lasting memory and example.

The National Front came together around two key issues – defence of democratic politics and the oil issue – backed by individuals and political groups of diverse, even divergent, views. They created links between political networks developed in and around Majlis and government and a range of party or partisan organisations and interests (reforming, patriotic, pious, leftist) among intellectuals, *bazaris* and modern professionals. These links emphasised shared hostility to court, military and elite power, desire for reform, opposition to privilege and corruption, and conviction that asserting Iranian rights to Iranian oil was central to national independence and self-respect. Such shared concerns emerged from political positions as diverse as those of the anti-British activist and popular religious figure Ayatollah Kashani, democratic modernising Shi'a reformers like Mehdi Bazargan, or the former communist Khalil Maleki, as well as less intellectualised but powerful hopes and fears of students and *bazaris*. The National Front took energy from the charismatic if ambivalent leadership of Muhammed Mussadeq. A politician and minister whose experience went back to the start of the century, known as an uncompromising and incorruptible opponent of royal autocracy and foreign intervention since the 1920s, his powerful oratory and self-conscious independence from faction and party were crucial to the movement. While his strengths and weaknesses are much debated, his idealism, patrician confidence, parliamentary and popular political talents, and blend of alertness to modernity with deft use of traditional skills and insights allowed him to operate in many modes with diverse constituencies.

The National Front mobilised support which expressed responses to the social and political changes of the 1930s and the events of the 1940s. The emphasis on constitutionalism and the popular will as proper checks on royal power and elite privilege spoke to frustrated hopes going back a generation. The emphasis on ending foreign interference and in particular foreign control of Iranian oil appealed to all who resented the overt role of British oil interests since the 1920s and the military and diplomatic interventions of British, Soviets and Americans during the 1940s. The reconnection of popular activism and parliamentary politics, which put pressure on ministers and Majlis members over oil concessions and electoral abuse from the mid-1940s, made sense to those who saw representative government mired in 'clan politics',[40] and the corruption of a small elite. The founding moment of the National Front in October 1949 was a protest joining politicians, *bazaris* and students under Mussadeq's leadership in a *bast* in the Shah's palace grounds, demanding free elections. The Front's tactics in the ensuing election included public meetings in both the *bazar* and Tehran University, and support for *bazari* anti-government protests. The small number of National Front deputies elected to the Majlis in 1950 wielded an influence much greater than the size of their group because they were seen to have strong support from key sectors of public opinion.

The particular combination of parliamentary influence and popular support wielded by the National Front was distinctive in several ways. Other politicians like Ahmad Qavam built support outside the Majlis through cliques and patronage networks, press publicity and links to particular interests (regional, propertied), the court or foreign embassies. In contrast, the Tudeh Party and its affiliates were effective in building activism and organisation among large groups of workers and intellectuals, and in providing expression for workplace grievances or desires for modern forms of social justice and equality. However, it was unable to wield parliamentary influence to match that base, since its communistic ideology challenged the vested interests dominating the Majlis, and raised suspicion of its pro-Soviet sympathies and anti-democratic tendencies. The National Front diverged from this pattern in two respects. First, in forming a coalition that was not solely an opportunistic alliance of interests, or an ideologically and programmatically focused party, the Front met a number of aspirations and fulfilled a number of aims. It provided political space in which the powerful but small and often isolated world of experienced politicians could intersect with the wider politics of civil society. It brought together the skills and experience of those in government and Majlis with the energy and breadth of public campaigns and party organisations. Second, the Front was a coalition of interests and ideologies as well as of parliamentary and extra-parliamentary movements. The broad assertion of anti-imperial nationalism embraced liberal patriotic views of 'negative equilibrium' or 'passive balance',[41] Shi'a Muslim responses to perceived threats to their culture and traditions, and leftist and reforming agendas for the development of a free, just and equal society. The critique of undemocratic elite control of power and debate appealed to old constitutionalist values, religious fears of state intervention, and leftist opposition to privilege and exploitation. Above all, the Front addressed what many politicised Iranians saw as bottom-line issues during the 1940s: oil nationalism and representative government.

The emergence of a coalition crossing the parliamentary/extra-parliamentary divide and an extensive political and ideological spectrum was no sudden development of the period that saw the formation of the Front (1949), the oil nationalism battle (1950–51) and Mussadeq's premiership (1951–53). It drew on the rising awareness of and involvement in the democratic and toil issues fostered by activists and *'ulama* like Kashani, the rise of the use of press and radio, and the mobilisation of sections of the urban population in protests, strikes and demonstrations during the 1940s. The 1942 'bread riots', the protests over Soviet oil concessions in 1944, the demonstrations supporting Mussadeq's protests over the 1947 elections, and against the Shah's candidate for prime minister in 1948, were occasions when specific material and political grievances were linked to the broader issues. They spread 'modern' political practices among participants in these events as well as making a modern political vocabulary of democracy, imperialism and exploitation available to them. For the National Front, they facilitated the development of a workable coalition which was neither inclusive or lasting, but was situated in key locations within Iranian urban society and politics. It brought together modernising professionals, both pious and secular (like those in the Iran party) *bazaris* and their religious allies (followers of Ayatollah Kashani, or Muzaffar Baqa'i's Toilers' Party) and intellectuals with varied views (Maleki the former communist, Bazargan the Islamic modernist engineer, Taleqani the socially conscious *mulla*). To later commentators, this combination of old and new established political interests and social groupings was the National Front's distinctive achievement.

This achievement should not be seen in isolation. The force and impact of the movement for oil nationalism which was central to Iranian politics between 1944 and 1953, and focused around Mussadeq and the National Front from 1949, rested on developments during and after Reza Shah's rule. The growth of new workforces, the spread of modern education from the 1920s, and the opening up of political life after 1941 reshaped the political environment. Pahlavi rule, the rise in oil prices, foreign occupation and aggressive Cold War diplomacy gave new force and meaning to the politics of democracy and nationalism. The expansion of the Tudeh Party into workplaces, intellectual life and local politics marked success for partisan politics and the spread of radical ideas and modern activism.

The electoral campaigns of late 1943 and early 1944 show how elite and professional politicians now had to deal with *bazaris*, wage workers, religious interests and radical activists, as well as military and foreign interference. Class grievances and democratic and nationalist aspirations intersected with vested interests and magnate power in open political contests in major urban centres. Intensified democratic politics coincided with the sharpening of the 'national question' with renewed foreign pressure for oil concessions, followed by the issues of the withdrawal of foreign troops and foreign involvement in the rise and fall of separatist movements in Kurdistan and Azerbaijan in 1945–46. This set the tone and agenda for the next few years with continuing conflicts over the role of the Shah and magnates (the so-called 'thousand families') in society and government, and the need for national unity and strength to resist great power pressure. These were issues for politicians, for the forces mobilised through the Tudeh and its affiliates, and for a frustrated and articulate cross-section of reforming, *bazar*-based and professional interests that identified with neither the outlook of the Tudeh movements nor the privileges and self-interest of the elite.

By 1949 this last element had coalesced around Mussadeq and his associates as vocal defenders of representative government and national autonomy. In that sense the National Front has been seen as resting on a 'middle-class' base composed of 'traditional' (*bazari* and religious) and 'modern' (secular professional/educated/intellectual) wings. This may describe its organised core and Mussadeq's administration, but neglects wider currents of ideas, experience and conflict producing broad political support for them from 1949 to 1953. Political debate, strikes, demonstrations and electoral activity during the 1940s fed popular enthusiasm for oil nationalisation and defiance to royal autocracy. Despite the anti-communism of most of the National Front coalition, and the ambivalent, often hostile, stance of the Tudeh Party to the Front and Mussadeq's government, the political energy and emotion backing the causes of oil and anti-Shah politics drew on forces and interests that the Tudeh helped to develop. This was recognised in the *melli* language of Mussadeq and his movement, and their recourse to popular sanctions and confirmation of their actions in government and Majlis on the streets. As one politician observed in disgust, street meetings, 'speaking to the people' and 'rabble rousing' consolidated the government's position against the Shah and political factions by mobilising popular expectation and middle-class idealism.[42] For a brief period the grievances and hopes of diverse groups combined in enthusiasm for the 'national' cause. While the reforming, patriotic and constitutionalist agenda of the Front expressed the demands of an educated professional group and their *bazari* peers for a role in government and reduced power for Shah, elite and army, they made links with a broader politics and larger constituencies.

A frequently discussed feature of the Mussadeqist movement is the making and breaking of the alliance between those with religious outlooks and aspirations and those with a secular approach. It is in the period from the 1920s to the 1950s that it first became possible to discern 'religious' and 'secular' as distinct cultural or political positions, although this distinction should not be over-interpreted. One effect of Reza Shah's rule was to embed and strengthen oppositions between 'religious' and secular. The expansion and secularisation of law, education and administration, and the professions associated with them, created a critical mass of employees and intellectuals formed by and occupied with secular activity. They had world-views significantly different from those of earlier generations, with a conscious investment in technology, secular reason, science and socially conscious cultural activities which had visible political consequences. Anti-clericalism and secular thinking went back to the work of Kermani and Malkom Khan, but did not dominate endeavours to reform society and policy in Iran before the 1920s. By the 1940s, the intelligentsia was likely to see secular scientific approaches as *central* to social and political change, whether influenced by official ideology or by western education, travel and reading. For those who wanted to combine piety and progress, this was now a matter of aligning the former with the latter rather than vice-versa. Awareness of boundaries and conflicts between religious and secular interests was more common among educated Iranians of the 1940s than their predecessors.

Accounts of this period reinforce this picture by emphasising the quietist, conservative, pro-establishment stance of the *'ulama*. In addition to the material and institutional changes of the Reza Shah regime, which reduced the *'ulama*'s public roles and resources, the official secularism of the regime and the expansion of a secular intelligentsia put them on the defensive. Their political energies were therefore concentrated on resisting further encroachment and demonstrating that their acquiescence could not be taken for granted, as they did in various protests in the 1920s and 1930s.[43] The circumstances of the period encouraged continuing political awareness among *mullas*, whether through pragmatic quiescence and concealment of opposition to the regime, or active management of what remained a highly political relationship between government and *'ulama*. This did not so much remove them from the political arena as reinforce and reposition their political significance.

Reza Shah's departure was an opportunity for *'ulama* and those with religious interests to make public demands and contribute to the partisan politics of the 1940s. By 1943, prime minister Soheili was wooing religious support with concessions to religious views on education, women's veiling and the independence of *madrasehs*. Activists like Ayatollah Kashani were opposing the Soviet and British occupations and propagating a Muslim view of nationalism. Organisations like the Feda'iyin i-Islam emerged among *bazar* youth and *tullab*, and *'ulama* deputies joined together as *Mujahedin i-Islam*. Groups of *mullas*, *bazaris* and committed Muslim intellectuals like those around Muhammad Nakhshab and Jamal al-Din Ashtiani in Tehran or Muhammad Taqi Shari'ati in Mashad argued for religious approaches to current political and social issues. These initiatives moved into organised participation in the nationalist and cultural politics of the later 1940s and early 1950s adding important Shi'a Muslim elements to the National Front. In considering the role of religious professionals, interests and cultures in the politics of this period it is important to appreciate their impact as autonomous influences opposing secular forces, *and* as allies whose aims and ideas co-existed if not converged with them.

The diversity of religious approaches to politics is a good starting point for this discussion. One important trend was a prudent distancing of the *'ulama* from explicit political activism. Famously, in 1949 a meeting of some 2,000 *mullas* of all ranks convened by the senior *mujtahed* Ayatollah Burujerdi in

Qum produced a resolution prohibiting clergy from joining political parties or taking up political activism. This is often taken as evidence that quietism and withdrawal were preferred options for the leadership and politically aware sections of the *'ulama*: it may well have represented a widespread view among religious specialists. However, it is misleading to suggest that this was an apolitical position, and there is evidence that senior *mujtaheds* like Burujerdi and others in Qum and other centres saw it politically. They might set their authority against open party political activity, but did not abandon the use of political influence and lobbying. They pressured the Mussadeq government to drop provisions to enfranchise women in 1952, and maintained discreet but traceable connections with the Shah, and active religious nationalist leaders like Kashani. The *fatwas* pronounced by a number of *mujtaheds* in support of oil nationalisation in 1951, very much in the spirit in which their forebears had opposed the Reuter and Tobacco concessions, indicate the willingness of some *'ulama* to take up a political stance.[44]

The protective and 'quietist' option proclaimed and widely practised by many *'ulama* should be understood as a *choice* among political alternatives, and hence itself political. Disengagement from explicitly political activism made political sense. It combined with other tactics using distinctively religious authority (*fatwas*), and techniques of lobbying and negotiation familiar to any interest group. Official/public non-participation by *mullas* in politics expressed tactical withdrawal and conscious self-preservation rather than refusal of politics. It signalled a shift towards a more defensive relationship between advocates of religious interests and wider political culture where convergent interests were not so easily established, sustained or assumed as in the past.

However, defensiveness, withdrawal or antagonism to other contemporary political trends and movements were not the only religious approaches to politics. Equally visible and significant were various alliances between those with religious and those with secular motivation, and the combination of Shi'a Muslim influences with others in political thought and activity. Most obvious was the linking of explicitly religious political groups with support among religiously observant Iranians, notably *bazaris*, with other partners to establish the National Front. Pious concern to defend Shi'a Islam from infidel attack found common cause with other strands of opposition to foreign dominance, just as *'ulama* and *bazari* resentment at the intrusive statism of Reza Shah's regime created sympathy for the cause of constitutional government against royal and elite power.

This convergence was expressed in the powerful if unstable partnership of religious organisations (Kashani's Association of Muslim Fighters, the *bazari* followers of Muzaffar Baqa'i) with parties pursuing more secular programmes (the professionals of the Iran Party, the intellectuals around Khalil Maleki). It focused on the leadership of Mussadeq with his record of patriotic anti-Pahlavi politics, and that of Ayatollah Kashani, who also had a record of anti-imperialist activism. The ability of this alliance to mobilise support among pious Iranians and more secularised groups came from blending religious elements into their campaigns for democracy, national autonomy and reform. The association of Islam with social justice and the cultural identity of the nation, like the language of struggle and martyrdom used by constitutionalists and nationalists of all kinds, were part of an exchange of political images and values. This exchange took practical form in the flow of *bazar* funds to religious leaders in the National Front, and the participation of *bazaris* and pious Iranians in the street politics that backed Mussadeq's government, even when leaders like Kashani distanced themselves from it. Broad-based support for oil nationalism and the containment of royal and elite power expressed the convergence of pragmatic and opportunistic decisions about how *bazaris* or educated modern professionals might best pursue their interests. It also expressed persistent traditions of coalition and interactive ideologies of reform and nationalism going back to the 1890s, as well as the effects of political and cultural circumstances in the 1940s.

Although there was hostility between those who took political stands as Shi'a Muslims and those who regarded themselves as politically secular, this should not obscure other relationships. References to the *division* between the 'traditional' and 'modern' social groups who formed the core of the National Front, exemplified in Abrahamian's eloquent account,[45] diverts attention away from the connections *between* them. Professionals, intellectuals and white-collar workers with modern/secular education and occupations were often part of *bazar* or *mulla* families whose other members still had *bazari*, business or religious roles. The real force of anti-clerical politics on the one side and oppositions to godless secularisation on the other were cross-cut and offset by familial and personal connections and experiences. In more practical terms, efforts to connect 'Islamic' and 'modern' political ideals and programmes discussed earlier were matched not just by the coalition politics of Kashani or Baqa'i, but by attempts by those like Mehdi Bazargan, Muhammad Taqi Shari'ati or Muhammad Nakhshab to work politically as Muslims within a modern movement.[46]

Such attempts had limited impact, which may suggest that the key political trend was towards conflict between self-defined and opposed 'religious' and 'secular' groups and interests. While some religious views might be compatible with the politics of reform, nationalism and democracy, open contention over religion was a growing feature of the period. As seen earlier, some of that took the form of ideological debate, but it also appeared in Majlis politics, street confrontations and clashes over particular policies with religious significance.

Attacks on Jews, Baha'is, and Zoroastrians during the 1940s showed the continuing force of Muslim zealotry in community politics, whether spontaneous or mobilised by activists.[47] By contrast, the establishment of the Feda'iyin i-Islam expressed both open anti-secularism and an updated populist religious nationalism focused on the 'affront to Islam' embodied in the oil concession, the foundation of Israel and the foreign presence in Iran. Their anti-secularism emphasised issues important to committed Shi'a Muslims, notably the use of *shari'a* law and women's dress codes. Although they used confrontational and ultimately violent methods, including assassination, not supported by other such Muslims, their ideological zeal and organisational energy attracted financial support from *bazaris* and allies among political *'ulama*.[48]

This specifically oppositional religious politics had several aspects. Although the anti-secularism of some *'ulama* and other religiously committed Iranians opposed various features of 'modern' society (secular law and education, changed treatment of women) and the critics or reformers of Shi'ism (Ahmad Kasravi, Shari'at-Sanglaji), they were in fact *within* that society and culture. The issues they pursued as defenders of established traditions were questions of the role of religion, the nature of knowledge and progress, and acceptable forms of politics and representation specific to 'modern times'. Contention over religion in the French Third Republic, over reform in Meiji Japan, or over both in inter-war Spain, brought supporters of established elites or religious institutions and practices into the world of modern political polemic, activism and organisation. So too in Iran, activists advocating Shi'a interests in the 1940s and 1950s involved themselves in the journalism, partisan organisation, campaigning and programme writing that was the stuff of that world.

In this sense even those religious activists most committed to oppose secular trends and assert Muslim interests had much in common with other participants in the politics of street, press and Majlis. Their conflicts with secularisers took place in that shared arena and contrasted with the stance of those religious leaders whose conscious choice was to stand aside from it. It is significant that the 'Mussadeqist' coalition, embracing leftists, political *mullas*, liberal nationalists, pious *bazaris* and educated young men of diverse views, was focused on the highly modern issue of oil nationalism, challenges to royal/elite power and Mussadeq's charismatic embodiment of these causes. The intransigent stance of the Feda'iyin i-Islam should likewise be understood in relation both to their practice of modern politics and to their place on a spectrum of Shi'a Muslim political activity. This spectrum spanned Ayatollah Burujerdi's manoeuvres with Mussadeq's government on behalf of the *'ulama* leadership, nuanced relationships between 'apolitical' members of that leadership and 'political' *mullas* such as Kashani, *'ulama* participation in elections and Majlis politics, and street support for religious issues and leaders. There were shifting tensions and alliances among these elements, with pious *bazaris* and street protesters being moved at different times by *mullas* to attack unveiled women or leftists, and by National Front polemics to mobilise behind Mussadeq against the Shah and the British.

This mosaic of religious inputs to the politics of the 1940s and early 1950s modifies assumptions about the positioning and relationship of 'politics' and 'religion'. First, any crude splitting off of 'religious' from 'secular' elements does not do justice either to the enduring use by activists of religious idiom for a *range* of political purposes and the alliances between explicitly religious and other interests, or to the immediate concerns or causes uniting them in the powerful, if unstable, 'Mussadeqist' coalition. Second, this should not obscure important countervailing developments. If the 'cross-class' mobilisation of the constitutional era involved groups of intellectuals and *bazaris* who shared much cultural capital, the patriot–popular coalition of 1947–53 embraced more diverse participants whose outlooks were not so consistent or coherent. The growth of secularised education and of professional, commercial and white-collar employment from the 1920s to the 1940s created strata of politically active Iranians with views and values shaped by those developments in numbers greater than those of the earlier period. Consequently, their contribution to political life in the 1940s and 1950s also had more impact, as did the contribution of those employed in a growing wage-labour sector. The much higher profile of secular forms of political debate and activity made confrontation between self-proclaimed critics of religion and its defenders more significant in the partisan politics and ideologies of the period.

In this confrontation the ideologically driven stereotypical linking of religion with 'backwardness' or reform with 'irreligion', foreshadowed in earlier debates, took fuller, clearer shape. It is difficult to estimate the broader impact of this ideological clash among overlapping groups of political activists in the Mussadeqist coalition, since these activists have tended to use the ideological categories and stereotypes in question. Nevertheless, the efforts of active leftists or Muslims to gather support for their views as Fedaiyan, communists or Shari'ati's anti-Kasravists did, certainly politicised the debate. While some Iranians emphasised convergence or possibilities for co-existence between religious and other convictions and forms of activism, more embattled and opposed stances either entwined with such attempts or developed independently. On the one hand were the cross-cutting influences on supporters of the Movement of God Worshipping Socialists, who connected themselves to the Iran Party, socialist ideas and the Mussadeqist coalition while actively combating irreligion. On the other hand groups like the Fedaiyan and anti-leftist *tullab* prioritised attacks on those forces as their defining objective with its own autonomous value. The 'Islamic' stance of the latter did not inhibit their use of modern approaches to politics, including, like the very different God Worshipping Socialists, confident use of 'lay' Muslim intellectuals. The real contrast was between Iranians for whom religious commitments interacted with commitments to nationalism and reform, and those for whom they were the dominant issue. Another contrast was between those for whom religious beliefs and practices could and should adapt and respond to changing circumstances, and those for whom they were an inheritance to be protected from change and posed against the corruption of those circumstances.

The small-scale and personalised character of many 'religious' elements in the politics of the 'Mussadeq era', and the compelling power of the patriotic and popular causes of oil and constitutional government, have understandably sustained a view of that politics as essentially 'secular'. Descriptions of a 'multi-class urban popular alliance' with its 'predominantly secular culture' by Foran, and of the coalition of 'modern' and 'traditional' middle class by Abrahamian, emphasise that view, basing themselves on analyses of changing social structures. Katouzian's analysis offers a political and ideological perspective, emphasising the contest of *mellat* (people/nation) and *doulat* (despotic corrupt government), and the goals of independence from both autocracy and external manipulation which he associates with the 'popular movement' of Iran at this time.[49] In each narrative there is dominant concern to place leftist and National Front politics in Iran between 1941 and 1953 in stories of modernity, dependency, state-building, or struggles over democracy and reform. In such stories the main issue is how far religious groups or influences opposed or supported these processes. However, the fragile co-existence of political *'ulama* and secularist professionals, the pragmatic management of Mussadeq's government of relations with Qum *mujtaheds*, and experiments of pious Shi'a with social radicalism or scientific reasoning, were as much part of those stories as more publicised antagonisms.

If Edward Browne's description of merchants, intellectuals and pious *bazaris* together in the British legation garden in 1906 is an iconic image of the key coalition of the Constitutional Movement, what would be its equivalent for the 'Mussadeq era'? It would need to depict three crucial aspects of politics in the period. First, it should express the hybridity of religious, reforming and nationalist concerns exemplified in references to 'holy war' and 'sacred cause' by secular politicians, and in the support of committed Shi'a believers to social reform, nationalism and 'modern' political issues. Second, it should depict the persistence of cultural/religious tropes of 'national' Iranian identity and visions of national well-being dating back to the 1880s alongside newer versions of these ideals. Third, it should show the new forms of activity through which wage workers, students, *bazaris* and white-collar workers pursued popular patriotic goals and redefined them. Activism informed by new views of 'Iran' and its confrontations with foreign powers, of reform and social justice, and of democracy and popular representation, spread from the limited circles where it had concentrated previously.

Whether seen as a period of disorder, of social struggle, or of popular confrontation with government and foreign powers, this era can also be understood in terms of conflicts, convergences and cohabitation, produced as much by the rich variety of Iranian experiences, outlooks and interests as by their antagonisms or incompatibilities. By the 1940s, the kaleidoscopic patterns of constitutional politics, shaken by internal and external changes over the following decades, reconfigured in a different but equally kaleidoscopic form. The political movements of that period were clearly not dominated by religious issues, interests or institutions, and challenge any simplistic view about their persistence or any 'inherent' propensity of Iranians to prefer them to other political objectives or modes of expression. Nevertheless, religious elements cohabited, contended with and contributed to the politics of the time.

The participation of Iranians with religious agendas and outlooks in the National Front coalition illustrates the power and the weakness of inclusive politics at both street and parliamentary levels, embodying the difficulties and opportunities involved in combining religious aspirations with other reforming or nationalist politics. Ultimately, these difficulties and weaknesses fractured the coalition, although the overt splits in the National Front owed as much, if not more, to factional and personal rivalries. Both division and conflict indicate ongoing and unresolved questions posed by the presence of religious elements within popular politics and reform activists and programmes – questions that were part and parcel of political reality. While there are conflicting views on the viability of such projects, they kept alive continuing overlaps, debates and links between religiously motivated political thinking and activity and other traditions and approaches. The apparently binary opposition of 'religious' and 'secular' interests, ideas and organisations, and the manifest conflicts between exponents of each, need to be located in a complex setting of cohabitation and convergence.

The politics of the 1940s and 1950s revealed processes of political change associated with the emergence of larger constituencies for nationalist and popular activism which transformed and moved on from existing patterns without obliterating them. The relatively restricted impact of popular political activity among Iranians as a whole, the external and internal obstacles to radical change, and the pressure of immediate political needs to confront the ruling elite and hostile great power intervention, all limited the transformative capacity of that politics, as did the many-sided and sometimes contradictory elements within political movements. While the Tudeh and National Front created and sustained new forms and levels of political mobilisation, their activities built on and accommodated to the diversity and established features of Iranian society as well as newer or changing aspects. Entwined with those explicitly innovative, reforming and nationalist initiatives were contests over religious and secular interests and world-views, attempts to synthesise them, and a range of tactical manoeuvres and compromises around them. The success of secularist politics, and the prominence or dominance of groups with secular outlooks, should not obscure these aspects.

Whatever aspects of those later movements are emphasised, their activity was cut short by the overthrow of the Mussadeq regime in 1953 and subsequent repression. The defeat of a regime partly reliant on popular and partisan support was only partly due to weaknesses and divisions in that support, being very much the product of mistakes made by the regime, and the intractability of US/British and Pahlavi/establishment opposition to it. The global power of the British and Americans mobilised in defence of oil interests and Cold War strategy was used to back the Shah and elite against Mussadeq's government, whose support was undermined by the contradictions and uncertainties of the Mussadeqist coalition.[50] Direct intervention by foreign powers short-circuited other possible outcomes to the contest between the government and its enemies. Nevertheless, without denying that the era of Mussadeqist nationalism and its end were powerfully shaped by external geopolitical realities, the legacy and afterlife of the movements, which flourished within Iran in that era, were also significant. For many of the intelligentsia it was the formative experience of 'progressive' nationalism, just as for leftists it was a key period of mass organisation and action. For Iranians who were, or subsequently became, politically aware and active, it was the most extensive period of *broad* political involvement for those wishing to challenge *doulat* and its relation to *mellat*. It was also the source of memories, stories, prejudices and aspirations based on political experiences between 1941 and 1953, and perceptions of the 'failures', 'success', 'betrayal', or inspiration of whichever causes Iranians had espoused during that time. The continued interweaving of religious ideas and images within languages of protest and anti-imperialism, and of contests over the extent to which religion could co-exist with modernity, sustained their discursive presence, implicit or explicit, into the future. Without exaggerating the scale or significance of legacies from the 1941–53 period, it is worth remembering that they remained available as a resource in the Iranian political repertoire.

Major changes and challenges to that repertoire were a feature of new situations created by the re-establishment of the Shah's power with domestic and American banking in 1953. In seeking to make sense of the politics of the 1970s, in which nationalistic, social and moral discontents converged, it is useful to consider developments over the whole quarter century from the overthrow of Mussadeq to that of the Shah who ousted him, and then the ingredients which fuelled the political revival of the 1970s. Much of this is rehearsed in the extensive literature on the revolution of 1977–81. The aim here is to signal the complex relationships between material and cultural developments in that quarter century and the whole era of modernity in Iran. While some narration of continuity and change is appropriate, it is provided as a basis for discussion of the conflicting, converging and co-habiting features of politics that were the outcomes/expressions of change and continuity. Iranians working with existing repertoires of nationalist, leftist and religious politics continued to use those familiar political modes, but also responded to the shifting circumstances within which politics was now pursued. Equally importantly, the pursuit of politics in the 1970s was transformed as the variety and number of Iranians touched by material and cultural change increased, creating new constituencies with new concerns.

Before the 1960s, Iranians' experience of modernity had been of sharply uneven processes of change. For some, global influences like the growth of foreign trade links and the oil industry had been highly significant in their lives, while many others were removed from such influences. The rise in literacy, the spread of money-based economic activity, or the impact of modern administrative and legal systems had been similarly limited to specific groups and locations, creating complex and discontinuous relations among Iranians with varying degrees of involvement in those processes. Such relationships were shaped by class difference, with 'modernising' elites interacting with dominated classes, and by the dynamics of government incursions into the lives of its subjects. The impact of social change was mediated by the strategies of resistance, evasion or adaptation deployed by subordinate groups towards such external and dominating interventions. The idea of uneven and complex patterns may be a more helpful framing concept for understanding Iranian modernity at this time than the binary contrast of 'continuity' and 'change'.

These varied and disjointed patterns of development changed in extent and intensity during the 1960s and 1970s. With the resources of growing oil revenues, encouragement from US governments, and the sense that the image and security of the restored regime were bound up with modernisation, the government embarked on major 'reform' programmes with widespread effects. As has been seen, the land reform programme, the spread of education, and of new manufacturing and service activities, led to sharp changes in the daily lives and social relations of many Iranians. New communities of urban migrants and squatters, state and market influences on rural communities, new groups of literate young people, white-collar workers and wage labourers created new cultural and political patterns as well as new productive structures and relations.[51] Their new activities and experiences gained political edge from two key

233

sources. Many changes affecting Iranians at this time were directly or indirectly the result of state intervention, and so re-posed questions about how they saw and dealt with the *doulat* which was reshaping their lives. The removal of landlord power following land reform, or new bureaucratic initiatives in education, health or urban planning might reinforce old images of the Shah as the source of solutions to people's problems. They might equally reinforce suspicions of an intrusive, uncomprehending and corruptly acquisitive government presence in the lives of agricultural, squatter or factory communities. Whether among the migrant squatters of Tehran, the cultivators of Khuzestan, or the pastoralists of the Qashgha'i and Shahsevan, state power figured ever more prominently as a force to be placated, avoided and manoeuvred.[52] While not creating organised opposition, they evolved a 'street-level' politics of negotiation, resistance or avoidance which kept them alert to the vagaries of state power while continuing subservient to it.

For some Iranians, tensions with the state were more overt than the everyday guerrilla manoeuvres of the groups just mentioned. These included high school graduates excluded from the university places for which they had qualified, wage workers resentful of the manipulations of management and police informers, and educated professionals required to constrain themselves within the repressive regulation of education, law, administration or cultural activity. It was among these groups, including some *'ulama* and *bazaris*, that political concerns from the pre-1953 era still resonated, finding outlets in political activism in the early 1960s triggered by the opening of some limited political opportunity, an economic downturn and proposed government reforms. They included a strike by poorly paid teachers in 1961, protests by successor groups to the National Front over election-rigging in 1960–61, and opposition to the reform programme from *'ulama*, political groups and *bazaris* in 1961–63.[53] These movements indicated the ability of some Iranians with grievances to respond to circumstances, and expressed workplace discontents and hostility to royal despotism and corruption familiar from the politics of earlier years. They included significant participation from students, *'ulama* and *tullab*, flagging the presence of political constituencies with important future roles. The emergence of an outspoken uncompromising version of populist religious opposition to the Shah in the voice of Ayatollah Khomeini showed the power of that tradition to produce new and astute political challenges.

Beyond this continuing thread of protest, the changes of the 1960s and 1970s produced more diffuse but significant political tensions. The arrival of modern communications, education, bureaucratic regulation and monetised market forces had material and cultural effects, but also raised political issues. Depending on their power, wealth, location and outlook (urban, well-connected, educated or their opposites), Iranians made *political* judgements and choices, allying cultural and political perceptions to practical survival strategies. The everyday behaviour of villagers and agricultural workers in Khuzestan towards officials was based on an articulate and developed understanding of their relations with the state, just as a Tehran soap factory worker, describing himself as 'unaware of politics', used newly acquired literacy to debate the distribution of bonus payments with managers. Grasp of power relations and the significance of experience was shown in the political perceptions of those manoeuvring through village hierarchies observed by Hegland and Loeffler, and the 'quiet encroachment' of the urban poor on living space and street trade described by Bayat.[54] From this perspective, political mobilisation in 1978–79 seems less mysterious.

For many ordinary Iranians, the authoritarian, interventionist and repressive features of the regime of Muhammad Reza Pahlavi were less a matter of ideological concern than of the pragmatic politics of the subordinate and unprivileged. This type of politics should not be forgotten in the search for an overview of the events and processes that ended his rule, both because there are important questions about the relationship of the two political arenas, and because the Shah's overthrow is not the only political narrative of the period. Turning to that narrative, several themes need to be addressed; first, there is the question of how the continuing and changing experiences of life in Iran generated political challenges to the regime; second, there are distinctive developments in religious politics to consider; third, insights from these discussions can be used to evaluate various views of the breakdown of the regime and suggest that issues of awkward cohabitation and the *contingent* features of that process may be as illuminating as social-scientific models.

The changes of the 1960s and 1970s also showed themselves in more obviously 'political' settings. Two expanded political constituencies were to be especially significant. One was the growing spectrum of urban workers in manufacturing, commercial or administrative jobs, new and old. Carving out often precarious lives, they were also responsive to the stimuli of workplace conflicts, religious influences and new forms of communication, education and entertainment and street life. Their activities, while not part of the explicit debates and interests of those concerned with despotism, national renewal and 'modern' religion, had their own kind of political agency. Reflecting on his political formation before 1979, a worker from a poor quarter of Tehran spoke of 'awareness' generated by a strike in a textile factory eight or ten years earlier – 'until then I didn't understand what the militia and SAVAK (the security forces) were'. He echoed workers in Isfahan recalling the daily conflicts and injustices of factory life, or a Tehran van-driver describing the influence of a three-year contract with a militant *mulla*. They might be moved by recollections of Mussadeq, which linked them to past activism, or on the contrary only by the cascading energies and achievements of protest by others in 1978–79, but participants in the politics of those years also drew on their own experience.[55]

The other group, who in the eyes of fellow participants formed the advance forces of the 1978–79 'revolution', were the hugely expanded number of Iranians in secondary and tertiary education in the 1970s. Here were Iranians who were frustrated by the constraints on and competition for opportunities supposedly opened up for them by education. They were readers and disseminators of the growing output of religious texts and political and intellectual writing of dissident reformers and leftists, and sometimes participants in networks and clandestine organisations challenging state repression, foreign influence or social injustice. Expanded access to secondary education and then colleges or universities (predominantly for urban children) by the later 1970s had a number of political effects. It enlarged the number of literate and educated participants in political debate and activity. By the late 1970s, there were some 2.5 million secondary school students (nearly one-third of the total school population) compared to about 100,000 in 1953, just under 300,000 (some 17 per cent of school pupils) and 1 million in 1970–1 (over 24 per cent). In the same period the number of students in higher education rose from 9,845 in 1953–54, to 22,856 in 1961–62, 97,338 in 1971, and 154,215 in 1976–77.

While expanding the numbers of the politically aware and articulate, the growing education system generated competition and frustrated expectations. Whereas over one-third of the high school graduates competing for university places in 1961–62 were successful, by the mid-1970s this had fallen to a mere 12 or 14 per cent. In the 1950s, and early 1960s, most higher education students (over 90 per cent) were studying in universities, the rest being in other lower-status tertiary colleges; by the 1970s the proportion had fallen to under 50 per cent. One survey of entrance examinees showed that 26 per cent had taken the exams *three or more* times previously, 62 per cent would try again if they failed on this occasion and 68 per cent would not stop trying to enter university, preferring to move from home, or study a less favoured subject rather than take another option.[56] The status and material gain associated with university study and the jobs to which it was supposed to lead, became a powerful driver for the important minority of young people and their families looking to advance by this route.

As the growth of education increased social change and social tension, it also raised or changed cultural and political awareness. Not only were aspiring young Iranians confronted with the competitive, financially restrictive and bureaucratically regimented process of admission to and progress through the system, they experienced and understood other aspects of that system. They might, like secondary school boys, form a 'squatter' community in Tehran, be forcibly aware of the barriers to their progress through school and into vocational training because of hostility to the aspirations of the poor 'third-class members like us'. They might, like university students in Shiraz, struggle with the inconsistent demands of the bureaucratic regime, their own and their families' ambitions, and the expectations of their American or American-educated teachers.[57] Students from pious and practising religious households confronted disparities between cultures and values there and those of universities and urban centres, or between codes of sexual propriety learned at home and adolescent responses to the stimuli and opportunities of streets and public parks.

These contexts illuminate important aspects of the anti-Shah movement of the late 1970s. Within a population that was predominantly young (two-thirds under thirty, half under sixteen), a large new pool of younger Iranians were acquiring the experience and resources that might sustain resentful dissident views and actions. The student population of the 1970s were audiences for religious reformers like Shari'ati, participants in critical discussion, and recruits or sympathisers with the new militant left groups. Coming from more diverse origins than in the past, they had different political connections. The significant number of students from *bazari* and less secular backgrounds can be related to greater student interest in the politics of religious reform and revival, and in the links between Shi'a Muslim ideas or images and anti-regime, anti-imperialist politics. Their links to *bazars* or rural areas, from where students might commute to nearby towns, provided channels for information, comment and political material like cassette tapes to reach wider sections of society.

The hopes, fears and debates stimulated by the changes of the 1960s and 1970s were added to the legacy of oppositional politics shaped by nationalism and desires for reform, as were varied religious critiques of corruption, injustice and western influence. Disaffection with the regime was a continuing feature of Iranian life expressed in pragmatic avoidance of its corrupt and inappropriate practices by the poor, or in political critiques of despotism and oppression by the educated. The spread of magazines, films, tapes and records, and the new ideas and images they carried, raised concerns among Iranians making important life decisions about prosperity and propriety and those struck by the cultural discordances of 'modern'/'traditional' and 'Iranian'/'foreign' in that material. This fuelled perceptions of the Shah's regime as the agent, ally or client of 'alien' American influence, and debates on the role of religion in 'patriotic', 'popular' or 'progressive' politics.

These debates drew on references to the politics of the 1940s or even of the constitutional era but gained new meanings and objectives in the 1960s and the 1970s. Much debate and protest was organised by groups of students abroad, free from the direct repression by the Iranian government. They questioned the leftists and nationalists who sought to achieve change by campaigning on the existing political terrain, establishing new groups committed to more confrontational ideologies and armed struggle. State elimination or control of most openings for protest and organisation, whether unions, professional bodies or political parties, left limited political space in schools, colleges or religious circles where critiques could be developed and disseminated. The legacy of politicised religion and the often hostile relations of government and 'ulama encouraged reassessment of the quietist stance of religious specialists in the 1950s. The force and clarity of 'ulama opposition exemplified by Khomeini's attacks on the regime in 1963–64, and the links to young radicals made by socially conscious, politically active 'ulama like Taleqani, or Shi'a activist/intellectuals like 'Ali Shari'ati, revived and refurbished Shi'a Muslim influence in oppositional policies.

Alongside the émigré and guerrilla politics emerging from the political disarray of the 1960s, and the growing networks of politicised 'ulama, were transformed versions of anti-imperial and working-class politics. As rising living standards for wage workers were undermined by inflation after 1973, and frustrations at the manipulations of management and government authorities in factories grew, so worker disputes increased during the mid-1970s despite state repression.[58] Focused on immediate material demands and informal organisation, they evidenced the political willingness and ingenuity of the workers in the 'modern' industries where most strikes took place. Writing on this kind of worker activism has emphasised the impact of military and police repression, and social and cultural constraints making worker protest and organisation localised and short-lived.[59] When extensive strikes among white-collar, oil and manufacturing workers contributed to the multi-faceted opposition to the Shah's regime during 1978, worker discontent entwined with the religious, bazari and activist oppositions which shaped the movement. There is polemic and scholarly discussion about the 'spontaneity', 'autonomy' or 'class' (as opposed to 'religious' or 'anti-regime') consciousness in the strikes which formed part of the 'cross-class' mobilisations of 1978–79, but it is also arguable that the expansion of core groups of modern industrial workers (over one-third of the urban wage-earning population) provided important patterns of political action.

Even more significant for the anti-regime movement was the changed emphasis and vocabulary of the anti-imperialist politics inherited from the 1940s and 1950s. Following the US role in the overthrow of Mussadeq, the subsequent consolidation of the Shah's regime and their ongoing support for the army, security forces and technical aid, 'America' and Americans became the main target for anti-imperialist polemic, replacing the British. This shift of focus to 'American' or generically 'western' imperialism was accompanied by new and powerful languages of cultural and religious critique of US/western influence and their support for Pahlavi despotism. As seen in Chapter 5, the political appeal of cultural nationalism grew with debates among Shi'a Muslims and exposure to new currents of cultural nationalism in the 1960s. It gave expression to the conflicted experiences of young Iranians negotiating indigenous and imported values and practices, and the unfulfilled promises of regime-led 'modernisation', and linked traditions of nationalist opposition to Pahlavi rule with those associating 'national' identity with religion. It gave voice to those seeking to connect Shi'a Islam with contemporary experience, social commitment and political activism, and to those seeking to expand older categories of anti-colonial politics. While the best-known exponents of cultural nationalism were small groups of intellectuals, writers and theorists, the themes they addressed chimed with ideas and experiences in the wider society.

It is in this context of material and cultural change and their associated discontents that the varied and contradictory roles of religious ideals and interests in the shaping of oppositional cultures can be appreciated. Among the *'ulama* the pressures of growing state encroachment on their domain and of the drive to secure an effective place in the world of 'modern' Iran stimulated a number of political or cultural initiatives. Some *'ulama* formed links to the pious nationalists of the anti-regime Liberation Movement of Iran, and with Muslim militants in underground movements of armed confrontation. Some maintained links with the networks of support for the intransigent opposition politics promulgated by Khomeini and his associates from exile. *'Ulama* positions and ideas of 'Islamic' opposition to the Shah ranged from the constitutionalist arguments of the Liberation Movement of Iran through the moral condemnations of a corrupt Americanised regime associated with Khomeini, to support for revolutionary activism. Furthermore, the expansion of religious practice which brought *mullas* together with other believers in *hay'ats* or religious gatherings in the 1970s, also had its political potential. It provided outlets for personal concerns or practical support for material needs, but also refashioned credibility for religion and religious specialists as advocates or intermediaries, and new critical moral language.

The political significance of these developments should not be exaggerated. As Bayat has noted, support for *hay'ats* and *rawzehs* did not necessarily translate into support for political Islam, just as views of Khomeini among the urban and rural underprivileged might stress his irrelevancy ('nothing changed') or his role as a source of futile disruption ('he'll just bring people on to the streets').[60] Despite the effective use by propagandists of the concept of the *mustaz'afin* (dispossessed/downtrodden) to signify both the beneficiaries and the agents of the Shah's overthrow, it was not the marginal poor who were necessarily mobilised by the religious condemnations of the regime. Where the relationships of *'ulama* and their constituencies was most politically significant was among *bazari* leaders and workers and the less marginal sections of the urban working population. Interviews with radicalised workers in both factory and workshop production in 1978–79 found that, alongside the material and class-based language of opposition, religiously influenced ideas of 'right', 'justice' and 'corruption' were powerful means of political expression. Sometimes personal devotion to Husein the martyred Imam shifted into devotion to the cause of resistance, now seen as 'his' cause.[61] Here the uncompromising vision of 'Islamic government' and resistance to the Pahlavi regime expressed by Khomeini and his associates converged with the vision of activist Muslim protest stemming from the thought of Shari'ati.

In a rather different milieu, established traditions of left-liberal nationalist opposition, with its Shi'a Muslim facets, was recrafted and cross-fertilised with languages of cultural authenticity and radical religious vision. This process was grounded in debate among the younger generation of anti-regime activists from educated and politically aware backgrounds, which were sometimes also actively pious. It expressed their frustrations with the resistance, or at least caution, of the Shi'a establishment towards innovation or political activism, and with the deficiencies of nationalist politics in the 1950s and 1960s. Organisationally it was sustained by semi-clandestine discussion and publication, by émigré networks of opposition in the overseas Muslim Student Associations, and dissemination of texts and ideas inside and outside Iran. Ideologically it fused anti-imperialist, socially committed tropes from established left-wing thinking with newer third-worldist and nativist ideas of cultural liberation and the regeneration of religion in an activist mode. It emphasised faith in the 'inner' resources of the committed individual and the 'imagined' Iranian community, as opposed to the role of external 'forces' or forms of leadership and organisation. As such, it inspired diverse protesters and activists, from the highly organised Mujahedin to factory workers, college students and urban politicos. The religious flavour of this approach, centred on Islam not on *mullas*, and on religious commitment to change rather than to established institutions or texts, was as dissident as its political outlook.

By the mid-1970s, the resistance of sections of the *'ulama* and their reforged connections with urban communities and political opposition, together with the impact of the denunciations of Khomeini and the ideals of Shari'ati were blending in what has been called 'the revolution's ideological primordial soup'.[62] While more 'orthodox' Shi'a Muslims opposed the innovative approach of Shari'ati, and Muslim liberals and constitutionalists were concerned by Khomeini's 'clericalism', there were also interactions. Learned *'ulama*, students, *bazaris* and radical intellectuals all participated at Huseinieh Ershad, where Shari'ati lectured, just as the Shah's prisons brought leftist students together with political *mullas* such as Taleqani. Dissident *'ulama* maintained links with Khomeini in exile and with overseas students' associations, just as the Liberation Movement maintained links with both religious and secular opposition. While it is important to distinguish between the conflicting and varied interactions of politics and religion in this period, it is equally important to be aware of the permeable boundaries between them. In an atmosphere of generalised dissatisfaction and opposition in which respected and inspiring languages of piety, martyrdom and struggle, old and new, were powerful political currencies, choice or competition between variant visions or discourse were less important than their polyvalence.

What these resources provided above all were political languages with familiar meanings but also the potential to express current concerns. Khomeini's reformulation of old invocations of ungodly/illegitimate rule and the foreign threat to 'Islam' in denunciations of the Shah and his ties to US interests matched the power of his usefully unspecific vision of Islamic government. It echoed challenges to earlier rulers demanding defence of the faith, but had entirely contemporary resonance in the world where the presence of American TV programmes and tens of thousands of American advisers and experts were part of Iranian experience. The liberationist and activist representation of 'being a Muslim' proclaimed by Shari'ati captured memories and narratives of resistance to oppression, whether internal or external, and frustration with the failures of previous resistance movements. It might use images from the Muslim and Iranian past and Shi'a thought, but spoke to contemporary tensions and criticisms of 'modern' life in Iran, and key issues of authenticity and identity. The authoritative force of Khomeini's language of rejection, the imaginative power of the Shari'ati's language of activism and liberation, and the shared commitment to struggle in both could be appropriated by *bazaris*, dissident *'ulama* or protesting workers and students when those changes came about.

In more practical ways, networks of covert Khomeini supporters, student and intellectual activists, and religious organisations provided the kernel of political infrastructure which helped to sustain the protests of 1978–79. Conventions of ritual mourning assemblies forty days after a death, or *'ulama* pronouncements and support for communal welfare, became templates for mass demonstrations, the rhetoric of opposition and local organisation. Workers in Isfahan after the Shah's overthrow spoke of the role of mosques and of leaflets using Shari'ati's texts, those in Qazvin of the inspiration of Taleqani and Khomeini (known to them since the mid-1970s) and their support for the *'ulama*, while Tehranis described experience in religious associations, and links to *mullas* as part of their politicisation.[63] Participants recorded their use of concepts of struggle and martyrdom, and of Shi'a ideals of anti-corruption and justice as goals of struggle, and described how activists (students and *mullas*) had spread this language in 1978–79, connecting it to established religious experience and vocabulary.

These accounts illustrate the embedding of religion in the revolutionary process. It is also clear from other accounts that these were not the only resources drawn on by participants. They were aware of the leftist politics of social revolution, of ideas and images of nationalism, and of a range of material and cultural discontents in their own immediate milieux.[64] Studies of the strike movements of 1978–79 suggest that many arose from such discontents and only became politicised and/or Islamised over time. Widely used images of 'right/justice' (*haqq*), while part of religious discourse, tapped into, and pre-empted, the appeal of secular leftist ideals, giving them religious direction.[65] The material failures of the Shah's regime for the working population, and for the educated classes, especially the younger generation, were matched by cultural discontents which went beyond the defence of religion as such. While it is important to understand how religion was embedded in the revolutionary activities of 1978–79 and so able to dominate their outcome, the actual dynamics of the upheaval had a denser, more complex character.

The speed and scale of the movements of 1977–79, and their largely unpredicted outcome in the Islamic Republic consolidated between 1979 and 1982 under the dominance of the particular religious trends associated with Khomeini, have provoked several large-scale interpretations.[66] They all share to some extent the use of a 'schema' or 'model' (of 'mobilisation', 'structural crisis', 'contradiction', 'crisis of legitimacy', 'cause' and 'process') to sustain their explanations. In so far as they rest on careful and revealing comparisons of and reflections on past protests and changes in Iran, or relevant experiences elsewhere, such approaches are useful, but they tend to underplay two significant themes. First, they neglect the *self-created* dynamic of events and decisions that are contingent but constitutive contributors to significant political change. Second, they are somewhat distant from the human individuals who singly or collectively 'make the difference' by their choices and actions.

A full appreciation of the causes and course of the mass movements of Iranians in 1978–79 needs to connect the structural and institutional aspects of material and political life and grand narratives of culture and ideology to the unstable dynamics of people's decisions and behaviour on the ground. Thus, it makes sense to depict the revolution of 1977–81 as embedded in the cultural and material development of the period following 1945, but also to see it as characterised by its own process and the immediate/contingent circumstances of those years. It was in a very real sense, and like comparable upheavals in France, Mexico or Russia, a revolution which made itself up as it went along. Just as the names and ideas of leaders and ideologues only became known or meaningful to Iranian protesters during the revolution itself, so the balances and combinations of leftist, Shi'a Muslim, nationalist and democratic aspirations and rhetoric shifted over that period. Workers in Qazvin commented that it was only in 1978–79 that their 'awareness' and 'understanding' (their words) were stimulated by the dissemination of Khomeini's proclamations by student activists, and by confidence born of successful protest on the streets. Hegland's account of the transformation of perceptions of Husein's martyrdom among villagers near Shiraz from a source of comfort and acquiescence with the status quo into the inspiration for political action stresses the impact of events and information among them during 1978–79. Reaction to the confrontations and killings seen or reported was the motivation for becoming participants, using an activist image of Husein's confrontation with injustice as their chosen rhetoric. To demonstrate was to take 'the way of justice ... for which Husein was killed' and to interpret his suffering as a model of how to 'fight' against repression and 'tyranny'.[67] The wearing of the *kaffan* (the shroud of the dead, asserting willingness to die for a cause) united villagers or Isfahani factory workers, and signified this activist appropriation of martyrdom, as in the 1906 constitutionalist campaigns; the slogan 'Husein is our saviour, Khomeini is our leader' carried in the Muharram demonstrations of December 1978 focused on demands for Khomeini's return around which many shades of opposition had united, sustaining current protests and activism.[68]

The comments of the participants in the movements of 1978–79 highlight not only the impetus of the developing cycle of protest, repression, politicisation and escalation, but also its human dimensions. A Tehrani electrician's personal knowledge of Ayatollah Taleqani, and personal gratitude to Husein for his 'grace' in a family crisis, interwove with involvements in communal charity, transformed into communal protection and demonstration during the revolution. Pious women in a village near Shiraz knew that in demonstrating against the Shah's regime they used accepted customs of religious participation and also seized a specific historic opportunity: 'If we don't speak this government will go on for hundreds of years or more.' The transitions had been effected by the radicalising impact of particular events, whether the news of women's participation in protests in the city of Shiraz, or the display of evidence of police torture.[69] The January 1978 confrontation of the Qum *tullab* with the regime as they protested the attack on Khomeini in the establishment press segued into 'mourning' protests in other centres which in turn led to demonstrations fuelled by news of violence, courageous protest and killings between January and May. Deaths of demonstrators in Mashad in July 1978 triggered mourning/memorial demonstrations and clashes with the authorities in most major towns. Marches and shootings in Tehran in early September fuelled the spread of strikes and street protests. Whether by listening to overseas broadcasts by the BBC, or responding to leaflets, phone calls and personal contacts with activists, neighbours and relatives, participants in the tide of public action emerged and developed through this unrolling process.[70]

The opening up of political opportunity through the civil and human rights campaign of progressive professionals in 1977, the revived intransigence of religious students and their allies in early 1978, and the range of grievances targeted on the regime by workers, political activists and outraged citizens of all ranks between mid-1978 and 1979, reinvigorated old ideals with new meanings. For Khomeini to label the Shah as Yazid, and for protesters to invoke Husein as 'our guide', did not just use familiar narratives of martyrdom, or repeat the rhetorical and ideological moves of activists in 1905–10 or the 1940s and 1950s, but renewed them. Familiarity supported the risky choice to move from acceptance of the status quo to resistance, and the immediate relevance and creative appropriation of honoured symbols affirmed the importance of their use in pursuit of change in the here and now. For the educated activist this might involve careful working out of relationships between the Karbala paradigm and the politics of social justice and anti-Americanism. For village women and urban workers, it might be the decision that a previously *zisht* (improper) activity – public protest – was permissible in the new context of religious marches for political ends, or that Husein, prince of martyrs, fought for the victory of the cause not just as a gesture.[71] Energy and commitment were built up through experience, solidarity or witness to struggle and suffering. A Tehran van-driver described the neighbour who built barricades in the face of twenty soldiers as a 'Karbala martyr'. An Isfahani steel-worker drew on arguments of student militants, anti-regime *'ulama* and the tapes of Khomeini to refocus workplace discontent and growing consciousness and solidarity. A young woman migrant from a village to Tehran uses ideas of 'true' Islam to assert autonomy from paternal authority and express class pride as she joins the revolution.[72]

However, the success of the growing challenges to the regime and its incapacity were also sustained by the equally contingent choices of the regime itself. Governments lose power as much if not more than their opponents win it. The indecision and ill-health of the Shah, divisions of opinion among those around him, their lack of understanding or knowledge of the character of the opposition, and uncertainty about the intentions of their powerful US protector/ally were all factors of this contingent kind. Alongside the structural difficulties of an oil-based *rentier* regime, and tensions with an aware, educated, often alienated populace, misjudgement and ignorance also played their roles. The sanctioning of the anti-Khomeini article, the oscillations between concessions (the release of political prisoners and reduction in censorship) and violent reprisals (creating 'martyrs'), or the triggering of workers' protests by the government-engineered recession, were government choices that increased the scale and intensity of opposition. Disagreements among various American advisers and policy-makers about whether or how to support the Shah introduced another set of contingent variables into the Shah's decisions and US government responses to his problems. The fears, hopes and misconceptions entertained by each party about the other shaped vacillations in policy and (as with President Carter's phone call to the

Shah after the 8 September shootings) confirmed Iranian perceptions of the regime's link to the US government.

In these senses the participants, processes and choices which came together to overthrow the Pahlavi regime in 1977–79 were not predetermined. Relationships between lay politicians and Khomeini supporters, or between organised political groups and the urban classes they sought to mobilise, changed in response to the unpredictable unrolling of the processes of opposition and protest. As where other regimes have been overthrown, the opposition was defined by shared views of what they were against (royal despotism, injustice, American influence) rather than by any shared vision of what should replace the regime. While 'Islamic government' was a slogan for mass protests against the Shah, the principle and forms of an Islamic Republic were established through political manoeuvres and conflicts *after* his departure.[73] From 1979 to 1982 the new regime was 'made' through such contests, in which the diversity and incompatibility of the agendas which Iranians brought to the anti-Shah movement were clearly visible. The conflicted relations and 'parallel struggles' of urban under-classes and organised political activists, and the shifting versions of 'Islam' invoked by *'ulama*, student radicals, politicised workers, or *bazari* and opposition leaders were obvious examples. This diversity gave power to the multi-group forces that mobilised against the Shah, but meant that the political culture of the 'revolutionary' years was built on unstable and improvised connections. Combinations of the familiar and the transformative, as with the meanings of Husein's martyrdom, or the contingent, the innovative and the well-established, as with the coalition of populist religiosity, traditions of anti-despotic politics and the organisational innovations of *'ulama* and students, gave the 1977–79 upheavals their particular character. The mediation of Khomeini's charisma through familiar images of the incorruptible leader, modern technologies of radio and tape, and new links between leading *'ulama*, their followers and the wider community illustrate similar combinations. These were shaped by the pressures to which political actors responded, the actors themselves and their modes of response.

The scale and speed of change in Iran from the 1960s and the difficulties and resentments it created by the mid-1970s generated a range of political pressures. The effects of inflation and unequal income distribution and the difficulties of urban life for migrants in the mid-1970s sharpened as a result of government attempts at deflation. Urban unemployment, more workplace disputes and squatter resistance to evictions in 1977 showed these pressures at work. Government attacks on 'corruption' and 'overpricing' in the *bazar* sector at the same period involved the fining, imprisonment and harassment of hundreds and thousands of *bazar* traders with a consequent rise in their hostility to the regime, already alienated by state attacks on the *'ulama*. Politically, the regime was also under pressure. It had growing problems managing

245

the contradictions of simultaneous co-option and repression of a large class of educated professionals and officials, who were both necessary to its existence and resentful of restrictions on their activities. Insulated by the oil wealth and repressive force at its disposal, and past political and material successes, the regime slid into what has been called a 'sultanistic' style,[74] informed by a limited circle of court and technocratic supporters of the Shah, rather than accurate appreciation of social and political change.

These pressures can be linked to others arising from Iranian relationships to the world system and global power. Reliance on oil as the main source of export earnings, state revenue and foreign exchange, not only created problems with economic development, but also made government stability and policy dependent on the world market and the strategic interests of oil purchasers, notably the USA. The changing complexion of US administrations and their internal rivalries and misunderstandings of the Iranian situation, like the dynamics of the world oil markets, could not be manipulated from Tehran. This long-term pattern of uncertainty and dependency also had contingent aspects, as President Carter opened up human rights issues in 1977 and the State Department and National Security Committee fought the turf wars over responses to the protest movements of 1978.[75] As Foran argues, the contrast between the US role in 1951–53 or 1961–63, when policy was decisively implemented, and in 1977–79, when policy never fully emerged, suggests that this external pressure, while not causing the overthrow of the regime, did affect the speed and character of the process.[76]

The range of pressures on the regime in the late 1970s is manifest by the diversity of Iranians who participated in mourning processions, strikes, *bazar* and university closures, street demonstrations, and organising collective protest and protection. Key features were the diversity and sometimes disparity of aims among the participants, and their gradual convergence around shared themes and demands, which were the product of the 'revolutionary process' itself and of overlaps among those who entered it. Different groups of Iranians pushed their own distinct and parallel agendas. The civil rights protests of professionals and old opposition groups in 1977 had no connection or similarity to the religiously inspired protests of early 1978, or the strike activities of that year. The interests of some in negotiated outcomes for protests, the establishment of constitutional constraints, or reform within the regime, clashed with the intransigence of those committed to confrontational struggle and regime change. The agendas of political activists and organisations had little resonance with the priorities and perceptions of shanty-town or rural communities. However, protesting constituencies did connect to one another. Politicised students returned to their urban neighbourhoods, entered factories, or went round campuses, just as workers attended mosques where activist *mullas*, *tullab* and lay leaders spread their messages, *bazaris* joined the *'ulama* and their educated offspring, and Khomeinist *'ulama* worked with 'lay' Muslims, and urban *hay'ats*. Together with personal and communication networks, these links allowed specific grievances and agendas to converge as well as compete.

This convergence was manifest in the adoption of demands or discourses with a polyvalent character. Anti-American, anti-colonial language appealed to nationalists focused on the autonomy and dignity of 'Iran', to Shi'a Muslims concerned to protect faith and identity, and to leftists committed to challenging dependency and imperialism. It tapped into material grievances over the favouring of American business interests, cultural resistance to 'western' influences in the name of 'Iranian' or Muslim authenticity, and political hostility to the subordination of the 'nation'/'people' to external power. It resonated with *bazaris* and modern professionals, and with 'secular'- as well as 'religious'-minded critics of the regime. Like the image of the 'Great Satan/America', generalised references to despotism and oppression addressed political concerns ranging from the grievances of wage workers to the democratic and leftist agendas of activists, the frustrated aspiration of youth, and the defensive agendas of the *'ulama*.

As already shown, the concerns and languages of Shi'a Islam also had a polyvalent character that allowed them to cross social and ideological differences. Their success in doing so further encouraged the adoption of a religious framework for political activity. Secular nationalists and democrats with their own traditions of linking patriotic and religious ideals and identities, like student activists reaching out to an 'Iranian people' they saw as religiously minded, responded to politicised religion/religious politics as relevant to their own agendas and as a proven powerful ally. Although the unexpected spread of the Qum protests over the anti-Khomeini article of January 1978 was partly the work of networks established over previous years by his adherents, it also testified to the mobilising power of religious condemnations of oppression/despotism. That this power was political is evidenced by situations in which larger numbers participated in events where 'religion' offered 'political' opportunities, than on occasions where the emphasis was on the established rituals and practices of the faith. When Ayatollah Taheri spoke on Islamic government and faced trial in Isfahan, he attracted larger groups than when he led a purely religious event at the same period. Protests against government violence in Mashad involving members of the *'ulama* dispersed when those same *'ulama* sought to organise collective prayers.[77]

The agency of religion in this context lay in the ability of religious practice (mourning rituals, Muharram, Ramadan, sermons) and institutions (mosques, *huseiniyehs*, welfare and *hay'at* associations) to sustain and focus protest. It also lay in protesters' ability to deploy religious values and associations for a range of purposes from challenging the government's illegitimacy and violence to seeking material change, social justice or moral regeneration. Demonstrations of this include Isfahani or Abadan workers linking workplace grievances to Mujahedin and Khomeinist ideas, a Hamadani driver spreading Khomeini's announcements in mosques to protesters, and activists using the slogan 'Every day Ashura, every place Karbala' to signify uncompromising struggle.[78] When the 'Patriotic Muslim Students of Tabriz University' ended their February 1978 leaflet with 'Down with the anti-God and anti-people Pahlavi regime', they gave religious opposition populist and democratic associations.[79] The spreading use of the term *mustaz'afin* (the oppressed ones) among those inspired by Shari'ati (who pioneered its use), but also by Khomeini and his supporters, associated political religion with the concerns of the powerless and unprivileged. As with the increased use of the term 'imperialism', it connected religiously inspired struggle to leftist, nationalist and democratic languages and programmes.[80]

While religious concerns and ideologies provided connecting frameworks for diverse groups to come together against the regime in a multi-class cross-generation alliance, they did not transcend either the differences among the varied elements in the opposition, or the indifference, doubts or hostility of some Iranians towards politicised religion/religious politics. Connections sustaining the alliance and the hegemony of populist Shi'a Islam were expressed in the widely used slogan 'Independence, Freedom, Islamic Government' joining significant, if vague, religious aspirations to anti-despotic, nationalist demands inherited from the 1950s. Analysis of the various slogans used in 1978–79 suggests that more (38 per cent) focused on a negative on which many came to agree ('the Shah must go') than on this positive demand for a Muslim, autonomous and democratic future (31 per cent). Nevertheless, the historic achievement of the alliance should not obscure the persistent alienation of the poor from *mulla* religiosity (as opposed to their own beliefs and practices), critiques by pious activists of both *'ulama* authority and popular 'superstition', or the ambiguity of organised workers towards 'Islamic' versions of their interests. The varied interpretations of the widely used concept of the *mustaz'afin* offered by various participants in the events of 1978–79 testify to the multi-sided contradictory aims and ideals expressed by such a term.[81]

The use of a number of generalised and polyvalent themes provided the means for expressing both diversity and common purpose. The opposition of the despotism and oppression of the regime to the freedom (*azadi*) and justice (*haqq*) to be established in its stead could have religious, democratic or socialistic meanings. The assertion of justice and morality against corruption and tyranny similarly had meanings for the urban poor confronting state indifference and repression, for educated activists with programmes of reform and social change, and for religiously minded Iranians hoping for godly rule and moral order.

The trope of martyrdom, so embedded in Shi'a Muslim culture and narratives of Iranian history, was echoed by traditions of popular leftist veneration of exemplary heroes sacrificing themselves for a cause. In the 1960s the Tudeh Party used the religious term *shahid* (martyr) for those who died in their political cause, while Khomeini only adopted this political usage during the 1978–79 period, having previously preferred the term *bichareh-ha* (unfortunate ones) for such persons, and reserved the designation *shahid* for the saintly sufferers of early Shi'a history, an interesting instance of fluid meaning shaped by contingent circumstances.[82] The image of the Shah as Yazid (destroyer of Husein), Satan or Pharaoh (who resisted Moses) linked familiar religious oppositions of good and evil with contemporary perceptions of his arbitrary power, rejection of moral values and lack of political legitimacy or social responsibility. 'Freedom' could signal desires for an end to a repressive undemocratic government, for removal of the material problems affecting *bazaris*, wage workers and the urban poor, or for rejection of foreign interference and threats to cultural and communal values. While the notion of the *mustaz'afin* entered Iranian political discourse through Shari'ati's translation of Fanon in the 1960s, by 1978 it was used in the language of Khomeinist populism and street or workplace protest.[83]

Just as the contingent pressures and opportunities of 1978–79 were the context in which Iranians reached for and remade the cultural resources of recent religious radicalisms (Shari'atist or Khomeinist) and of older left, religious and reform politics, so too they produced the revival and reconfiguration of gendered political discourse and the politics of gender. The status, role and conduct of women were powerful signifiers in male-dominated political contests over religion, progress and authority. As in the struggles of 1905–11, the presence and voices of women made their distinctive political contribution. Changing access to education, changing codes of conduct for middle- and upper-class women, and shifts in work and residence for lower-class women during the 1960s and 1970s produced new concerns, demands and experiences. These included a larger pool of articulate educated women aspiring to use their skills and qualifications, tensions between changing circumstances and established gender conventions for women from religious and traditional backgrounds and families, and the difficulties of sustaining material and cultural stability in poor urban neighbourhoods. Their political significance had a number of aspects. At the level of action, the presence of women as well as men in movements of 1978–19 was a significant phenomenon with its own impact on those movements. At the level of political discourse and rhetoric, the use of gendered sexualised language and image was an important feature. At the level of gender politics contests over both action and discourse expressed the conflicted character of the anti-Shah movements as well as their gendered forms and content.

The entry of women alongside men into the movements of 1977–79 was shaped by the gendered context of society and politics in late Pahlavi Iran and women's varied locations within it. Among educated activist circles, leftist organisations, intellectual dissidents or Muslims influenced by Shari'ati, women with similar backgrounds, education or family connections to male activists played a part. Shaped by the leftist, religious and anti-despotic/anti-imperialist politics of these groupings, and sometimes by the feminist ideas of the period, their experience and roles were often limited by the persistence of established gender differences or explicit sexism in anti-reform organisations. As urban and rural communities became politicised, many women negotiated their participation in protests within accepted conventions of modesty and respectability, but responded to the increasingly radical context in new ways. They legitimised their actions by aligning them to established patterns of female religious activity, using arguments from religious texts to justify their choices, and accepting the constraints of established codes of female behaviour. The women of 'Aliabad' who joined marches in 1979 linked their decision to their existing practice as devout Shi'a Muslims and to the need to respond to the unfolding confrontations of people and government. While accepting protection and segregation on marches, they also claimed the right to act innovatively (joining the political demonstration on Ashura, rather than keeping their traditional place as witnesses/spectators).[84]

This pressing on the boundaries of convention while also recognising its power was both the product of the developing political drama, and a refiguring of 'being a Muslim' around thought, study and choice, rather than acceptance of established views or practices. In urban settings in the mid-late 1970s, women from a range of backgrounds were developing self-created autonomous relationships to religion. Just as some women of white-collar, professional or middle-class backgrounds attended religious classes run by *'ulama* and learned religious women, others were drawn into the study and political circles around universities. For less privileged women, the climate of politicised religion and escalating politics might itself be the context for change. Someone like Sakineh, village girl turned domestic servant in Tehran, could challenge parental and communal convention in the name of the 'real' Islam which revolutionised their thinking and justified taking autonomous political action.[85] In all these situations there were significant interactions between women's agency, gender-based power relations and conventions, and the contingent circumstances of widespread politicisation. The wearing of *chadors* or headscarves by women who did not otherwise do so, and the turn to religion as an expression of oppositional identity, like the contradictions faced by women inspired by gender as well as opposition politics, were products of such interactions.

Such acknowledgements of dress codes and gender roles as defined within Shi'a Islam indicate the centrality of gendered discourses to the politics of the revolution. Two key elements in these discourses were the symbolic issue of 'veiling' and the centrality of sexual corruption in indictments of the Pahlavi regime. Questions of veiling had been iconic topics in the discourses of elite modernisers since the late nineteenth century where they had signifying roles in the creation of ideas of progress, as discussed above.[86] These tropes were revisited in nativist and radical Muslim discourses as well as by politicised *'ulama* in the 1960s and 1970s. The Pahlavi regime was castigated for material and cultural corruption symbolised by the more visible presence of women and the decline of *chador*-wearing among middle-class or 'modern' women. Arguments for veiling were recast in terms of the needs of 'nature' (Ayatollah Mutahhari), or in terms of fulfilment through commitment to an activist Islam (Shari'ati). The readoption of the *chador* or new 'modest' (*hejab*) dress became signifying gestures of activism, decency and patriotic opposition to a hyper-westernised, corrupt, ungodly regime rather than of conformity to traditional codes of female dress and modesty. For some women it also signified the acceptance of arguments for the need for a populist connection to women who normally wore *chadors* and the classes or communities from which they came.[87]

Discursively speaking, the focus of attention on dress codes and their sexualised connotations went beyond the practice of those who maintained or adopted the conventions of female body covering. Ideological western discussions of 'veiling' as a marker of the oppressive and backward character of Islam/'Islamic' societies provoked nativist/third worldist accusations of cultural imperialism. Veiling thus figured as a political symbol and discursive theme as well as an issue of cultural or political choice. Descriptions of non-veiled women as 'naked' or 'prostitutes' added a powerful sexual charge to condemnations of regime-led modernisation, and advocacy of a 'pure' alternative. Reference to the 'painted dolls' and consumerist degradation of women by an alien modernity imposed by an illegitimate government featured in the language of 'lay' Muslim radicals and of reformist or populist *'ulama*.[88] This masculine discourse of purity/corruption appealed not only to Iranians who saw long-established gender codes challenged by recent change, or to those young men uncertain of where they stood in relation to such change, but also to possibilities of female self-assertion and self-respect. There is sharp disagreement, especially among feminist scholars, as to how to understand this appeal, but it did enter the experience of some Iranian women.[89]

It was in this context that apparently surprising combinations of celebration of female activism and autonomy with obsessive concerns for decency, modesty, convention and respectability flourished. If *hejab* could be idealised/ideologised as anti-Pahlavi, anti-western, 'properly' Islamic and Iranian, that placed ideological and discursive power in the hands of its advocates. If it met aspirations for commitment and self-assertion alongside communal and moral acceptance, it would appeal to a range of activist constituencies. If women's progress or freedom could be figured into visions of popular, national or Muslim freedom, that could attract support for organisations pursuing those aims. Conversely, claims for the importance of female interests, rights or needs which challenged those aims or sought autonomous space beside them could be denigrated and suppressed as 'diversions' from the 'real' class, Muslim or anti-imperialist struggle. Alongside the possibilities for female participation and even innovation created in the political 'moment' of 1977–82 were the pressures to direct, constrain, or even dismiss them.

The interactions and incompatibilities of gender, leftist, religious and nationalist movements and discourses exemplify convergence, conflict and cohabitation in the stories of Iranian politics. Approaching relationships between disparate political elements through these three modes allows the complexity of political experience and action to be better appreciated and understood. It opens up discussion of the political upheavals of 1905–11, 1941–53 and 1977–82 at the level of human experience and choice, the level of social relations and contradictions, and the level of processes of political change and mobilisation. Returning to the historiographical challenge noted at the start of this chapter, it offers a route into the study of contingency and history in the domain of political movements. The Qajar repertoire of Mussadeq combined with day-to-day dealings with political rivals or supporters and foreign powers, as the Mussadeqist inheritance of Shari'ati combined with in-fighting among religious reformers and student radicals, or the Shi'a dissident backgrounds of early constitutionalists with involvement in parliamentary politics. Such combinations were relevant for the unnamed artisans, women, students and *'ulama* who protested, wrote, organised and took risks to realise their many aspirations, as much as for well-known individuals. The dynamic of familiar values and practices, inherited patterns of work and thought, and creative response to new situations was woven into political activity of all kinds. It shaped the encounter of early social democracy with Iranian constitutional politics, the struggles of committed Shi'a Muslims to defend or extend their cultural and political domain, and the vicissitudes of reforming, nationalist and leftist politics since the 1920s. It also shaped individual or group decisions to join or avoid political activities, with all their local, personal and communal implications. It is certainly not the only dynamic useful for analysing political movements, but offers a framework which can include others and enrich understanding.

Concluding some stories (and starting others)

In a real sense, the end of this book is a beginning. Its discussion of insights and difficulties encountered in the study of Iranians' past experience opens the way to further narratives. By setting the anti-Shah politics of 1977–82 among stories which extend over longer periods of time, it provides perspectives for thinking about the inherited resources available to those taking political action or making political choices in particular circumstances. By presenting stories of religious practices, specialists and institutions entwined with narratives of material change, political ideas and activities, and cultural forms and practices, it poses questions about how best to capture such relationships in a historical text. By setting the experiences and attitudes of particular Iranians within structures of power, culture and material life, it draws attention to the challenge of depicting the workings of that insightful nineteenth-century proposition that 'people make their history but not in circumstances of their own choosing'. It joins other texts on Iranian history in a conversation about these issues, and seeks to clarify difficulties rather than claiming to resolve them.

The choice of a holistic approach connects developments across time and also developments in different areas of Iranians' lives (material, political, cultural), suggesting that interpretations of particular aspects of Iranian history should combine appreciation of their uniqueness with understanding of their place in a structured whole. The civic and popular nationalist politics of the 1941–53 period can be set in the context of past and present circumstances, and of a rich matrix of contested experience ranging from new media and political organisations to the changed working lives of urban Iranians. The religiously inflected anti-American and anti-Pahlavi politics of the 1970s can be compared to earlier periods by looking at how they both drew on their political legacy and broke from it, and by examining the particular mix of influences at work in 1977–82. Rather than claiming to generalise or offer some unarguable 'truth' about why Iranians chose to express their grievances and aspirations in particular ways, the narratives here emphasise the connecting threads and specificities of each historical 'moment'.

In recounting stories of religious thought and practice in their various settings, this text has attended to the active agency of different Iranians, the contingent situations in which they exercised that agency, and conditions and influences inherited from the past. The urban traders, intelligentsia and artisans who joined in demands for and defence of constitutional government in 1905–11 made choices which distinguished them from those who resisted such developments, or kept out of political conflict. They created innovative forms of expression, extending existing traditions of protest to new locations and purposes, and combining recently encountered political ideas with established languages of dissidence and martyrdom. They undertook these initiatives at a moment of contingent opportunity created by conflicts among government and elite, rising foreign intervention, and disruptive material and cultural change. They did so in a setting shaped by decades of Iranian concern with modernisation and external economic pressures, and by new links with a wider world of political debate and action from England to Central Asia. The 'Constitutional Revolution' of 1905–11 is best understood by appreciating the influence and interaction of these three elements.

Similar arguments apply to the 'Islamic Revolution' seven decades later. Rural Iranians who joined anti-Shah demonstrations in 1978–79 made real choices and creative innovations like those of the Aliabad women inventing their own patterns of respectable militancy, or Isfahani factory workers linking workplace grievances to the rhetoric and inspiration of a new generation of student activists and politicised *'ulama*. They did so in response to immediate developments (display of evidence of government torture, news of demonstrations and successful challenges to authority). They were influenced by the longer-term development of resources (educational opportunity, modern ideas of Muslim activism, patterns of migration, encounters between recent and established indigenous and imported cultural influences) and constraints (competition for entry to higher education, repression of political opposition, material inequalities). Anti-regime views and actions incorporated all these elements, and analyses of the coalition which overthrew the Shah should likewise incorporate their specific contributions and influence on one another.

One aim of this book has been to examine and explain large-scale upheavals and changes without either under- or over-emphasising human agency, contingency or long-established structures and influences. Giving due weight to all aspects of change also helps to meet the challenge of providing explanations which establish an informed and convincing interpretation, but recognise other possible outcomes. The analyses of the Mussadeqist, constitutionalist or 1977–82 anti-Shah movements explain why those movements achieved, or failed to achieve, what they did, but also suggest that things could have turned out otherwise. These events were not predictable or determinable, which is where immediacy and contingency play their part.

The text also contributes to the tradition of historical scholarship in which past thoughts and beliefs are studied as elements *within* lived experience rather than external to it. As argued in Chapters 1 and 5, ideas, images, words, beliefs and rituals shape as well as being shaped by involvement in productive work, social relationships and political activity. They are integral to life, not optional or decorative extras. There are real intellectual challenges involved in recounting narratives based on the view that human experience is culturally and linguistically as well as materially and politically constituted, but such narratives give due respect and autonomy to *all* relevant aspects of human activity.

This is particularly significant in a text which re-evaluates the role of religious practices, ideas, specialists and institutions in the cultural politics and political culture of Iran between the late nineteenth and late twentieth centuries. It has shown how Iranians integrated their religious and anti-religious thought and activities within their lives. It argues that just as divisions of labour and communal or family interests shaped religious activity, so religious discourses and practices shaped work and life in households, political groups and communities. This allows an appreciation of the role of religious elements in different social settings and periods, and an understanding of their contested and unstable character. For villagers losing, defending and remaking religious practices in Khuzestan in the 1970s, urban activists linking anti-clericalism, leftist ideas and Shi'a rhetoric in political activity before the First World War, or the politics of gender difference and veiling through the whole century, social circumstances, political conflict and religious culture intereacted.

This draws attention to the interplay and tension within and between religious and non-religious interests and outlooks (communal and official, orthodox and dissident, learned and popular). Khomeinists, leftists and Mujahidin in the 1970s, like pious Shi'a and secular nationalists in the 1940s, or prominent *mujtaheds*, dissident preachers and secular constitutionalists in the 1910s, proclaimed and contested differing versions of nation-making, social reform and identity while also forming alliances. The political significance of religion for some Iranians does not belie the scepticism or hostility of others, nor its uneven impact. The suspicions of poor rural and urban women about the self-interest or indifference of *mullas*, and the opportunistic use of religious interests and idioms by ruling elites were significant parts of the picture of religion in society and politics.

Alongside the dominant and pervasive stories of religious influences in Iranian history from the 1870s to the 1970s are others which can be overshadowed by that powerful narrative. The suggestion here is that there are powerful stories of material and cultural change, of political radicalism and nationalism, and also neglected stories of subaltern groups, of roads not taken, or interests disregarded and denigrated. The sense of popular alienation from interventionist governments, even if accompanied by willingness to take the opportunities they offered,

255

is a significant counterpoint to stories of 'reform' or 'modernisation'. The specific communal or ethnic experiences and marginalisation of Kurds, nomad pastoralists or Azeris are likewise counterpoints to accounts of nationalism and nation-making. One revealing approach, not undertaken in this book, would be the construction of *counter*-national or subaltern narratives of Iranian pasts.

Gendered histories of Iran in this period, touched on in this text, are examples of stories currently in some uneasy position between marginality and centrality. The learning and insight so effectively deployed by scholars of gender in Iranian history has been recognised among gender-aware scholars and readers, but not mainstreamed within dominant narratives of that history. It is treated as an interesting and valid specialised contribution rather than transformative of core historical practice, replicating the gender-resistant character of mainstream history writing about other areas of the world. Again, narratives of political activity, religious culture or modernising communities in Iran would read very differently if written on a gendered basis.

While the treatment of the Iranian past in this text suggests the potential for creating alternative histories without realising it, it has also revisited and reframed some existing structured approaches to accounts of that past. Thus, John Foran's use of world system and dependency theory, or Homa Katouzian's stress on the clash of state and subject as connecting threads, have been treated as useful themes to keep in mind rather than all-embracing explanatory or narrative frameworks. Similar caveats apply to analyses which focus on class mobilisation or the role of the *'ulama* as definitive drivers of events and changes in Iran in this period.

The narratives have shown that religious practice and belief should be considered as *part of* their 'modern' settings (whether the 1890s, 1940s or 1970s) rather than counterposed to modernity. It has been argued here that religious reformers, specialists and believers were within modernity, but experienced and created their own distinctive versions of it. They were situated in specific circumstances (the difficulties of ruling regimes, urban migration, new forms of culture and learning, foreign interventions); they were heirs to particular patterns of material, political or cultural relationships and activity (links to *bazari* interests and resources, roles and status in urban or rural religious practice, histories of political challenge and negotiation, discourses of renewal or opposition to innovation); in such contexts they had choices to make and a range of options to choose from. Both situation and choice were *contemporary* situations in which hostility or resistance to present circumstances were located *in the present*. As argued at the start of Chapter 4, Iranians in the nineteenth and twentieth centuries actively experienced and made their particular versions of modernity. For those who saw Islam in danger, defended the ruling regime, or their own established interests and privileges, the conflicts in which they might play a 'conservative' role or defend 'tradition' were immediate, and their responses to them created change and innovation. Aristocrats using parliamentary politics to protect land and power, *mujtaheds* using the press or cassette tapes to attack secularism, the urban poor joining pro-regime demonstrations, all combined attachment to existing systems and creative adaptability in defending them.

Returning to the question that stimulated work on this book, we can revisit the issue of the role of 'religious' elements in Iranian lives, actions and experiences between the late nineteenth and late twentieth centuries. On the one hand, it is important to assert the flux, complexity and contingency of that role, and to challenge over-structural or deterministic interpretations of its persistence or inevitability. On the other hand, it is important to recognise religious practices and ideas as powerful and durable resources for various groups and communities in Iran, for material and political links between the *'ulama* and other sections of society, and for the polyvalent role of religious discourse in the politics of nationalism, reform and protest. The ability of Iranians to adapt and vary religious practices, ideas and institutions to changing needs, and the ownership of much regular practice by believers rather than specialists, as well as the richly varied repertoire of Shi'a Muslim language, custom and ritual allowed rural families as well as urban intellectuals to make meaningful and innovative use of these resources.

This did not mean that religious resources were not deployed to defend privilege or the status quo. Community control of its members, gender and status divisions, and the established authority of elders and employers as well as the legitimacy of ruling regimes were underpinned by religious sanctions as much as such sanctions were invoked by those seeking change. It is in that context that contingency and agency have played their role, shaping contrasting outcomes to political contests in the constitutionalist era, the 1940s and the 1970s. While religious influences were sustained by the political, material and cultural resources described in the text, they contended with both other long-established relations and practices in society and politics, from family and community structures to ethnic or class identities and interests. Any appreciation of the role of the 'religious' elements in society, culture and politics should take full account of the other influences present. The dynamics of government intervention and the resistance of the governed, of generation and gender power, and of material need, or occupational and communal interest, had their own impact on Iranians' lives and choices.

Finally, the stories told here have sought to recognise the density and richness of the many resources, relationships and activities with which Iranians were involved in the period that has been examined. While it may be ambitious to try to do justice to that richness in a single text, this approach has been central to addressing the issues of oversimplification raised in the introduction. Fuller

257

understanding of Iranians in this period rests on finding ways to present them as complex many-sided human beings rather than impersonal social actors or two-dimensional stereotypes. If the text has achieved even partial success in this endeavour, then it will have served a useful purpose.

Notes

Introduction

1. Abrahamian, *Iran between Two Revolutions*; Ansari, *Modern Iran since 1921*.

2. Gilsenan, *MERIP (Middle East Research and Information Project) Reports*, 102, special issue on *Islam and politics*, p. 30.

3. Fischer, *Iran: From Religious Dispute to Revolution*, p. 136.

4. See, for example, Shirazi, *The Veil Unveiled: The Hijab in Modern Culture*; El Guindi, *Veil: Modesty, Privacy and Resistance*; Gole, *The Forbidden Modern: Civilisation and Veiling*; Ozdalga, *The Veiling Issue: Official Secularism and Popular Islam in Turkey*.

5. I take this idea appreciatively from Scarcia, 'Kerman 1905', pp. 195–238; the term appears on p. 233.

1 A story of cultures and communities

1. Examples are noted in Consul Abbott's reports in Amanat (ed.), *Cities and Trade: Consul Abbott on the Economy and Society of Iran 1847–1866*, pp. 10, 18, 50, 64, 68, 70, 93, 100, 106; Sykes, *Report on the Agriculture of Khorasan*; Vaziri, *Jughrafiya yi-Kerman* (ed.) Bastani-Parizi, pp. 39, 89–90, 96–7, 104, 117, 119, 122, 125, 133, 135, 141, 144, 146–7, 152–3, 161–3, 168, 176, 178, 183, 185, 188–9; al-Mulk, *Safar-Nameh yi-Khuzestan* (ed. Siyaqi), p. 64.

2. See Gilbar, 'The Persian economy in the mid-nineteenth century'; Okazaki, 'The great Persian famine of 1870–71'.

3. Fasa'i, *Farsnameh*; Tahvildar, *Tarikh-i-Isfahan* (ed. Sutudeh); Zarrabi,

Tarikh i-Kashan (ed. Afshar), pp. 236–41, 271–403; Vaziri, *Jughrafiya yi-Kerman*, pp. 32, 77–80.

4. See Fasa'i, *Farsnameh*, vol. 2, p. 22; Vaziri, *Jughrafiya*, pp. 27, 32, 40–1; Browne, *A Year Among the Persians*, pp. 404–8; Wills, *Land of the Lion and the Sun*, pp. 135–8, 141–4; Sykes, *Ten Thousand Miles in Persia*, pp. 193, 195, 197–8.

5. Farmanfarma, *Safar-nameh yi-Kerman va Baluchestan* (ed. Nezam-Mafi), pp. 11, 29, 31–2, 38, 57, 62, 66–8, 72–4, 76–8, 84; Berard, *Les revolutions de la Perse*, pp. 321–3.

6. Tapper, *Frontier Nomads*, pp. 188, 237–8; Abbott, 'Notes taken on a journey eastwards from Shiraz', pp. 170–1; and in Amanat, *Cities and Trade*, p. 194; Garthwaite, *Khans*, pp. 34–6, 83–6.

7. See Ashraf and Hekmat, 'Merchants and artisans in the developmental processes of nineteenth-century Iran'.

8. Mahdavi, *For God, Mammon, and Country*, pp. 19–21, 31, 35–7, 70–5, 82–5, 172–5.

9. See Vaziri, *Jughrafiya*, pp. 33–5, 178, 189; Zarrabi, *Tarikh i-Kashan*, pp. 236–41; Abbott, in Amanat (ed.), *Cities and Trade*, pp. 122, 128, 151; Wills, *Land of the Lion and Sun*, pp. 82–3, 110, 122, 183–4.

10. Vaziri, *Jughrafiya*, pp. 41, 136, 172, 183; Tahvildar, *Tarikh i-Isfahan*; Beeman, *Language, Status and Power in Iran*; Nouraei, 'Census, revenue and the lower classes of Mashad in the later nineteenth century, based on the Zein al-'Abd-din report', unpublished paper, 2006, pp. 3–7.

11. Vaziri, *Tarikh*, pp. 389–90, 405, 407–9; Fasa'i, *History of Persia under Qajar Rule*, pp. 263–6, 342–3, 350–1,

356–7; Floyer, *Unexplored Baluchistan*,
p. 349; Eastwick, *Journal of a Diplomat's
Three Years Residence in Persia*,
pp. 288–90; Foreign Office, FO60, vol. 278,
Rawlinson to Wood, April 1869.

12. See Ravandi, *Tarikh i-ijtema'i yi-
Iran*, vol. 3, pp. 4, 186, 200, 403; Mustaufi,
*Social and Administrative History of
Iran*, vol. 1, pp. 104, 106, 109, 143; Wills,
Lion and Sun, p. 67; Wigham, *The Persian
Problem*, p. 301; MacLean, 'Report on the
conditions and prospects of British trade
in Persia', *Parliamentary Accounts and
Papers*, 1904, vol. XCV; Vaziri, *Jughrafiya*,
p. 81.

13. See, for example, Tapper,
Frontier Nomads, p. 178; Gurney, 'A Qajar
household and its estates'; Mahdavi, 'The
structure and function of the household of
a Qajar merchant', pp. 560–5.

14. Consul Preece, 'Visit to Yazd and
Kerman', *Parliamentary Accounts and
Papers*, 1894, vol. LXXXVII, pp. 340–9.

15. Vaziri, *Jughrafiya*, pp. 54–71,
98–100; Mahdavi, *God, Mammon*, pp. 31,
43–4, 52–6; Tapper, *Frontier Nomads*,
pp. 237–42.

16. Abbott in Amanat (ed.), *Cities and
Trade*, pp. 76, 94, 164; Vaziri, *Jughrafiya*,
pp. 35–6, 89, 91, 150, 152, 147, 161, 168,
176, 178.

17. Abbott in Amanat (ed.), *Cities and
Trade, passim*; Vaziri, *Jughrafiya*, pp. 33–7,
77–8, 90–1, 95, 102, 138, 161, 169, 178,
188–9; Tahvildar, *Jughrafiya*, pp. 95, 102;
see also Kazembeyki, *Society, Politics and
Economics in Mazanderan 1848–1914*,
pp. 22–8.

18. Abbott in Amanat (ed.), *Cities and
Trade*, p. 94; Vaziri, *Jughrafiya*, pp. 79, 172.

19. Foran, 'The concept of dependence
as a key to the political economy of Qajar
Iran'; Enayat, 'The problem of imperialism
in nineteenth century Iran'; Nowshir-
vani, 'The beginnings of commercialized
agriculture in Iran'; Gilbar, 'The Persian
economy'; Seyf, 'The commercialisation
of agriculture: production and trade of
opium in Persia'; Kazembeyki, *Mazan-*

deran, pp. 104–14; de Groot, 'Kerman in
the later nineteenth century', pp. 332–49.

20. See Neshat, 'From bazaar to
market: foreign trade and economic
development in nineteenth-century Iran';
Hakimian, 'Wage labour and migration:
Persian workers in southern Russia
1880–1914'.

21. A useful account is Amanat,
'Between the *madrasa* and the market-
place: the designation of clerical leadership in modern Shi'ism'.

22. See, for example, Sykes' plan of
Kerman in *Ten Thousand Miles*, p. 188;
of Shiraz in Clarke, *The Iranian City of
Shiraz*, pp. 14, 16, 17, 19; of Kcrmanshah
in Clarke and Clark, *Kermanshah: An
Iranian Provincial City*, p. 21; Tehran
in Wirth, 'Der bazaar Tehran'; and of
Taft near Yazd in Ehlers and Momeni,
'Religiose Stiftungen und Stadtentwicklung
das Beispiel Taft, ZentralIran'.

23. Mirjafari, 'The Haydari/Ni'amati
conflicts in Persia'; Sheil, *Glimpses of Life
and Manners in Persia*, pp. 322–6.

24. There is evidence of the growth
of a shrine at Sekhunj near Kerman
city in English, *City and Village in Iran:
Settlement and Economy in the Kirman
Basin*, pp. 53, 55; and of continuing use
of shrines in Zarrabi, *Tarikh i-Kashan*,
pp. 428–35; Vaziri, *Jughrafiya*, p. 95; Nadir
Mirza, *Tarikh va Jughrafiya-yi Dar al
Saltanat-i Tabriz*, p. 109.

25. Vaziri, *Tarikh*, p. 342; *Jughrafiya*,
p. 157; Sykes, *Ten Thousand Miles*, p. 78;
Minorsky, 'The sect of Ahl i-Hakk', in his
Iranica, p. 314; Wills, *Lion and Sun*, p. 131;
Browne, *A Year*, p. 394; Wilson, *Persian
Life and Customs*, pp. 127–31.

26. See depictions in Wills, *Lion and
Sun*, facing p. 283; Momen, *An Introduction to Shi'i Islam*, figs 40, 41, 44, 47;
Skrine, *World War in Iran*, plates 9, 10; the
nineteenth-century evolution of *ta'ziyeh* is
discussed in Calmard, 'Le mecenat des representations de *ta'ziyeh*' 1 and 2, *Le monde
Iranien et l'Islam*, vol. 2, pp. 73–126; vol.
4, pp. 133–62, and 'Muharram ceremonies

and diplomacy'; see also Chelkowski (ed.), *Ta'ziyeh: Ritual and Drama in Iran*.

27. See Sheil, *Glimpses*, pp. 125–30; Wills, *Lion and Sun*, pp. 279–84; Gobineau, *Les religions et les philosophies dans l'Asie centrale*, pp. 339–59.

28. Fischer, *Iran: From Religious Dispute to Revolution*, pp. 136–8.

29. Browne, *A Year*, pp. 180–1, 202, 221, 290–1; Sheil, *Glimpses*, pp. 102, 139–40, 192–6.

30. See Sheil, *Glimpses*, pp. 324–6; Fasa'i, *Farsnameh*, vol. 1, p. 264; vol. 2, p. 22; Mirjafari, 'The Haydari/Nimati conflicts'.

31. Hume-Griffiths, *Behind the Veil in Persia and Turkish Arabia*, p. 112; Floyer, *Unexplored Baluchistan*, p. 349; Kerman consular records FO248 vol. 846 (October 1906), vol. 906 (June, December 1907), vol. 1030 (January 1911); Gobineau, *Depeches diplomatiques*, p. 53.

32. See Vaziri, *Tarikh*, pp. 331–4; I'timad al-Sultana, *Mirat al-Buldan i-Nasiri*, vol. 2, pp. 22–3; Amin al-Douleh, *Khatirat-i Siasi* (ed. Farmanfarmaiyan), p. 167; Vaziri, *Jughrafiya*, pp. 51, 67, 70, 84, 159.

33. Algar, 'The revolt of the Aqa Khan Mahallati'; on wealthy *mujtaheds/'ulama*, see Tunakabuni, *Qisas al-'ulama*, pp. 104–9; Vaziri, *Jughrafiya*, pp. 44–5, 46 (on an *'alim* with merchant and landed interests in Kerman and acquisition of property).

34. Wilson, *Persian Life*, pp. 218–25; Browne, *A Year*, pp. 159–60, 180–1, 194, 221, 290–1, 422–3.

35. Wills, *Lion and Sun*, p. 338.

36. Tapper, *Frontier Nomads*, pp. 186–9, 334–40; Garthwaite, *Khans and Shahs*, pp. 34–42; Vaziri, *Jughrafiya*, pp. 58–63; Fasa'i, *Farsnameh*, vol. 2, pp. 29, 30–7, 231.

37. Wills, *Lion and Sun*, pp. 122, 275; FO60/212, memo from Stevens (Tehran) to Clarendon (London), October 1886.

38. Amanat, *Resurrection and Renewal* is the fullest account of early Babism,

whose innovative aspects are summarised on pp. 405–16; Cole, *Modernity and the Millennium*, sets the later movement in a wider context, ch. 3 dealing with Iran; Bayat, *Mysticism and Dissent*, chs 4–6 looks at changes in dissenting thought.

39. Ringer, *Education, Religion, and the Discourse of Cultural Reform in Qajar Iran*, pp. 5–16, 213–72; Bakhash, *Iran: Monarchy, Bureaucracy and Reform under the Qajars*, chs 1, 6; Nashat, *The Origins of Modern Reform in Iran*; Najmabadi, *Women with Mustaches and Men without Beards*, chs 1, 2, 4–6.

40. See Katouzian, 'Reza Shah's political legitimacy and social base'; and 'The Pahlavi regime in Iran'; Abrahamian, *Iran*, pp. 149–56.

41. Bharier, *Economic Development in Iran*; Floor, *Industrialisation in Iran 1900–1941*; and *Labour Unions, Law, and Conditions in Iran 1900–1941*, chs 3–5; Abrahamian, 'The strengths and weaknesses of the labour movement in Iran 1941–53'.

42. See Menashri, *Education and the Making of Modern Iran*, Part 2; Matthee, 'Transforming dangerous nomads into useful artisans, technicians, agriculturalists: education in the Reza Shah period'.

43. For adaptation by old-style career bureaucrats, see Mostofi, *The Story of My Life/Administrative History of the Qajar Period*, vol. 2, pp. 548–50, 576–7, 704–7; vol. 3, pp. 896, 919, 1028–36, 1130–2, 1159–60, 1176 and also the career of Muhammad Mussadeq described in Katouzian, *Mussadiq*, chs 1–3, and Diba, *Mossadegh: A Political Biography*, chs 1–4; see also Majd, *Resistance to the Shah: Landowners and Ulama in Iran*, pp. 15–21, 40–8; for new entrants to education and the professions, see Menashri, *loc. cit.*; Good, 'The transformation of health care in modern Iranian history', pp. 61–72; and the careers of politicians like Mehdi Bazargan, described in Chehabi, *Iranian Politics and Religious Modernism*, pp. 107–10; on recruitment to the oilfields and factories

see Abrahamian, *Iran*, pp. 146–7, Bharier, *Economic Development*; Floor, *Industrialisation*.

44. See Pavlovich, 'La situation agraire en Perse a la veille de la Revolution'; Kazembeyki, *Mazanderan*, pp. 100–2; Vaziri, *Jughrafiya*, pp. 58, 87, 107, 158, 168–9, 171; Stack, *Six Months in Persia*, vol. 1, p. 219; Bakhtiari, 'Kitabcheh 1873–82', trans. in Garthwaite, *Khans and Shahs*, pp. 147–69, p. 148; Noshirvani, 'The beginnings of commercialised agriculture in Iran'.

45. Haidari, 'The agrarian reform problem in Iran'; Lambton, *Landlord and Peasant in Persia*, chs 13, 14; Majd, *Resistance*, chs 1–3; Hooglund, *Land and Revolution in Iran, 1960–1980*, pp. 12–17; Khosrovi, 'La stratification sociale rurale'.

46. Biographical examples can be found in the lives of Mustawfi and Mussadeq via the citations in footnote 44, plus intellectuals like Ahmad Kasravi, sketched in Mottahedeh, *The Mantle of the Prophet*, pp. 98–105, and Abrahamian 'Kasravi: the integrative nationalist of Iran', pp. 101–7.

47. Photographic material in, for example, Majd, *Resistance to the Shah*, pp. 6, 17, 18, 42, 43, 54, 64, 66; Milani, *Tales of Two Cities*, pp. 45–51; Cronin, *Modern Iran*, plates 2, 3, 6, 8–12 illustrate the interactions of cultural change, class, occupation, and political pressure for dress reform from the Shah in the shifts of soldiers and professionals to uniforms, suits and ties.

48. See Goodell, *Elementary Structures*, p. 20; Lambton, *Landlord and Peasant in Persia*; Loeffler, 'Tribal order and the state: the political organisation of Boir Ahmad', for local perspectives, plus Abrahamian, *Iran*, pp. 149–50; Majd, *Resistance*, pp. 15–19, 40–8; Katouzian, *State and Society*, pp. 306–8 for elite/metropolitan perspectives.

49. On tribes see Cronin, *Modern Iran*, part V; on state management of religion

see below; and on religious practice see Donaldson, *The Wild Rue: A Study of Muhammedan Magic and Folklore in Iran*, chs 4–9, 13, 16, 25, 26; Merritt-Hawkes, *Persia: Romance and Reality*, pp. 261–2; Rosen, *Persian Pilgrimage*, pp. 279–86; Aghaie, *The Martyrs of Karbala*, pp. 51–2, 54–5.

50. Floor, *Labour Relations*, pp. 34–58; Foran, *Fragile Resistance*, pp. 238, 252.

51. Contrast Goodell, *Elementary Structures*; Forbes-Leith, *Checkmate: Fighting Tradition in Central Persia*; Banani, *The Modernization of Iran 1921–41*, pp. 58–61; and Abrahamian, *Iran*, pp. 136–7; see also Loeffler, 'Tribal order'; Goodell, *Elementary Structures*, pp. 20–3, 109; Majd, *Resistance to the Shah*, pp. 20, 36; McClachlan, *The Neglected Garden*, pp. 32–5; Foran, *Fragile Resistance*, pp. 228–34; Tapper, *Frontier Nomads*, pp. 283–94; and 'The case of the Shahsevan'; Cronin, 'Riza Shah and the disintegration of Bakhtiari power 1921–34'; Oberling, *The Qashqai Nomads of Fars*, ch. 12; Beck, *Nomad: A Year in the Life of a Qashqai Tribesman*, pp. 90–1, 232, 287–9.

52. See the statistics in Ferrier, 'The Iranian oil industry', pp. 690–2; Katouzian, *The Political Economy of Modern Iran*, pp. 92–4, 117–19; Foran, *Fragile Resistance*, pp. 245–6; more generally for a 'company' view, see Ferrier, *History of the British Petroleum Company*, vol. 1, *The Developing Years 1901–32*; Bamberg, *History of the British Petroleum Company*, vol. 2, *The Anglo-Iranian Years 1928–54*.

53. The 1933 negotiations are discussed in Katouzian, *Political Economy*, pp. 118–19; Ferrier, 'Oil industry', pp. 643–51; and Beck, 'The Anglo–Persian dispute of 1932–3'.

54. Donaldson, *The Wild Rue*; Rosen, *Persian Pilgrimage*; and Merritt-Hawkes, *Persia*; memoir material by Iranians growing up in the 1920s and 1930s (and later) indicates the persistence of domestic *rawzehs*, Muharram Ramadan rituals, and

pilgrimage in professional and educated families as well as the less privileged.

55. See Kamshad, *Modern Persian Prose Literature*, pp. 59–68, 73–6, 142–64, 184–98; Gheissari, *Iranian Intellectuals in the 20th Century*, pp. 54–60, 69–73; Katouzian, *Sadeq Hedayat: The Life and Legend of an Iranian Writer*, chs 4–6, 9–11.

56. See Hooglund, *Land and Revolution*, pp. 72–3, 88–99 and, more generally, chs 5, 6; Najmabadi, *Land Reform and Social Change in Iran*, ch 6; Moghadam, *From Land Reform to Revolution*.

57. Hoogland, *Land and Revolution*, pp. 115–21 and table 8.

58. Ibid.; Najmabadi, *Land Reform*, pp. 106–7.

59. Loeffler, *Islam in Practice*; Friedl, *Women of Deh Koh*; and *Children of Deh Koh*; Tapper, *Frontier Nomads*, pp. 298–314; and *Pasture and Politics: Economics, Conflict, and Ritual among the Shahsevan*; Goodell, *Elementary Structures*.

60. Friedl, *Women of Deh Koh*, pp. 88–109, 122; 'The dynamics of women's spheres of action'; and *Women in Middle Eastern History*; 'Women and the division of labour in an Iranian village', pp. 12–18, 31; my own contact with a modest Kermani *bazari* family between 1973 and 1978 allowed me to observe their decision to permit a daughter, who had stayed in the parental home and been urged to follow the conventions governing modesty at the start of that time, to move to Tehran, undertake secretarial work, and live in a flat with other young women as well as adopting fashionable dress and hairstyles. The question of whether parental control would affect her marriage choices loomed large but, interestingly, remained unresolved for her.

61. See Goodell, *Elementary Structures*, pp. 39–48, 126–30, 199–210, 230–3; Lahsaeizadeh, *Contemporary Rural Iran*, chs 9, 10.

62. Najmabadi, *Land Reform*, p. 162 quotes surveys showing that, in the 1970s some 52 per cent of rural households had radios, 11 per cent had tape recorders and, in one village, over 40 per cent had televisions; see also Lambton, *Persian Land Reform*, p. 190.

63. Afshar, 'Women's labour'; Hegland, '"Traditional" Iranian women: how they cope'; Hooglund, 'Women of Aliabad'.

64. Goodell, *Elementary Structures*, p. 92; Friedl, *Women of Deh Koh*, p. 122.

65. Hooglund, 'Women of Aliabad', pp. 33–6; Goodell, *Elementary Structures*, pp. 69–70; Loeffler, *Islam in Practice*, introduces each of his informants by placing them within hierarchies of political influence, material affluence and respect within the community, see pp. 51, 78–9, 91–2, 118, 152, 175, 202, 208; see also Friedl, *Women of Deh Koh*, pp. 31–46, 234–7.

66. Hooglund, *op. cit.*; Najmabadi, *Land Reform*, pp. 106–7.

67. Loeffler, *Islam in Practice*, pp. 69, 75, 83, 85, 86, 115–17, 127, 176, 180.

68. Goodell, *Elementary Structures*; Loeffler, *Islam*, pp. 17, 86.

69. Fischer, *Iran*, p. 137; Goodell, *Elementary Structures*, pp. 283–5.

70. Hegland, 'Traditional Iranian Women', pp. 496–7; Hooglund, 'Women of Aliabad', pp. 33–5; Hooglund, *Land and Revolution*, pp. 145–6; and 'Rural participation in the revolution'.

71. Keshavjee, *Mysticism and the Pluralism of Meaning*, pp. 11–19.

72. Loeffler, *Islam*, pp. 152, 198, on village study group, pp. 37–8, 54–5, 118–19, 172, 195, 203–4, 216–17, on active 'lay' religious activities; Goodell, *Elementary Structures*, p. 144 on village religious study, pp. 64, 96–7, 119–24, 151, 278–9, 287–94, 300–1, on village religious practices; Friedl, *Women of Deh Koh*, pp. 13–15, 19–21, 51–61, 92–3, 97, 106–7, 218–20 on old and new practices; for analyses see Loeffler, *Islam*, pp. 256–7, 259–63, 268–70, 276–9; Goodell, *Elementary Structures*, 119–20, 291, 297–300.

73. Goodell, *Elementary Structures*, pp. 123–4, 280–94, 299–300.

74. See English, *Kerman*, p. 47; Clarke, *Shiraz*, pp. 16, 17, 19, 24; Clarke and Clark, *Kermanshah*, pp. 28, 70, 80, 116, 117, 121; Wirth, 'Tehran bazar'; Bonine, *Yazd and Its Hinterland*; and 'Shops and shopkeepers: the dynamics of an Iranian provincial bazar', p. 212.

75. Bonine, 'Shops and shopkeepers', pp. 208–9, 211–13, 217–24.

76. Fischer, *Iran*, p. 137; Goodell, *Elementary Structures*, pp. 283–5.

77. Interview with squatter in the 'Professor Brown settlement', 1974, published in Kazemi, *Poverty and Revolution in Iran*, pp. 120–32, p. 128; the respondent's clear view of a class structure and his family's place in it compares interestingly with the limited perceptions recorded from a survey of migrants, ibid., pp. 101–2.

78. Interviews held in 1978–79 recorded in Vieille and Khosrokhavar, *Le discours populaire de la revolution iranienne*, vol. 2, pp. 10–11, 270.

79. See Moaddel, *Class Politics and Ideology in the Iranian Revolution*, pp. 126–7; Parsa, *Social Origins of the Iranian Revolution*, pp. 136, 142–4; Halliday, *Iran: Dictatorship and Development*, pp. 206–10; Bayat, *Workers and Revolution in Iran*, ch. 4; Foran, *Fragile Resistance*, pp. 332–3; Moghadam, 'Industrial development, culture, and working class politics'.

80. Bayat, *Workers*, pp. 40–1 shows 86 per cent of factory workers from non-wage-earning backgrounds in 1961 (65 per cent of peasant origin) and nearly 70 per cent similarly in 1981 (almost 56 per cent of peasant origin), but with those of wage-earning backgrounds now forming over 26 per cent of the total.

81. Sreberny-Mohammadi and Mohammadi, *Small Media, Big Revolution: Communication, Culture, and the Iranian Revolution*, p. 68; Bayat, *Workers*, p. 50; Kazemi, *Poverty*, p. 63.

82. Kazemi, *Poverty*, pp. 80–1, 126–7; Bayat, *Workers*, pp. 152–3 on workers using the Shah's portrait to legitimise protest.

83. See Beeman, *Language, Status, and Power in Iran*, pp. 75–92, 141–69, 174–91.

84. Bauer, 'Poor women and social consciousness in revolutionary Iran', pp. 41–71, 145–7, 152; my Kermani contact described in note 60.

85. Bauer, 'Poor women and social consciousness in revolutionary Iran', pp. 146, 153–5; Kazemi (Professor Brown interviews), p. 131; Bayat, *Street Politics: Poor People's Movements in Iran*, p. 15.

86. Menashri, *Education*, pp. 191, 192, 216, 218.

87. Ibid., pp. 262–3.

88. Arjomand, 'Traditionalism in twentieth-century Iran', pp. 213–16.

89. Fischer, *Iran*, p. 139.

90. Bayat, *Workers*, p. 51.

91. Kazemi, *Poverty*, pp. 63, 93, 126; Bayat, *Workers*, p. 50; Arjomand, 'Traditionalism', pp. 216–18; Fischer, *Iran*, p. 177.

92. Sadri and Sadri, 'The mantle of the prophet: a critical perspective', pp. 143–6; Zubaida and Vali, 'The *hojjatiyyeh* organisation'.

93. Betteridge, 'To veil or not to veil', pp. 111–17, 119–24.

94. Mottahadeh, *The Mantle of the Prophet*, p. 27

2 A story of material relationships

1. See Chapter 1.

2. See Gilbar, 'The Persian economy in the mid-nineteenth century'; Lambton, 'Persian trade under the early Qajars' in her *Qajar Persia*; Malcolm, 'The Melville papers' (1801), in Issawi, *The Economic History of Iran*; Amanat, *Cities and Trade: Consul Abbott on the Economy and Society of Iran, 1847–1866*.

3. See urban descriptions in Vaziri, *Jughrafiya yi-Kerman* (ed. M. Bastani-Parizi); Tahvildar, *Jughrafiya yi-Isfahan* (ed. Sotudeh); Mirza, *Tarikh va Jughrafiya yi-Dar al-Saltaneh yi-Tabri*; Fasa'i, *Farsnameh yi-Fasa'i*, vol. 2; Zarrabi, *Tarikh i-Kashan* (ed. Afshar), as well as those by foreign visitors.

4. Seen in the consular records of the British government as well as the Iranian texts in note 3.

5. As recognized by nineteenth-century Iranian writers who list *'ulama* as part of the urban notability.

6. This draws on the urban descriptions already mentioned, and plans of Tehran, Kerman, Semnan and Shiraz.

7. See Amanat, 'Between the *madrasa* and the marketplace: the designation of clerical leadership in modern Shi'ism'.

8. Fraser, *Narrative of Journey into Khorasan in the Years 1821 and 1822*, p. 457.

9. Amanat, 'Between the *madrasa* and the marketplace'; Cole, 'Imami jurisprudence and the role of the *'ulama*: Morteza Ansari on imitating the supreme exemplar'.

10. Fraser, *Narrative*, pp. 457–9; Kazembeyki, *Society, Economy and Politics in Mazanderan, Iran, 1848–1914*, p. 38.

11. See, for example, Fasa'i, *History of Persia under Qajar rule* (vol. 1 of his *Farsnameh*), p. 351.

12. Vaziri, *Jughrafiya*, pp. 87, 172; Mahdavi, *For God, Mammon, and Country*, p. 103.

13. Vaziri, *Jughrafiya*, p. 95; Zarrabi, *Tarikh i-Kashan*, pp. 432–3; Sayyah, *Khaterat i-Hajji Sayyah* (ed. Sayyah), p. 165.

14. Sayyah, *Khaterat*, pp. 164–5; Browne, *A Year among the Persians*, pp. 505–6.

15. al-Hukama, *Rustam al-Tavarikh* (ed. Mushiri), has literary examples of such criticism.

16. Vaziri, *Jughrafiya*, pp. 32, 45, 50.

17. Ibid., pp. 86, 135–6, 147, 160; Bastani-Parizi, *Peighambar i-Dozdan*, p. 129; Abbott in Amanat (ed.), *Cities and Trade*, pp. 66; Sykes, *Ten Thousand Miles*, pp. 209, 432, 435.

18. See Chapter 1.

19. Menashri, *Education and the Making of Modern Iran*, pp. 102, 110, 121, 191, 199.

20. See the changing shape of Kermanshah, Shiraz and Yazd shown in Clarke and Clark, *Kermanshah: An Iranian Provincial City*, p. 21, 24, 26, 30; Clarke, *The Iranian City of Shiraz*, pp. 14, 26, 17, 19; Bonine, 'Shops and shopkeepers: the dynamics of an Iranian provincial bazar', pp. 203–28, p. 212.

21. See Foran, *Fragile Resistance: Social Transformation in Iran from 1500 to the Revolution*, pp. 226–51; Abrahamian, *Iran between Two Revolutions*, pp. 140–54.

22. von Rosen, *Persian Pilgrimage*, pp. 279–86.

23. Foran, *Fragile Resistance*, p. 342.

24. This is most fully dealt with in Hooglund, *Land and Revolution in Iran 1960–80*, part 2; Najmabadi, *Land Reform and Social Change in Iran*, chs 3, 6, 8.

25. Goodell, *The Elementary Structures of Political Life*, pp. 42–9, 65–74, 135–7.

26. Foran, *Fragile Resistance*, pp. 325–9; Abrahamian, *Iran*, pp. 430–5; Katouzian, *The Political Economy of Modern Iran*, pp. 275–85.

27. Katouzian, *Political Economy*, pp. 325–6.

28. Bonine, 'Shops and shopkeepers'.

29. Kazemi, *Poverty and Revolution in Iran*, pp. 90–1.

30. Goodell, *Elementary Structures*; Friedl, *Women of Deh Koh*; and 'The division of labour in an Iranian village'; Hegland, '"Traditional" Iranian women: how they cope', pp. 483–501; Beck, *Nomad: A Year in the Life of a Qashqa'i Tribesman*; Tapper, *Pasture and Politics: Economics, Conflict, and Ritual among the Shahsevan*; Bayat, *Street Politics*, chs 1, 2; and *Workers and Revolution in Iran*, chs 3–5; Bauer, 'Poor women and social consciousness in revolutionary Iran'.

31. Lambton, *Landlord and Peasant in Persia*, pp. 126–7, 261; and *The Persian Land Reform 1962–1966*, p. 144; Akhavi, *Religion and Politics in Contemporary Iran* pp. 96–7.

32. Lambton, *Land Reform*, pp. 195–6, 234–9; Hooglund, *Land*, pp. 80–1.

33. Akhavi, *Religion*, pp. 132–4.

34. Hooglund, *Land*, pp. 29, 149.

35. Fischer, *Iran from Religious Dispute to Revolution*, p. 259; contrast this with the extensive landholdings of the shrine of Imam Reza at Mashad.

36. Ibid., pp. 96–7, 170–1; Good, 'The changing status and composition of an Iranian provincial elite', p. 247; Chehabi, *Iranian Politics and Religious Modernism*, pp. 203–8; Mottahedeh, *The Mantle of the Prophet*, pp. 349–52; Sadri and Sadri, 'The mantle of the prophet: a critical postscript', pp. 143, 145.

37. Clarke, *Shiraz*; Bonine, *Yazd*; Clarke and Clark, *Kermanshah*; Fischer, *Iran from Religious Dispute to Revolution*, pp. 121–3.

38. Fischer, *Iran from Religious Dispute to Revolution*, p. 78.

39. Ibid., p. 94.

40. Ibid., pp. 96, 122.

41. Ibid., pp. 95–7.

42. Mottahedeh, *The Mantle of the Prophet*, pp. 351–2.

43. Akhavi, *Religion and Politics in Contemporary Iran*, p. 141.

44. Foran, *Fragile Resistance*, p. 336.

3 A story of distinctive institutions and vested interests

1. See Fischer, *Iran: From Religious Dispute to Revolution*, pp. 32–5, 42–50.

2. Momen, *Introduction to Shi'a Islam*, p. 123; Arjomand, *The Shadow of God and the Hidden Imam*; *Religion, Political Order and Societal Change in Shi'ite Islam from the Beginning to 1890*, pp. 107, 128.

3. Arjomand, *The Shadow of God*, pp. 126–30 and chs 5, 6 more generally; Newman, 'The myth of clerical migration to Safavid Iran'; and 'Towards a reconsideration of the "Isfahan school" of philosophy: Shaykh Baha'i and the role of the Safavid 'ulama'; Babayan, 'The Safavid synthesis: from Qizilbash Islam to Imamite Shi'ism', pp. 135–61; and 'Sufis, dervishes and mullas'; Aubin, 'La politique religieuse des Safavides'.

4. Arjomand, *The Shadow of God*, p. 185.

5. See Momen, *Introduction to Shi'a Islam*, pp. 127–8; Arjomand, *The Shadow of God*, pp. 215–17; Scarcia, 'Intorno alle controversie tra Ahbari e Usuli presso gli imamiti di Persia', pp. 211–50.

6. Cole, 'Shi'i clerics in Iraq and Iran 1722–80'; and 'Ideology, ethics, and discourse in eighteenth century Iran'.

7. Vaziri, *Tarikh-i Kerman* (ed. Bastani-Parizi), pp. 332–69; Hedayat, *Rawzat al-Safa*, vol. 9, pp. 254–61.

8. Arjomand, *The Shadow of God*, p. 246.

9. See Tunakabuni, *Qisas al-'ulama*, pp. 125–98.

10. See note 7 and Malcolm, *History of Persia*, vol. 2, pp. 422–3; Arjomand, *The Shadow of God*, pp. 243–4.

11. Scarcia, 'Intorno'; Cole, 'Shi'a clerics'; Arjomand, *The Shadow of God*, chs 10, 11.

12. See Amanat, *Resurrection and Renewal*, especially chs 1, 6, 9; MacEoin, 'Changes in charismatic authority in Qajar Shi'ism'; Arjomand, *The Shadow of God*, p. 245.

13. Vaziri, *Jughrafiya yi-Kerman*, pp. 41, 44–54, 157, 159, 191; Amanat, *Resurrection and Renewal*, pp. 62–89; Bayat, *Mysticism and Dissent: Socio-religious Thought in Qajar Iran*.

14. Cole, *Modernity and the Millennium*, ch. 3; Bayat, *Mysticism and Dissent*; and *Iran's First Revolution*.

15. Amanat, 'Madrasa and market-place'.

16. Ibid.; Amanat, *Resurrection and Renewal*, pp. 34–69; Cole, 'Imami jurisprudence and the role of the 'ulama'.

17. Amanat, 'Madrasa and market-place'; and *Resurrection and Renewal*, p. 294.

18. Browne, *The Persian Revolution*, pp. 31–58; Keddie, *Religion and Rebellion in Iran: The Iranian Tobacco Protest of 1891–92*; Lambton, 'The Tobacco Regie: prelude to revolution', vol. 12, pp. 110–57

and vol. 13, pp. 71–90; Moaddel, 'Shi'i political discourse and class mobilization in the Tobacco movement of 1891–92'.

19. The chapter titles in her *Mysticism and Dissent* track what she sees as the shift in socio-religious thought from 'socialisation' through 'politicisation' to 'secularisation'.

20. Kermani, *Tarikh i-Bidari yi-Iranian* (ed. Saidi Sirjani); de Groot, 'Kerman in the later nineteenth century: a regional study of society and social change', pp. 435–67; Arjomand, 'The 'ulama's traditionalist opposition to parliamentarianism', pp. 174–90; Martin, *Islam and Modernism: The Iranian Revolution of 1906*; and 'Shaykh Fazlallah Nuri and the Iranian revolution 1906–9', pp. 39–53.

21. Bayat, *Iran's First Revolution*, ch. 8; Afary, *The Iranian Constitutional Revolution 1906–11*, chs 4, 5; Arjomand, 'Traditionalist opposition'.

22. Menashri, *Education and the Making of Modern Iran*, ch. 5; Akhavi, *Religion and Politics in Contemporary Iran*, pp. 33–7, 44–55.

23. Matthee, 'Transforming dangerous nomads into useful artisans, technicians, agriculturalists: education in the Reza Shah period', pp. 123–45; Menashri, *Education*.

24. Menashri, *Education*, p. 102; Akhavi, *Religion*, pp. 187–9.

25. The text is in Mustawfi, *The Administrative and Social History of the Qajar Period*, vol. 3, pp. 1125–6; and Akhavi, *Religion*, pp. 29–30; see Martin, 'Mudarres, republicanism, and the rise to power of Riza Khan'; Ghani, *Iran and the Rise of Reza Shah*, pp. 307–19.

26. Cronin, 'Conscription and popular resistance in Iran 1925–41'; Akhavi, *Religion*, pp. 37–8, 58; Faghfoory, ''Ulama–state relations in Iran 1921–41'.

27. Chehabi, 'Staging the emperor's new clothes: dress codes and nation building under Reza Shah'; Akhavi, *Religion*, pp. 58–9, 44, quoting the telegram from Razi, *Asar i-Hujjah*, pp. 48–51.

28. Chehabi, 'Staging' and 'The banning of the veil and its consequences' pp. 193–210; Baker, 'Politics of dress: the dress reform laws of 1920s/30s Iran'; Fischer, *Iran*, pp. 97–100; Amin, *The Making of the New Iranian Woman: Gender, State Policy, and Popular Culture 1865–1946*.

29. Fischer, *Iran*, p. 85, Akhavi, *Religion*, p. 228, citing Mutahhari, 'Moshkei-i asasi dar sazman-i ruhaniyat', in *Bahsi dar bareh-yi marja'iyat va ruhaniyat*.

30. Akhavi, *Religion*, pp. 24, 63–4, 66, 100, 102, 122; and 'The role of the clergy in Iranian politics', pp. 91–117; Fischer, *Iran*, pp. 69, 109, 164–5; Martin, *Creating an Islamic State: Khomeini and the Making of a New Iran*, pp. 18–20, 50–6; Yazdi, 'Patterns of clerical behaviour in postwar Iran 1941–53', pp. 281–307.

31. Akhavi, 'Role of the clergy'; Yazdi, 'Patterns of clerical behaviour'; Richard, 'Ayatollah Kashani: precursor of the Islamic Republic'; Kazemi, 'The *Fada'iy yi Islam*; fanaticism, politics and terror', pp. 158–75; Moin, *Khomeini: Life of the Ayatollah*, pp. 60–3.

32. Richard, 'Shari'at Sangalaji, a reformist theologian of the Riza Shah period'; Borujerdi, *Iranian Intellectuals and the West*, pp. 63, 88, 95; Fischer, *Iran*, p. 277.

33. Rahnema, *An Islamic Utopian: A Political Biography of 'Ali Shari'ati*, pp. 11–34, 51–3, 63–4; Chehabi, *Iranian Politics and Religious Modernism*, pp. 113–14, 120, 127–30, 138–9, 187.

34. Algar, 'The oppositional role of the *'ulama* in twentieth century Iran'; Floor, 'The revolutionary character of the *'ulama*: wishful thinking or reality?'; Chehabi, *Iranian Politics*, pp. 175–85; Akhavi, *Religion*, pp. 91–105.

35. Rahnema, *Islamic Utopian*, p. 274; Martin, *Creating an Islamic State*, p. 126; Akhavi, *Religion*, p. 234, n. 94; Chehabi, *Iranian Politics*, p. 210.

36. Fischer, *Iran*, ch. 5; Akhavi, *Religion*, pp. 117–29, 143–58; Chehabi, *Iranian*

Politics, pp. 169–74, 202–10; Borujerdi, *Iranian Intellectuals*, pp. 85–105.

37. Fischer, *Iran*, pp. 136–7, 174–5, 177; Kazemi, *Poverty and Revolution in Iran: The Migrant Poor, Urban Marginality and Politics*, pp. 63, 93, 126; Mottahedeh, *Mantle*, pp. 341–4, 347–53, 355–6; Arjomand, *The Turban for the Crown: The Islamic Revolution in Iran*, pp. 91–3.

38. Abrahamian, *Iran*, p. 433; Fischer, *Iran*, pp. 101, 137–8; Goodell, *Elementary Structures*, pp. 44, 46, 96, 121–2, 123–4, 281–7; Loeffler, *Islam in Practice: Religious Beliefs in a Persian Village*, pp. 17–19, 69, 75, 83, 85, 86, 115–17, 127, 176, 180.

39. Rahnema, *Islamic Utopian*, chs 16–21; Chehabi, *Iranian Politics*, pp. 202–8.

40. Rahnema, *Islamic Utopian*, pp. 267–74 (condemnations), p. 275 (Khomeini's response); Akhavi, *Religion*, pp. 146, 150; Chehabi, *Iranian Politics*, pp. 205–6, 207–8; Fischer, *Iran*, pp. 165–9.

41. Akhavi, *Religion*, p. 229, n. 31.

42. Paidar, *Women and the Political Process in Twentieth-century Iran*, pp. 32–7, 172–82; Amin, *Making of the Modern Iranian Woman*, pp. 20–47, 58–60, 87–8, 239–42; Najmabadi, *Women with Mustaches and Men without Beards*, chs 2–4.

43. Yeganeh and Keddie, 'Sexuality and social protest in Iran'.

4 The life, death and afterlife of political issues

1. Babayan, 'The Safavi synthesis: from *qizilbash* Islam to imamite shi'ism'; and *Mystics, Monarchs and Messiahs: Cultural Landscapes of Early Modern Iran*, chs 1, 6, 7, 9–11; Calmard, 'Les rituals Shiites et le pouvoir'; and 'Shi'i rituals and power: II'; Newman, 'The myth of clerical migration to Safavid Iran'; Lockhart, *Nadir Shah*, ch. 9 (drawing on the contemporary histories Muhammad Kazem Marvi, *Kitab i-Nadiri*, and Mirza Muhammad Mehdi Astarabadi, *Tarikh i-Nadiri*); Perry, *Karim Khan Zand*, pp. 214–18; and 'The last Safavids'; and 'Justice for the underprivileged: the

ombudsman tradition of Iran'; Meredith, 'Early Qajar administration'; Lambton, 'Tribal resurgence and the decline of the bureaucracy'.

2. On railways see Mustashar al-Douleh's letter written in 1864 when consul in Tiflis, quoted by Bakhash, *Iran: Monarchy, Bureaucracy, and Reform under the Qajars*, p. 29 ('the establishment of a railroad in Iran will in three years revolutionise the country, bring order and civilisation to the state and nation, and be the greatest source of power. In one word Iran will become a paradise'). On law see his *Yek kalameh*, *passim*; and Talebof, *Kitab i-Ahmad/Ahmad's book*, vol. 2, p. 136 ('if we had the rule of law we would be masters of knowledge, wealth, order and independence'); Khan, *Qanun* (ed. Nateq), no. 3, p. 3 (Ramazan 1307/April 1890) 'it is clear as the sun that all that amazing prosperity ... and those endless conquests ... that we witness in foreign countries, all of it is the result of the establishment of law'.

3. Talebof, *Kitab i-Ahmad*, vol. 2, pp. 92–4 (need for modern 'European' curriculum), 122–3 (education and European success), 98–9, 136 (Iran needs schools and educators); Marageh'i, *Siyahat-nameh yi Ibrahim Beg*, pp. 165–7, 359 (importance of useful knowledge), 293–5 (links between education, rule of law, and prosperity).

4. Abu Taleb Behbehani, author of a reform text, *Minhaj al-'Ala/The lofty way* (discussed and quoted in Adamiyat and Nateq [eds], *Social and Political Ideas from Unpublished Sources of the Qajar Period*, pp. 99–114), was an official who lived in the Ottoman Empire and Egypt; Mirza Yusuf Khan Mustashar al-Douleh was a diplomat in Tiflis, St Petersburg and Paris and served in the justice ministry; Mirza Malkom Khan worked as a government translator and diplomat; Mirza Husein Khan Mushir al Douleh became chief minister after a series of diplomatic and ministerial posts.

5. On Kermani, see Bayat, 'Mirza Aqa Khan Kermani'; and *Mysticism and Dissent: Socio-religious Thought in Qajar Iran*, ch. 5; the quotation is cited in Adamiyat, *Andisheh-ha yi Mirza Aqa Kermani*, p. 241.

6. There are contemporary parallels worth pursuing here with the reforming intellectual groups developing in Egypt, India and the Ottoman Empire, and with the traditions of politically engaged intelligentsia emerging as part of opposition to Tsarist autocracy in Russia or around the Dreyfus affair in France.

7. Mirza Husein Khan, writing from Istanbul to the Foreign Minister, July 1869, quoted in Neshat, *The Origins of Modern Reform in Iran 1870–80*, p. 137.

8. *Yek kalameh* and letter to Akhundzadeh quoted by Bakhash, *Iran: Monarchy, Bureaucracy and Reform under the Qajars*, pp. 40–1; Talebof, *Ketab-i Ahmad*, vol. 2, pp. 124–5; Maragheh'i, *Siyahat-nameh*, p. 299.

9. See 'A story of nation and nationalism', this chapter.

10. See Martin, *Islam and Modernism: the Iranian Revolution of 1906*, chs 3, 4; Bayat, *Iran's First Revolution: Shi'ism and the Constitutional Revolution of 1905–9*, chs 5, 6, 8, 9; Hairi, *Shi'ism and Constitutionalism in Iran*, chs 2, 3; Lambton, 'The Persian *'ulama* and constitutional reform'.

11. On the 'dissident' strand, see Bayat, *First Revolution*, chs 3, 5–8; Afary, *The Iranian Constitutional Revolution 1906–11*, chs 2, 4; Cole, 'Iranian millenarianism and democratic thought in the nineteenth century'; on opposition to reform, see Bayat, *op. cit.*, chs 8, 9; Martin, *Islam and Modernism*, chs 5–7; and 'Shakh Fazlallah Nuri and the Iranian revolution'; Hairi, 'Shaikh Fazlullah Nuri's refutation of the idea of constitutionalism'; Arjomand, 'The *'ulama*'s traditionalist opposition to parliamentarism 1907–9'.

12. Afary, *Constitutional Revolution*, chs 6, 7, pp. 70, 88, 104–5, 267–9; Bayat, *First Revolution*, ch. 4; Berberian, *Armenians and the Constitutional Revolution of 1905–11*, pp. 94–100, 116–23, 129–40; Najmabadi, '*Zan-ha yi-millat*: women or wives of the nation?'; and '"Is our name remembered?": writing the history of Iranian constitutionalism as if women and gender mattered'; Mansur, 'Chehreh yi-zan dar jaraid-i mashrutiyat/ The image of woman in constitutional journals'.

13. Katouzian, 'Riza Shah's legitimacy and social base'; and 'Liberty and licence in the constitutional revolution of Iran'; Gheissari, *Iranian Intellectuals in the Twentieth Century*, pp. 40–50.

14. See Maraghehi, *Siyahat-nameh*, pp. 293–5; Talebof, *Kitab i-Ahmad*, vol. 2, pp. 121–4 on the need for informed political participation and active citizenship; on the need for 'constitutional' frameworks and public support for state power, see *Qanun*, nos 2, 18, 22, 25, 35; letter from Mustshar al-Douleh to the heir apparent 1888/89, quoted in Kermani, *Tarikh i Bidari yi Iranian/History of the Awakening of the Iranians* p. 176; for the constitutional period see Afary, *Constitutional Revolution*, chs 3, 5, 10.

15. Editorial, *Sur i Israfil*, 4 December 1907, p. 2; Nazem al-Islam, *Bidari*, vol. 2, p. 100.

16. Afary, *Constitutional Revolution*, pp. 73–92, 95–109, 151–76, 264–83; Bayat, *First Revolution*, pp. 97–105, 148–53, 201–9; Chaqueri, *Origins of Social Democracy in Iran*, chs 4–7.

17. Floor, *Labour Unions*, part 1; Abrahamian, *Iran*, pp. 154–64; Cronin, 'Conscription and popular resistance in Iran, 1925–41'.

18. Keddie, *Sayyid Jamal al-din 'al Afghani': A Political Biography*, ch. 6 on Afghani; Hairi, *Shi'ism and Constitutionalism*, on Na'ini; Martin, *Islam and Modernism*, ch. 3 on Tabataba'i.

19. Bayat, *First Revolution*, ch. 3, pp. 263–5.

20. Nazem al-Islam, *Bidari*, vol. 1, pp. 309–24; Scarcia, 'Kerman 1905: la

guerra tra Seihi e Balasari'; Bayat, *First Revolution*, pp. 105, 149–52, 172–4.

21. On Mudarris, see Martin, 'Mudarris, republicanism, and the rise to power of Riza Shah'; Bani-Sadr, *Vaz'iyat i-Iran va naqsh i-Mudarris*; Khajehnuri, *Bazigaran i-asr i-tala'I: Sayyid Hasan Mudarris*; on Kashani, see Richard, 'Ayatollah Kashani: precursor of the Islamic Republic?'; Akhavi, 'The role of the clergy in Iranian politics 1949–54'; and *Religion and Politics in Contemporary Iran*, pp. 60–72.

22. Akhavi, *Religion and Politics*, pp. 144–58.

23. See Martin, *Creating an Islamic State*, pp. 103–28, Abrahamian, *Khomeinism*, chs 1, 2.

24. Goodell, *Elementary Structures*, pp. 42–8, 63–5, 126–8; Loeffler, *Islam in Practice*, pp. 9–11; and 'Tribal order and the state'; Tapper, *Frontier Nomads*, pp. 298–311; and *Pasture and Politics*; Beck, *Nomad: A Year in the Life of a Qashqai Tribesman in Iran*; and 'Economic transformations among Qashqai nomads 1962–78'; Bayat, *Street Politics: Poor People's Politics in Iran*, pp. 24–32, 44–8; Kazemi, *Poverty and Revolution*, pp. 59–63, 123–32; Bauer, 'Poor women and social consciousness'.

25. Instances of peasant relations with landlords and officials being shaped by protest, bargaining and concession can be found in Farmanfarma, *Safar-nameh yi Kerman va Baluchestan* (ed. Nezam-Mafi), pp. 31–2, 62, 66–7, 73, 76–7, and British consular diaries for Kerman for 1905, 1907, 1908; a general view is offered by Gobineau, *Trois ans en Asie*, pp. 289–90.

26. Amanat, *Pivot of the Universe: Nasir al-din Shah Qajar and the Iranian Monarchy 1831–96*, p. 8.

27. Avery and Simmons, 'Persia on a cross of silver 1880–90'; Mahdavi, *For God, Mammon, and Country: A Nineteenth-century Persian Merchant*, pp. 16–17, 73–8, 82–3, 138–45; see also ch. 1.

28. See the references to the consent and/or involvement of the governed/*mellat*

in *Qanun*, issues 11, 16 and Mustashar al-Douleh's *Yek kalameh*, pp. 8, 12; an unpublished dictionary from the reign of Muzaffar al-din Shah (1896–1906) translated *mellat* as 'peuple, nation' (quoted in Kashani-Sabet, *Frontier Fictions*, p. 252).

29. See Sipihr, *Nasikh al-tavarikh: Qajariyeh* (ed. Bihbudi), vol. 4, pp. 208–11; and Hedayat, *Rawzat al-Safa yi Nasiri* (ed. Kitabforushi Markazi), vol. 10, pp. 702–4 for Nasir al-din Shah's use of the image of 'Ali; Vaziri, *Jughrafiya yi-Kerman*, p. 83; and *Rauzat al-Safa*, vol. 10, pp. 811, 817–18 on the repair of mosques and shrines; on royal pilgrimages see Fasai, *History of Persia under Qajar Rule*, pp. 168, 261, 358, 368–72.

30. Amanat, *Resurrection and Renewal*; Cole, 'Iranian millenarianism and democratic thought in the nineteenth century'; Bayat, *Iran's First Revolution*, chs 3, 5–7.

31. See de Groot, 'Kerman in the later nineteenth century', pp. 454–9, quoting British consular diaries on events in Kerman, 1905–13; Afary, *The Iranian Constitutional Revolution 1905–11*, ch. 6; Najmabadi, *The Story of the Daughters of Quchan: Gender and National Memory in Iranian History*, pp. 13–26.

32. See Kermani, *Tarikh-i Bidari-yi Iranian*, vol. 1, pp. 265–73, 280–308; Torkaman, *Shaykh i shahid Fazlallah Nuri*, pp. 231–368; Lambton, 'Secret societies and the Persian Revolution of 1905–6'; Martin, *Islam and Modernism*, pp. 117–38.

33. See Abrahamian, *Iran between Two Revolutions*, chs 4–6; and 'The strengths and weaknesses of the labour movement in Iran 1941–53'; Azimi, *Iran: The Crisis of Democracy*; Gasiorowski (ed.), *Muhammad Mossadeq and the 1953 Coup in Iran*, chs 1–3; Atabaki, *Azerbaijan: Ethnicity and the Struggle for Power in Iran*, chs 4–6.

34. See Richard, 'Ayatollah Kashani: precursor of the Islamic republic?'; Faghfoory 'Patterns of clerical behaviour in postwar Iran 1941–53'; Akhavi, 'The role of the clergy in Iranian politics 1949–54'.

35. Vaziri, *Iran as Imagined Nation:*

The Construction of National Identity examines the mismatch between early uses of terms like Iran, Iran-shahr, or Iran-zamin, and the misleading and essentialist use of those terms by European orientalists and Iranian nationalists. Kashani-Sabet, *Frontier Fictions: Shaping the Iranian Nation 1804–1946*, pp. 11–19, offers a more nuanced view of the pre-history of ideas of an 'Iranian' nation or territory, and draws attention to the significance of boundaries and territoriality in nation-making throughout the text; see also Tavakoli-Targhi, *Refashioning Iran: Orientalism, Occidentalism and Historiography*, ch. 6.

36. Correspondence quoted in Adamiyat, *Amir Kabir va Iran*, p. 53; Nashat, *The Origins of Modern Reform in Iran 1870–80*, pp. 145, 151–3; and Bakhash, *Iran: Monarchy, Bureaucracy and Reform under the Qajars*, pp. 29, 30, 352; a sensitive discussion of early official and patriarchal views of *vatan* is in Tavakoli Targhi, *Refashioning Iran*, pp. 113–18; see also Bayat, *Iran's First Revolution*, pp. 34–44.

37. See Bakhash, *Iran*, ch. 6; Bayat, *Mysticism and Dissent: Socio-religious Thought in Qajar Iran*, chs 5, 6; and *Iran's First Revolution*, pp. 80, 98–9; Keddie, *Sayyid Jamal al-din 'al Afghani: A Political Biography*; Algar, *Mirza Malkom Khan: A Biographical Study in Iranian Modernism*; Hairi, *Shi'ism and Constitutionalism in Iran*, ch. 1; Ringer, *Education, Religion, and the Discourse of Cultural Reform in Qajar Iran*, ch. 7.

38. The text is in al-Saltaneh, *Tarikh i-Muntazem i-Nasiri*, vol. 1, p. 250; an earlier example is quoted in Adamiyat, *Andisheh-ha yi taraqqi va hukumat i-qanun/dar asr i-Sepah Salar*, pp. 57–60.

39. Quoted in Bakhash, *Iran*, pp. 224–5.

40. Classic examples are Mustashar al-Douleh's *Yek Kalameh* (1871); Maragheh'i's *Siyahat-nameh yi-Ibrahim Beg* (c. 1888–90); Talebof's *Kitab i-Ahmad* (c. 1894); and the writings of Mirza Malkom Khan (see *Majmu'eh yi-Athar i-Malkom Khan*) and Mirza Aqa Kermani, *Sad ketabeh* and *Seh maktub* (1890s).

41. See Ringer, *Education, Religion*, ch. 7 and conclusion; Bayat, *First Revolution*, ch. 2.

42. See Keddie, *Religion and Rebellion in Iran: The Iranian Tobacco Protest 1891–92*; Adamiyat, *Shuresh bar imtiaz-nameh yi rezhi*; an early account, Browne, *The Persian Revolution 1905–9*, ch. 2; source material can be found in Adamiyat and Nateq (eds), *Afkhar i–ijtema'l va siyasi dar athar i-muntasher-nashodeh yi-dauran i-Qajar*; and 'Correspondence respecting the Persian tobacco concession', Great Britain, Parliamentary Sessional Papers, 1891, 1892; Moaddel, 'Shi'i political discourse and class movements in the Tobacco Movement of 1890–92'.

43. See Zarcone and Zarinebaf-Shahr (eds), *Les iraniens d'Istanbul*; Keddie, *'al-Afghani*, chs 12, 13; Bayat, 'Mirza Aqa Kermani: a nineteenth-century nationalist'; and *Mysticism and Dissent*, pp. 140–2; Bayat, *First Revolution*, pp. 68–70; Browne, *Persian Revolution*, pp. 93–5.

44. See Bayat, *First Revolution*, ch. 4; Swietochowski, *Russan Azerbaijan 1905–20*; Atabaki, *Azerbaijan*, ch. 2.

45. See documents in Adamiyat and Nateq, *Afkar i-ijtema'i*, pp. 299–371; Jamal al-din Isfahani, *Lebas i-Taqva*; Dadkhah, 'Lebas o taqva: an early twentieth century [sic] treatise on the economy'; Mahdavi, *For God, Mammon, and Country: A Nineteenth-century Persian Merchant*, chs 4, 5, 7.

46. See the Calcutta-based Iranian journal *Habl al-Matin*, no. 2, p. 13 (2 July 1900); a thoughtful discussion of the whole issue is Najmabadi, 'The erotic *vatan* [homeland] as beloved and mother: to love, to possess, to protect'.

47. *Qanun*, no. 15, p. 4; *Akhtar*, vol. 3, no. 9, pp. 33–4 (March 1877); see also nos 8, 10 (February/March 1977); on the role of *Akhtar* see Kologlu, 'Un journal Persan

d'Istanbul: *Akhtar*'; and Pistor-Hatam, 'The Persian newsletter *Akhtar* as a transmitter of Ottoman political ideas'.

48. Akhundzadeh's own account of his multicultural identity is in *Alifba yi-jadid va maktubat*, pp. 104, 249, 349–51, quoted in Hairi, *Shi'ism and Constitutionalism in Iran*, p. 25; see also Adamiyat, *Andisheh-ha yi Mirza Fath 'Ali Akhundzadeh*, 1970–71, pp. 15–25.

49. Kermani, *Seh maktub*, pp. 10–11, 14; and *Sad Khataba*, no. 41.

50. This view appears in Haji Muhammad Karim Khan Kermani (Qajar prince and leader of the heterodox Shaikhi sect in Kerman), *Risalah yi Nasiriyeh*, pp. 388–91.

51. De Groot '"Brothers of the Iranian race": manhood, nationhood and modernity in Iran c. 1870–1914'.

52. *Qanun*, nos 1, 10, 12.

53. See Tavakoli-Targhi, *Refashioning Iran*, pp. 122–34; de Groot, '"Brothers of the Iranian race"'; Najmabadi, 'The erotic *vatan*'; and '*Zan ha yi-mellat*: women or wives of the nation'; plus *Women with Mustaches and Men without Beards: Gender and Sexual Anxieties of Iranian Modernity*, chs 3, 4, 8; Paidar, *Women and the Political Process in Twentieth-century Iran*, chs 1, 2.

54. Full recent accounts are Bayat, *Iran's First Revolution*; and Afary, *The Iranian Constitutional Revolution 1906–11*; contemporary narratives are Kermani, *Tarikh-i Bidari-yi Iranian*; and Browne, *The Persian Revolution*; see also Kasravi, *Tarikh-mashruteh yi Iran*.

55. Browne, *The Persian Revolution*, pp. 329–30, *Habl al-matin*, 3 October 1910; Malekzadeh, *Tarikh i-Inqilab i-mashrutiyat i-Iran*, vol. 6, pp. 212–19.

56. Quoted in Arjomand, 'The *'ulama*'s traditionalist opposition'.

57. *Muzakirat i-majlis: doureh yi avval*, p. 228.

58. Hairi, *Shi'ism and Constitutionalism*, pp. 83–7; *Muzakirat*, p. 179; *Anjuman*, 28 May 1907, p. 3; *Sur i-Israfil*, no. 14, 18 September 1907.

59. Reproduced in Nezam-Mafi (ed.), *Majmu'eh yi-Mutun va Asnad i-Tarikhi*, vol. 4, p. 76.

60. See the 1906 Electoral Law of September 1906, articles 4, 5, the Supplementary Fundamental Laws of October 1907, articles 1–3, 18, 20, 21, 27, 39, 58 and the new Electoral Law of July 1909, articles 4, 5, 7, reproduced in Browne, *Persian Revolution*, pp. 356, 372–9, 386–7.

61. See Agulhon, *Marianne into Battle*; Sarkar, *Hindu Wife, Hindu Nation*; Reading, *Polish Women, Solidarity and Feminism*; Baron, 'The construction of national honour in Egypt'; and *Egypt as a Woman*; Innes, *Women and Nation in Iran Literature and Society 1880–1935*.

62. See *Kaveh*, no. 1 (24 January 1916) p. 8, no. 2 (8 February 1916) p. 3, no. 3 (29 February 1916) p. 3; Bourne and Watt (eds), *British Documents on Foreign Affairs: Reports and Papers from the Foreign Office Confidential Prints; Persia I: The Anglo-Persian Agreement*, pp. 85–7.

63. The fullest accounts are Ghani, *Iran and the Rise of Reza Shah: From Qajar Collapse to Pahlavi Power*; Katouzian, *State and Society in Iran: The Eclipse of the Qajars and the Emergence of the Pahlavis*; Zirinsky, 'The rise of Reza Khan'; and 'Imperial power and dictatorship: Britain and the rise of Reza Shah'.

64. As suggested in Cronin, *The Army and the Creation of the Pahlavi State in Iran 1910–26*.

65. *Habl al-matin*, no. 49, 16 June 1908, pp. 1–2; *Kaveh*, no. 1, 24 January 1916, p. 2; Kashani-Sabet, *Frontier Fictions*, pp. 146–7, quoting British consular sources in 1915–16; *Nahid*, no. 2, April 1921, pp. 1–2, quoted in *Frontier Fictions*, p. 157.

66. Kashani-Sabet, *Frontier Fictions*, p. 160.

67. On Isa Sadiq, see Mottahedeh, *The Mantle of the Prophet*, pp. 54–67; on Kasravi see ibid., pp. 98–105; his own *Zendigani yi man*; and Abrahamian, 'Kasravi: the integrative nationalist of Iran'.

68. See footnote 65, Kashani-Sabet, *Frontier Fictions*, pp. 208–11; Mathee, 'Transforming dangerous nomads into useful artisans, technicians, agriculturalists: education in the Reza Shah period'.

69. See Abrahamian, *Iran*, chs 4, 5; Azimi, *Iran: The Crisis of Democracy*; Lytle, *The Origins of the Iranian–American Alliance 1941–53*; McFarland, 'A peripheral view of the origins of the Cold War: Iran 1941–47'; Millspaugh, *Americans in Persia*; Lenczowski, *Russia and the West in Iran 1918–48: A Study in Big Power Rivalry*; Goode, *The United States and Iran 1946–51: The Diplomacy of Neglect*.

70. Abrahamian, *Iran*, pp. 210–12; Ramazani, *Iran's Foreign Policy 1941–73: A Study of Foreign Policy in Modernising Nations*; Millspaugh, *Americans*, pp. 187–90 gives a Cold War American view; a glimpse of the period from a regional vantage-point inflected with a British official outlook is in Skrine, *World War in Iran*, chs 19, 20.

71. Majlis Proceedings, 28 February 1949, quoted in Abrahamian, *Iran*, p. 246; Azimi, *Crisis of Democracy*.

72. These issues are discussed in Gheissari, *Iranian Intellectuals in the Twentieth Century*, ch. 5, Boroujerdi, *Iranian Intellectuals and the West: The Tormented Triumph of Nativism*, chs 2, 3, 5, 6; Mirsepassi, *Intellectual Discourse and the Politics of Modernization: Negotiating Modernity in Iran*, chs 2–4; Jahanbegloo (ed.), *Iran between Tradition and Modernity*, chs 1 (Behnam), 7 (Dabashi), 8 (Sadri).

73. Shariati, 'What should we lean on?', p. 5.

74. Khomeini, *Islam and Revolution: Writings and Declarations of Imam Khomeini*, pp. 176, 187–8, 195–8.

75. Vieille and Khosrokhavar, *Le discours populaire de la revolution iranienne*, vol. 2; 'Interviews', pp. 133 (Tehran van driver), 144, 149, 151 (Qazvin workers), 195 (clerk), 257 (migrant worker), 283 (electrician), 354 (female domestic servant moved to Tehran from a rural area).

5 A story of language, symbol and discourse

1. Sipihr, *Nasikh al-tavarikh: Qajariya*, vol. 1, p. 79, vol. 3, p. 189.

2. Ibid., vol. 4, pp. 208–11; Hedayat, *Rauzat al-safa yi Nasiri*; vol. 10, pp. 702–4; portraits of the Shah wearing the medallion from the 1850s and 1860s appear in Diba and Ekhtiar (eds), *Royal Persian Paintings*, 1998, pp. 244, 246.

3. Thus the Shah published the diary of his pilgrimage to the shrine cities of Iraq, promoted *ta'zieh*, commissioning the grand Tekkieh yi-Doulat for performances, invoked religious rhetoric in his dealings with foreign diplomats and recorded dreams with religious themes, as well as showing his religiosity in correspondence. See Amanat, *Pivot of the Universe: Nasir al-din Shah and the Iranian Monarchy*, pp. 234, 265, 276, 299–300; Calmard, 'Le mecenat des representations de *ta'ziyeh*: II'; and on religious court ceremonial, Feuvrier, *Trois ans à la cour de Perse*, pp. 205, 208.

4. See, for example, Vaziri, *Tarikh i-Kerman*, pp. 397, 407; Fasai, *Farsnameh yi-Nasiri*, vol. 1, pp. 236–7, 267, 342.

5. Hume-Griffiths, *Behind the Veil in Persia and Turkish Arabia*, p. 112; Foreign Office records consular series, FO248 vol. 1072, Kerman consular diary, 8–15 December 1913.

6. Fasai, *Farsnameh yi-Nasiri*, pp. 220, 237, 264, 309; FO248, vol. 820, Kerman consular diary, September 1904; vol. 840, June 1905; Floyer, *Unexplored Baluchistan*, p. 349.

7. Discussed in Amanat, *Pivot of the Universe*, pp. 265–74, drawing on the Shah's correspondence, British diplomatic sources and documents in Gharavi (ed.), *Majareh yi-Doulat Inglis va Mirza Hashem Khan*, 1984.

8. This concept is developed in Fischer, *Iran from Religious Dispute to Revolution*, pp. 13–27.

9. Ibid.

10. see Tinkabuni, *Qisas al-'ulama*, pp. 71–3, 93–4, 99–100; a different testi-

mony to the role of *'ulama* in checking oppression is in Fasa'i, *Farsnameh yi-Nasiri*, p. 263.

11. Brugsch, *Reise der Konigliche Preussischen Gesandschaft nach Persien 1860–1861*, vol. 2, p. 330; Eastwick, *Journal of a Diplomat's Three Years' Residence in Persia*, pp. 288–91; the Qazvin incident is recorded in Gobineau, *Dépêches diplomatiques*, p. 95.

12. Kashani-Sabet, *Frontier Fictions: Shaping the Iranian Nation, 1804–1946*, pp. 59–62, quoting government and *'ulama* sources; Fasai, *Farsnameh yi-Nasiri*, pp. 127–8, 174; Algar, *Religion and the State in Iran 1785–1906: The Role of the 'Ulama in the Qajar Period*, pp. 82–93.

13. Amanat, *Resurrection and Renewal*, pp. 93–105, 141–52, 413–16; Cole, *Modernity and the Millennium: The Genesis of the Bahai Faith in the Middle East*, pp. 91–7, 101–8, 190–6.

14. This episode is covered in Keddie, *Religion and Rebellion in Iran: The Iranian Tobacco Protest of 1891–2*; Adamiyat, *Shuresh bar imtiyaz-nameh yi rezhi*; see also Browne, *Persian Revolution*, ch. 2.

15. Quoted from protest material gathered by British diplomats in Keddie, *Religion and Rebellion*, pp. 46–7, 57, 58; Moaddel, 'Shi'i political discourse and class mobilization in the Tobacco Movement of 1890–2', quoting Karbalai, *Qarar-dad i-rezhi yi 1890 miladi*, p. 46.

16. The text is given in Nazem al-islam, *Tarikh i-Bidari yi-Iranian*, p. 19; Browne, *The Persian Revolution*, p. 22; Keddie, *Religion and Rebellion*, pp. 95–6.

17. Feuvrier, *Trois ans à la cour de Perse*, p. 284.

18. Moaddel, 'Shi'i political discourse' emphasises class issues; Algar, *Religion and the State*, ch. 12, *'ulama* leadership; Keddie, *Religion and Rebellion*, cross-group alliances; Keddie *op. cit.* and Lambton, 'The Tobacco Regie: prelude to revolution', also deal with the role of Russian diplomatic interests.

19. Keddie, *Sayyid Jamal al-din: A Political Biography*, pp. 37–8, 45 (quoting a British diplomatic source on Afghani wearing 'Nogai' dress in Afghanistan), 79–80, 189–95, 215–36, 336–69; and 'Symbol and sincerity in Islam'; and 'Islamic philosophy and Islamic modernism'.

20. Foran, 'The strengths and weaknesses of Iran's populist alliance'.

21. Nazem al-Islam, *Bidari*, vol. 1, pp. 609, 611 quoting a 1906 leaflet; vol. 2, pp. 214, 215, 223, 399, 469, quoting leaflets and telegrams; Browne, *Persian Revolution*, pp. 118, 120; Foreign Office, FO371, vol. 112, July 1906.

22. Nazem al-Islam, *Bidari*, vol. 1, pp. 243–5, 444–53; Hairi, *Shi'ism and constitutionalism*, pp. 72–87; Martin, *Islam and Modernism: The Iranian Revolution of 1906*, ch. 3.

23. See Bayat, *First Revolution*, ch. 4; Afary, 'Social democracy and the Iranian constitutional revolution of 1906–11' in Foran, *Century of Revolution*; Chaqueri, *The Origins of Social Democracy in Modern Iran*, chs 3–7; Afghani, in Browne, *Persian Revolution*, pp. 28–9; and Nazem al-Islam, *Bidari*, vol. 1, pp. 87–8; Kermani in Bayat, 'Mirza Aqa Kermani', pp. 84, 85–6; Browne, *Persian Revolution*, p. 143.

24. *Sur i-Israfil*, no. 18, 27 November 1907; no. 29, 14 May 1908.

25. See Nazem al-Islam, *Bidari*, vol. 1, pp. 331–3, 443–54.

26. Bayat, *First Revolution*, chs 8, 9; Afary, *Constitutional Revolution*, chs 4, 6, 10, 11.

27. Kermani, *Sah Maktub*, p. 17, 88, quoted in Bayat, 'Mirza Aqa Kermani'; and *Salar-nameh*, p. 12; and *Ayineh yi-sikandari*, quoted in Tavakoli, *Refashioning Iran: Orientalism, Occidentalism, and Historiography*, p. 99; Akhundzadeh, *Maktubat i-Mirza Fath 'Ali Akhundzadeh*, pp. 20–1, 249–51.

28. See, for example, the letter from 'a Shirazi' in *Nida yi vatan*, 18 June 1908, p. 4; *Rahnema*, 18 August, 1907, p. 8; the complex hybridity of nationalist discourses is carefully analysed in Tavakoli-Targhi,

Refashioning Iran, chs 6, 7; and Kashani-Sabet, *Frontier Fictions*, ch. 4; Kermani, *Bidari*, vol. 1, p. 364, records the first instance of popular hailing of the 'nation' without reference to the Shah or Islam.

29. See the cartoons in Kashani-Sabet, *Frontier Fictions*, pp. 136, 138; and Afari, *Constitutional Revolution*, figs 6, 11; Najmabadi, *The Story of the Daughters of Quchan: Gender and National Memory in Iranian History*; and 'The erotic *vatan* as beloved and mother: to love, to possess, and to protect'; Tavakoli-Targhi, *Refashioning Iran*, ch. 7.

30. See, for example, the language of a leading opponent Shaikh Fazlallah Nuri accusing constitutionalists of encouraging prostitution (quoted in Bayat, *First Revolution*, p. 187) and attacking the establishment of girls' schools (Malikzadeh, *Tarikh i-inqilab i-mashrutiyat*, vol. 3, p. 182); on honour, gender and patriotism, see Bidari, vol. 1, pp. 610–11, vol. 2, pp. 224–6; see also de Groot '"Brothers of the Iranian race": manhood, nationhood and modernity in Iran 1870–1914'.

31. See Afary, *Constitutional Revolution*, ch. 7; Najmabadi, '*Zanha yi millat*: women or wives of the nation?'; Tavakoli-Targhi, *Refashioning Iran*, chs 7, 8.

32. See Kashani-Sabet, *Frontier Fictions*, pp. 157–79; Katouzian, *State and Society in Iran: The Eclipse of the Qajars and the Rise of the Pahlavis*, chs 9, 10.

33. Kashani-Sabet, *Frontier Fictions*, pp. 144–57.

34. *Nahid*, no. 2, 19 April 1921, p. 1, quoted *loc. cit.*, p. 157; Reza Khan's statement is in Bourne andCameron Watt (eds), *British Documents on Foreign Affairs: Reports and Papers from Foreign Office Confidential Prints*, vol. 13, p. 378.

35. See Rejali, *Torture and Modernity in Iran: Self, Society, and State in Modern Iran*, ch. 4, and on Reza Pahlavi, pp. 52–3, 54–5, 57–60, and figures on pp. 188–9; Menashri, *Education and the Making of Modern Iran*, pp. 93–8; Mathee, 'Transforming dangerous nomads into use-ful artisans, technicians, agriculturalists: education in the Reza Shah period'.

36. See Chapter 4.

37. See Ghods, 'Iranian nationalism and Reza Shah'; and 'Government and society in Iran 1926–34'; Kashani-Sabet, *Frontier Fictions*, ch. 6; Katouzian, *State and Society*, pp. 324–8.

38. See Mathee, 'Transforming dangerous nomads'; Abrahamian, *Iran between Two Revolutions*, pp. 140–1, 152–3.

39. Akhavi, *Religion and Politics in Contemporary Iran*, p. 58, quoting a Russian account.

40. See *op. cit.*, pp. 28–31; Cronin, *The Army and the Creation of the Pahlavi State in Iran, 1910–26*, pp. 157–67; Martin, 'Mudarris, republicanism, and the rise to power of Reza Shah'; Faghfoory, 'The 'ulama–state relations in Iran 1921–41', pp. 425–6.

41. While there were twenty-four *'ulama* in the fifth Majlis (1924–25), by the tenth and eleventh in the 1930s there were ten and none respectively.

42. See Fischer, *Iran*, pp. 97–9, 186; Chehabi, 'Staging the emperor's new clothes: dress codes and nation building under Reza Shah'; a nuanced reading of the conflicts over dress code is in Amin, *The Making of the Modern Iranian Woman: Gender, State Policy and Popular Culture 1865–1946*, ch. 4.

43. Akhavi, *Religion and Politics*, p. 44.

44. On Mudarris, see Martin, 'Mudarris, republicanism and the rise to power of Riza Khan'; Chehabi, *Iranian Politics and Religious Modernism: The Liberation Movement of Iran under the Shah and Khomeini*, pp. 45–6; on Kashani, see Richard, 'Ayatollah Kashani: precursor of the Islamic Republic?'; Abrahamian, *Iran*, p. 234, n. 20.

45. Momen, *An Introduction to Shi'i Islam*, p. 251; Fischer, *Iran from Religious Dispute*, pp. 276–7; Richard, 'Shari'at-Sangalaji: a reformist theologian of the Reza Shah period'.

46. The date of publication of this

275

work is variously given as 1941 to 1945 and is uncertain; see Martin, *Creating an Islamic state: Khomeini and the Making of a New Iran*, p. 217, n. 10.

47. Richard, 'Shari'at-Sangalaji', pp. 160–1; Fischer, *Iran from Religious Dispute*, p. 85.

48. Rahnema, *An Islamic Utopian: A Political Biography of 'Ali Shari'ati*, pp. 10, 47; Chehabi, *Iranian Politics and Religious Modernism*, pp. 104–5.

49. Kashani-Sabet, *Frontier Fictions*, pp. 195–202.

50. *Op. cit.*, pp. 186–95; Najmabadi, 'Crafting an educated housewife in Iran'; Amin, *Making of the Modern Iranian Woman*, chs 3–6.

51. This is most interestingly argued in Najmabadi, *Women with Mustaches and Men without Beards: Gender and Sexual Anxieties of Iranian Modernity*.

52. See Chapter 4 and Chapter 6; Elwell-Sutton, 'The Iranian press 1941–47'.

53. See Abrahamian, *Iran*, chs 6, 7 and 'The strengths and weaknesses of the labour movement in Iran 1941–53'; an example is given in Ansari, *Modern Iran since 1921: The Pahlavis and After*, p. 77, quoting Iranian correspondence with the British Embassy on the radicalisation of rural Iranians, and pp. 79–80 and 90 on similar developments in Azerbaijan, referring to the local leftist press.

54. On 'negative equilibrium' (the policy of offering no concessions to either of the major powers pressuring Iran), see Katouzian, *Musaddiq and the Struggle for Power in Iran*, pp. 56–8; Diba, *Mossadegh: A Political Biography*, pp. 84–5, quoting Mussadeq's collected speeches.

55. See Taleqani, 'Introduction' to the 1955 edition of the pro-constitutional *mujtahed*; Mirza Muhammad Husein Na'ini's 1909 *Tanbeh al-ummah wa tanzeh al-millah*, pp. 4–6; Chehabi, *Iranian Politics*, pp. 55–6, 58, 117–24.

56. Chehabi, *Iranian Politics*, p. 124.

57. Rahnema, *Islamic Utopian*, pp. 6–10.

58. On the Feda'iyan-i-Islam, see Kazemi, 'The Fada'iyan e-Islam: fanaticism, politics and terror'; and 'State and society in the ideology of the Devotees of Islam'.

59. Richard, 'Ayatollah Kashani'; Abrahamian, *Iran*, pp. 234, 248, 265–6.

60. Quoted in Akhavi, 'The role of the clergy in Iranian politics 1949–53', p. 102; see also Abrahamian, *Iran*, pp. 265–6.

61. Ghods, *Iran in the Twentieth Century*, p. 172; Ansari, *Modern Iran*, p. 91 and n. 72.

62. Taken from a speech of Mussadeq at his trial, in *Mussadeq dar mahkameh yi nizami*, vol. 2, book 1, p. 418; Abrahamian, *Iran*, p. 282.

63. Chehabi, *Iranian Politics*, p. 158, quoting 'How the Liberation Movement of Iran was founded' in *Documents from the Liberation Movement of Iran*, vol. 1, pp. 17–18.

64. Abrahamian, 'History used and abused' in his *Khomeinism: Essays on the Islamic Republic*, pp. 104–10; Rajaee, 'Islam, nationalism, and Musaddiq's era: post-revolutionary historiography in Iran'.

65. See Rahnema, *Islamic Utopian*, ch. 9, pp. 231, 251; Abrahamian, *Radical Islam: The Iranian Mojahedin*, ch. 4.

66. See Borujerdi, *Iranian Intellectuals and the West: The Tormented Triumph of Nativism*; Mirsepassi, *Intellectual Discourse and the Politics of Modernization: Negotiating Modernity in Iran*; Gheissari, *Iranian Intellectuals in the Twentieth Century*, ch. 5.

67. See Bauer, 'Poor women and social consciousness in revolutionary Iran'.

68. Recorded in Vieille and Khosrokhavar, *Le discours populaire de la revolution iranienne*, vol. 2, 'Interviews', pp. 108, 174.

69. See Rahnema, *Islamic Utopian*, chs 2, 3, 5–9.

70. Ibid., p. 258, quoting a meditation on Ashura written by Shari'ati in 1971 from his *Collected Works*, vol. 19, pp. 3–13.

71. Quoted in *Yad-nameh yi-shahid i-javid 'Ali Shari'ati*, pp. 77–80.

72. Compare and contrast Akhavi, *Religion and Politics*, pp. 143–58, and 'Shari'ati's social thought', in Keddie (ed.), *Religion and Politics in Iran*; Rahnema, *Islamic Utopian*, chs 11, 12, 19–21; Abrahamian, *Radical Islam*, ch. 4; Boorujerdi, *Iranian Intellectuals*, pp. 105–15; Mirsepassi, *Intellectual Discourse*, pp. 114–27; Bayat, 'Shi'ism in contemporary politics: the case of 'Ali Shari'ati'; Fischer, *Iran*, pp. 165–70.

73. Hegland, 'Two images of Husein: accommodation and revolution in an Iranian village' looks at specific political shifts in 1978–79; a general context is suggested in the testimonies in Loeffler, *Islam in Practice*, pp. 42, 98–9, 108–9, 159–60, 171–2 and counter views on pp. 75 and 82.

74. Khomeini, 'Islamic government', p. 31 and his Muharram declaration of November 1978, pp. 242–5: Mojahedin, *Nazhat-Huseini*; Vieille and Khosrokhavar, *Discours populaire*, vol. 2, pp. 132–3; conversations with the author, Tehran, Bam, 1978.

75. Hegland, 'Two images'; Sreberny-Mohammadi and Mohammadi, *Small Media, Big Revolution: Communication, Culture and the Iranian Revolution*, pp. 119–21, Hooglund, *Land and Revolution in Iran 1960–80*, pp. 142–8; Vieille and Khosrokhavar, *Discours populaire*, vol. 2, p. 81.

76. Vieille and Khosrokhavar, *Discours populaire*, vol. 2, pp. 223, 279, 283; Abrahamian, *Khomeinism*, pp. 26–32, 47–9.

77. Vieille and Khosrokhavar, vol. 2, pp. 47, 72, 81, 311, 319.

78. Ibid., pp. 350–1, 354–5; on generational issues, see Khosrokhavar, *Anthropologie de la révolution iranienne: le rêve impossible*, pp. 91–100, 239–48.

79. Goodell, *The Elementary Structures of Political Life: Rural Development in Pahlavi Iran*, p. 73 shows rural Khuzestanis judging Khomeini a demagogue, matched by their indifference to the notion that they were part of a 'nation', seeing themselves rather as members of their village *mamlekat* (p. 118); Friedl, 'State ideology and village women', charts the distance between villagers' understanding of what it might be to be 'a Muslim' and that of the supporters and agents of the Islamic Republic.

80. A term coined by James Bill in his article 'The plasticity of informal politics: the case of Iran'.

6 A story of movements and struggles

1. Dadkah, 'Lebas i-taqva: an early twentieth century treatise on the economy'; Bayat, *Iran's First Revolution*, pp. 89–90; there is evidence of merchant interest in and support for critical reformist journals like *Habl al-matin* and *Qanun* published abroad in the 1890s.

2. See Cole, *Modernity and the Millennium: The Genesis of the Baha'i Faith in the Nineteenth Century Middle East*, ch. 3; and 'Iranian millenarianism and democratic thought in the nineteenth century'; the role of religious dissidents is most fully argued in Bayat, *First Revolution*, ch. 3 – she notes how records and studies of leading activists like Yahya Doulatabadi and Jamal al-din Va'ez have obscured their dissident and Babi connections.

3. See Afary, *The Iranian Constitutional Revolution*, ch. 7; Bayat, 'Women and revolution in Iran'; Najmabadi, '*Zanha yi millat*: women or wives of the nation'; Sanasarian, *The Women's Rights Movement in Iran: Mutiny, Appeasement, and Repression from 1900 to Khomeini*, ch. 2; Paidar, *Women and the Political Process in Twentieth Century Iran*, ch. 2; Nateq, 'Negah be barkhi yi-neveshteh-ha va mubarezat i-zan dar doureh yi-mashrutiyat'.

4. See, for example, Rendall, *Origins of Modern Feminism*; and 'Introduction' and ch. 4 art in Rendall (ed.), *Equal or Different*; Yellin, *Sisters and Citizens*; Gleadle, *Early Feminists: Radical Unitarians and the Emergence of the Women's Rights*

Movement; Moses, *French Feminism in the Nineteenth Century*.

5. *Musavat*, 22 March 1908, pp. 5–6, quoted in Afary, *Constitutional Revolution*, p. 190; Mu'ali is quoted in Bamdad, *From Darkness*, pp. 48–9.

6. See Najmabadi, 'Zan-ha'; and *The Story of the Daughters of Quchan: Gender and National Memory in Iranian History*, ch. 6; and 'The erotic *vatan* (homeland) as beloved and mother: to love, possess, and protect'; de Groot '"Brothers of the Iranian race": manhood, nationhood and modernity in Iran c. 1870–1914'; and 'The dialectics of gender: men, women and political discourses in Iran c. 1890–1930'; Amin, *The Making of the Modern Iranian Woman: Gender, State Policy, and Popular Culture*, pp. 25–40; Nateq, 'Masaleh yi zan az mudavenat i-chap az nezhat i-mashrtiyat ta asr i-Reza Khan'.

7. Kermani, *Bidari*, vol. 1, p. 539, vol. 2, pp. 92–3; Kasravi, *Mashruteh*, vol. 1, pp. 180–2, 354–5, vol. 2, pp. 646; Browne, *Persian Revolution*, pp. 131–2.

8. See Foran, 'The strengths and weaknesses of Iran's populist alliance: a class analysis of the constitutional revolution of 1905–11'; Abrahamian, 'The crowd in the Persian revolution; Afary, *Constitutional Revolution*, pp. 39, 78–88, 98–104, 220–4, draws attention to conflicts between more or less radical or privileged groups in the 'hybrid coalition of constitutionalists' (p. 88); Bayat, *First Revolution*, pp. 123–53, 161–74, 178–83, 192–204, 210–31, illustrates networks of personal contact and rivalry which shaped political initiatives and mobilisations; work by Heidi Walcher on Isfahan and Joanna de Groot on Kerman give local perspectives.

9. 'The first attack on the press', *Iran i-no*, no. 216, 28 May 1910, p. 1.

10. Nateq quoted in Afary, *Constitutional Revolution*, p. 170; the view of an official surfaces in Mostowfi, *The Administrative and Social History of the Qajar Period (The Story of My Life)*, vol. 2, pp. 456–8, 461.

11. Poem quoted in Najmabadi, *Daughters of Quchan*, pp. 76–7; *Majlis*, vol. 1, no. 62, 30 March 1907, p. 4.

12. Noted by Browne's informant, *The Persian Revolution*, p. 143, the constitutionalist journal *Musavat*, no. 16, 3 March 1908, p. 6, and in reports from villages quoted in Afary, *Constitutional Revolution*, p. 152.

13. See Chapter 4.

14. Martin, *Islam and Modernism: The Iranian Revolution of 1906*, chs 5, 7; Arjomand, 'The *ulama*'s traditionalist opposition to parliamentarism 1907–9'; on Nuri's use of *bast* and of his established networks and authority among *tullab*, elite contacts, and fellow *'ulama* alongside newer tactics of pamphleteering and leafleting see Bayat, *First Revolution*, pp. 98–105, 148–53, 220–2, 236–43; see Afary, *Constitutional Revolution*, ch. 8, and pp. 73–88, 99–103, 237–48, 264–82; and 'Social democracy and the Iranian constitutional revolution of 1906–11'; Chaqueri, *The Origins of Social Democracy in Modern Iran*, chs 4–7 on the development of various party and protest activities.

15. See Martin, *Islam and Modernism*, ch. 3; Hairi, *Shi'ism and Constitutionalism in Iran*, ch. 2; and Bayat, *First Revolution*, ch. 3, and pp. 254–8, 263–6 on 'modern', 'reforming' and dissident trends among *'ulama* and those with religious education.

16. Sattar Khan's comment is given in the report of a French officer based in Tabriz in 1908, printed in Chaqueri (ed.), *La social-democratie en Iran: articles et documents*, p. 112; Taherzadeh-Behzad (a participant in the struggles in Tabriz), *Qiyam i-Azerbaijan dar Enqelab i-mashrutiyat i-Iran*, pp. 177–80, 216–18, 442–8; Browne, *Persian Revolution*, pp. 249–50, 269–70, 441–2 (the last quoting a critical assessment by a British source); see also Afary, *Constitutional Revolution*, pp. 214–21, 291–2, 299–301.

17. Adamiyat, *Fekr i-demokrasi yi-ejtema' dar nezhat i-mashrutiyat i-Iran*,

pp. 3–4; Tavakoli-Targhi, 'Athar agahi az enqelab i-franseh dar shekl-giri yi-engareh yi mashrutiyat dar Iran'; and 'Refashioning Iran: language and culture during the constitutional revolution'.

18. See the programmes of the Mujahedin, Social Democrat and Hemmat parties reproduced in Chaqueri, 'Social Democracy', pp. 125–6, 129–32, 159–60; on social democratic activity and ideas generally, see Afary, 'Social Democracy'; and *Constitutional Revolution*, pp. 81–7, 126–31, 264–71.

19. Kerman consular diary FO248, vol. 906, diary for 13–19 September 1907; vol. 1030, diary for 10–30 July 1911; vol. 1072, diaries for 17 April, 7–14 April, 19–26 May 1913, and *The Times*, 19 July 1910, p. 7 on labour issues; more generally, see Floor, *Labour Unions, Law and Conditions in Iran, 1900–1941*, pp. 4–11; Chaqueri, *Origins of Social Democracy*, pp. 90–5.

20. See *Revue du monde musulman*, February 1910, p. 319 (social democrats welcoming *mullas* as allies and describing themselves as 'defenders of Islam'); Chaqueri, *Documents*, p. 129 (reference to Sa'adi), *Iran–no*, 15 January 1911 (in *op. cit.*, pp. 136–7) for use of religious formulas.

21. Browne, *Persian Revolution*, pp. 119–20, 164; Kasravi, *Tarikh i-Mashruteh*, vol. 1, p. 158; Kermani, *Bidari*, vol. 2, p. 171.

22. See Bayat, *First Revolution*, pp. 152, 173, 179, 209–10, 237, 239–40, 249; Afary, *Constitutional Revolution*, pp. 81, 97.

23. Nazem al-Islam, *Bidari*, vol. 2, pp. 154–8; Kasravi, *Tarikh i-Mashruteh*, vol. 2, pp. 587–9.

24. See Taherzadeh-Behzad, *Qiyam i-Azerbaijan*; Kerman consular diaries FO248, vol. 906, diaries for 13–19 September 1907, 15–28 November 1907, 5–12 December 1907; vol. 938, diaries for 12–20 February 1908, 17–23 April 1908; vol. 969, telegrams 10 March, 16 April, 1909; com-

parable divisions among Isfahan merchants are noted in Doulatabadi, *Hayat i-Yahya*, vol. 2, pp. 213–17.

25. Katouzian, *The Political Economy of Modern Iran 1926–1979*, p. 98, n. 17, quotes two speeches of Mudarris of 1921 and 1923 in the former of which he said, 'Muslim Iran must be Muslim and Iranian', and in the latter, 'Our religious practice is our very politics, and our politics are our very religious practice'.

26. See Afshari, 'The historians of the constitutional movement and the making of the Iranian popular tradition'; Najmabadi, *Daughters of Quchan*, ch. 9; Afary, *Constitutional Revolution*, pp. 341–2; Bayat, *First Revolution*, pp. 3–10; Foran, *Fragile Resistance*, pp. 170, 194; and 'The strengths and weaknesses of Iran's populist alliance', for views of the historiography.

27. See Abrahamian, *Iran between Two Revolutions*, pp. 117–35; Katouzian, 'Reza Shah's political legitimacy and social base'; Zirinsky, 'The rise of Reza Khan'.

28. Abrahamian, *Iran between Two Revolutions*, p. 329.

29. See Chapter 4.

30. See Gheissari, *Iranian Intellectuals in the Twentieth Century*, pp. 45–52, 61–71; Abrahamian, *Iran between Two Revolutions*, pp. 153–62, 330–6, 339–47; Ramazani, 'Intellectual trends in the politics and history of the Mussadiq era'.

31. See Chapter 4.

32. Katouzian, *Political Economy*, pp. 182–3; Ferrier, 'The Iranian oil industry', p. 690, based on oil company sources.

33. See Table in ibid., pp. 693–4.

34. Zirinsky, 'The Rise of Reza Shah'; and 'Imperial power and dictatorship: Britain and the rise of Reza Shah 1921–26'; Ghani, *Iran and the Rise of Reza Shah: From Qajar Collapse to Pahlavi Power*, chs 6, 7, 12–14.

35. Bill, *The Eagle and the Lion: The Tragedy of American–Iranian Relations*, chs 1, 2; Lytle, *The Origins of the Iranian–American Alliance, 1941–53*; and Goode, *The United States and Iran 1941–51: the*

Diplomacy of Neglect; Heiss, *Empire and Nationhood: The United States, Great Britain, and Iranian Oil*, ch. 1; Kuniholm, *The Origins of the Cold War in the Near East: Great Power Diplomacy in Iran, Turkey, and Greece*.

36. Louis, *The British Empire in the Middle East: Arab Nationalism, the United States, and Postwar Imperialism*; McBeth, *British Oil Policy 1919–39*; Bamberg, *The History of the British Petroleum Company*, vol. 2, *The Anglo-Iranian Years*.

37. Azimi, *Iran: The Crisis of Democracy*, p. 87; Abrahamian, *Iran between Two Revolutions*, pp. 172, 178–81, 186–7, 195–8, 304; and, for a different view, Azimi, 'On shaky ground: concerning the absence or weakness of political parties in Iran'.

38. Figures from Menashri, *Education and the Making of Modern Iran*, pp. 96, 121.

39. Abrahamian, *Iran between Two Revolutions*, chs 6–8.

40. A term used by Azimi, see *Iran: The Crisis of Democracy*, p. 26.

41. Katouzian, *Mussadiq and the Struggle for Power in Iran*, p. 274, n. 10, argues that the latter is a more expressive translation of the term *muvazaneh yi-manfi* used to describe a policy of avoiding or rejecting making concessions to powerful outsiders which Mussadeq and others opposed to conventional (and unsuccessful) policies of playing one foreign power off against another. Katouzian takes the origin of this approach back to critiques by Sayyid Hasan Mudarris in the 1920s (p. 56).

42. Speech by Jamal Emami, recorded in the *Majlis Proceedings*, 3 November 1951, quoted in Abrahamian, *Iran between Two Revolutions*, pp. 267–8.

43. See Akhavi, *Religion and Politics in Contemporary Iran: Clergy–State Relations in the Pahlavi Period*, chs 2, 3; and 'The role of the clergy in Iranian politics 1949–54'; Faghfoory, 'The *'ulama*–state relations in Iran 1921–41'; Yazdi, 'Patterns

of clerical political behaviour on postwar Iran, 1941–53'.

44. Akhavi, 'Role of the clergy', pp. 93, 95, 103, quoting the newspaper *Ittil'at* 13 February, 8, 14, 17, 18 March, 8 April 1951, 29 December 1952 and *Religion and Politics*, p. 63, quoting *Ittil'at*, 5 January 1953; Yazdi, 'Clerical political behaviour', pp. 286, 287.

45. Abrahamian, *Iran between Two Revolutions*, pp. 259–60.

46. On Bazargan in the 1940s, see Chehabi, *Iranian Politics and Religious Modernism: The Liberation Movement of Iran under the Shah and Khomeini*, pp. 117–26; on Muhammad Taqi Shari'ati and the God-worshipping socialists, see ibid., pp. 113–14, 120, 127, 129–30; and Rahnema, *An Islamic Utopian: A Political Biography of 'Ali Shari'ati*, pp. 13–34.

47. Abrahamian, *Iran between Two Revolutions*, p. 174.

48. See Kazemi, 'The *Fada'iyan i-Islam*: fanaticism, politics and terror'; Chehabi, *Religious Modernism*, pp. 115–17, 126–7; Yazdi, 'Clerical political behaviour', pp. 294–9.

49. See Foran, *Fragile Resistance*, pp. 286–7, 298–9; Abrahamian, *Iran between Two Revolutions*, pp. 259–60, 276–8; Katouzian, *Mussadiq*, pp. 256–61, and *Political Economy*, ch. 9.

50. As eloquently delineated in Azimi, 'Unseating Mossadeq', and Gasiorowski, 'Why did Mossadeq fall?'.

51. See Chapter 1.

52. Goodell, *The Elementary Structures of Political Life*; Kazemi, *Poverty and Revolution in Iran: The Migrant Poor, Urban Marginality, and Politics*; Friedl, *Women of Deh Koh*; Beck, 'Economic transformations among the Qashqai nomads'.

53. Parsa, 'Mosque of last resort: state reform and social change in the early 1960s'.

54. Loeffler, *Islam in Practice*; Bayat, *Street Politics: Poor People's Movements in Iran*; Hegland, '"Traditional" Iranian

women: how they cope'; interview with 'Mansur', October 1979, in Vieille and Khosrokhavar, *Le discours populaire de la révolution Iranienne*, vol. 2, p. 186.

55. Interview with 'Mammade' (September 1979), 'Abu'lfazl' (October 1979), Isfahani factory workers (October 1979), 'Asghar' (February 1980), Darya factory workers (February 1979), Qazvin workers (October 1979), in *Discours populaire*, vol. 2, pp. 10–11, 22–4, 74–5, 132–3, 154–5, 281.

56. Menashri, *Education*, pp. 206, 216–17.

57. Squatter youth interviewed and quoted in Kazemi, *Poverty and Revolution*, pp. 129–30.

58. Halliday, *Iran: Dictatorship and Development*, pp. 206–8; Jalil, *Workers Say No to the Shah*, pp. 75–82.

59. Compare Bayat, *Workers and Revolution in Iran*, pp. 85–94; Foran, *Fragile Resistance*, p. 387; Abrahamian, *Iran between Two Revolutions*, pp. 510–13; and Moghadam, 'Industrial development, culture and working class politics, a case study of Tabriz'.

60. Bayat, *Workers and Revolution*, pp. 50–1.

61. Interview with 'Asghar', in Vieille and Khosokhavar, *Discours populaire*, vol. 2, pp. 281–3.

62. Sadri and Sadri, '*The Mantle of the Prophet*: a critical postscript', p. 145.

63. Interviews with Isfahani workers, Qazvin workers and Tehran van-driver, in Vieille and Khosrokhavar, *Discours populaire*, vol. 2, pp. 72, 132, 154, 158, 162.

64. Interview with factory workers near Isfahan and with 'Mammade' (Tehrani worker), in *op. cit.*, pp. 11, 16, 17, 23–4, 30.

65. See interviews with 'Taghi' (Hamadan), 'Eskander' and 'Ghaffar' (Qazvin), 'Asghar' (Tehrani electrician), in *op. cit.*, pp. 153–4, 223, 284.

66. Abrahamian, *Iran between Two Revolutions*, pp. 435–49, 530–7; Chehabi, *Iranian Politics and Religious Modernism: The Liberation Movement of Iran under*

the Shah and Khomeini, ch. 1; Skocpol, 'Rentier state and Shi'a Islam in the Iranian Revolution'; Parsa, *Social Origins of the Iranian Revolution*, ch. 1, p 10; Arjomand, *The Turban for the Crown: The Islamic Revolution in Iran*, ch. 10; Foran, *Fragile Resistance*, pp. 358–64, 367–77, 384–97; Moghadam, 'Populist revolution and the Islamic state in Iran'.

67. Interview, October 1979, in Vieille and Khosrokhavar, *Discours populaire*, vol. 2, pp. 155–7; Hegland, 'Two images of Husain: accommodation and revolution in an Iranian village'.

68. Sreberny-Mohammadi and Mohammadi, *Small Media*, p. 156 and fig. 9.6; interview with Isfahani workers, October 1979, in Vieille and Khosrokhavar, *Discours populaire*, vol. 2, p. 83; the wearing of *kaffans* in the 1906 protests is noted in Malikzadeh, *Tarikh i-enqelab i-mashrutiyat i-Iran* (ed. Tehran), vol. 2, pp. 364–6.

69. Hegland 'Aliabad women', pp. 180–1; the woman is quoted on p. 185.

70. Foran, *Fragile Resistance*, p. 380.

71. Hegland, 'Aliabad women', pp. 182–3; and 'Two images of Husein', p. 229; 'Ghaffar' (Qazvin worker), quoted in Vieille and Khosrokhavar, *Discours populaire*, vol. 2, p. 151.

72. 'Abu'lfazl', quoted in Vieille and Khosrokhavar, *Discours populaire*, vol. 2, p. 108; interview with Isfahani steel-workers, *op. cit.*, pp. 78–82, and with 'Sakineh', pp. 350–1.

73. See Bakhash, *The Reign of the Ayatollahs: Iran and the Islamic Revolution*; Moaddel, 'Class struggles in post-revolutionary Iran'; Moghadam, 'Islamic populism, class and gender in post-revolutionary Iran'; Bayat, *Workers and Revolution*; Schirazi, *The Constitution of Iran: Politics and the State*.

74. A term applied to the Shah's reliance on a blend of fear and reward to bind key supporters to his increasingly personalised rule in Chehabi, *Iranian Politics*, pp. 17–18, 39 (drawing on a defini-

tion developed by the political theorist Juan Linz).

75. See Bill, *The Eagle and the Lion: The Tragedy of American–Iranian Relations*, pp. 226–60.

76. Foran, *Fragile Resistance*, pp. 394–5.

77. Parsa, *Social Origins*, pp. 110, 214; Fischer, *Iran from Religious Dispute to Revolution*, p. 208.

78. Parsa, *Social Origins*, pp. 160–1; interview with Isfahani workers, in Vieille and Khosrokhavar, *Discours populaire*, vol. 2, pp. 81–2 and with 'Taghi', pp. 226–7.

79. Leaflet reproduced in *Review of Iranian Political Economy and History*, vol. 2, no. 2 (June 1978), pp. 60–78.

80. See Abrahamian, *Khomeinism: Essays on the Islamic Republic*, pp. 26–7, 47–8; interviews with 'Taghi', 'Asghar', *pasdars*, in Vieille and Khosrokhavar, *Discours populaire*, vol. 2, pp. 224, 284, 313.

81. Vieille and Khosrokhavar, *Discours populaire*, vol. 2, pp. 99–100 (Isfahani workers), 189, 202 (office worker), 313 (*pasdars*), 346 (domestic servant).

82. Abrahamian, *Khomeinism*, pp. 27–30.

83. Rahnema, *Islamic Utopian*, pp. 105, 119, 126–7.

84. Hegland, 'Aliabad women', pp. 179–80, 185.

85. Interview reproduced in Vieille and Khosrokhavar, *Discours populaire*, pp. 354–5.

86. See above; Amin, *Making of the Modern Iranian Woman*; Najmabadi, *Women with Mustaches and Men without Beards: Gender and Sexual Anxieties of Iranian Modernity*, chs 5, 7, 8.

87. See Yeganeh and Keddie, 'Sexuality and Shi'i social protest in Iran'; Betteridge, 'To veil or not to veil: a matter of protest'.

88. Interestingly, Shari'ati's thought on women and veiling is not discussed in the otherwise full treatment of his life and thought in Rahnema, *Islamic Utopian*; Paidar, *Women and the Political Process in Twentieth Century Iran*, pp. 178–81, summarises key points; on Khomeini's views, see Algar, *Islam and Revolution: Writings and Declarations of Imam Khomeini*, pp. 171–2 (1940s), 222–3 (1978), 263–4 (1979), 273 (1979).

89. See, for example, Moghissi, *Feminism and Islamic Fundamentalism: The Limits of Post-modern Analysis*; Naghibi, 'Bad feminist or bad-hejab: moving outside the *hejab* debate'.

Bibliography

Archives

The National Archives (Public Record Office)
Foreign Office Records: FO60, FO248, FO371

Newspapers

Habl al-Matin, Iran i-no, Kaveh, Musavat, Nida yi-vatan, Qanun, Rahnema, Sur i-Esrafil

Published material

Abbott, K., 'Notes taken on a journey eastwards from Shiraz', *Journal of the Royal Geographical Society*, 1857

Abrahamian, E., *Khomeinism: Essays on the Islamic Republic*, California University Press, 1993

— *Radical Islam: The Iranian Mojahedin*, I.B.Tauris, 1989

— *Iran between Two Revolutions*, Princeton University Press, 1982

— 'The strengths and weaknesses of the labour movement in Iran 1941–53', in Bonine and Keddie (eds), *Continuity and Change in Modern Iran*, 1981

— 'Kasravi: the integrative nationalist of Iran', in Kedourie and Haim (eds), *Towards a Modern Iran*, 1980

— 'The crowd in the Persian revolution', *Iranian Studies*, 1969

Abu-Lughod, L. (ed.), *Remaking Women: Feminism and Modernity in the Middle East*, Princeton University Press, 1998

Adamiyat, F., *Shuresh bar imtiaz-nameh yi rezhi*, Payam, 1981

— *Fekr i-demokrasi yi-ejtema' dar nezhat i-mashrutiyat i-Iran*, Payam, 1976

— *Andisheh-ha yi taraqqi va hukumat i-qanun dar asr i-Sepah Salar*, Khwarazmi, 1972

— *Amir Kabir va Iran*, Khwarazmi, 1969

— *Andisheh-ha yi Mirza Aqa Kermani/ The ideas of Mirza Aqa Kermani*, Payam, 1967

Adamiyat, F. and H. Nateq (eds), *Afkhar i-ijtema'i va siyasi dar athar i-muntasher-nashodeh yi-dauran i-Qajar*, Agah, 1977

Afary, J., *The Iranian Constitutional Revolution 1906–11*, Columbia University Press, 1996

— 'Social democracy and the Iranian constitutional revolution of 1906–11', in Foran (ed.), *A Century of Revolution: Social Movements in Iran*, 1994

— 'Cartoons from the journal Mulla Nasreddin', *Nimeh yi-Digar*, 1993

— 'Peasant rebellions of the Caspian region during the Iranian constitutional revolution', *International Review of Middle East Studies*, 1991

— 'On the origins of feminism in early twentieth century Iran', *Journal of Women's History*, 1989

Afshari, R., 'The historians of the constitutional movement and the making of the Iranian popular tradition', *International Journal of Middle East Studies*, 1993

Aghaie, K., *The Martyrs of Karbala*, Washington University Press, 2004

Agulhon, M., *Marianne into Battle*, Cambridge University Press, 1981

Akhavi, S., 'The role of the clergy in Iranian politics 1949–54', in Bill and Louis (eds), *Musaddiq, Iranian Nationalism and Oil*, 1988

— 'Shari'ati's social thought', in Keddie (ed.), *Religion and Politics in Iran*, 1983

— *Religion and Politics in Contemporary Iran*, State University of New York Press, 1980

Akhundzadeh, F., *Maktubat i-Mirza Fath' Ali Akhundzadeh* (ed. M. Sobhdam), Mard i-Emruz, 1985

Algar, H., 'Amir Kabir', in *Encyclopaedia Iranica*, Routledge/Mazda 1982–

— *Mirza Malkom Khan: A Biographical Study in Iranian Modernism*, California University Press, 1973

— 'The oppositional role of the *'ulama* in twentieth century Iran', in Keddie (ed.), *Scholars, Saints and Sufis*, 1972

— *Religion and the State in Iran 1785–1906: The Role of the 'Ulama in the Qajar Period*, California University Press, 1969

— 'The revolt of the Aqa Khan Mahallati', *Studia Islamica*, 1969

Amanat, A., 'Introduction', in *Crowning Anguish: Memoirs of a Persian Princess from the Harem to Modernity*, Mage Press, 1999

— *Pivot of the Universe: Nasir al-din Qajar and the Iranian Monarchy 1831–96*, I.B.Tauris, 1997

— 'The downfall of Mirza Taqi Khan Amir Kabir and the problem of ministerial authority in Iran', *International Journal of Middle East Studies*, 1991

— *Resurrection and Renewal: The Making of the Babi Movement in Iran 1844–1850*, Cornell University Press, 1989

— 'Between the *madrasa* and the marketplace: the designation of clerical leadership in modern Shi'ism', in Arjomand (ed.), *Authority and Political Culture in Shi'ism*, SUNY Press, 1988

— (ed.), *Cities and Trade: Consul Abbott on the Economy and Society of Iran 1847–1866*, Ithaca Press, 1983

Amin, C., *The Making of the Modern Iranian Woman: Gender, State Policy and Popular Culture 1865–1946*, Florida University Press, 2002

Ansari, A., *Modern Iran since 1921: The Pahlavis and After*, Longman, 2003

Arjomand, S., *The Turban for the Crown: The Islamic Revolution in Iran*, Oxford University Press, 1988

— (ed.), *Authority and Political Culture in Shi'ism*, State University of New York Press, 1988

— *The Shadow of God and the Hidden Imam: Religion, Political Order, and Societal Change in Shi'ite Islam from the Beginning to 1890*, Chicago University Press, 1984

— 'Traditionalism in twentieth-century Iran', in Arjomand (ed.), *From Nationalism to Revolutionary Islam*, 1984

— (ed.), *From Nationalism to Revolutionary Islam*, State University of New York Press, 1984

— 'The 'ulama's traditionalist opposition to parliamentarianism 1907–9', *Middle Eastern Studies*, 1981

Ashraf, A., 'The roots of emerging dual class relations in nineteenth century Iran', *Iranian Studies*, 1981

Ashraf, A. and H. Hekmat, 'Merchants and artisans in the developmental processes of nineteenth century Iran', in Udovitch (ed.), *The Islamic Middle East from 700–1900*, 1981

Atabaki, T., *Azerbaijan: Ethnicity and the Struggle for Power in Iran*, I.B.Tauris, 2000

Aubin, E., *La Perse d'aujourd'hui*, Colin, 1908

Aubin, J., 'La politique religieuse des Safavides', in Fahd (ed.), *Le shi'isme imamite*, Presses Universitaires de France, 1970

Avery, P. and J. Simmons, 'Persia on a cross of silver 1880–90', in Kedourie and Haim (eds), *Towards a Modern Iran*, F. Cass, 1980

Azimi, F., 'Unseating Mossadeq: the configuration and role of domestic forces', in Gasiorowski and Byrne (eds), *Muhammad Mossadeq and the 1953 Coup in Iran*, Syracuse University Press, 2004

— 'On shaky ground: concerning the absence or weakness of political parties in Iran', *Iranian Studies*, 1997–98

— *Iran: The Crisis of Democracy*, I.B.Tauris, 1989

Babayan, K., *Mystics, Monarchs, and Messiahs: Cultural Landscapes of Early Modern Iran*, Harvard University Press, 2002

— 'Sufis, dervishes and mullas', in Melville (ed.), *Safavid Persia*, 1996

— 'The Safavid synthesis: from Qizilbash Islam to Imamite Shi'ism', *Iranian Studies*, 1994

Bahadur, A. M. Khan, 'Some new notes on Babism', *Journal of the Royal Asiatic Society*, 1927

Baker, P., 'Politics of dress: the dress reform laws of 1920's/30's Iran', in Lindisfarne-Tapper and Ingham (eds), *Languages of Dress in the Middle East*, Curzon, 1997

Bakhash, S., *The Reign of the Ayatollahs: Iran and the Islamic Revolution*, Unwin, 1986

— *Iran: Monarchy, Bureaucracy And Reform under the Qajars*, Ithaca Press, 1978

Bakhtiari, Husein Quli Khan Ilkhani, 'Kitabcheh 1873–82', translated in Garthwaite, *Khans and Shahs*, 1983

Balaghi, S., 'Political culture in the Iranian revolution of 1906 and the cartoons of *Kashkul*', in F. Gocek (ed.), *Political Cartoons: Cultural Representations in the Middle East*, Markus Wiener, 1997

Bamberg, J., *History of the British Petroleum Company*, vol. 2: *The Anglo-Iranian Years 1928–54*, Cambridge University Press, 1994

Bamdad, B., *From Darkness into Light: Women's Emancipation in Iran* [1967], ed./trans. F. Bagley, Exposition Press, 1977

— 'La femme persane', *Revue du monde musulman*, 1910

Banani, A., *The Modernization of Iran 1921–41*, Stanford University Press, 1961, 1977

Bani-Sadr, A., *Vaz'iyat i-Iran va naq sh-i Mudarris*, Paris, 1977

Baron, B., *Egypt as a Woman*, California University Press, 2005

— 'The women's awakening in Egypt', *Gender in History*, 1994

— 'The construction of national honour in Egypt', *Gender and History*, 1993

Bastani-Parizi, M., *Paighambar-i-ozdan*, Nigah, 1967

Bauer, J., 'Poor women and social consciousness in revolutionary Iran', in Nashat (ed.), *Women and Revolution in Iran*, Westview Press

Bayat, A., *Street Politics: Poor People's Movements in Iran*, Columbia University Press, 1997

— *Workers and Revolution in Iran*, Zed Books, 1987

Bayat, M., *Iran's First Revolution: Shi'ism and the Constitutional Revolution of 1905–9*, Oxford University Press, 1991

— *Mysticism and Dissent: Socio-religious Thought in Qajar Iran*, Syracuse University Press, 1982

— 'Mirza Aqa Kermani', in Kedourie and Haim (eds), *Towards a Modern Iran*, 1980

— 'Shi'ism in contemporary politics: the case of 'Ali Shari'ati', in Kedourie and Haim (eds), *Towards a Modern Iran*, 1980

— 'Women and revolution in Iran', in Keddie and Beck (eds), *Women in the Muslim World*, Harvard University Press, 1978

— 'Mirza Aqa Khan Kermani', *Middle Eastern Studies*, 1974

Beck, L., *Nomad: A Year in the Life of a Qashqai Tribesman in Iran*, I.B.Tauris, 1991

— 'Economic transformations among Qashqai nomads 1962–78', in Bonine and Keddie (eds), *Continuity and Change in Modern Iran*, State University of New York Press, 1981

Beck, P. 'The Anglo-Persian dispute of 1932–3', *Journal of Contemporary History*, 1974

Beeman, W., *Language, Status, and Power in Iran*, Indiana University Press, 1986

Berard, V., *Les revolutions de la Perse*, Armand Colin, 1910

Berberian, H. *Armenians and the Constitutional Revolution of 1905–11*, Westview Press, 2001

Betteridge, A., 'To veil or not to veil: a matter of protest or policy', in Nashat (ed.), *Women and Revolution in Iran*, 1983

Bharier, J., *Economic Development in Iran*, Oxford University Press, 1971

Bill, J., *The Eagle and the Lion: The Tragedy of American–Iranian Relations*, Yale University Press, 1988

— 'The plasticity of informal politics: the case of Iran', *Middle East Journal*, 1973

Bill, J., and W. Louis (eds), *Mussadiq, Iranian Nationalism, and Oil*, Texas University Press, 1988

Bonine, M., 'Shops and shopkeepers: the dynamics of an Iranian provincial *bazar*', in Bonine and Keddie (eds), *Continuity and Change in Modern Iran*, State University of New York Press, 1981

— *Yazd and Its Hinterland*, Marburg, 1980

Bonine, M., and N. Keddie (eds), *Continuity and Change in Modern Iran*, State University of New York Press, 1981

Borujerdi, M., *Iranian Intellectuals and the West: The Tormented Triumph of Nativism*, Syracuse University Press, 1996

Bourne, K., and C. Watt (eds), *British Documents on Foreign Affairs: Reports and Papers from the Foreign Office Confidential Prints; Persia I: The Anglo-Persian Agreement*, University Publications of America, 1984

Browne, E. G., *The Press and Poetry of Modern Persia* [1914], Kalimat Press, 1983

— *The Persian Revolution*, Cambridge University Press, 1910

— *A Year among the Persians*, A. and C. Black, 1893

Brugsch, H., *Reise der Konigliche Preussischen Gesandschaft nach Persien 1860–1861*, Leipzig, 1862–63

Busse, H., 'Abbas Mirza', in *Encyclopaedia Iranica*, vol. 1, Routledge/Mazda, 1985

Calmard, J., 'Shi'i rituals and power: II', in C. Melville (ed.), *Safavid Persia: The History and Politics of an Islamic Society*, I. B. Tauris, 1996

— 'Les rituels Shiites et le pouvoir', in Calmard (ed.), *Etudes safavides*, Institut Français de Recherche en Iran, 1993

— 'Muharram ceremonies and diplomacy', in E. Bosworth and C. Hillenbrand (eds), *Qajar Iran*, Edinburgh University Press, 1983

— 'Le mecenat des representations de *ta'ziyeh*', 1 and 2, *Le monde Iranien et l'Islam*, 1974, 1976–7

Chaqueri, C. (ed.), *Origins of Social Democracy in Iran*, University of Washington Press, 2001

— *La social-democratie en Iran: articles et documents*, Edition Mazdak, 1979

Chehabi, H., 'The banning of the veil and its consequences', in Cronin (ed.), *The Making of Modern Iran*, 2003

— 'Staging the emperor's new clothes: dress codes and nation building under Reza Shah', *Iranian Studies*, 1993

— *Iranian Politics and Religious Modernism: The Liberation Movement of Iran under the Shah and Khomeini*, I.B. Tauris, 1990

Chelkowski, P., (ed.), *Ta'ziyeh: Ritual and Drama in Iran*, New York University Press, 1979

Clark, A., *The Struggle for the Breeches*, University of California Press, 1995

Clarke, J., *The Iranian City of Shiraz*, Durham University, 1963

Clarke, J., and B. Clark, *Kermanshah: An Iranian Provincial City*, Durham University, 1969

Cole, J., *Modernity and the Millennium: The Genesis of the Bahai Faith in the Nineteenth-century Middle East*, Columbia University Press, 1998

— 'Iranian millenarianism and democratic thought in the nineteenth century', *International Journal of Middle East Studies*, 1992

— 'Ideology, ethics, and discourse in eighteenth century Iran', *Iranian Studies*, 1989

— 'Shi'i clerics in Iraq and Iran 1722–80: the Akhbari–Usuli conflict reconsidered', *Iranian Studies*, 1985

— 'Imami jurisprudence and the role of the *'ulama*: Morteza Ansari on imitating the supreme exemplar', in Keddie (ed.), *Religion and Politics in Iran*, Yale University Press, 1983

Cronin, S., 'Riza Shah and the disintegration of Bakhtiari power 1921–34', in Cronin (ed.), *The Making of Modern Iran*, 2003

— *The Making of Modern Iran: State and Society under Riza Shah, 1921–41*, Routledge/Curzon, 2003

— 'Conscription and popular resistance in Iran 1925–41', *International Review of Social History*, 1998

— 'The Pahlavi regime in Iran', in Chehabi and Linz (eds), *Sultanistic Regimes*, Johns Hopkins University Press, 1998

— *The Army and the Creation of the Pahlavi State in Iran*, Tauris Academic, 1997

Dabashi, H., review of W. Beeman, *Language, Status and Power in Iran*, *Iranian Studies*, 1988

Dadkhah, K., '*Lebas-i-taqva*: an early twentieth century [sic] treatise on the economy', *Middle Eastern Studies*, 1992

Davidoff, L., 'Class and gender in Victorian England: the case of Hannah Cullwick and Arthur Munby' [1979], reprinted in L. Davidoff, *Worlds Between: Historical Perspectives on Gender and Class*, Polity Press, 1995

Diba, F., *Mossadegh: A Political Biography*, Croom Helm, 1986

Diba, L., and M. Ekhtiar (eds), *Royal Persian Paintings*, I.B.Tauris, 1998

Documents from the Liberation Movement of Iran, Tehran, 1982

Donaldson, B., *The Wild Rue: A Study of Muhammedan Magic and Folklore in Iran*, Luzac, 1938

Doulatabadi, Y., *Hayat i-Yahya*, Ibn Sina, 1952

Douleh, Amin al-, *Khaterat i-Siasi*, ed. H. Farmanfarmayan, Amir Kabir, 1962, 1977

Douleh, Mustashar al-, *Yek kalameh* [1868–71], Tehran, 1982

Eastwick, E., *Journal of a Diplomat's Three Years' Residence in Persia*, Smith, Elder, 1864

Ehlers, E., and M. Momeni, 'Religiose Stiftungen und Stadtentwicklung das Beispiel Taft, ZentralIran', *Erdkunde*, 1989

Elwell-Sutton, L., 'The Iranian press 1941–47', *Middle East Journal*, 1968

Enayat, A., 'The problem of imperialism in nineteenth century Iran', *Ripeh*, 1977

English, P., *City and Village in Iran: Settlement and Economy in the Kirman Basin*, Wisconsin University Press, 1966

Faghfoory, M., 'Patterns of clerical behaviour in postwar Iran 1941–53', *Middle Eastern Studies*, 1990

— '*Ulama*–state relations in Iran 1921–41', *International Journal of Middle East Studies*, 1987

Fahd, T. (ed.), *Le shi'isme imamite*, Presses Universitaires de France, 1970

Farmanfarma, Firuz Mirza, *Safar-nameh yi-Kerman va Baluchestan* [1888], ed. M. Nezam-Mafi, Persian Book Co., 1963

Fasa'i, H., *History of Persia under Qajar Rule* (from the *Farsnameh yi-Nasiri*, 1887–88) trans./ed. H. Busse, Columbia University Press, 1972

— *Fars-Nameh yi-Fasa'i*, Amir Kabir, 1965

Fathi, A., 'The role of the "rebels" in the constitutional movement in Iran', *International Journal of Middle East Studies*, 1979

Ferrier, R., 'The Iranian oil industry', in P. Avery, G. Hambly and C. Melville (eds), *The Cambridge History of Iran*, Vol. 7, *From Nadir Shah to the Islamic*

Republic, Cambridge University Press, 1991

— *History of the British Petroleum Company,* vol. 1: *The Developing Years, 1901–32,* Cambridge University Press, 1982

Feuvrier, J., *Trois ans a la cour de Perse,* Juven, 1899

Fischer, M., *Iran: From Religious Dispute to Revolution,* Harvard University Press, 1980

Floor, W., *Labour Unions, Law, and Conditions in Iran 1900–1941,* Durham University (Centre for Middle Eastern and Islamic Studies Occasional Papers, no. 26), 1985

— *Industrialisation in Iran 1900–1941,* Durham University, 1984

— 'The revolutionary character of the *'ulama*: wishful thinking or reality?' in Keddie (ed.), *Religion and Politics in Iran,* Yale University Press, 1983

Floyer, E., *Unexplored Baluchistan,* Griffith and Farran, 1882

Foran, J. (ed.), *A Century of Revolution: Social Movements in Iran,* University of California Press, 1994

— *Fragile Resistance: Social Transformation in Iran from 1500 to the Revolution,* Westview Press, 1993

— 'The strengths and weaknesses of Iran's populist alliance: a class analysis of the Constitutional Revolution, 1905–11', *Theory and Society,* 1991

— 'The concept of dependence as a key to the political economy of Qajar Iran', *Iranian Studies,* 1989

Forbes-Leith, F., *Checkmate: Fighting Tradition in Central Persia,* Harrap, 1927

Fraser, J. B., *Narrative of Journey into Khorasan in the Years 1821 and 1822* [1825], reprint Oxford University Press (India), 1994

Friedl, E., *Children of Deh Koh,* Syracuse University Press, 1997

— 'The dynamics of women's spheres of action', in Keddie and Baron (eds), *Women in Middle Eastern History,* Yale University Press, 1991

— *Women of Deh Koh,* Smithsonian Institution Press, 1989

— 'State ideology and village women', in G. Nashat (ed.), *Women and Revolution in Iran,* Westview Press, 1983

— 'Women and the division of labour in an Iranian village', *MERIP Reports,* no. 95, 1981

Garthwaite, G., *Khans and Shahs: A Documentary Analysis of the Bakhtiari,* Cambridge University Press, 1983

Gasiorowski, M., 'Why did Mossadeq fall?', in Gasiorowski and Byrne (eds), *Mohammad Mossadeq and the 1953 Coup in Iran,* Syracuse University Press, 2004

Gasiorowski, M. and M. Byrne (eds), *Muhammad Mossadeq and the 1953 Coup in Iran,* Syracuse University Press, 2004

Ghani, C., *Iran and the Rise of Reza Shah: From Qajar Collapse to Pahlavi Power,* I.B.Tauris, 1998

Gharavi, M. (ed.), *Majareh yi doulat – Inglis va Mirza Hashem Khan,* Nashr i-Tarikh i-Iran, 1984

Gheissari, A., *Iranian Intellectuals in the Twentieth Century,* Texas University Press, 1998

Ghods, M., 'Government and society in Iran 1926–34', *Middle Eastern Studies,* 1991

— 'Iranian nationalism and Reza Shah', *Middle Eastern Studies,* 1991

Ghods, R., *Iran in the Twentieth Century: A Political History,* Rienner/Adamantine, 1989

Gilbar, G., 'The Persian economy in the mid-nineteenth century', *Die Welt des Islams,* n.s., 1979

Gleadle, K., *Early Feminists: Radical Unitarians and the Emergence of the Women's Rights Movement,* Macmillan, 1995

Gobineau, A., *Depeches diplomatiques,* ed. A. Hytier, Ambilly-Annemasse, 1959

— *Les religions et les philosophies dans l'Asie centrale* [1865], Gallimard, 1957

— *Trois ans en Asie* [1859], Grasset, 1980

Gole, N., *The Forbidden Modern: Civilisation and Veiling*, University of Michigan Press, 1996

Good, B., 'The transformation of health care in modern Iranian history', in Bonine and Keddie (eds), *Continuity and Change in Modern Iran*, Syracuse University Press, 1981

Good, M. del Vecchio, 'The changing status and composition of an Iranian provincial elite', in Bonine and Keddie (eds), *Continuity and Change in Modern Iran*, 1981

Goode, J., *The United States and Iran 1946–51: The Diplomacy of Neglect*, St Martin's Press, 1989

Goodell, G., *The Elementary Structures of Political Life: Rural Development in Pahlavi Iran*, Oxford University Press, 1986

Groot, J. de, '"Brothers of the Iranian race": manhood, nationhood and modernity in Iran c.1870–1914', in S. Dudink, K. Hagemann and J. Tosh (eds), *Masculinities in Politics and War*, Manchester University Press, 2004

— 'The dialectics of gender: men, women and political discourses in Iran c. 1890–1930' *Gender and History*, 1993

— 'The formation and reformation of popular protest in Iran', in K. Brown et al. (eds), *Urban Crises and Social Movements in the Middle East*, Harmattan, 1990

— '"Sex" and "race": the construction of image and language in the nineteenth century', in S. Mendus and J. Rendall (eds), *Sexuality and Subordination: Interdisciplinary Studies of Gender in the Nineteenth Century*, Routledge, 1989

— 'Kerman in the later nineteenth century: a regional study of society and social change', D.Phil thesis, Oxford, 1978

Guindi, F. El, *Veil: Modesty, Privacy and Resistance*, Berg, 1991

Gurney, J., 'A Qajar household and its estates', *Iranian Studies*, 1983

Hadari, G., 'The agrarian reform problem in Iran', *Middle East Journal*, 1951

Hairi, A., 'The legitimacy of early Qajar rule as viewed by Shi'i religious leaders', *Middle Eastern Studies*, 1988

— 'Shaikh Fazlullah Nuri's refutation of the idea of constitutionalism', *Middle Eastern Studies*, 1977

— *Shi'ism and Constitutionalism in Iran*, Brill, 1977

Hakimian, H., 'Wage labour and migration: Persian workers in southern Russia 1880–1914', *International Journal of Middle East Studies*, 1985

Halliday, F., *Iran: Dictatorship and Development*, Penguin, 1979

Hedayat, R., *Rawzat al-Safa yi Nasiri* [1853–56], Kitabforushi Markazi, 1959–60

Hegland, M., 'Two images of Husein: accommodation and revolution in an Iranian village', in Keddie (ed.), *Religion and politics in Iran*, 1983

— '"Traditional" Iranian women: how they cope', *Middle East Journal*, 1982

Heiss, M., *Empire and Nationhood: The United States, Great Britain, and Iranian Oil*, Columbia University Press, 1997

Hooglund, E., *Land and Revolution in Iran, 1960–1980*, Texas University Press, 1982

— 'Rural Iran and the clerics', *MERIP Reports*, 1982

Hooglund, M., 'Women of Aliabad', *Review of Iranian Political Economy*, 1981

— 'Rural participation in the revolution', *MERIP Reports*, 1980

Hourcade, B., 'Iran, revolution islamiste ou tiers-mondiste?', *Herodote*, 1985

Hukama, Rustam al-, *Rustam al-Tavarikh*, ed. M. Mushiri, Chap-i Taban, 1969

Hume-Griffiths, M., *Behind the Veil in Persia and Turkish Arabia*, Seeley and Co., 1909

Hunt, L., *Eroticism and the Body Politic*, Johns Hopkins University Press, 1991

Innes, C., *Woman and Nation in Irish*

Society and Literature 1880–1935, Harvester Press, 1993

Isfahani, Jamal al-din, *Lebas i-Taqva* [1900], ed. H. Rizvani, Tehran, 1984

I'timad al-Saltaneh, *Tarikh i-Muntazem i-Nasiri*, Tehran, 1881–3

— *Mirat al-Buldan-i Nasiri*, Tehran, 1877–80

Jafri, S. H., *The Origins and Early Development of Islam*, Longman, 1979

Jahanbegloo, R. (ed.), *Iran between Tradition and Modernity*, Lexington Books, 2004

Jalil', T., *Workers Say No to the Shah: Labour Law and Strikes in Iran*, London, Campaign for the Restoration of Trade Union Rights in Iran, 1977

Kamshad, H., *Modern Persian Prose Literature*, Cambridge University Press, 1966

Karbalai, S., *Qarar-dad i-rezhi yi 1890 miladi*, Mubarizan, 1982

Kashani-Sabet, F., *Frontier Fictions: Shaping the Iranian Nation 1804–1946*, Princeton University Press, 1999

Kasravi, A., *Tarikh-mashruteh yi-Iran* [1938–39], Amir Kabir, 1977–78

— *Zendigani yi man*, Tehran, 1944–46

Katouzian, H., 'Reza Shah's political legitimacy and social base', in Cronin (ed.), *The Making of Modern Iran*, 2003

— *State and Society In Iran: The Eclipse of the Qajars and the Emergence of the Pahlavis*, I.B.Tauris, 2000

— 'Liberty and licence in the constitutional revolution of Iran', *Journal of the Royal Asiatic Society*, 1998

— 'The Pahlavi regime in Iran', in Chehabi and Linz (eds), *Sultanistic Regimes*, Johns Hopkins University Press, 1998

— *Sadeq Hedayat: The Life and Legend of an Iranian Writer*, I.B.Tauris, 1991

— *Mussadiq and the Struggle for Power in Iran*, I.B.Tauris, 1990

— *The Political Economy of Modern Iran: Despotism and Pseudo-modernism 1926–1979*, Macmillan, 1981

Kaur, M., *Women in India's Freedom Struggle*, Sterling Publishers, 1985

Kazembeyki, M., *Society, Politics and Economics in Mazanderan 1848–1914*, Routledge/Curzon, 2003

Kazemi, F. 'State and society in the ideology of the Devotees of Islam', *State, Culture, and Society*, 1985

— 'The *Fada'iy yi Islam*; fanaticism, politics and terror', in S. Arjomand (ed.), *From Nationalism to Revolutionary Islam*, State University of New York Press, 1984

— *Poverty and Revolution in Iran: The Migrant Poor, Urban Marginality and Politics*, New York University Press, 1980

Keddie, N., *Qajar Iran and the Rise of Reza Shah*, California University Press, 1999

— (ed.), *Religion and Politics in Iran*, Yale University Press, 1983

— *Roots of Revolution*, Yale University Press, 1981

— *Sayyid Jamal al-din 'al Afghani': A Political Biography*, California University Press, 1972

— 'Pan-Islam as proto-nationalism', *Journal of Modern History*, 1969

— 'Islamic philosophy and Islamic modernism', *Iran: Journal of the British Institute of Persian Studies*, 1968

— 'The origins of the religious/radical alliance in Iran', *Past and Present*, 1966

— *Religion and Rebellion in Iran: The Iranian Tobacco Protest of 1891–2*, F. Cass, 1966

— 'Symbol and sincerity in Islam', *Studia Islamica*, 1963

— 'Religion and irreligion in early Iranian nationalism', *Comparative Studies in Society and History*, 1962

Kedourie, E. and S. Haim (eds), *Towards a Modern Iran*, F. Cass, 1980

Kermani, Haji Muhammad Karim Khan, *Risalah yi Nasiriyeh* [1850s], Kerman, 1955

Kermani, Mirza Aqa, *Salar-nameh*, vol. 1, Matba' yi- Ahmadi (Shiraz), 1898

Kermani, Nazem al-Islam, *Tarikh i-bidari-yi-Iranian/History of the Awakening of* the Iranians, ed. A. Saidi-Sirjani, Agah, 1977

Keshavjee, R., *Mysticism and the Pluralism of Meaning*, I.B.Tauris/Institute of Ismaili Studies, 1998

Khajehnuri, I., *Bazigaran i -asr i-tala'i: Sayyed Hasan Mudarris*, Tehran 1979

Khomeini, R., *Sahifa yi-nur*, Sazman-i Madarik-i Farhang-i Ingilab-i Islami, 1990

— *Islam and Revolution: Writings and Declarations of Imam Khomeini*, ed. and trans. H. Algar, Mizan Press, 1981

Khosrokhavar, F., *Anthropologie de la revolution iranienne: le reve impossible*, L'Harmattan, 1997

Khosrovi, K., 'La stratification sociale rurale', *Etudes Rurales*, 1966

Kia, M., 'Nationalism, modernisation, and Islam in the writings of Talibov', *Middle Eastern Studies*, 1994

Kingsley Kent, S., *Sex and Suffrage in Britain, 1860–1914*, Princeton University Press, 1987

Kologlu, O., 'Un journal Persan d'Istanbul: Akhtar', in Zarcone and Zarinebaf-shahr (eds), *Les iraniens d'Istanbul*, Institut Français d'Etudes en Iran, 1993

Kuniholm, B., *The Origins of the Cold War in the Near East: Great Power Diplomacy in Iran, Turkey, and Greece*, Princeton University Press, 1980

Lahsaeizadeh, A., *Contemporary Rural Iran*, Avebury, 1993

Lambton, A., *Qajar Persia: Eleven Studies*, I.B.Tauris, 1987

— 'Tribal resurgence and the decline of the bureaucracy', in T. Naff and R. Owen (eds), *Studies in Eighteenth Century Islamic History*, Carbondale, 1977

— 'The Persian 'ulama and constitutional reform', in T. Fahd (ed.), *Le shi'isme imamite*, Presses Universitaires de France, 1970

— *The Persian Land Reform 1962–1966*, Oxford University Press, 1969

— 'The Tobacco Regie: prelude to revolution', *Studia Islamica*, 1965

— 'Persian societies 1906–11', *Middle*

Eastern Affairs, 3 (*St Antony's Papers*, no. 16), Chatto and Windus, 1963

— *Landlord and Peasant in Persia*, Oxford University Press, 1953

Layard, H., *Early Adventures in Persia, Susiana, and Babylonia*, John Murray, 1887

Lenczowski, G., *Russia and The West in Iran 1918–48: A Study in Big Power Rivalry*, Greenwood Press, 1968

Lockhart, L., *Nadir Shah*, Luzac, 1938

Loeffler, R., *Islam in Practice: Religious Beliefs in a Persian Village*, State University of New York Press, 1988

— 'Tribal order and the state: the political organisation of Boir Ahmad', *Iranian Studies*, 1978

Lorentz, J., 'Iran's greatest reformer of the nineteenth century', *Iranian Studies*, 1971

Louis, W., *The British Empire in the Middle East: Arab Nationalism, the United States, and Postwar Imperialism*, Oxford University Press, 1984

Lytle, M., *The Origins of the Iranian–American Alliance 1941–53*, Holmes and Maier, 1987

McBeth, B., *British Oil Policy 1919–39*, F. Cass, 1986

McClachlan, K., *The Neglected Garden*, I.B.Tauris, 1988

McDaniel, R., *The Shuster Mission and the Persian Constitutional Revolution*, Minnesota, Biblioteca Islamica, 1974

MacEoin, D. 'Changes in charismatic authority in Qajar Shi'ism', in E. Bosworth and C. Hillenbrand (eds), *Qajar Iran*, Edinburgh University Press, 1983

McFarland, S., 'A peripheral view of the origins of the Cold War: Iran 1941–47', *Diplomatic History*, 1980

MacLean, H., 'Report on the conditions and prospects of British trade in Persia', *Great Britain: Parliamentary Accounts and Papers*, 1904, vol. 95

Mahdavi, S., *For God, Mammon, and Country: A Nineteenth-century Persian Merchant*, Westview Press, 1999

— 'The structure and function of the

household of a Qajar merchant', *Iranian Studies*, 1999

Majd, M., *Resistance to the Shah: Land-owners and 'ulama in Iran*, Florida University Press, 2000

Malcolm, J., 'The Melville papers', in C. Issawi (ed.), *The Economic History of Iran*, Chicago University Press, 1971

— *History of Persia*, Murray, 1815

Malekzadeh, M., *Tarikh i-Inqilab i-mashrutiyat i-Iran* [1948–50], 'Ilmi, 1984

Malkom Khan, *Qanun*, 1890s, reprint, ed. H. Nateq, Tehran, 1977

— 'Ketabcheh yi- ghaybi' (Secret manual), *Majmu'eh yi-Asar*, ed. M. Tabataba'i, Kitabkhaneh yi Danesh, 1948–49

Mansur, R., 'Chehreh yi zan dar jaraid-i mashrutiyat/The image of woman in constitutional journals', *Nimeh yi digar/The other half*, 1984

Maragheh'i, Zein al-'Abedin, *Siyahat-nameh yi Ibrahim Beg* [1880s], Tehran, 1984

Martin, V., *The Qajar Pact*, I.B.Tauris, 2005

— *Creating an Islamic State: Kho-meini and the Making of a New Iran*, I.B.Tauris, 2003

— 'Mudarres, republicanism, and the rise to power of Riza Khan', in Cronin (ed.), *The Making of Modern Iran*, 2003

— *Islam and Modernism: The Iranian Revolution of 1906*, I.B.Tauris, 1989

— 'Shaykh Fazlallah Nuri and the Iranian revolution 1906–9', *Middle Eastern Studies*, 1987

Matthee, R., 'Transforming dangerous nomads into useful artisans, techni-cians, agriculturalists: education in the Reza Shah period', in Cronin (ed.), *The Making of Modern Iran*, 2003

Melville, C. (ed.), *Safavid Persia: The His-tory and Politics of an Islamic Society*, I.B.Tauris, 1996

Menashri, D., *Education and the Making of Modern Iran*, Cornell University Press, 1992

Meredith, C., 'Early Qajar administra-tion', *Iranian Studies*, 1971

Merritt-Hawkes, O., *Persia: Romance and Reality*, Nicolson and Watson, 1935

Milani, A., *Tales of Two Cities*, Kodan-sha, 1997

Millspaugh, A., *Americans in Persia* [1946], Da Capo Press, 1976

Minorsky, V., 'The sect of Ahl-I Hakk', in Minorsky, *Iranica: Twenty Articles*, University of Tehran, 1964

Mirjafari, H., 'The Haydari/Ni'mati con-flicts in Iran', *Iranian Studies*, 1979

Mirsepassi, A., *Intellectual Discourse and the Politics of Modernization: Nego-tiating Modernity in Iran*, Cambridge University Press, 2000

Mirza, Nadir, *Tarikh va Jughrafiya yi-Dar al-Saltana i-Tabriz* [1905], Tehran, 1977

Moaddel, M., 'Shi'i political discourse and class mobilization in the Tobacco movement of 1891–2', in J. Foran (ed.), *A Century of Revolution*, University of California Press, 1994

— *Class Politics and Ideology in the Iranian Revolution*, Columbia Univer-sity Press, 1993

— 'Class struggles in post-revolutionary Iran', *International Journal of Middle East Studies*, 1991

Moghadam, F., *From Land Reform to Revolution*, Tauris Academic, 1996

Moghadam, V., 'Islamic populism, class and gender in post-revolutionary Iran', in J. Foran (ed.), *A Century of Revolu-tion*, University of California Press, 1994

— 'Populist revolution and the Islamic state in Iran', in T. Boswell (ed.), *Revo-lution in the World System*, Greenwood Press, 1989

— 'Industrial development, culture, and working class politics: a case study of Tabriz industrial workers in the Iranian revolution', *International Sociology*, 1987

Moghissi, H., *Feminism and Islamic Fundamentalism: The Limits of Post-modern Analysis*, Zed Books, 1999

Moin, B., *Khomeini: A Life of the Ayatol-lah*, St Martin's Press, 1999

Mojahedin, *Nazhat–Huseini*, Liberation Movement Press, 1976

Momen, M., *An Introduction to Shi'i Islam*, Yale University Press, 1985

Moses, C., *French Feminism in the Nineteenth century*, SUNY Press, 1981

Mostowfi, A., *The Story of My Life/Social and Administrative History of the Qajar Period*, [1943], trans. N. Mostowfi Glenn, Mazda Press, 1997

Mottahedeh, R., *The Mantle of the Prophet: Religion and Politics in Iran*, Chatto and Windus, 1986

Mulk, Najm al-, *Safar-Nameh yi-Khuzestan* [1880s], ed. M. Siyaqi, Mu'asasseh yi-Matbu'at i-'Ilmi, 1962

Mutahhari, M., 'Moshkel-I asasi dar saz-man-I ruhaniyat', in *Bahsi dar bareh-yi marja'iyat va ruhaniyat*, Tehran, 1962

Muzakirat i-majlis: doureh yi avval, ed. Hashimi, Tehran, 1946

Naghibi, N., 'Bad feminist or bad-hejab: moving outside the *hejab* debate', in A. Donnell (ed.), *The Veil: Postcolonialism and the Politics of Dress* (special edition of *Interventions: International Journal of Postcolonial Studies*), Routledge, 1999

Na'ini, Mirza Muhammad Husein, *Tanbih al-ummah wa tanzeh al-millah* [1909], ed. M. Taleqani, Intishar, 1955, 1979

Najmabadi, A., *Women with Mustaches and Men without Beards: Gender and Sexual Anxieties of Iranian Modernity*, California University Press, 2005

— *The Story of the Daughters of Quchan: Gender and National Memory in Iranian History*, Syracuse University Press, 1998

— 'Crafting an educated housewife in Iran', in L. Abu-Lughod (ed.), *Remaking Women: Feminism and Modernity in the Middle East*, Princeton University Press, 1998

— 'The erotic *vatan* (homeland) as beloved and mother: to love, to possess, to protect', *Comparative Studies in Society and History*, 1997

— '"Is our name remembered?": writing the history of Iranian constitutionalism as if women and gender mattered', *Iranian Studies*, 1996

— '*Zan-ha yi millat*: women or wives of the nation?', *Iranian Studies*, 1993

— *Land Reform and Social Change in Iran*, Utah University Press, 1987

Najmi, N., *Iran dar miyan i-tufan ya sharh-i zendegani yi Abbas Mirza Naib al-Saltaneh*, Kanun i-Ma'arifat, 1957

Nateq, H., 'Masaleh yi zan dar barkhi az mudavenat i-chap az nezhat i-mashrutiyat ta asr i-Reza Khan'/'The woman question in some "left" publications from the constitutional period until the Reza shah period', *Zaman i-no*, 1983

— 'Negahi be barkhi neveshteh-ha va mubarezat i-zan dar doureh yi mashrutiat'/'A look at some women's writings and movements in the constitutional period', *Ketab i-Jomeh*, 1980

Nashat, G. (ed.), *Women and Revolution in Iran*, Westview Press, 1983

— *The Origins of Modern Reform in Iran 1870–80*, Illinois University Press, 1982

— 'From bazaar to market: foreign trade and economic development in nineteenth-century Iran', *Iranian Studies*, 1981

Newman, A., *Safavid Iran: The Rebirth of a Persian Empire*, I.B.Tauris, 2006

— 'The myth of clerical migration to Safavid Iran', *Die Welt des Islams*, 1993

— 'Towards a reconsideration of the "Isfahan school of philosophy": Shaykh Baha'i and the role of the Safavid 'ulama', *Studia Iranica*, 1986

Nicolas, A., *Essai sur le Cheikhisme* (4 vols), Geuthner, 1910–14

Noshirvani, V., 'The beginnings of commercialized agriculture in Iran', in A. Udovitch (ed.), *The Islamic Middle East 700–1900*, Darwin Press, 1977

Oberling, P., *The Qashqa'i Nomads of Fars*, Mouton, 1974

Okazaki, S., 'The great Persian famine of 1870–71', *Bulletin of the School of Oriental and African Studies*, 1986

Ozdalga, E., *The Veiling Issue: Official*

Secularism and Popular Islam in Turkey, Curzon Press, 1998

Paidar, P., *Women and the Political Process in Twentieth Century Iran*, Cambridge University Press, 1995

Parsa, M., 'Mosque of last resort: state reform and social change in the early 1960s', in Foran (ed.), *A Century of Revolution*, UCL Press, 1994

— *Social Origins of the Iranian Revolution*, Rutgers University Press, 1989

Pavlovich, M., 'La situation agraire en Perse a la veille de la Revolution', *Revue du Monde Musulman*, 1910

Perry, J., *Karim Khan Zand*, Chicago University Press, 1979

— 'Justice for the underprivileged: the ombudsman tradition of Iran', *Journal of Near Eastern Studies*, 1978

— 'The last Safavids', *Iran: Journal of the British Institute of Persian Studies*, 1971

Pistor-Hatam, A., 'The Persian newsletter *Akhtar* as a transmitter of Ottoman political ideas', in Zarcone and Zarinebaf-shahr (eds), *Les iraniens d'Istanbul*, 1993

Preece, Consul, 'Visit to Yazd and Kerman', *Great Britain: Parliamentary Accounts and Papers*, 1894, vol. 87, pp. 340–9

Rahnema, A., *An Islamic Utopian: A Political Biography of 'Ali Shari'ati*, I.B.Tauris, 2000

Rajaee, F., 'Islam, nationalism, and Musaddiq's era: post-revolutionary historiography in Iran', in Bill and Louis (eds), *Mussadiq, Iranian Nationalism and Oil*, 1988

Ramazani, R., 'Intellectual trends in the politics and history of the Mussadiq era', in Bill and Louis (eds), *Musaddiq, Iranian Nationalism and Oil*, 1988

— *Iran's Foreign Policy 1941–73: A Study of Foreign Policy in Modernising Nations*, Virginia University Press, 1975

Ravandi, M., *Tarikh i-Ijtema'i yi-Iran*, Tehran, Jibi, 1979

Razi, M., *Asar i-Hujjah*, Qum, 1953

Reading, A., *Polish Women, Solidarity, and Feminism*, Macmillan, 1992

Rejali, D., *Torture and Modernity in Iran: Self, Society, and State in Modern Iran*, Westview Press, 1994

Rendall, J. (ed.), *Equal or Different: Women's Politics 1800–1914*, Blackwell, 1987

— *The Origins of Modern Feminism*, Macmillan, 1985

Richard, Y., 'Shari'at Sangalaji a reformist theologian of the Riza Shah period', in Arjomand (ed.), *Authority and Political Culture in Shi'ism*, State University of New York Press, 1988

— 'Ayatollah Kashani: precursor of the Islamic Republic', in Keddie (ed.), *Religion and Politics in Iran*, 1983

Ringer, M., *Education, Religion, and the Discourse of Cultural Reform in Qajar Iran*, Mazda Press, 2001

Rosen, M. von, *Persian Pilgrimage*, Hale, 1937

Rotblat, H., 'Social organisation and development in an Iranian provincial *bazar*', *Economic Development and Cultural Change*, 1975

Sadri, M. and A., '*The mantle of the prophet*: a critical perspective', *State Culture and Society*, 1985

Sanasarian, E., *The Womens' Rights Movement in Iran: Mutiny, Appeasement, and Repression from 1900 to Khomeini*, Praeger, 1983

Sarkar, T., *Hindu Wife, Hindu Nation: Community, Religion and Cultural Nationalism*, Indiana University Press, 2001

Sayyah, M., *Khaterat i-Haji Sayyah*, ed. H. Sayyah, Ibn Sina, 1967

Scarcia, G., 'Kerman 1905: la guerra tra Sheihi e Balasiri', *Annali del Istituto Universitario Orientale di Napoli*, 1963

— 'Intorno alle controversie tra Ahbari e Usuli presso gli imamiti di Persia', *Rivista degli Studi Orientali*, 1958

Schirazi, A., *The Constitution of Iran: Politics and the State*, I.B.Tauris, 1997

Schweizer, G., 'Tabriz (Nordwest Iran) und der Tabrizer bazar', *Erdkunde*, 1972

Seyf, A., 'The commercialisation of agriculture: production and trade of opium in Persia', *International Journal of Middle East Studies*, 1984

Shari'ati, A., 'What should we lean on?', *Nashrieh yi sazeman i-daneshjuyan*, no. 2, 1962

Sheikholislami, A., 'The patrimonial character of Iranian bureaucracy', *Iranian Studies*, 1978

— 'The sale of office in Qajar Iran', *Iranian Studies*, 1971

Sheil, M., *Glimpses of Life and Manners in Persia*, John Murray, 1856

Shirazi, F., *The Veil Unveiled: The Hijab in Modern Culture*, Florida University Press, 2001

Sinha, M., *Colonial Masculinity: The 'Manly Englishman' and the 'Effeminate Bengali' in the Late Nineteenth Century*, Manchester University Press, 1995

Sipihr, M., *Nasikh al-tavarikh: Qajariyeh*, ed. M. Bihbudi, Kitabforushi Islamiyyeh, 1965–66

Skocpol, T., 'Rentier state and Shi'a Islam in the Iranian Revolution', *Theory and Society*, 1982

Skrine, C., *World War in Iran*, Constable, 1962

Sreberny-Mohammadi, A. and A. Mohammadi, *Small Media, Big Revolution: Communication, Culture, and the Iranian Revolution*, Minnesota University Press, 1994

Stack, E., *Six Months in Persia*, Sampson Low, 1882

Sullivan, Z., 'Eluding the feminist, overthrowing the modern? Transformations in twentieth-century Iran', in L. Abu Lughod (ed.), *Remaking Women: Feminism and Modernity in the Middle East*, Princeton University Press, 1998

Swietochowski, T., *Russan Azerbaijan 1905–20*, Cambridge University Press, 1985

Sykes, P., *Report on the Agriculture of Khorasan*, Government of India, 1910

— *Ten Thousand Miles in Persia*, John Murray, 1902

Taherzadeh-Behzad, K., *Qiyam i-Azerbaijan dar enqelab i-mashrutiyat i-Iran*, Iqbal, 1955

Tahvildar, M., *Jughrafiya-yi-Isfahan*, ed. M. Sutudeh, Muasasseh-yi Mutala't va Tahqiqat-i Ijtima'i, 1963

Taj al-Saltaneh, *Crowning Anguish: Memoirs of a Persian Princess from the Harem to Modernity* (trans. A. Vanzan and M. Neshati; ed. A. Amanat), Mage Press, 1999

Talebof, 'Abd al-Rahim, *Azadi va siyahat*, ed. I. Afshar, Sahar, 1978

— *Kitab i-Ahmad/Ahmad's Book* [c. 1894], Shabgir, 1966, 1977

Talib, 'Ali ibn Abu, *Nahj al balagheh*, trans. S. Askari Jafery, Elmhurst Press, 1977

Tapper, R., 'The case of the Shahsevan', in Cronin (ed.), *The Making of Modern Iran*, 2003

— *Frontier Nomads: A Political and Social History of the Shahsevan*, Cambridge University Press, 1997

— *Pasture and Politics: Economics, Conflict, and Ritual among the Shahsevan*, Academic Press, 1979

Tavakoli-Targhi, M., *Refashioning Iran: Orientalism, Occidentalism and Historiography*, Palgrave, 2001

— 'Athar agahi az enqelab i-franseh dar shekl-giri yi-engareh yi mashrutiyat dar Iran', *Iran-nameh*, 1990

— 'Refashioning Iran: language and culture during the constitutional revolution', *Iranian Studies*, 1990

Tinkkabuni, Mirza Muhammad, *Qisas al-'ulama* [1886], 'Ilmiyya yi-Islami, 1984

Torkaman, M., *Shaykh i shahid Fazlallah Nuri*, Rasa, 1984

Udovich, A. (ed.), *The Islamic Middle East 700–1900: Studies in Economic and Social History*, Darwin Press, 1977

Vali, A. and Zubaida, 'Factionalism and political discourse in the Islamic Republic of Iran: the case of the *Hujjatiyyeh* organisation', *Economy and Society*, 1985

Vaziri, A., *Jughrafiya yi-Kerman* [1874–96)] (ed. M. Bastani-Parizi), 1967
— *Tarikh-i Kerman*, [1890s], (ed. M. Bastani-Parizi), Kitab-ha yi-Iran, 1961
Vaziri, M., *Iran as Imagined Nation: The Construction of National Identity*, Paragon House, 1993
Vieille, P. and F. Khosrokhavar, *Le discours populaire de la revolution iranienne*, Contemporaneite, 1990
Wheeler, G., 'The journal *Molla Nasreddin* and its influence in revolutionary Persia 1906–11', *Central Asian Review*, 1959
Wigham, H., *The Persian Problem*, Isbister and Co., 1903
Wills, C. J., *Land of the Lion and the Sun*, Macmillan, 1883
Wirth, E., 'Der bazaar Tehran', *Erlanger geographische arbeiten*, 1976
Yazdi, M., 'Patterns of clerical behaviour in postwar Iran, 1941–53', *Middle Eastern Studies*, 1990
Yeganeh, N., and N. Keddie, 'Sexuality and Shi'i social protest in Iran', in J. Cole and N. Keddie (eds), *Shi'ism and Social Protest*, Yale University Press, 1986
Yellin, J., *Women and Sisters: The Anti-Slavery Feminists in American Culture*, Yale University Press, 1989
Zarcone, T., and F. Zarinebaf-Shahr (eds), *Les iraniens d'Istanbul*, Institut Français des Etudes en Iran, 1993
Zarrabi, 'Abd al-Rahim, *Tarikh-i Kashan*, ed. Iraj Afshar, Intisharat i-farhang i-Iran zamin, 1978
Zirinsky, M., 'The rise of Reza Khan', in Foran (ed.), *A Century of Revolution*, 1994
— 'Imperial power and dictatorship: Britain and the rise of Reza Shah', *International Journal of Middle East Studies*, 1992

Index

Index

Index

303

to religion, 250; capacities of, 15; constitution of, 55; excluded from *madraseh* education, 94; in carpet production, 74; in Islam, 53; in relation to nationalism, 151–2; in work, conflict over, 55; involvement in politics, 243; opportunities for, 52–3; paid employment of, 76; political activism of, 181, 205, 207, 249–50; productive activity of, 44; protests of, 173; religious commitment of, 4; religious study by, 58; reproductive issues, 48; rights of, 140, 181; strikes of, 211; voting rights of, 110, 140, 226; working outside the home, 52

women question, 205–6
workers: organisations of, 37, 53; urban, 235; waged, 34, 41, 42, 65, 123, 138, 220, 233, 244 (growth of, 69, 70; in oil industry, 215, 219; interviews with, 239–40; politics of, 238)

Yazd, 75–6, 91, 173
Yeganeh, N., 110

zakat (poor rate levy), 22, 23, 65, 66, 72, 80, 96
Zand, Karim Khan, 88
Zill al-Sultan, prince, 147, 203
Zoroastrians, 130; attacks on, 228

Index